24.28

KV-575-204

Create Microsoft®
Fro   )2

PRIMA
TECH

A [W.I.T.   IG

A Division of Prima Publishing

Prima Publishing, colophon, and In a Weekend are registered trademarks of Prima Communications, Inc. PRIMA TECH is a trademark of Prima Communications, Inc., Roseville, California 95661.

Publisher: Stacy L. Hiquet

Associate Marketing Manager: Jennifer Breece

Managing Editor: Sandy Doell

Project Editor: Cathleen D. Snyder

Technical Reviewer: Bob Breece

Copy Editor: Geneil Breeze

Interior Layout: Shawn Morningstar

Cover Design: Prima Design Team

Indexer: Sharon Shock

Proofreader: Kelly Marshall

ISBN: 0-7615-3447-4

Library of Congress Catalog Card Number: 2001-086682

Printed in the United States of America

00 01 02 03 04 BB 10 9 8 7 6 5 4 3 2 1

For Brandon Teena and all self-made men

ACKNOWLEDGMENTS

People are often impressed when I tell them I've written more than a dozen books, but I quickly assure them it is nothing to get excited about. Technical publishing is a grueling and tedious job at times. It's also often a thankless one. Thus, it is vitally important to recognize all the blood, sweat, and tears that went into producing this 400-and-some-page book you now hold in your hands. Were it not for the hard work and dedication of the many people "behind the curtain," this book would not have happened.

To Debbie Abshier, my longtime friend and favorite Acquisitions Editor: Thank you for your continued support and trust in my work. You don't know how much it means to me.

Thanks also to Project Editor Cathleen Snyder and Copy Editor Geneil Breeze, who smoothed out all the rough edges and made me sound like a much better writer than I really am.

Technical Editor Bob Breece did an excellent step-by-step review of the manuscript and kept me on my toes at all times.

A very special thank you to Managing Editor Sandy Doell and Publisher Stacy Hiquet, whose understanding, patience, and compassion never go unnoticed.

Mom and Dad and Bryan, I am truly a blessed man to call you family. Don't worry, be happy!

I regret leaving behind all of my many wonderful friends for my new adventure in the desert. Please know I miss each and every one of you terribly. Hope you'll come to visit soon and often—but not all at once!

To the Indy Boyz, my extended family: YOU ROCK! Thanks for being there.

And finally, to my best friend, muse, soul mate—and fellow author!—Lori Swan: Tucson's sunshine is no match for the warmth and brightness of your smile. Hurry, baby, the mountain awaits.

ABOUT THE AUTHOR

C. Michael Woodward recently moved to Tucson, Arizona after spending the first 37 years of his life in Indianapolis. He is a Senior Technical Writer for Analysts International, Inc., and is the founder of Echelon Editorial and Publishing Services, which provides freelance writing, editing, and project management services to the technical publishing industry. Michael has authored or contributed to more than a dozen computer books, including *Microsoft Outlook 2002 Fast & Easy*, *Adobe Illustrator 9 Fast & Easy*, *Microsoft Outlook 2000 Fast & Easy*, *Create FrontPage 2000 Web Pages in a Weekend*, *Microsoft Windows 2000 Fast & Easy*, and many others. He's currently spending all his free time exploring his new home state, which is a full-time job in itself.

CONTENTS

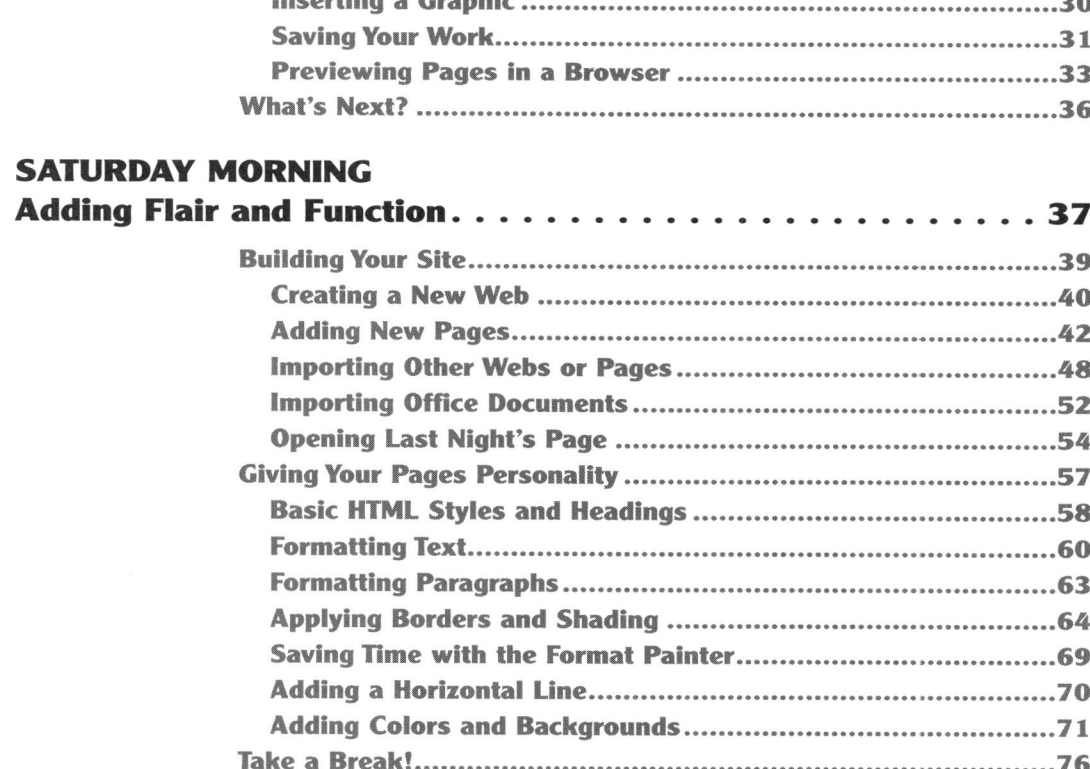

Introduction

When I was a kid, I used to think about how very, very old I would be in the year 2000. Now that it's been here and gone, I don't feel so old. Back then, the Internet was in its infancy, known only to government officials and university scholars working on top-secret national security projects, and the World Wide Web didn't even exist!

Today, it's hard to find anyone who hasn't at least heard of the Internet. Millions of people all over the planet are online, and the numbers grow exponentially every year. Thanks to companies like Microsoft and products like FrontPage 2002, anyone with a computer and a phone line can not only surf the Web, but also build a nice, cozy Web site of their own. What's more, the Internet closes the gap between small companies and big corporations. A Web-savvy business owner can make millions of dollars online—even in a modest, home office environment.

What This Book Is About

Create Microsoft FrontPage 2002 Web Pages In a Weekend is a hands-on, easy-to-read guide to building a Web site of which you can be proud. In seven structured sections beginning on Friday evening and ending on Sunday evening, you'll create your own collection of attractive, professional-looking Web pages, enhance them with exciting features like dynamic tables of contents and animated graphics, and get your new site all set up to publish in your own little corner of cyberspace. Along the way, you'll get tips and shortcuts to make your project go smoothly from beginning to end.

Who Should Read This Book

Let's make an agreement right now. If you pick up this book, I'm going to assume you're ready to get down to business. You don't need a fifty-page lecture on how to use a mouse, and you understand the difference between the keyboard and the monitor. You've had some experience using other Windows applications—Word, perhaps, or maybe WordPerfect. You know why you want to build a Web site, but you don't have the first clue how to get started.

This book includes step-by-step directions and clear explanations written in a friendly, comfortable style. I've tried to write this book as if you were sitting right here next to me at the computer in my home-based office, because that's often the best way to learn quickly—hands-on, try-it-as-you-go, with one-on-one guidance from a knowledgeable friend.

Microsoft FrontPage levels the Web-design playing field, giving even people with limited computer skills the ability to create great Web sites. With the help of this book and a weekend of your time, you can build an exciting Web site too.

Who Should *Not* Read This Book

The goal of this book is not to make you a professional Web designer or Internet architect, or to teach you all the intimate details about the electronic publishing universe. If that's what you're seeking, this book is probably not your best choice.

On the other hand, if you want a jumpstart on building a nice, tidy Web site for the first time, then you will find this book fits perfectly into your Web design toolkit. Remember, we're only talking about a weekend of your time. You can always learn and explore the multitude of FrontPage features later, when you have a *lot* more time to study.

Power users, I appreciate your needs too, and I would rather have you buy a more appropriate book than buy mine and be disappointed. For more detailed coverage on advanced Web design topics, I'd like to recommend the following books, also from Prima Publishing:

- *Learn HTML In a Weekend, 3rd Edtion* (Prima, 2000)
- *Java 2 Fast & Easy Web Development* (Prima, 2000)
- *CGI Fast & Easy Web Development* (Prima, 2000)
- *Dreamweaver 4 Fast & Easy Web Development* (Prima, 2001)
- *Electrify Your Web Site In a Weekend* (Prima, 1999)
- *Web Advertising and Marketing, 3rd Edition* (Prima, 2000)

Visit your local bookseller or Prima's website at http://www.prima-tech.com for details on these and other great books.

How This Book Is Organized

You can easily complete the seven sessions in this book over the course of one weekend. Each session will take about three or four hours to complete. Unless you're already experienced in HTML and Web design, I recommend that you follow them in order so you don't miss any important information along the way. Here's a general itinerary for your weekend adventure.

Friday Evening: Laying the Foundation. In this session, you'll learn the basics of planning a Web site, get familiar with the FrontPage interface, and then jump right into creating your first page. By the end of the evening, you'll have your initial page set up and ready to build on for Saturday.

Saturday Morning: Adding Flair and Function. After breakfast, you'll learn how to add new pages to your Web site. You'll also learn

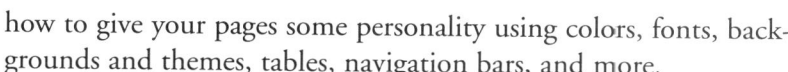

how to give your pages some personality using colors, fonts, backgrounds and themes, tables, navigation bars, and more.

Saturday Afternoon: Putting the Web in World Wide Web. You'll break for lunch, and then learn how to create hyperlinks, bookmarks, and image maps.

Saturday Evening: Working with Tables and Frames. If you thought fancy features like frames and forms were beyond your abilities, you'll be singing a different tune as you drift off to sleep Saturday night. In this session, you'll add a frame layout to your Web site, and then design online forms you can use to get feedback and input from your visitors.

Sunday Morning: Putting the Power of Components to Work. FrontPage includes many automated components you can insert into your Web pages, including hit counters, hover buttons, include pages, timestamps, search forms, and more. In this session, you'll learn how to implement them quickly and easily.

Sunday Afternoon: Finalizing and Maintaining Your Pages. To complete your project, you'll clean up and polish your pages, finish your to-do list, and compile some reports that will help keep your Web site fresh and updated in the future.

Sunday Evening: Bonus Session: Creating Web Art Special Effects. As a special bonus session, you'll find tips and techniques for creating and enhancing your own personalized Web art using Jasc Paint Shop Pro, a popular third-party art program.

In the appendixes, you'll learn everything you need to know about selecting your Internet services and publishing your Web site online. You'll also find coverage of advanced features and additional techniques, such as adding audio and video to your Web site and securing your site with passwords. Finally, you get a no-nonsense glossary that explains terms and concepts that might be new to you.

Special Features of This Book

Throughout this book, you'll find special text formats and icons to help you work faster, avoid problems, and learn more on your own.

 Notes provide additional information or enhance a discussion in the text by emphasizing a particular point.

 Tips offer helpful hints, suggestions, or alternative methods for a procedure.

 **Cautions** warn you about mistakes and pitfalls that inexperienced users often encounter.

 *Buzzwords* are new terms. The new terms are identified in italics in the text and then defined in the Buzzwords section. You'll also find these words in the glossary.

 This graphic appears next to paragraphs that contain an address for a Web site that might be helpful to the discussion.

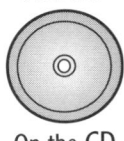 This graphic appears next to paragraphs that relate to material included on the *Create Microsoft FrontPage 2002 Web Pages In a Weekend* CD-ROM.

Are You Ready?

It's Friday night. Your significant other is out with the gang, the kids are having a sleepover at the neighbor's house, and you're itching to get started. Stock up the fridge with some healthy snacks, make a fresh pot of coffee, then settle down at the keyboard and brace yourself: The fun is about to begin!

Laying the Foundation

- Getting Ready
- Planning Your Site
- Working in FrontPage 2002
- Creating a Quick and Simple Web Page

When the Internet first became popular in the early 1990s, publishing Web sites was a daunting task best left to the experts. Today, however, advances in technology have simplified Web site design. Just about anyone with a computer and a modem can create and publish great-looking Web sites with advanced features, often without too much effort or training.

Microsoft FrontPage takes simplicity even further, making Web site design almost as easy as using a word processor. So, if you've wanted to build your own Web site but were afraid you didn't know enough, relax! By the time you finish this book, you'll have created a site in which you can take pride. Your site will have links, graphics, buttons, and all those other features you've seen and admired out there on the Internet—and you'll wonder why you didn't do it sooner.

Getting Ready

As with any well-planned project, it's best to have everything on hand that you will need to work on the project. Then you won't have to interrupt what you're doing later to find something.

 TIP Get some paper and a pen right now to jot down notes as you go You'll use it more than you think you will!

Preparing Your Computer

First, you'll want to make sure that your computer is ready to handle your project, because you're dead in the water without it. Here are a few things you should check before you start.

Is the FrontPage Software Installed and Working?

To determine whether FrontPage is already properly installed on your machine, just attempt to find and open the program from the Start menu. If it's not there, you'll need to install it from your Microsoft Office or Microsoft FrontPage CD-ROM.

 TIP

If this is the first time you've started FrontPage, it might not appear on the Programs submenu. Expand the Programs menu by clicking on the down arrow at the bottom of the menu.

 **NOTE**

Throughout this book, most of the examples are built based on a full installation of Microsoft FrontPage 2002 and the Office XP suite, running on Windows 2000 Professional on a small network. If you have a different configuration, don't worry. You can still use most features with no trouble.

Can You Get Online?

Have you already set up an account with an ISP (*Internet Service Provider*) and Web Host? It's not vital that you establish these accounts before you begin, but I highly recommend it. You'll want to be able to at least get online to check the functionality of your site, verify links, download free artwork, and so on. It's also helpful to know who your Web Host will be—not all servers support everything FrontPage has to offer.

If you need help, Appendix A, "Publishing Your FrontPage 2002 Web Pages," will help you get connected. I tucked it away in the back of the book so it wouldn't get in the way for the majority of readers, who are already primed and ready for action.

◄ ◄

A *Web Host*, also called a *Web Presence Provider* (WPP), is the company that you hire to store your Web site so that other users can access it on the Internet. Essentially, you're simply renting space on the host's server, which has a continuous live connection to the Internet. Some Web hosts are available for free if you're willing to put up with advertising on your site.

Do not confuse a Web hosting service with an ISP. An ISP is the company that gives you dial-up access to the Internet, whether or not you have a Web site of your own. Your ISP and your Web Host can be the same company, but they don't have to be. See Appendix A, "Publishing Your FrontPage 2002 Web Pages," for more details about ISPs and Web Hosts.

◄ ◄

• •

Don't forget to also verify that your modem or connection device is connected and working properly. There's nothing more frustrating than hunting for some errant setting buried in the software and discovering three hours later that the doggone phone cord wasn't snapped into the modem all the way.

• •

Do You Need to Update Your Browser(s)?

As the Web matures from infant to toddler, it becomes smarter and more sophisticated. Every new version of Microsoft FrontPage is designed to take full advantage of the latest and greatest features available in today's Web technology. Some features are so new, in fact, that older browsers don't even understand them. Thus, it's important to keep your Web browsing software up to date, whether you're a developer or just a frequent surfer.

In fact, if you can afford the hard disk space, you might want to keep more than one brand of browser on your computer, including versions of both Microsoft Internet Explorer and Netscape Navigator. Computers come in all sizes, speeds, and configurations, so it's no surprise that Web pages, colors, and text formatting can display slightly differently from browser to browser—sometimes even on the same computer. The more browsers you use to preview your site as you work, the more obvious these common but unexpected differences become.

> **TIP**   To check your browser's version number, select Help, About from the browser's menu bar.

FIND IT ▶ You can download both current and older versions of the two most
ONLINE   popular browsers from the following Web sites:

Microsoft Internet Explorer: http://www.microsoft.com/ie

Netscape Navigator: http://www.netscape.com

Planning Your Site

Although you might not know exactly how you want your Web site to look, you've probably at least given some thought to what you want. If your site is business-related, you might want to include information about your company and what it offers. Or maybe you have some great panoramic photos from your vacation you want to post and share with friends and family.

Before you actually leap into creating pages, spend a little time thinking about what you want your site to look like. You don't have to plan each page right now, but some initial planning will save you time (see Figure 1.1). The next sections give you some good food for thought.

What's the Point?

You should have an overall theme or topic for your site, even if the site is just a personal one. Don't try to include too many different topics—you'll just confuse the reader and lose his or her interest quickly. Remember that you can always build another site for another topic.

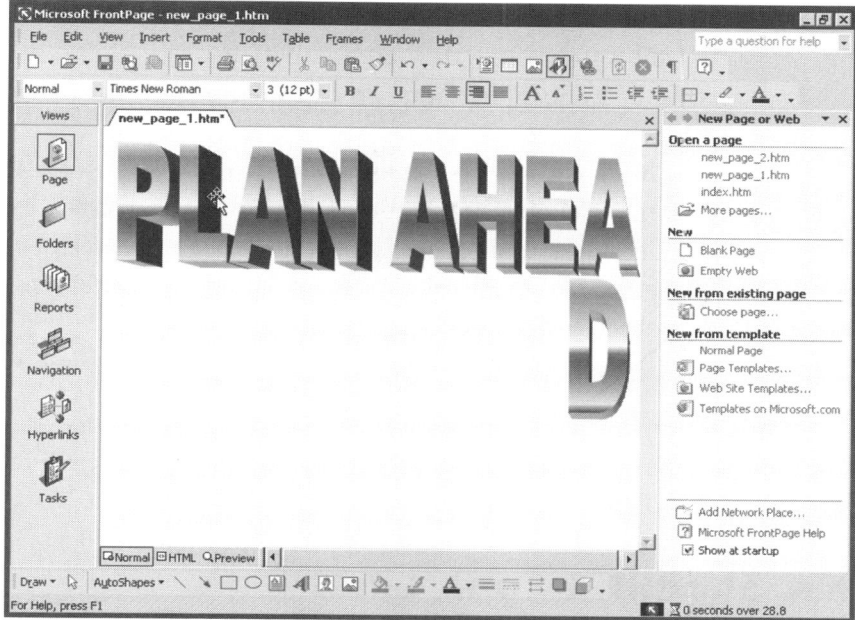

Figure 1.1

There's a lot to be said for advance planning.

TIP

Don't bite off more than you can chew. Start with a reasonably simple design. As you learn more about Web site design and management, you can change and enhance your site with more advanced features and functions. It's easy to commit to a large project when you first get started. It's also easy to get discouraged if the project drags on too long. The techniques you'll learn this weekend are easily manageable with a few hours' work.

Collect or create any documents or graphics you think you want to use. You can always change or add more later. If you want to use photos or other art (your logo, for example), make sure that you have them in digital form, such as on a photo CD or stored as a graphic file on your computer. If you don't have a way to do this yourself, ask your friends. Scanners and digital cameras are becoming more popular and affordable every day, so the odds are good that someone you know can help you. If not, check with your local photo processing company or quick printer. Many businesses offer photo conversion services at reasonable prices.

If you're going to use files already stored on your computer, make sure you know where they are located, and that they're as complete and finished as possible. (You can edit them later if necessary.)

CAUTION   Be mindful of international copyright laws. Using materials created by other people without their permission is against the law. You can download free clip art and images that you can use without violating any laws from many Web sites. You'll find more information about some of these sites later in this book.

If you have a collection of hyperlinks related to your content that you want to share with others, bookmark or make a note of them as well. You'll insert the links on a separate page later.

What Should It Look Like?

Surf the Internet for ideas and examples. When you find a page or site design you like, add it to your Favorites folder or bookmark it so that you can return later to study its layout and structure. I'll show you later how to imitate the style of a Web site you like.

Sketch out by hand some basic ideas for your layout. Sometimes putting a few things down on paper can help stimulate other ideas as you go along. You might even want to use a program like Word or Visio to draw up an outline or storyboard for the site structure.

Who Cares?

Think about the purpose of your site and your intended audience. Are they likely to be computer-savvy people or regular Joes? The more technically oriented your viewers are, the more sophisticated your site should be. If you're just posting a personal home page, you can keep your design simple.

Also, what do you want to know about the people who visit your site? Will you need to provide a way for them to give you feedback? Do you want them to sign your guest book?

Keep in mind that the larger your site is and the more pages, graphics, and supporting files you include, the more storage space you'll need, which could cost you more money. The same is true for traffic. If your goal is to make millions via high-volume online sales, you'll need a much different site than if you're just posting a small autobiographical site to occasionally share with new friends you meet online.

To Frame or Not To Frame?

Some sites, like the one shown in Figure 1.2, use frames to organize the site and make it easier for users to navigate. Some users, however, find frames cumbersome or confusing (or sometimes their tired, old computer's browser doesn't support frames), and they might not spend much time exploring your site. Will your site use frames? (You can also simulate frames using FrontPage's Shared Borders feature, thereby simplifying your Web structure.)

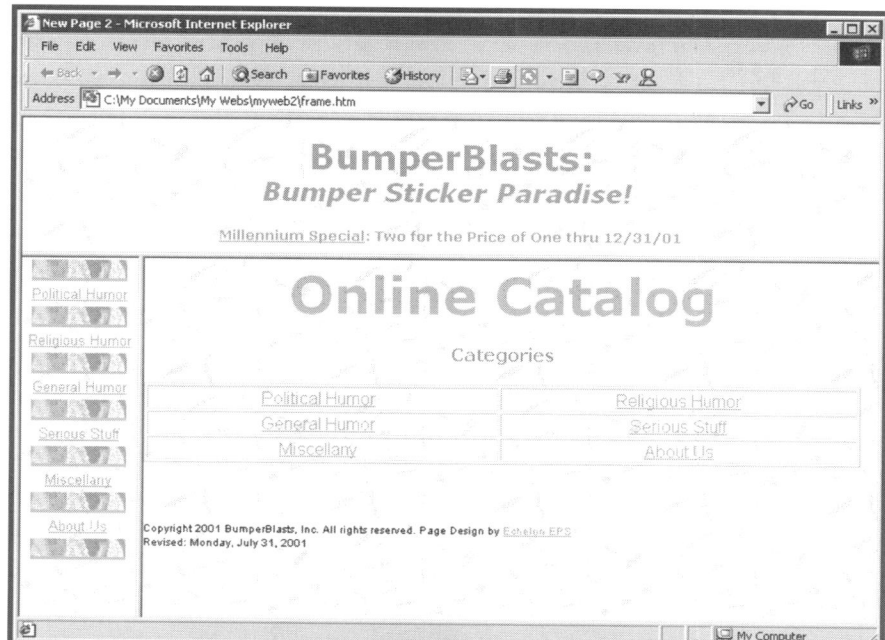

Figure 1.2

You can pack more punch with a frame-based layout.

◄ ◄

A *frame-based* Web site displays multiple Web pages at the same time in separate frame windows within a Web page.

◄ ◄

Are You Selling Something?

If you're selling a product or products, do you want your customers to be able to order directly from the Web site using a credit card? I'll cover some basic design concepts for commercial sites and point you toward some tools to help establish your business online. Conducting business over the Internet usually requires some complex security procedures and equipment setup, however, and the intricacies of e-commerce are beyond the scope of this book. If you need to add these features to your Web site, consult your WPP's technical support department for help. Most WPPs provide design and implementation services—usually for an extra fee.

■ ■

If you're interested in learning more about e-commerce, be sure to check out *Web Enable Your Small Business In a Weekend* (Prima, 2000).

■ ■

Working in FrontPage 2002

One of the best things about FrontPage 2002 is that it's easy to use, even for novices. The interface is similar to the other Microsoft Office XP applications, such as Word and Excel. You'll recognize buttons such as Open, Bold, and Print on the toolbars, as well as the familiar File, Edit, and Help menus, among others. Take a quick look at FrontPage now, and get to know its basic features.

Starting FrontPage

When you're ready to begin, fire up the computer, get comfortable in your chair, and start FrontPage. Like most Windows applications, it all begins at the Start button. To open FrontPage, follow these steps.

1. Click on the Windows Start button.

2. Click on Programs and then select Microsoft FrontPage from the submenu. FrontPage 2002 opens and the Task pane appears.

3. Click on Blank Page under the New category. FrontPage displays a blank document called new_page_1.htm in Normal view, ready for editing (see Figure 1.3).

TIP

Use the tabs at the top of the work area to switch between open pages.

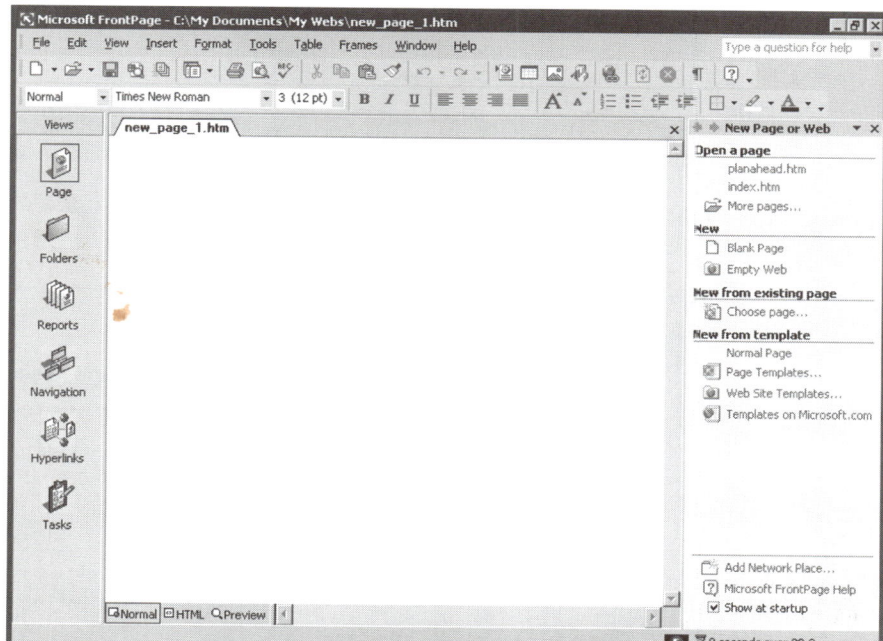

Figure 1.3

Just open a new document and start typing to get rolling on your first Web page.

Getting Familiar with FrontPage

When you look at the FrontPage 2002 interface for the first time, you'll see some things that look familiar. For example, FrontPage's Standard and Formatting toolbars are similar to those you've seen in Word and other Office applications (see Figure 1.4). The Views bar on the left looks similar to Outlook's Shortcut bar. The View tabs at the bottom work like worksheet tabs in Excel.

You'll learn more about the specific tools and features of FrontPage later. For now, just familiarize yourself with the layout of the screen.

TIP

If you have trouble identifying a tool or other screen element in the FrontPage environment, just point to it with the mouse pointer to see the name in a ToolTip. For detailed help with a tool, click on Help, What's This?, then click on the item in question to view a brief explanation.

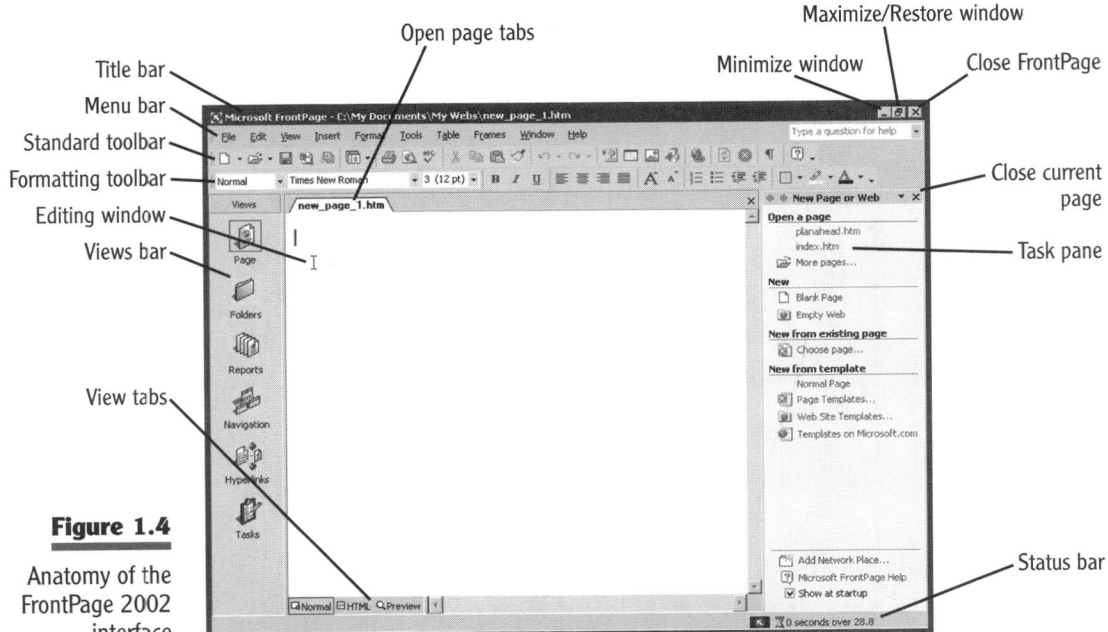

Figure 1.4

Anatomy of the
FrontPage 2002
interface

Understanding FrontPage Views

One nice feature of FrontPage 2002 is that it gives you quick access to a variety of views, reports, and other information related to your site. Using different views, you can quickly move from editing a page to checking the status of your Tasks list to listing all the files and folders in your site.

Page View

You'll use Page view when creating and editing Web pages. Within Page view, you have three different ways to see the page on which you're working. Use the View tabs at the bottom of the work area to switch between the different views available in Page view.

✪ **Normal.** The Normal view is your main working view (see Figure 1.5). In Normal view, you can enter and edit text, apply formatting, insert graphics and links, and more.

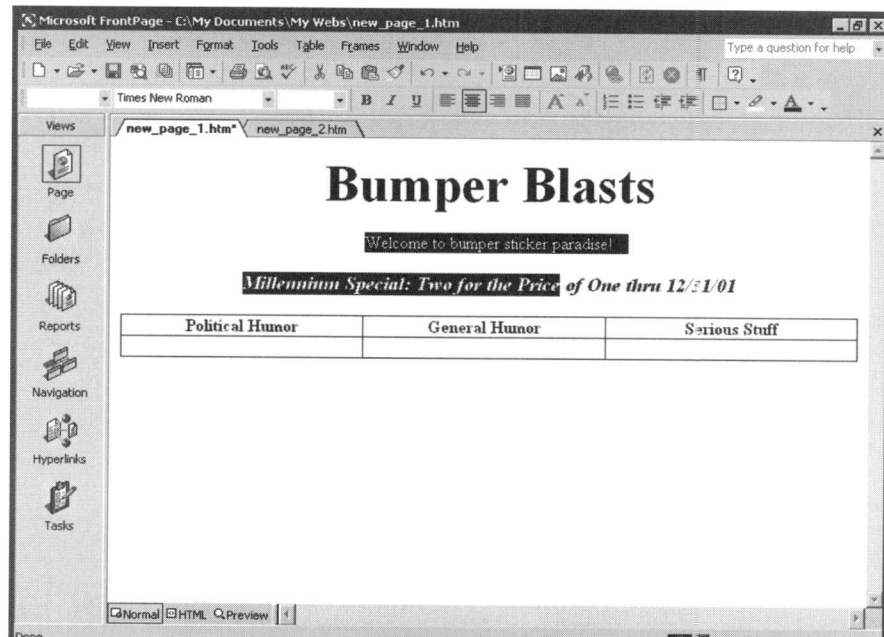

Figure 1.5

Edit your pages in Normal view, but don't rely on it to reflect how a page will look in a browser.

✿ HTML. Web pages are based on a programming language called HTML. However, you don't have to know anything about HTML to create Web pages. FrontPage automatically generates the HTML code in the background while you work in Normal view. If you want to take a peek at this mysterious language—or if you want to edit the code yourself (not recommended for beginners)—click on the HTML tab. You'll see something similar to what's shown in Figure 1.6.

BUZZ WORD

◄ ◄

HTML (Hypertext Markup Language) is the programming language understood by Web browsers. HTML is much easier to learn and understand than typical programming languages.

◄ ◄

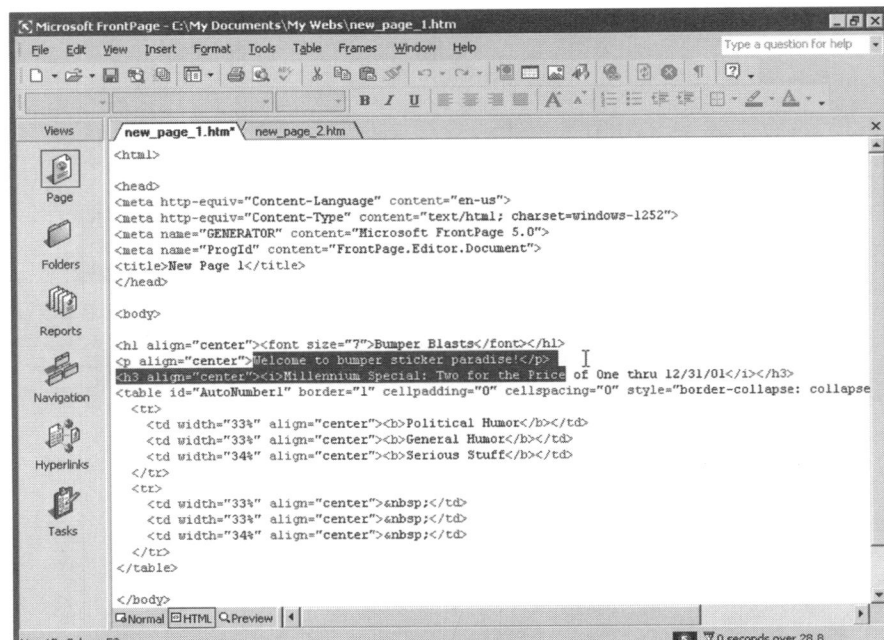

Figure 1.6

You can edit the HTML code, but do so with caution— you might get unexpected results.

NOTE

HTML coding employs *tags* to "mark up" the text. Tags are embedded within the Web page text, and they work as on/off toggle switches. HTML tags are surrounded by brackets (< and >). Typically, the "on" tag appears before the text being formatted, and the "off" tag (which is the same tag, preceded by a /) appears after the text. For example, to show text in boldface, the HTML code would look something like this:

```
<b>This is boldface text</b>
```

The resulting text would appear as:

This is boldface text

○ **Preview.** The Preview tab gives you a quick look at how your page will appear in your visitor's browser. Preview saves you a lot of time. You don't have to save and close your file and then open it again in a stand-alone browser such as Internet Explorer or Netscape Navigator. It's not a perfect simulator and it might take a moment to render the view, but it does a great job on most pages (see Figure 1.7).

Folders View

The Folders view, shown in Figure 1.8, gives you Windows Explorer-like access to all of the files contained in your Web site. From here, you can manage all of your files; for example, you can rename, move, delete, or copy files. You don't need to worry too much about tracking your files—FrontPage automatically does it for you.

Folder/Navigation Toggle Pane

Even when you're not working in the Folders view, you can still see the existing files in your Web. Click on the Toggle Pane button to open a narrow window just to the right of the Views bar to display the Folder List pane. Click the down arrow next to the Toggle Pane button to switch from the Folder List to the Navigation pane. The Navigation pane, shown in Figure 1.9, gives you access to the navigational structure of your

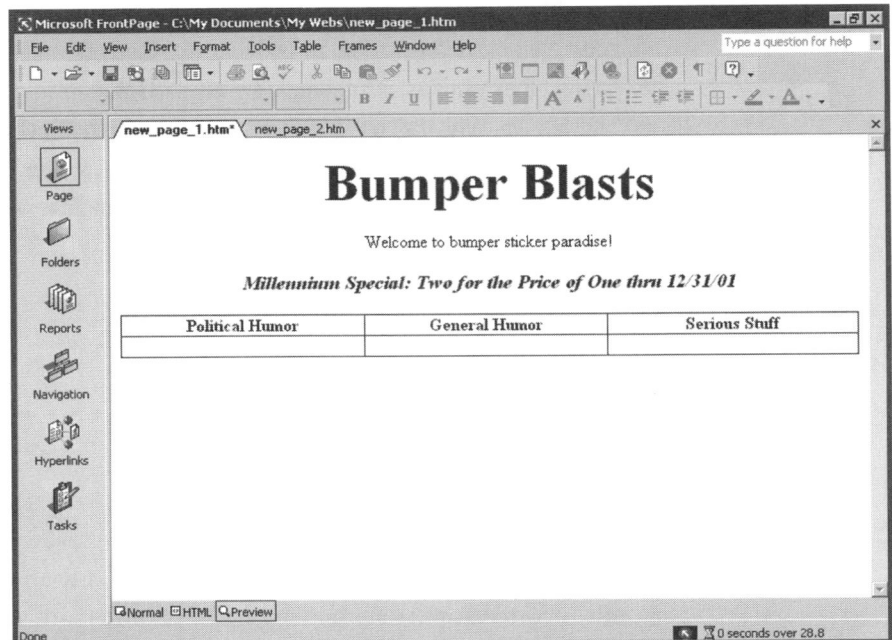

Figure 1.7

The Preview tab approximates how the page will look in a browser.

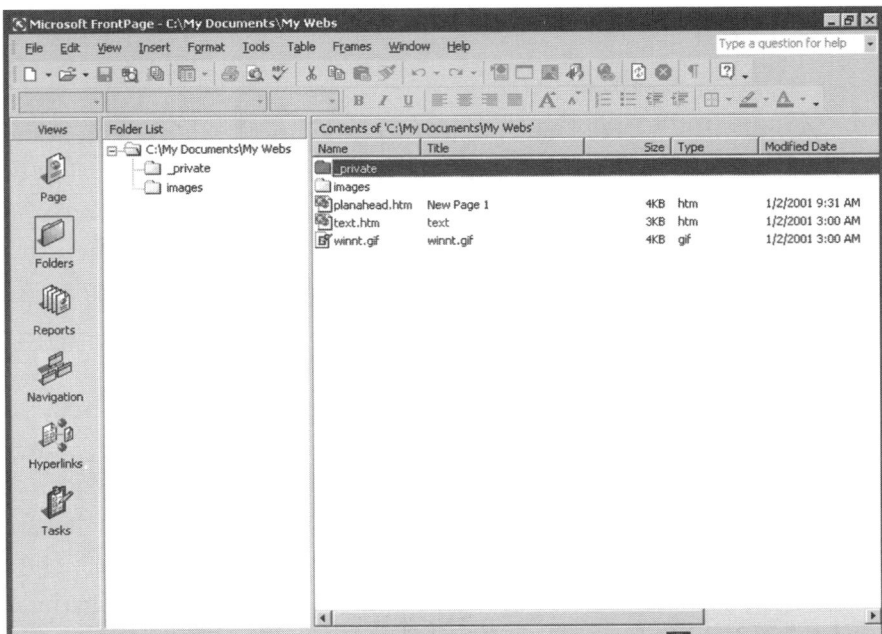

Figure 1.8

The Folders view helps you manage the files in your Web site.

Toggle Pane button

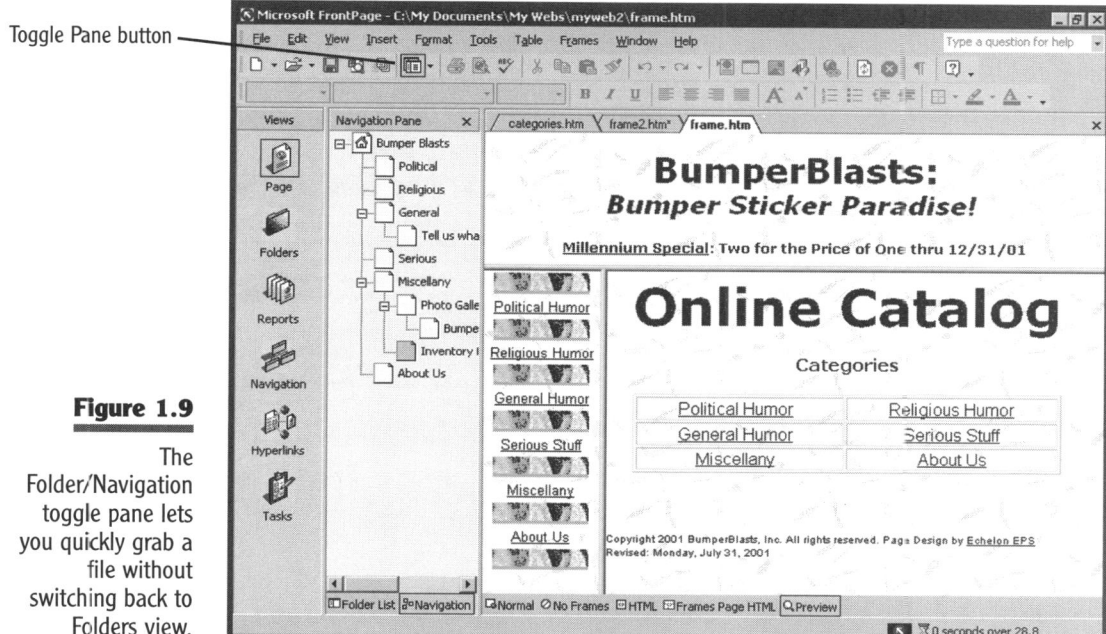

Figure 1.9

The
Folder/Navigation
toggle pane lets
you quickly grab a
file without
switching back to
Folders view.

site when you're not in Navigation view. Drag and drop files from the Folder or Navigation toggle pane onto the FrontPage workspace to link the file to the open page, or drag and drop the file over the tabs area to open the page for editing.

Reports View

You can get detailed information about your Web site in Reports view (see Figure 1.10). You can find the number and size of all your pictures and graphic images. (Just remember that a large graphic file might be slow to load.)

The first time you go to Reports view, you'll see the Site Summary, listing 15 different available reports. Double-click on any report to open it. Reports are handy for finding problems and ensuring that everything in your site is complete and working properly.

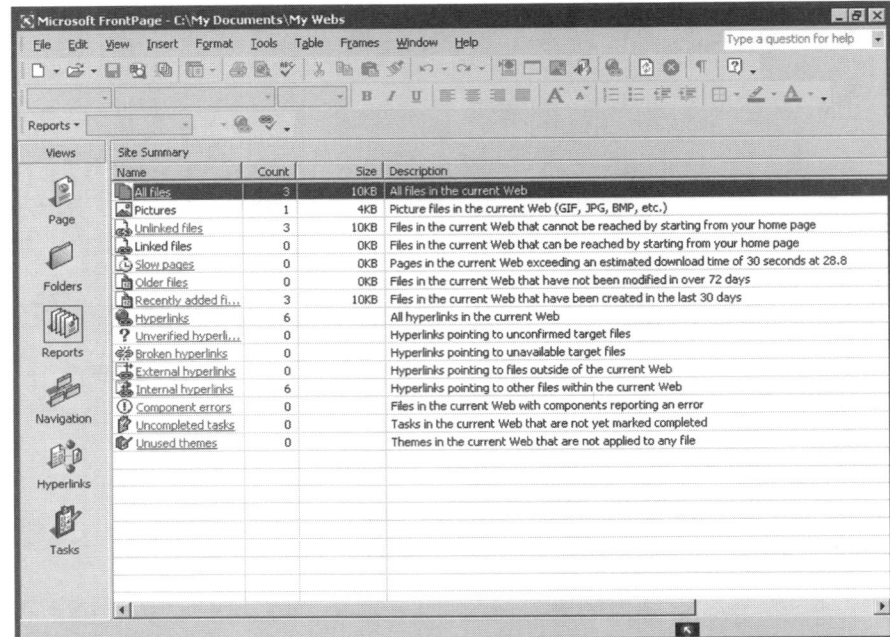

Figure 1.10

FrontPage's Reports feature is a Web site manager's best friend.

TIP

■ ■

Returning to Reports view takes you back to the last report you viewed onscreen. To return to the Site Summary, select View, Reports, Site Summary.

■ ■

Navigation View

Use the Navigation view, shown in Figure 1.11, to see or change the structure of your pages and to quickly add navigation bars to some or all of your pages.

TIP

■ ■

Sometimes you need to see the list of files when you're not in the Folders view. Click on View, Folder List or click on the Toggle Pane button to show the list of files in your site. You can use the Folder List pane in Page, Navigation, and Hyperlinks views. Just drag and drop files from the Folder List onto the FrontPage workspace (see Figure 1.12).

■ ■

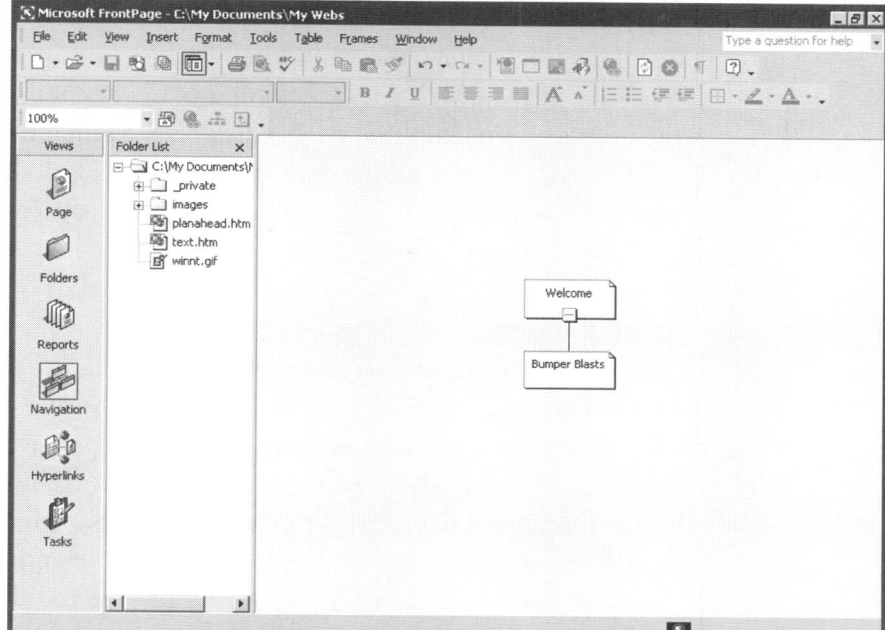

Figure 1.11

The Navigation view is a quick way to link the pages of your Web site.

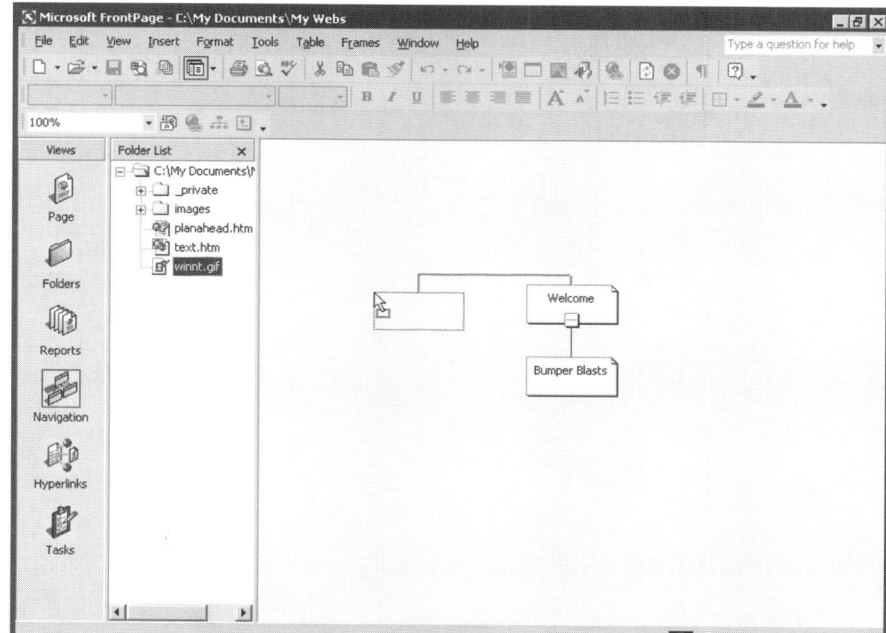

Figure 1.12

You can drag files from the Folder List pane onto the FrontPage workspace to edit them.

Hyperlinks View

The Hyperlinks view, shown in Figure 1.13, gives you a visual map of all the links in your Web site. Click on any file in the Folder List to see all the links contained on that page. Click on the Expand button (+) to show the links on other pages in the current group. Hyperlinks view makes it easy to see the available paths to and from any page, as well as any external links contained on your pages.

Tasks View

The Tasks view gives you a complete list of all the "to-do" items remaining for your project (see Figure 1.14). This might be one of the handiest features of FrontPage, because it automatically keeps track of the details you need to fix or check later. After you get a sizable Web site underway, there might be quite a few of these details. In the Sunday Afternoon session, "Finalizing and Maintaining Your Pages," you'll learn just how helpful the Tasks list is as you clean up your site and prepare to publish it online.

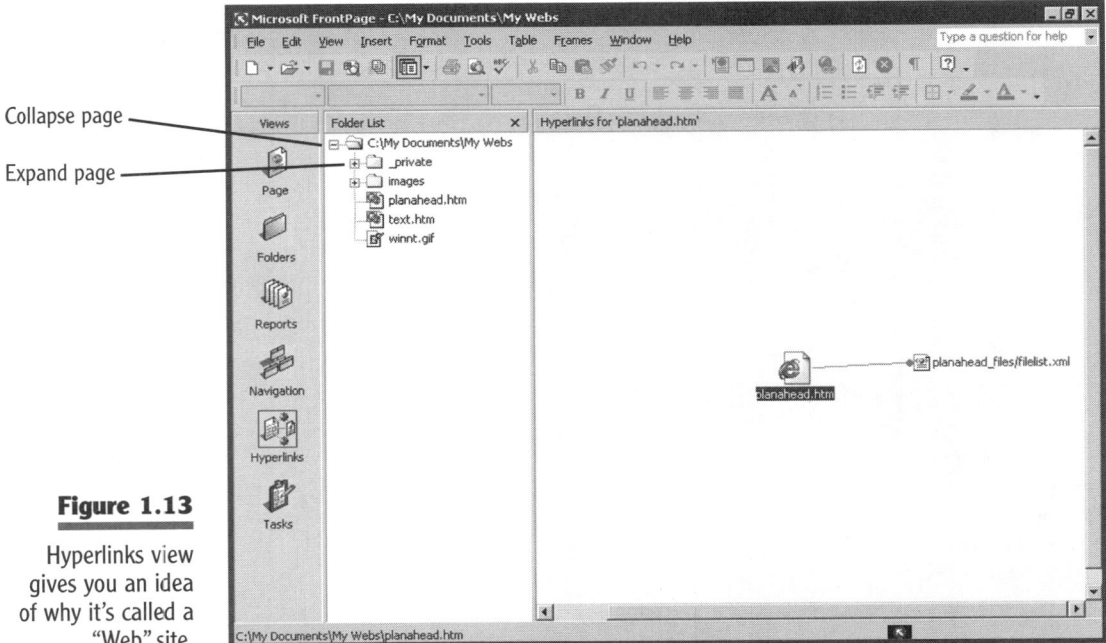

Figure 1.13

Hyperlinks view gives you an idea of why it's called a "Web" site.

Figure 1.14

If you're forgetful by nature, you'll appreciate the Tasks view.

TIP

You might need to click on the Views bar's down arrow to see additional Views buttons.

Closing FrontPage

If you were experimenting and exploring as you followed along through the first part of this session, you'll want to close any open documents or Webs you might have created. Again, you might find this procedure similar to that in Word, Excel, or other Microsoft applications. If prompted to save a file, choose No for now. You'll learn how to save your work later, when you finish for the evening. There are a few different ways to close various parts of FrontPage.

○ To close a single page (Page view only), click on the Close Current Page button. (Remember, this button is at the top of the document, below the FrontPage toolbars.)

- To close an entire Web, select File, Close Web.

- To close FrontPage, click on the Close FrontPage button (in the upper-right corner of the screen) or select Exit from the File menu.

Take a Break!

Okay, now you have a basic understanding of how FrontPage works, and you have a general idea of what you want your Web site to look like. But you haven't done any real work yet. So, take a few minutes to stretch, walk the dog, maybe grab a carrot stick or two. When you come back, you'll get down to the business of creating your first Web page!

Creating a Quick and Simple Web Page

By the time you finish this session, you'll have created your first Web page, inserted a graphic, checked your spelling, and saved the file. You'll be ready to build your Web site from there tomorrow morning. Ready? Get to it!

Creating a New Web Page

Before you start, make sure that you're starting from a fresh, new page. Open FrontPage from the Start menu as you learned earlier in the evening, and FrontPage will present you with a new, blank document.

If a new page doesn't open automatically, just switch to Page view (if necessary) and then click on the New button on the toolbar. You should end up with a blank page, ready for you to fill with all kinds of good stuff.

Entering and Editing Text

If you've ever used Microsoft Word (or any other word processor, for that matter), you won't have any trouble using the FrontPage editor. All the usual tools are available: bold, italic, and underline buttons; alignment and formatting tools; and so on. Most common Word keyboard commands apply to FrontPage as well.

 **NOTE** In this book, I will use examples built for a Web site for a small bumper-sticker company. Bumper Blasts is a home-based online business with relatively simple site needs. With the ideas for your own Web site in mind, you're ready to get started.

All you have to do to begin your first Web page is start typing. To enter the text for your first page, do the following:

1. Type an opening heading for your Web page and press Enter.
2. Type a short sentence or phrase of introductory text and press Enter.
3. Enter a few subheadings that you want to designate as the main categories for your Web site.

Your screen should look similar to the one in Figure 1.15.

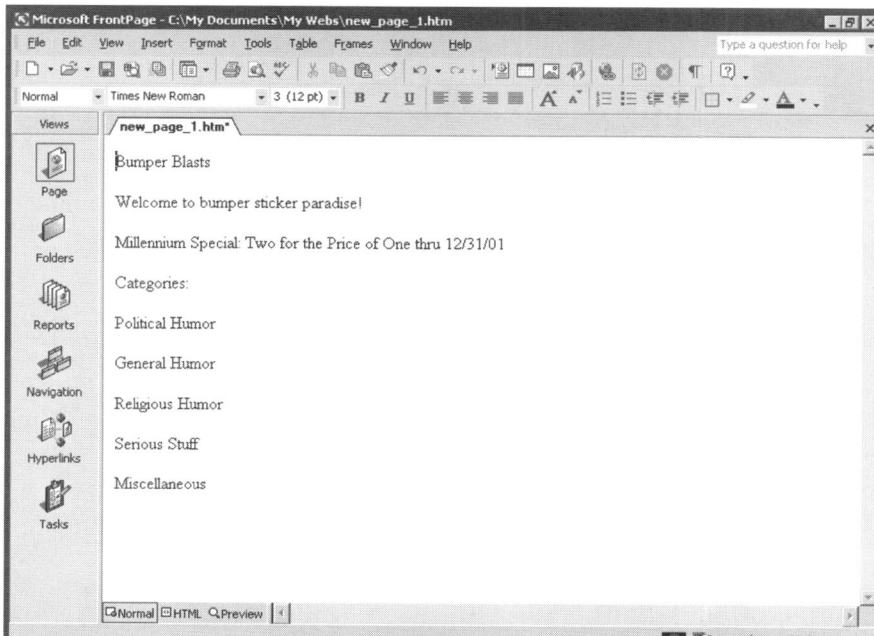

Figure 1.15

The beginnings of the first Web page

Now apply some formatting to the text:

1. Click anywhere in the main heading to select the paragraph.
2. Click on the down arrow next to the Style drop-down list and then select Heading 1 (see Figure 1.16).
3. Select your second line of text and apply the Heading 2 style.

If you're following my sample text, skip the third and fourth lines of the example for now. Next, turn the list of subheadings into a bulleted list.

1. Click just to the left of the first character in the first subheading, press and hold the Shift key, and drag the pointer to the end of the last subheading. All your subheadings should be selected.
2. Click on the Bullets button on the Formatting toolbar. FrontPage automatically indents the paragraphs and adds bullets to each item (see Figure 1.17).

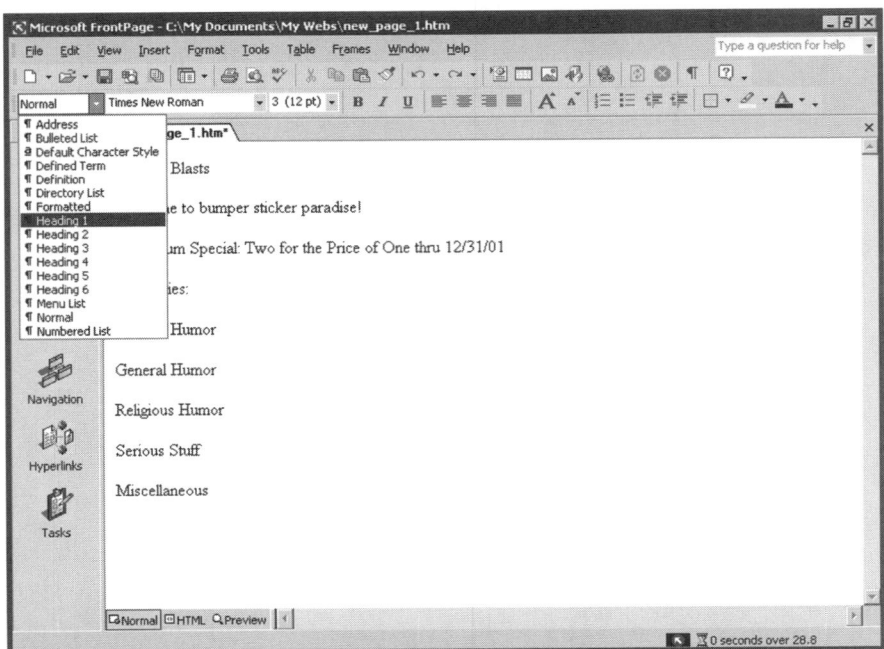

Figure 1.16

Apply a paragraph style just as you would in Word.

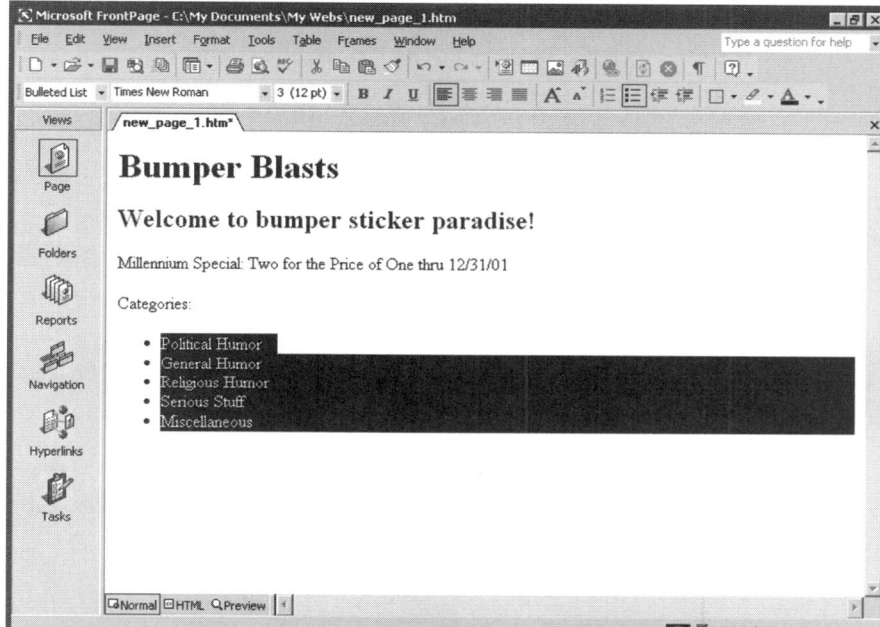

Figure 1.17

One quick click turns these paragraphs into a bulleted list.

You can add, move, or delete text and formatting at any time.

- Select the last item in your bulleted list and click on the Bullets button again to remove the bullet point. The paragraph changes back to Normal text.
- To delete text, select the text to remove and then press Delete.
- To add new text, click where you want to insert text and begin typing. Existing text will move to the right.
- Use the shortcut menus to cut, copy, and paste selections.

You can use normal cut-and-paste or drag-and-drop editing procedures to move text around in your document.

1. Select the first item in your bulleted list and press Ctrl+X to cut the paragraph.

2. Right-click at the start of the last bulleted paragraph and then select Paste from the shortcut menu that appears (see Figure 1.18). The text appears, along with the Paste Options button.

3. Click on the Paste Options button to reveal a drop-down list of options (see Figure 1.19). You can choose to keep the original formatting intact or keep only the text itself and apply the formatting of the current paragraph to the text you're inserting. After you make a selection and move on to your next edits, the Paste Options button will disappear.

4. Click in the margin to the left of your last bullet point to select the entire paragraph.

5. Click again on the highlighted text and hold down the left mouse button. When you next move the mouse, the cursor changes to the drag pointer.

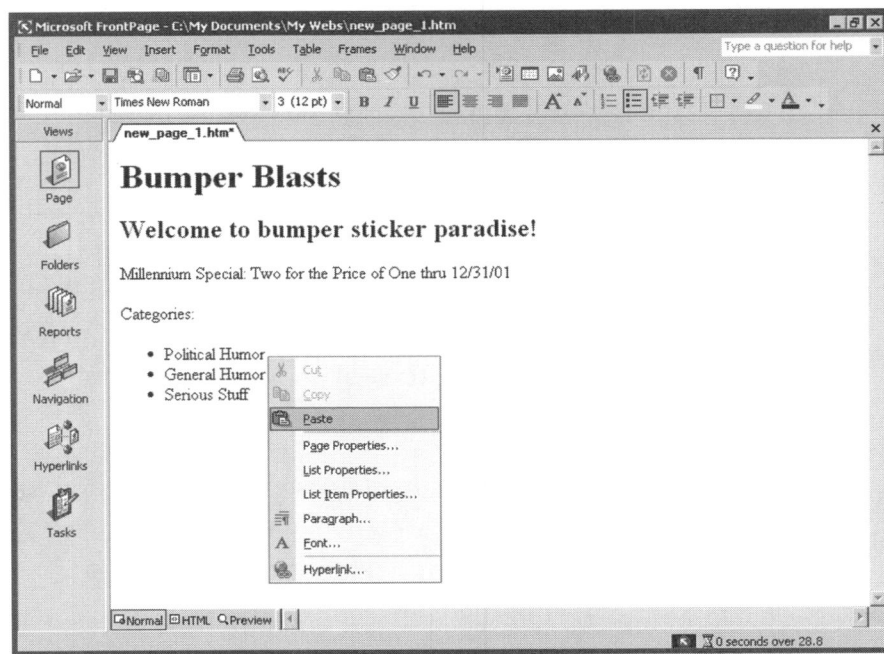

Figure 1.18

Use the shortcut menus for easy cut-and-paste operations.

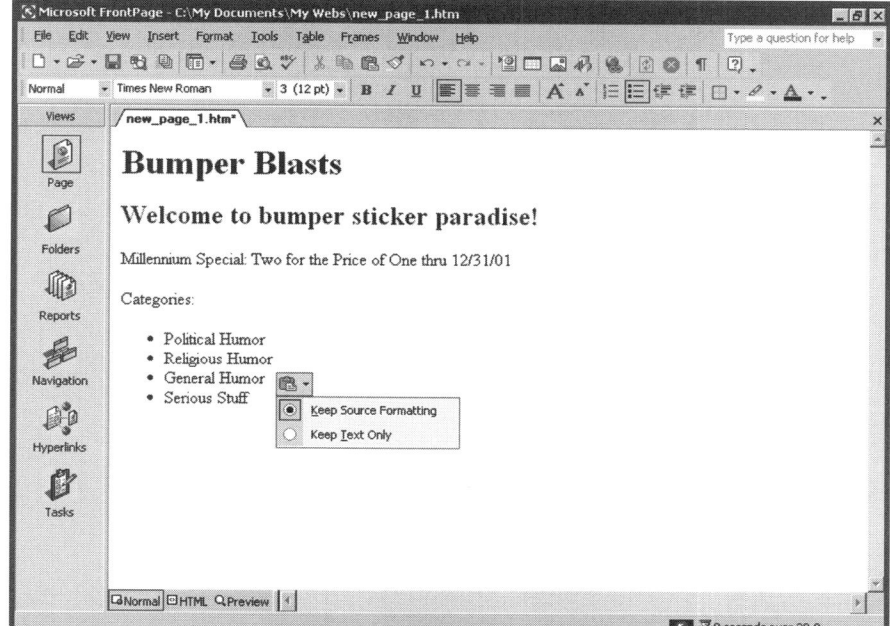

Figure 1.19

The Paste Options button, new in Office XP, helps to eliminate confusion when you're moving text from one place to another.

6. Drag the highlighted text to the start of the first bulleted paragraph and release the mouse button. FrontPage drops the line of text in its new location. Press Enter if you want to separate the moved text as a new paragraph.

7. Click at the end of the last bulleted paragraph and press Enter. FrontPage creates a new bulleted paragraph, as shown in Figure 1.20.

8. Changed your mind about that new line? No problem. Press the Backspace key once to remove the bullet, and press Backspace again to remove the line you just created.

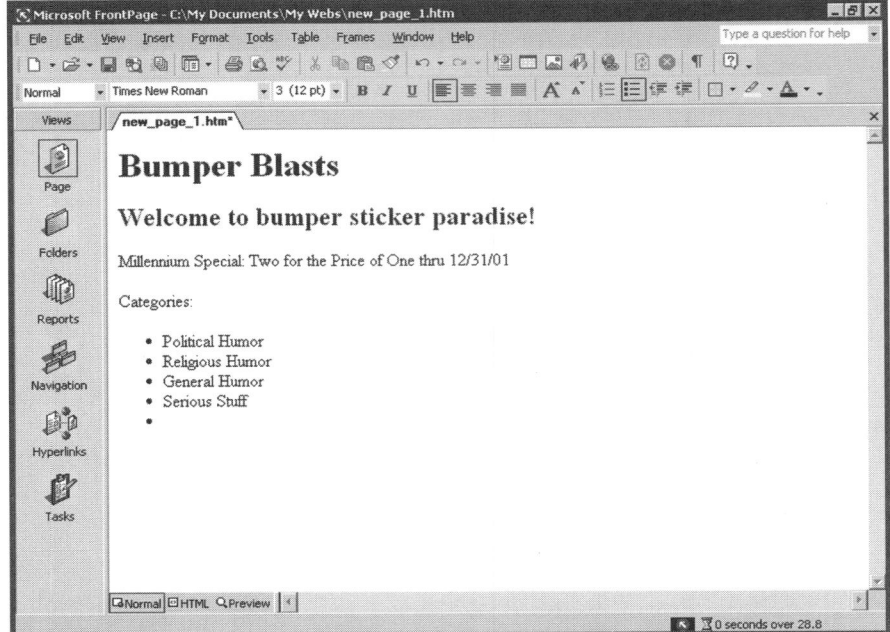

Figure 1.20

FrontPage guesses that the new paragraph you're adding should be another item in your bulleted list.

Checking for Spelling Errors

After you're satisfied with the text, make sure that you didn't make any typing errors. Follow these steps to spell-check your document.

1. Click on the Spelling button on the toolbar (the button marked "ABC" with a check mark). FrontPage begins the spelling check.

2. If FrontPage finds a word it doesn't recognize, the Spelling dialog box opens and the word in question appears in the Not in Dictionary text box, as shown in Figure 1.21.

3. You have several choices for correcting words the spelling checker identifies as misspelled.

   • **Ignore**. The spelling is correct; ignore this instance of it.

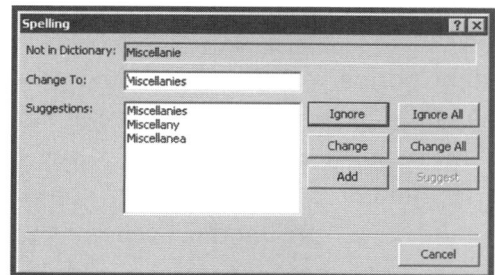

Figure 1.21

Use the spelling
checker to check
your work.

- **Ignore All**. The spelling is correct; ignore all instances of the
  word in this document.

- **Change**. The spelling is incorrect; change this instance of it.
  Enter your own correction or select one from the Suggestions list.

- **Change All**. The spelling is incorrect; change all instances of it in
  this document. Enter your own correction or select one from the
  Suggestions list.

- **Add**. The spelling is correct; recognize this word in all documents
  by adding it to the dictionary.

- **Suggest**. The spelling is incorrect, but none of the suggestions
  are correct. Select a suggested word and then click on Suggest
  for alternatives.

- **Cancel**. End the spelling check.

4. When the spelling check is finished, a message appears (see
   Figure 1.22). Click on OK to close the message box.

Figure 1.22

Where would you
be today without
your trusty spelling
checker?

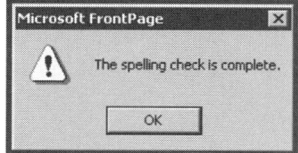

Inserting a Graphic

Your Web site will be boring without some visual elements. Those image files you collected earlier in the evening will come in handy now. As the Insert Picture submenu suggests in Figure 1.23, you can insert graphics from files stored on your computer, place them from FrontPage's built-in Clip Art Gallery, copy them from another Web site, capture them directly from a digital camera, or create the graphic right in FrontPage using drawing tools that are considerably enhanced over those in previous versions of FrontPage. For this example, I simply inserted a Windows JPG file from my hard drive. You'll have time to explore the fun stuff later.

1. Click where you want to insert the graphic.

2. Select Insert, Picture, and then select From File. The Picture dialog box appears.

3. Navigate to the desired file, select the file name, and then click on OK. FrontPage inserts the picture on your Web page, as shown in Figure 1.24.

4. If you want to change the alignment of your graphic, select the object and then click on the Left, Center, or Right Align buttons on the toolbar.

Congratulations—you've just created your first Web page! I told you it was easy. You're far from finished, but you've done enough to get an idea of where you're headed. Enough creativity for now; take a look at the results of your efforts so far and then close up shop for the night.

Figure 1.23

FrontPage supports a wide variety of graphic file formats.

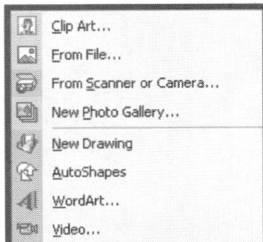

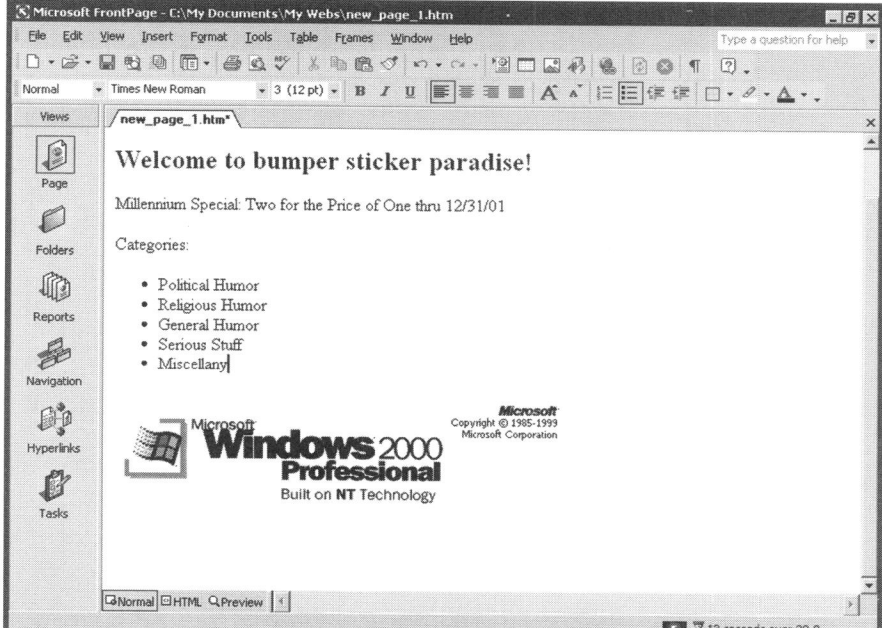

Figure 1.24

Let the world know
you only use the
best: Microsoft!

Saving Your Work

Before you go any further, you need to save your work so that you can
come back to it later. To save this file to a folder on your hard drive,
follow these steps.

1. Click on the Save button on the toolbar. If this is the first time
   you've saved the file, the Save As dialog box appears, as shown in
   Figure 1.25. (If this is not the first time you've saved the file, Front-
   Page saves the file in the background while you continue working.)

2. Enter the name you want to give the file in the File Name box.
   (FrontPage will suggest a file name; feel free to use it if you want.
   If this will be your front or home page, keep in mind that most
   Web servers need the site's opening page to be named index.htm
   or index.html. Check with your service provider to be sure.)

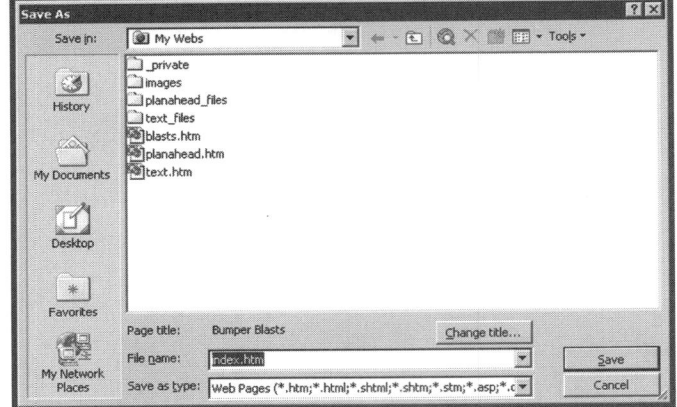

Figure 1.25

Use the file name
FrontPage suggests
or enter your own.

3. Navigate to the folder on your hard drive where you want to save the file.

4. FrontPage assigns a Page Title to your document based on the first line of text. The Page Title is the name that appears on the title bar of your browser when this page is open. To change the title, click on Change and enter the new name in the Set Page Title dialog box, then click on OK.

TIP

It's a good idea to be as descriptive with page titles as possible. Some Web search engines display only page titles when reporting a user's search results. If you want a noticeable Web site, you need to give the user a hint about your site's content. You're much more likely to draw a visitor with a title like "Bumper Blasts: Bumper Stickers with Attitude for Today's Road Warrior" than with the suggested default title.

5. Click on Save to save the file. If you have a graphic in the file, FrontPage prompts you to also save the embedded file (see Figure 1.26). Feel free to rename the file or change the default save location or action using the buttons near the bottom of the dialog box. Click on OK to close the dialog box.

CAUTION

◆ ◆

Save frequently, not just when you're finished working. You never know when your computer might crash, the power might go out, or any number of other anomalies might occur. If something like that happens, all your hard work will go down the drain, and you'll have to start over from the point when you last saved the file.

◆ ◆

Previewing Pages in a Browser

Although working in FrontPage's Normal view gives you a general idea of how your text will look online, it's not completely accurate. For a better representation of how a visitor will see your page, click on the Preview tab (see Figure 1.27). The differences at this point might be subtle or nonexistent. As your site develops, however, the differences will be more obvious as you compare views.

As I said earlier, though, sometimes even the Preview view doesn't tell the whole story. You'll want to check your progress in a real browser (or two

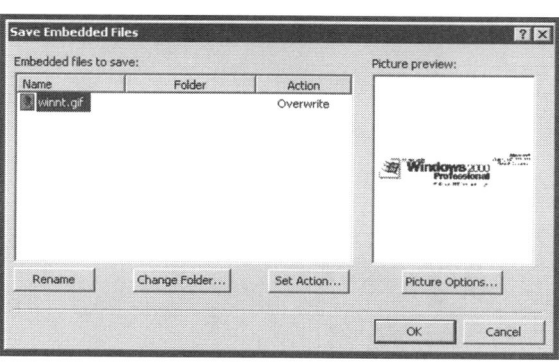

Figure 1.26

FrontPage needs to copy files you've embedded into its file list.

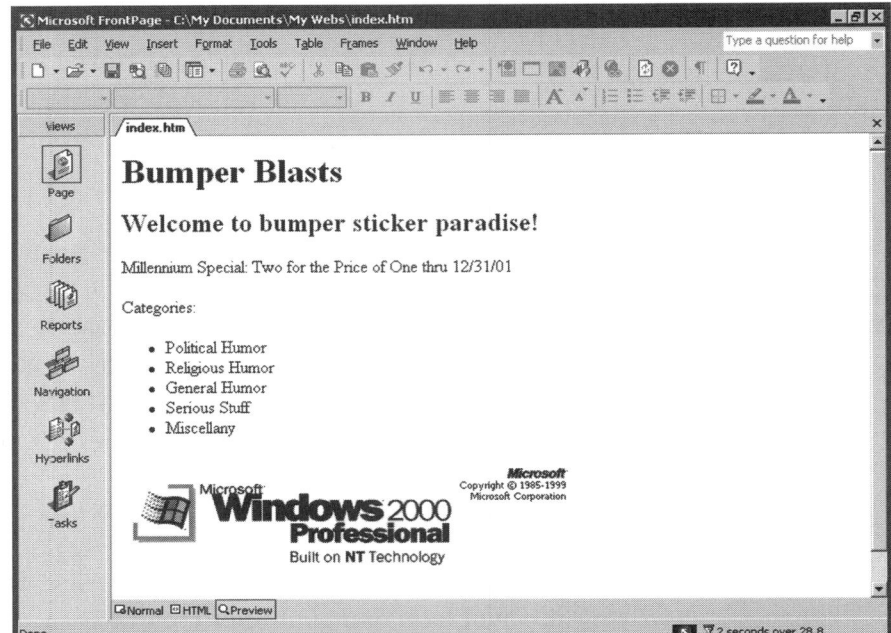

Figure 1.27

Take a quick peek
at the browser view
on the Preview tab.

or three) from time to time, just to ensure you're getting the results you
want. To view your new page, save any changes and then follow these
steps.

1. Select File, Preview in Browser. The Preview in Browser dialog box
   opens, giving you a list of browsers you can use to view the file (see
   Figure 1.28).

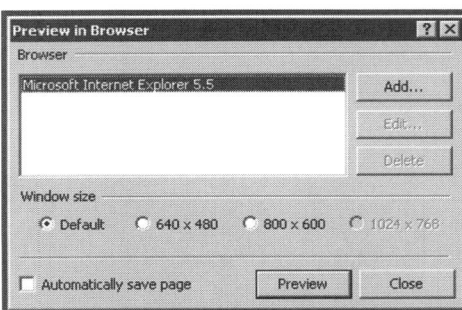

Figure 1.28

You can check the
appearance of your
page using a
variety of browsers.

2. To add another browser to the list, click on the Add button and enter the browser's name and location in the Add Browser dialog box.

3. Under Window size, choose either Default or 800 × 600, which is the most common display size on the average user's computer. This will help you make sure the browser displays your page in the same dimensions as your visitor will probably view it. Then, click on OK.

4. Select the browser you want to use and then click on Preview. The selected browser opens and displays your Web page, as shown in Figure 1.29.

5. When you're finished, click on the browser's Close button to return to FrontPage.

6. Repeat steps 1 through 4 to view the file in a different browser.

Whew! Your Web site is well on its way to becoming a reality, and you've only been working for a few hours. Not bad for an evening's work, eh?

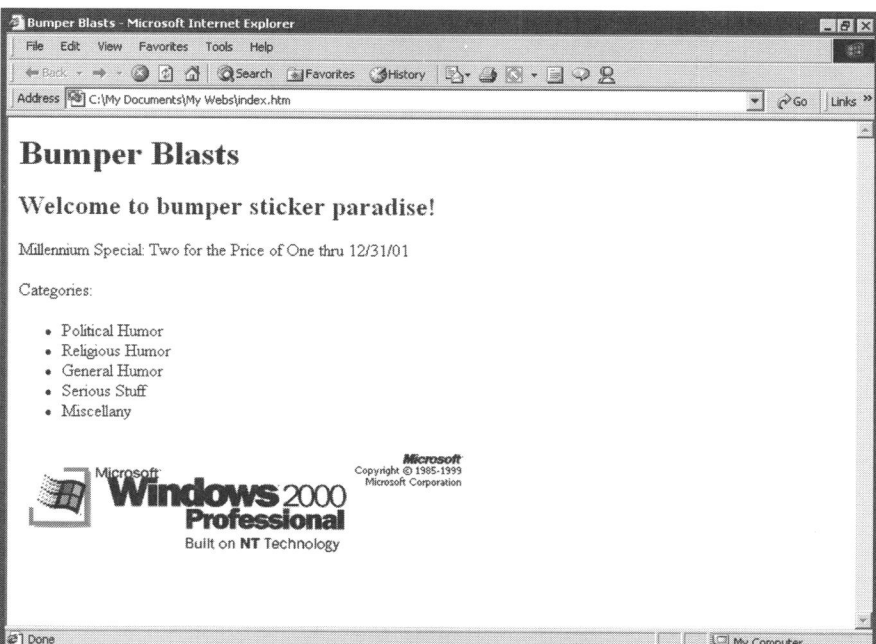

Figure 1.29

Here's how my opening page looks in Internet Explorer 5.

What's Next?

You now have one great-looking page, but you have a long way to go before your Web site is complete. Tomorrow, you'll learn more about enhancing your pages, including how to add common features such as links and backgrounds. You'll also explore more advanced Web site design features such as forms and frames. On Sunday, you'll add marquees, hit counters, and a dynamic table of contents that automatically changes as your content changes. Then, you'll put on the finishing touches and, at last, publish your Web site online.

For now, save any new work you've done, close FrontPage, shut down your computer, and go relax. You've earned it!

Adding Flair and Function

- ✿ Building Your Site
- ✿ Giving Your Pages Personality
- ✿ All about Lists
- ✿ Getting a Cohesive Look with Themes

Good morning! While you were sleeping, another few thousand people logged on to the Internet for the first time. Each one of them is a potential visitor to your Web site, so get rolling!

Last night you learned a lot about planning your Web site and working in FrontPage. You also built your first Web page, added a few embellishments, and saw how your new page looked in a browser. Today, you'll build on what you learned last night. By the end of the day, you'll have many new pages to show off your growing skills as a Web designer. So, throw on your favorite baggy sweats, grab a bagel and some juice, and put on some background tunes. You have a lot of exciting work to do today!

Building Your Site

In last night's session, you worked on a single Web page. Most Web sites consist of several pages. FrontPage makes it easy to manage your entire Web site. You can make the same change to multiple pages, update links, and perform other tedious chores, but only if you store all the information about your site in one place. That one place is a FrontPage Web. Your first task this morning is to create a new Web and learn how to import any existing Web sites, pages, or other documents you might already have tucked away somewhere. After that, you'll add the page you created last night and get to work on sprucing it up and adding more pages.

Creating a New Web

A FrontPage Web is a collection of Web pages, graphics, documents, and other files needed to operate your Web site. It's also the place where you manage your site by adding or removing pages, updating hyperlinks in one fell swoop, and making other changes.

NOTE Depending on your situation, you might be able to manage your FrontPage Web directly from your company's network or your Web Host's server. Most individuals and small businesses, however, store their site on their computer's hard drive and only publish the completed site or updates to the server as needed. In this book, I'll assume that's your story as well. If not, you'll want to check out other options in Appendix A, "Publishing Your FrontPage 2002 Web Pages," now, rather than later.

You'll want to start every new project by first creating a new FrontPage Web. To create a new FrontPage Web, follow these steps.

1. Open FrontPage from the Start menu. Close any Webs or pages that might open automatically (such as the one you created last night) by clicking File, Close (for single pages) or File, Close Web (for Web sites).

TIP If you manage only one Web site, you can tell FrontPage to always open the last Web you used. Select Tools, Options to open the Options dialog box, and then check the box next to Open Last Web Automatically when FrontPage Starts. Click on OK to close the dialog box.

If you work on several sites, you're better off disabling this option and opening Front-Page to a blank page. Use the File, Recent Files or Recent Webs menus to quickly open the desired Web. Your most recently opened files will be listed in the Task pane; if you do indeed want to work on them again, just point and click.

2. On the Task pane, click on Web Site Templates. The Web Site Templates dialog box opens, presenting a variety of options for your new site (see Figure 2.1). Depending on which one you choose, FrontPage might ask you a series of questions so that it can build a skeleton site that includes several pages with the basic content you need to get started. For now, just select the One Page Web template.

TIP

■■■■■■■■■■■■■■■■■■■■■■■■■■■■■■■■■■■■■

If the Task pane is not already open, you can pop it up quickly by choosing File, New, Page or Web. Click on the Task pane's Close button to get rid of it when you're finished, or to buy some more precious workspace.

■■■■■■■■■■■■■■■■■■■■■■■■■■■■■■■■■■■■■

3. Tell FrontPage where to store this Web by entering the path name in the edit box. Specify the location of the new Web. The default location (C:\My Webs\) is as good a place as any.

Figure 2.1

Create a basic one-page Web in a flash.

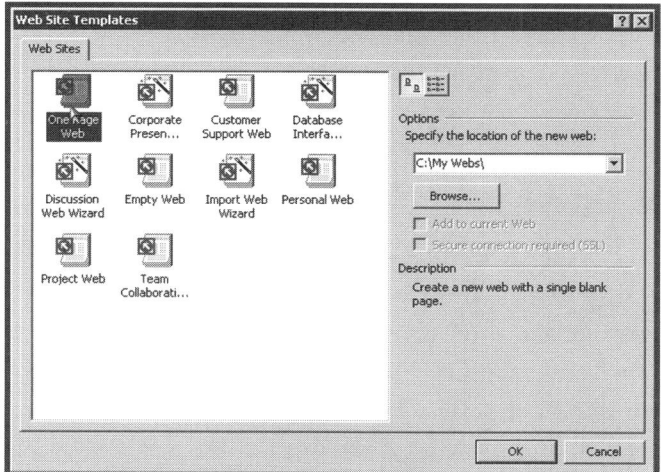

TIP

I store all my Webs in appropriately labeled subfolders under the My Webs folder (usually found in the My Documents folder) on my computer's hard drive. The examples in this book reflect that location. It doesn't really matter where you store your files as long as you can easily organize and keep track of them.

4. Click on OK. FrontPage opens your new Web and creates a folder structure. You'll notice that FrontPage has already created a new, blank page called index.htm, as shown in Figure 2.2.

NOTE

The file containing the opening page of any Web should always be called index.htm (or another variation, such as index.html, default.htm, default.asp, and so on, depending on your server needs). When you type the URL to go to a Web site, you usually just have to type the domain's Web site address to open the site, such as http://www.mysite.com. The browser knows to automatically open the index or default page if it finds it. In reality, however, the full address you're pointing to is something like http://www.mysite.com/index.html.

You might also see index pages with the extension .asp instead of .htm or .html. Pages using this extension are Active Server Pages. Most of the examples in this book use the .htm extension. Be sure you check with your Web Host to see which you need to use—otherwise you might have to invest some time in renaming everything.

Adding New Pages

Unless you have only the most basic one-page "billboard" Web site in mind, you will want to add new pages to your site. You can add new pages one at a time as you develop your site, or you can add all your pages at once and then develop them individually. The latter method works fine if you know exactly which pages you'll need from the start, but chances are you'll add some later anyway.

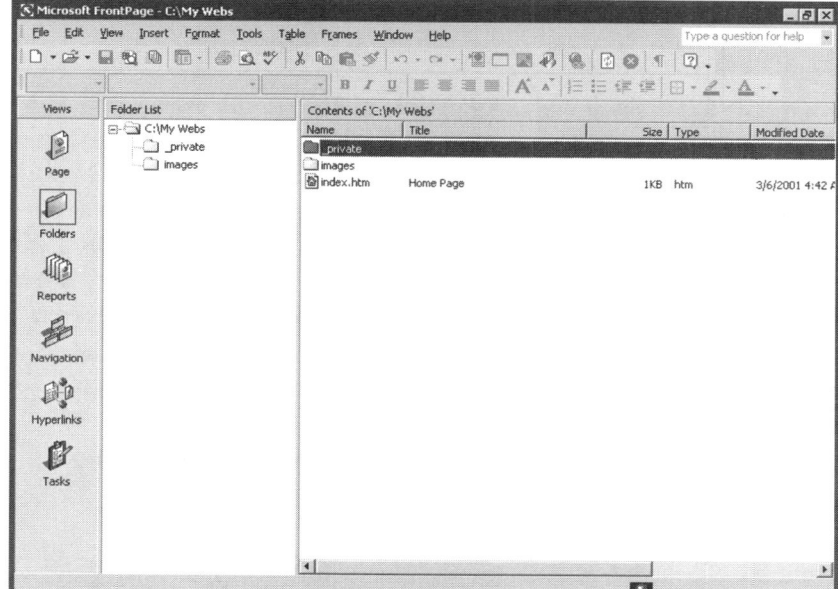

Figure 2.2

Here's your Web, with a blank index (home) page to get you started.

Adding a New Page to Edit Later

If all you want to do is create a blank page now and work on it later, you can. In fact, you can even ask FrontPage to remind you to edit the page later so that you don't forget.

It's a good idea to add a to-do item to your Tasks list any time you need to go back and finish something. Once you have several pages in your Web, it can be hard to remember all those little details by yourself!

 **NOTE** You'll work more with the Tasks list when you finish your Web on Sunday afternoon.

1. Click on the Folders view to see the list of files and folders in your Web.

2. In the Folder List pane, click on the folder in which you want to add the new page. For now, just select the top-level folder.

WHAT GOOD ARE TEMPLATES?

FrontPage is all about making your job easier. Templates can save you time by doing some of the development work for you. For example, if you want to set up a discussion-based Web site complete with user submission forms, search capabilities, and reply threads, double-click on the Discussion Web Wizard. FrontPage will ask you a series of questions about your intended Web site and then generate all the pages you need to get started (see Figure 2.3). What's more, you can even choose an overall theme for your Web site's look and feel. (You'll learn more about themes later this evening.) All you have to do is customize the content to suit your needs, insert your own graphics, create additional pages as needed, and apply any special formatting.

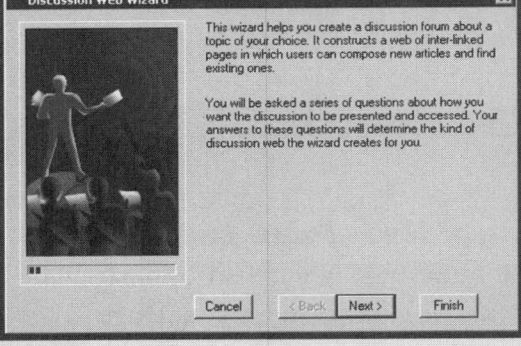

Figure 2.3

The template wizards provide quick shortcuts to creating the basic structure of your Web site and pages.

When the wizard completes the setup, it offers to take you straight to the Tasks lists. That's FrontPage's way of saying, "Okay, I did my part; now it's your turn."

It's okay to use these templates if they provide what you need. Your work is far from finished, however. You still need the skills you learn in this book to edit the templates, insert advanced features, and personalize the Web site.

3. Click on the New button on the toolbar. FrontPage creates a new page and adds it to the Contents pane of the Folders view (see Figure 2.4). The default file name, new_page_x.htm, is highlighted, so that you can give it your own file name. X represents the new page number; each page you create is numbered successively.

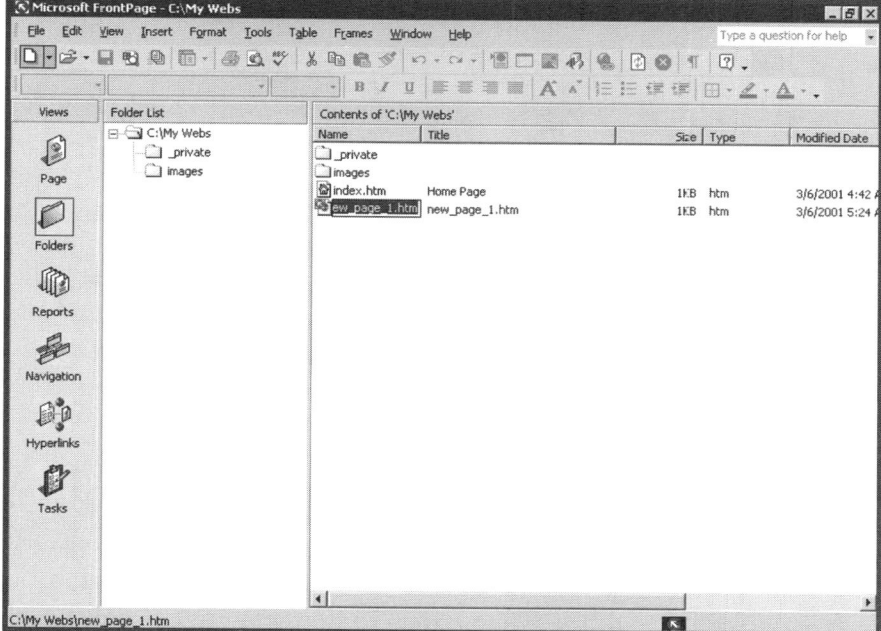

Figure 2.4

Rename your page right here and save an extra step later.

4. Type the desired file name, using .htm as the extension. The name you enter here will be part of the URL you will enter or link to when viewing the page online. If you use spaces in the file name, FrontPage replaces them with underscores.

5. Press the Tab key. FrontPage accepts your change and highlights the new page's title.

6. Type a title for the page. The page title will appear in the title bar of the visitor's browser when the page is viewed online.

7. Press Tab again. FrontPage accepts your new title and highlights the new page's Comments field. Type any comments you want and press Enter.

8. Now tell FrontPage to remind you to work on this page later. Select the new page and then click on Edit, Tasks, Add Task. The New Task dialog box opens, as shown in Figure 2.5.

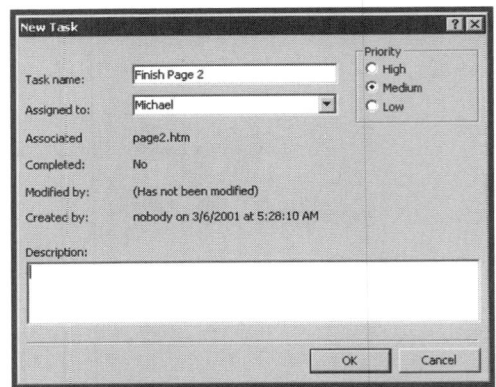

Figure 2.5

If you don't want
to edit a new page
immediately, add it
to your list of tasks.

9. Type a descriptive name in the Task Name text box and assign
   someone to the task. (You can leave it blank in this case, because
   you're the only one on the project.) Click on OK. FrontPage closes
   the dialog box, adds the task to your Tasks list, and takes you back
   to the Folders view so that you can continue working.

TIP

Another quick way to create a new task is to click on the new page and hold down the
mouse button. While you hold the button, point to the Tasks button on the Views bar.
FrontPage will switch to Tasks view. While you are still holding the mouse button, drag
back to the Editing window and notice that the pointer will change to a small arrow surrounded by a box and a + sign. When you see the new cursor shape, release the mouse
button. Complete the task as described in Step 9. It took a lengthy explanation to
describe this shortcut, but actually performing it takes only a second.

Adding a New Page to Edit Immediately

Sometimes you'll want to work on a new page as soon as you create it. In
the Bumper Blasts Web site, I need to create a Frequently Asked Questions page. I think I'll let FrontPage do some of the work, so this time I'll
use a template to set up the page's basic elements for me. You should add
a page appropriate to your own content, such as a guest book, a table of
contents, or just a blank normal page to develop from scratch.

1. Click on Page view to change to the editing view.

2. Click on the down arrow next to the New button on the toolbar and choose Page. The Page Templates dialog box cpens and displays a list of available page templates, as shown in Figure 2.6.

3. Select the desired page style and click on OK. FrontPage instantly creates your new page based on the chosen template and opens it for editing.

Type the text you want on the new page. It's a good idea to save your work frequently, so do that now. You'll be prompted to save the file and give it a title, if you haven't already.

If you used a template, read the comments FrontPage displays on the page. These tips help you edit the template-based page to suit your needs (see Figure 2.7).

TIP

If you change your mind and don't want to keep the page you just created, just click on the page's Close button. Poof! The page is gone just as quickly as it was created.

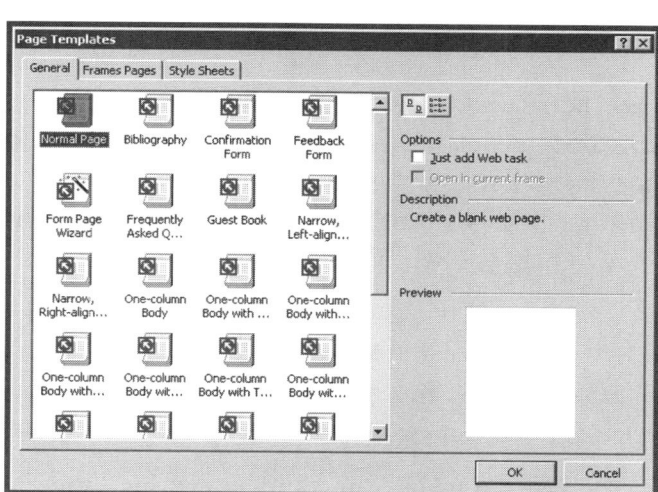

Figure 2.6

Add a blank new page, or let FrontPage assist you with a template.

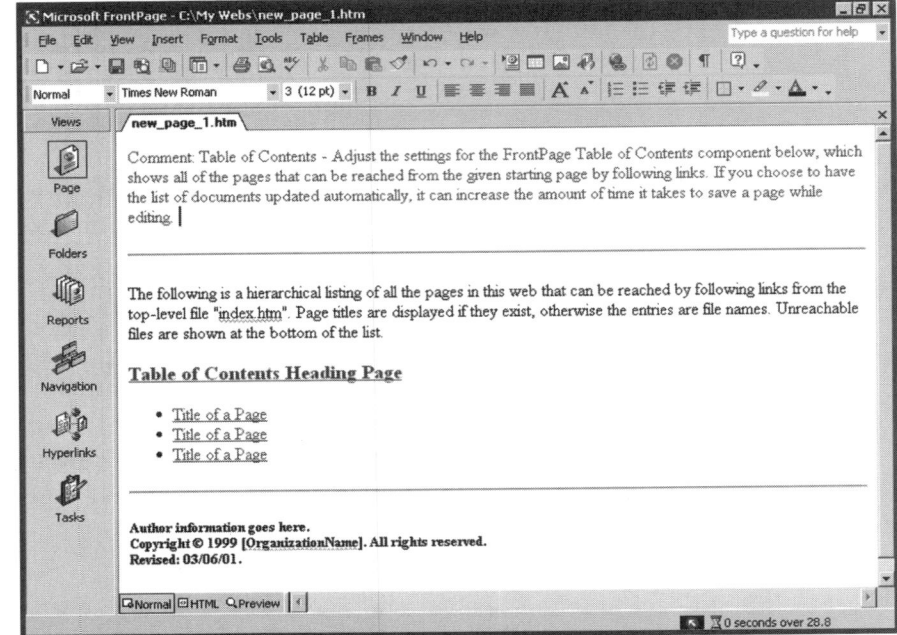

Figure 2.7

FrontPage includes instructions and tips in a template so that you can personalize your page's content.

By now, you should have a couple of new pages in your Web, in addition to the index.htm file that FrontPage created for you. They're not very detailed, but that's okay. Next, you'll work on fine-tuning these pages.

In the next sections, you'll focus on importing existing Web pages or Office documents. If all you have to import to your new Web is the page you created last night, skip the next few sections and go straight to "Opening Last Night's Page." Make a mental note that the information is here to help you when you need it.

Importing Other Webs or Pages

You can import existing Web sites and pages into your Web. Why would you want to? For any number of reasons:

○ You want to make changes to an existing FrontPage Web but keep an unchanged copy of the site available.

- Your existing site was created in another program, and you want to begin using FrontPage to manage the site.

- You want to take just a few pages of an existing Web site and add them to your new site.

- You want to import a sample Web site to study its structure and learn how certain features were implemented.

Whatever the reason, FrontPage makes it easy to import existing Web sites or pages into your new site.

Importing Existing Pages from Your Computer or Network

You might have some stand-alone Web pages or HTML documents on your hard drive that you want to use in your new Web site. To import just one or two pages into your current Web, follow these steps.

1. With your current Web open, select File, Import. The Import dialog box appears (see Figure 2.8).

2. To import a file, select Add File. The Add File to Import List dialog box opens.

3. Change the Files of Type setting to HTML Files. Navigate to the desired file and click on it to select it. Click on Open to add the file to the list.

Figure 2.8

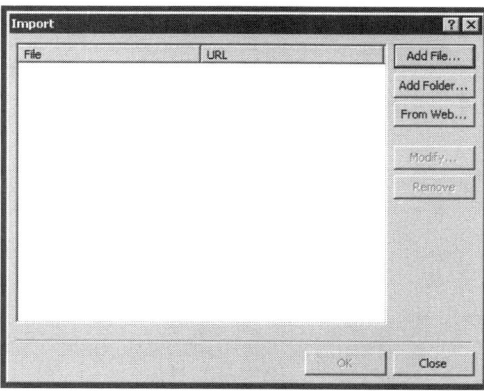

Importing single pages from other Webs or folders is another way to save time in your site development.

TIP

Hold down the Control key while you click on files to select more than one file. To import an entire folder, click on Add Folder, select the desired folder, and click on OK. FrontPage adds all the files in the chosen folder to the import list.

4. Remove from the list any files you don't want to import by highlighting the file or files and clicking on Remove.

5. When you've listed all the files you want to import, click on OK to close the dialog box and begin the import.

Importing Existing Pages from the World Wide Web

If you find a page on the Web that you particularly like and want to download and modify for your own use, you can do so as long as you're mindful of copyright laws. To import just one or two pages into your current Web, follow these steps.

1. With your current Web open, select File, Import. The Import dialog box appears.

2. Click on From Web to start the wizard. The Choose Source page appears first (see Figure 2.9). Select From a World Wide Web Site, then type the URL of the page in the Location text box. Be sure to enter the full address including the file name, such as http://www.mysite.com/mypage.htm, or you might end up accidentally importing the entire site!

TIP

To be absolutely sure that you get a lengthy path name or URL right, you might want to open the page in your browser, copy the URL from the Address field, press Alt+Tab to return to FrontPage, and then paste the URL into the wizard's Location field.

3. Click on Next to complete the wizard's questions, then click on Finish to start the import. FrontPage imports the designated file into your Web. You might be prompted to connect, if you need to log on to the Internet.

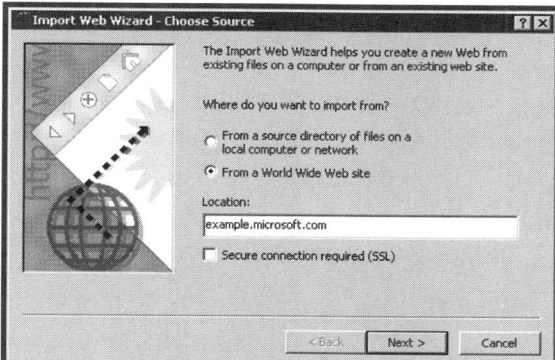

Figure 2.9

Copying a design is usually okay, but using someone else's content or graphics without permission is against the law.

Importing an Entire Site

To import an existing Web site for use as a new Web site, follow these steps. For this example, you'll import a sample Web site from Microsoft's sample collection.

1. Make sure that all existing Webs and pages are closed.

2. Select File, Import. The New dialog box opens. Click on Import Web Wizard and click on OK. The Import Web Wizard opens.

3. Enter the location or path name for the site in the appropriate box. The http://example.microsoft.com address really is a site; go ahead and use that address for this example.

❖ ❖

CAUTION Be very, very careful about importing files from someone else's Web site. Web sites are protected by copyright laws just like written documents, and plagiarism is plagiarism. It's acceptable to borrow some basic ideas (who was it that said "There's no such thing as an original design"?), but never, *never* publish someone else's work as your own. That goes for photos, graphics, or any other file you might find. If it is not clearly marked that the files can be freely distributed or copied, always ask permission from the site owner. It's not only the law; it's good manners. (Mom would be so proud!)

❖ ❖

4. Click on Next. If you're importing from a site out in cyberspace, you'll next be asked to choose how much of the site you want to import (see Figure 2.10). You can choose to stop at a certain level of the navigation structure, limit the total size of the files downloaded, or import only text and graphics files (leaving out hidden files and the like). Or, you can choose any combination of the three.

5. Click on Finish to begin the import. When the import is completed, switch to Folders view to see a list of the files and folders imported (see Figure 2.11). From there, you can open and edit any file.

Importing Office Documents

One of the most exciting developments of Microsoft Office over the last few versions has been its growth in "Web friendliness." All the primary Office applications are fully integrated and Internet-compatible. Create an animated PowerPoint presentation complete with transitions and sound effects. Import that presentation into FrontPage and publish it to your Web site, no tweaking necessary. People using Internet Explorer 4.0 or later can view the slide show in their browsers just as they would see it on the screen. Netscape users can play the slide show in their own installation of PowerPoint or the PowerPoint Viewer. To import an Office document into your Web, follow these steps.

1. With your current Web open, select File, Import. The Import dialog box appears.

Figure 2.10

You can set limitations on the site import—not a bad idea if you're just using the import to study site design.

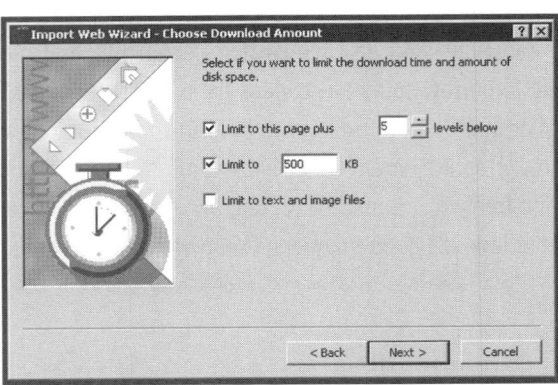

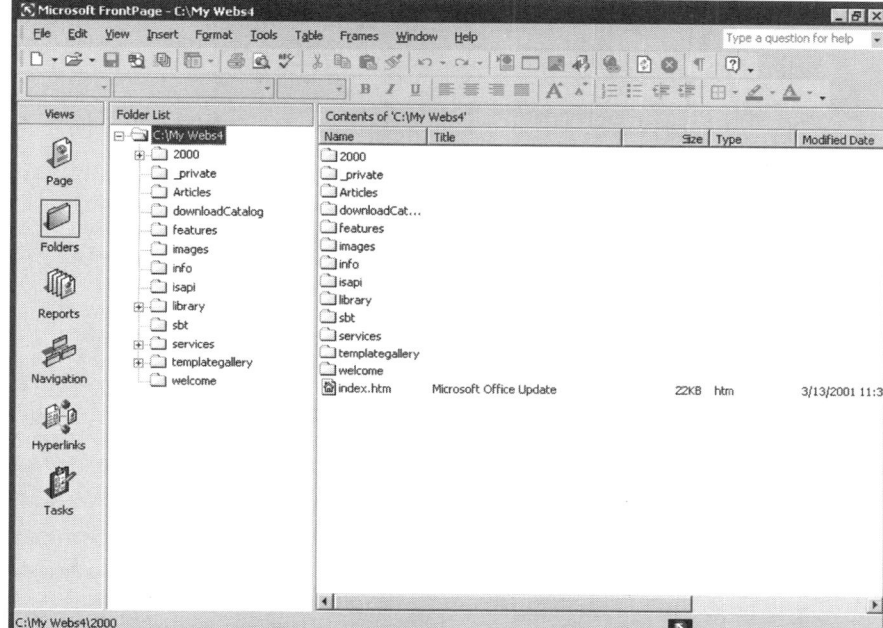

Figure 2.11

Get a jumpstart on your Web site by importing a site from somewhere else and modifying it to fit your needs and design preferences.

2. To import a file, select Add File. The Add File to Import List dialog box opens.

3. Change the Files of Type to Microsoft Office Files (see Figure 2.12). Navigate to the desired file and select it. Click on Open to add the file to the list.

4. When you've listed all the files you want to import, click on OK to close the dialog box and begin the import.

Switch to Folders view and delete any unwanted files you might have inserted as an experiment. Save your work and close all open Webs except your main project.

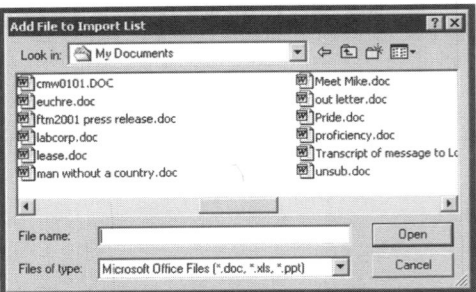

Figure 2.12

Import Office documents into your Web just as you would import any other Web page or graphic.

DON'T USE A SCREWDRIVER TO DRIVE A NAIL....

For Web pages that are primarily text-based, it makes sense to use the right tool for the right job. Create your text document in Word so that you can take advantage of Word's robust word processing features, then import the file into FrontPage to publish it on your Web site.

Do the same for complex tables. Use Excel to create a spreadsheet, then select Insert, File to insert the spreadsheet into an open FrontPage Web page. FrontPage automatically converts the document to HTML format and inserts it as a table in your open Web page, as shown in Figure 2.13.

Opening Last Night's Page

When you created your new Web this morning, FrontPage automatically added a starter file called index.htm. You already have the starter page you created in last night's session, so you'll just drop it in, literally. Herein lies another shortcut for building your site: drag-and-drop. To import last night's page into your new Web, try this:

1. Open your FrontPage Web and click on Folders view.

2. Open Windows Explorer and use it to locate the file you worked on last night. Click on the file to select it.

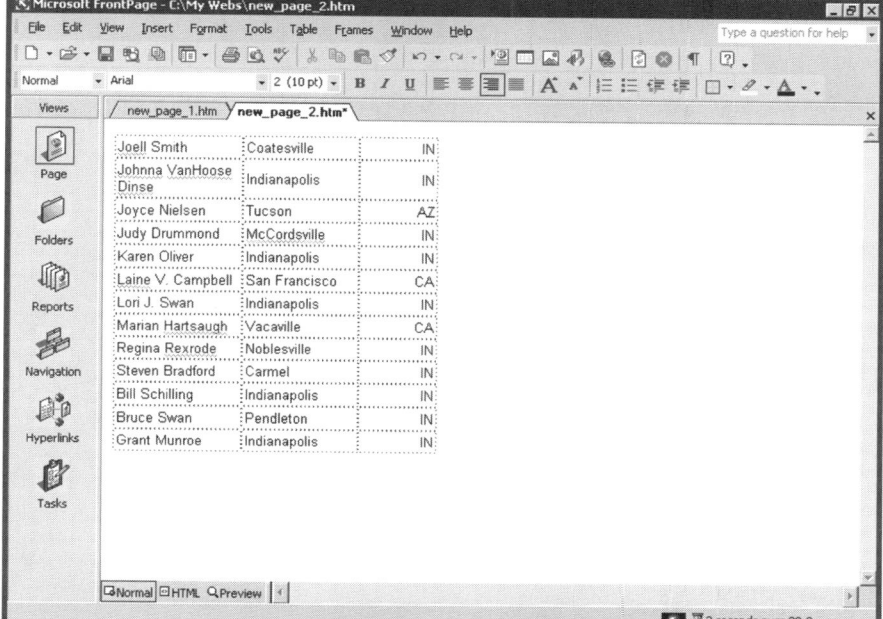

Figure 2.13

Use Insert rather than Import to add an Office document directly to an existing Web.

3. Drag the file to the FrontPage icon on the Windows taskbar (see Figure 2.14), but don't release the mouse button. Hold the pointer over the icon. After a moment, the FrontPage window will come to the front. Drag the pointer to the Contents pane and release the mouse button. The page imports instantly.

4. Repeat steps 1 through 3 to import the graphic file you inserted in last night's page. If you don't import the graphic, you'll get an empty box with an X where the graphic should be.

Remember, however, that you must name a Web site's opening page index.htm. You already have one with that name—the blank one installed by the wizard. You don't really need that one now, so delete the existing index file and then rename last night's page index.htm.

1. To delete the existing file, just select it and press Delete.

Drag to import the
Web page

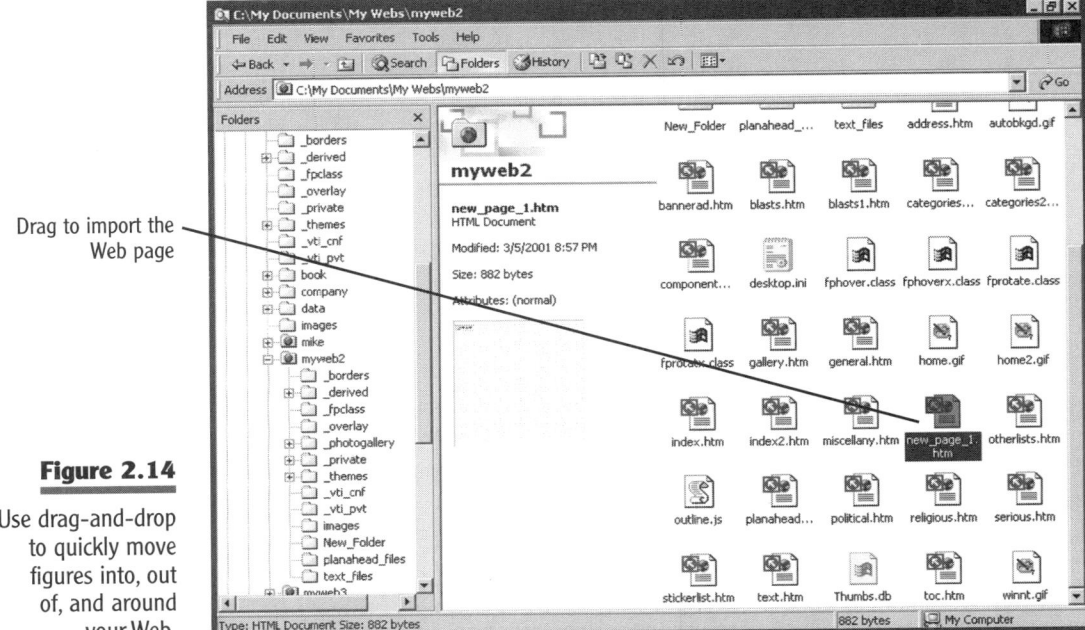

Figure 2.14

Use drag-and-drop
to quickly move
figures into, out
of, and around
your Web.

2. To rename last night's file, click on Folders view and then click on the file you want to change.

3. Right-click on the file name and select Rename.

4. Type the new file name and press Enter (see Figure 2.15).

Notice that FrontPage pauses a moment to update not just the file name, but also any links or references to that file name in your Web (see Figure 2.16). If you have a fast computer, you might miss it. It's more noticeable when your Web site is larger because it takes longer. This is one of FrontPage's most outstanding features. You don't have to search and replace page after page to find all the links to that particular reference.

That long and not-so-exciting lesson on setting up your new Web site is finished (no applause, please). Ready to move on to something a little more creative and fun?

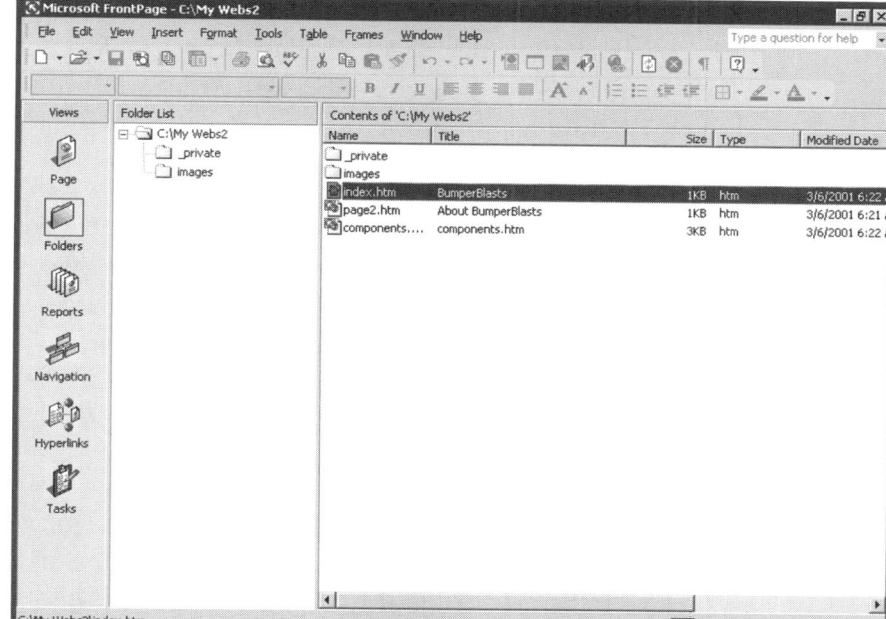

Figure 2.15

Rename the file you created last night to index.htm. That tells browsers to open this page first when users visit your Web site.

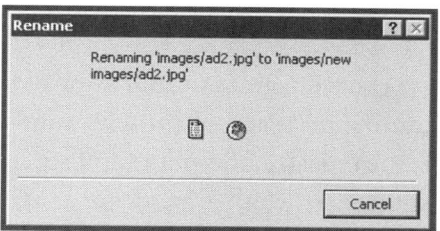

Figure 2.16

FrontPage updates all references and links whenever you move, rename, or delete a page.

Giving Your Pages Personality

Open the index.htm file from the Folders view and take a look at the page you created last night. Nice start, but pretty plain so far, eh? Plain black text on a plain white background just isn't very exciting.

The rest of this morning's session will deal with making your pages look good. You'll add background colors and patterns, apply new styles and fonts, and create a sophisticated multilevel bulleted list with graphics in place of the bullets. Finally, you'll learn how to spice up your site's overall appearance by applying a theme. A theme enables you to assign the same page-formatting characteristics, such as identical headings and buttons, background color, and so on, to any or every page in your site.

 **NOTE** Throughout the remainder of this session, I'll demonstrate the techniques using the original page I created last night, just so that you can see the difference each treatment has to the same content. Feel free to continue building new pages as appropriate for your Web site and apply these techniques to any or all of them.

Basic HTML Styles and Headings

HTML began as a structured programming language without a lot of options. You had a handful of available heading styles, a few styles to make indented lists, and some other options. Although the basic styles have not changed, now there's a lot more flexibility in what you can do within the confines of those styles. Nevertheless, you should have a basic understanding of HTML styles, because you will use them.

In a word processor, you have a great deal of control over paragraph and heading styles. You can define exactly how you want them to appear by choosing the font size, the typeface, the amount of space between lines, and other styles. HTML styles, on the other hand, are a bit more cut and dried. You can change all these attributes using FrontPage's formatting techniques, but it's a lot more work. In addition to the extra work, not every browser will be able to display your embellishments, and unless you are using CSS (*Cascading Style Sheets*), you'll have to make the same change to every affected page. (You'll learn a little bit more about CSS later this morning.)

 TIP Last night you learned how to assign a style, remember? Click somewhere in the paragraph you want to change and then pick a style from the Style drop-down menu.

There are six basic HTML heading styles. Each of them is left-aligned, and their individual characteristics are described in Table 2.1. Think of heading styles in terms of an outline. Heading 1 holds your top-level topic, Heading 2 indicates subtopics under Heading 1, Heading 3 is for topics under Heading 2, and so on. The lower the level, the higher the number, and the smaller the heading. However, unlike 8th grade English class, there are no rules regarding when to use which heading, so use your best judgment and design instincts when assigning a style.

TABLE 2.1 BUILT-IN HTML PARAGRAPH STYLE ATTRIBUTES

Style Name	Attributes
Normal	12 pt text, left-aligned, one line of space before and after the paragraph. This is the main style for all your body text.
Heading 1	24 pt boldface, left-aligned, one line of spacing before and after the paragraph. In general, use it for only the highest level of your topic. On some browsers, the Heading 1 style can be overwhelming, so use it sparingly.
Heading 2	18 pt boldface, left-aligned, one line of spacing before and after the paragraph. I usually use Heading 2 as my main heading because it's not as large as the Heading 1 font.
Heading 3	14 pt boldface, left-aligned, one line of space before and after the paragraph.
Heading 4	12 pt boldface, left-aligned, one line of space before and after the paragraph. A good "subhead" style choice.
Heading 5	10 pt boldface, left-aligned, one line of space before and after the paragraph. This heading style is actually smaller than Normal text.
Heading 6	8 pt boldface, one line of space before and after the paragraph. Heading 6 is tiny onscreen, which makes it ideal for headers, footers, legal mumbo-jumbo, and "the fine print."

The default font for most browsers is Times New Roman. However, the font and sizes may vary depending on the visitor's browser. You can use CSS styles to redefine what the "default" appearance is, too.

BUZZ WORD

As in a Word document, the bulk of the text in your Web page is usually in Normal style. In HTML, Normal text is called *body text*. Any text not designated as a Heading or other style defaults to body text.

In addition to Normal, you might occasionally use other styles, such as Bulleted List, but you'll generally use Normal and Headings 1-6. FrontPage also allows you to create new paragraph styles using the techniques you'll learn this morning, but always keep in mind that older browsers might not support them. Anything the browser can't interpret will default back to Normal style, and your Web page won't look like the one you designed.

That doesn't mean don't use them; just be aware. It's difficult to judge how many people out there are using out-of-date browsers, slow modems, and tired old computers, but it's more than you think. (What's more, for purely competitive reasons, even newer versions of Netscape Navigator don't support some Microsoft Internet Explorer features and vice versa.) Consider your audience. Are they computer junkies or regular Joes? The junkie most definitely has the latest and greatest browser, and will be impressed with well-designed sites. Joe just wants the information and probably doesn't care or even realize that he's using a four-year-old browser.

Formatting Text

The limitations of early browsers have not stopped the rest of the world from seeing just how creative they can be with their Web sites. Commercial sites

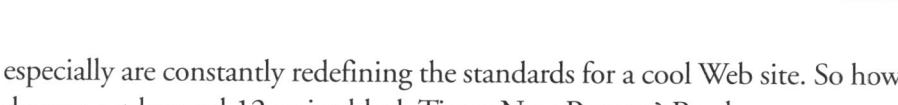

especially are constantly redefining the standards for a cool Web site. So how do you get beyond 12-point black Times New Roman? Read on.

I'm more of a sans serif kind of person, so I want to change the main headings of the Bumper Blasts site to a nice, clean sans serif font. I'm not sure which one yet, but I'll let FrontPage help me decide. (You can read more about sans serif fonts in the sidebar later in this chapter.)

1. Select the text you want to change. If you're changing an entire paragraph, click in the left margin next to the paragraph to quickly select it. Otherwise, select the desired words.

2. Select Format, Font to open the Font dialog box. This dialog box, shown in Figure 2.17, looks much like the Font dialog box in Microsoft Word, but the available options differ.

3. Select a font from the Font list. Notice in the Preview area that FrontPage gives you a sample of your selection. If you're not sure what a font looks like, the preview is a big help. After taking a peek at several, I've decided to choose Arial Rounded MT Bold. Choose whatever you like—but remember that you might not have that font.

Figure 2.17

Déjà vu? This dialog box looks similar to the Font dialog box in Word.

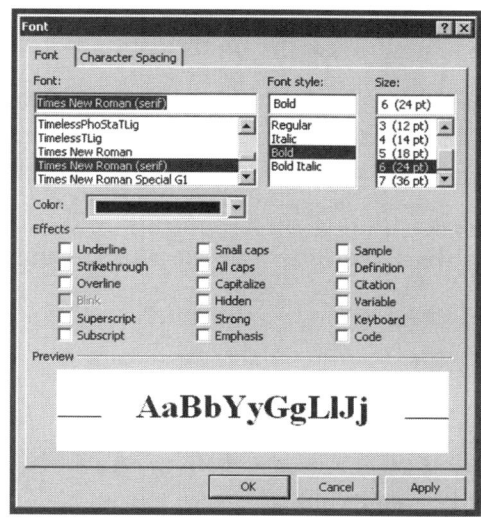

4. Select a Font style. Some fonts look better in bold, and sometimes italic makes them hard to read. Again, the Preview area is a good marker.

5. The Size list includes available sizes 1–7. Size 1 is the smallest size (8 point); 7 is the largest (36 point). For reference, Heading 1 is size 6, and Normal style is size 3.

6. Pick a color for your text by clicking on the down arrow next to the Color box and selecting a color from the color palette. When choosing a font color, keep in mind your background color. Blue text on a black background will be nearly impossible to read no matter how good your monitor is. Stick with high-contrast colors (see Figure 2.18).

7. Choose from a variety of effects. Some you'll recognize; others are holdovers from early HTML days. (Emphasis, for example, is the same thing as italic.) When applying effects, remember that a little goes a long way. Especially Blink, which makes your text blink off and on in Netscape Navigator.

8. When you're satisfied with your choices, click on OK to close the dialog box. Your page will update to reflect the changes.

PLAIN OR FANCY, STRAIGHT OR CURLY?

A *sans serif* font style has flat, plain edges rather than fancy tips or flourishes. Sans serif fonts are great for headings, but text-heavy pages in a sans serif font can be more difficult to read than those set in a serif font. Arial is a common sans serif font you've probably used before. Our dear old friend Times New Roman is a serif font.

It's easiest to see the difference when you compare them one-on-one.

This is Arial (san serif).

Notice the perfectly straight T, I, and i.

This is Times New Roman (serif).

Notice the little points on each end of the T, N, and s. These are the serifs. Thus, sans serif is French for "without little fancy points" (or something like that).

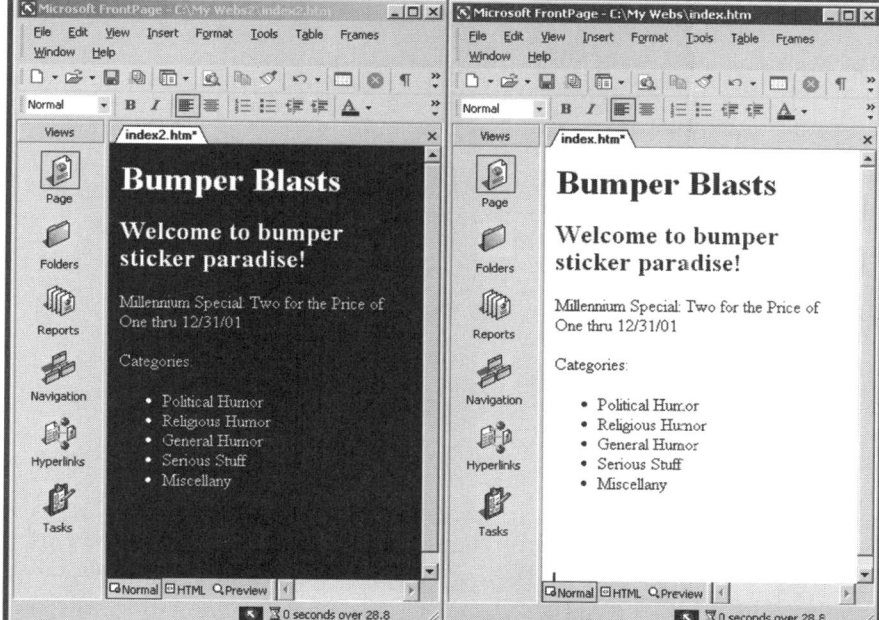

Figure 2.18

High-contrast colors are much easier to read onscreen.

Formatting Paragraphs

In addition to the look of the text, you can also control the spacing around it. There's no space between the lines of the bulleted list on my Bumper Blasts page, but I think there should be. (The last line is fine, however, so I won't select it.)

1. Select the paragraph(s) you want to change.

2. Select Format, Paragraph to open the Paragraph dialog box, as shown in Figure 2.19.

3. Again, this dialog box resembles its cousin in Word. In the Alignment drop-down list, you can change from the default left-aligned text to right, centered, or justified.

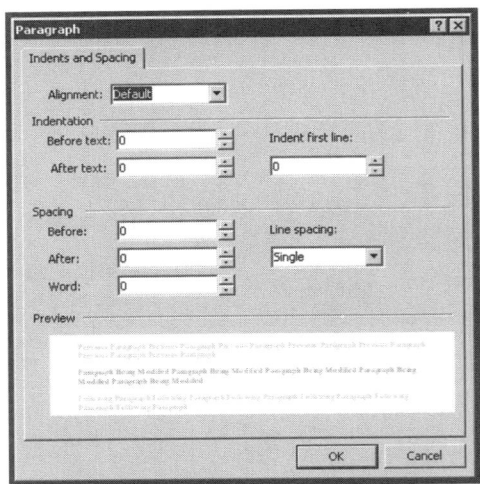

Figure 2.19

Change the line
and paragraph
spacing if you don't
like the default
settings.

4. To change the indentation of a paragraph, adjust the settings in the Before Text (to add space to the left) and After Text (to add space to the right) boxes. To indent only the first line of a paragraph, adjust the number in the Indent First Line box.

5. To add or remove space before or after a paragraph, between words, or between lines, adjust the appropriate values in the Spacing area.

6. Click on OK when you're finished, to close the dialog box and see the changes (see Figure 2.20)

Applying Borders and Shading

You can apply borders to a line of text, too. In addition to your standard black line, you can be a little more creative. Borders can have depth and dimension, which can go a long way in adding visual interest to your pages.

1. Select the desired paragraph in its entirety by clicking in the margin to the left of the paragraph.

2. Select Format, Borders and Shading to open the Borders and Shading dialog box, as shown in Figure 2.21.

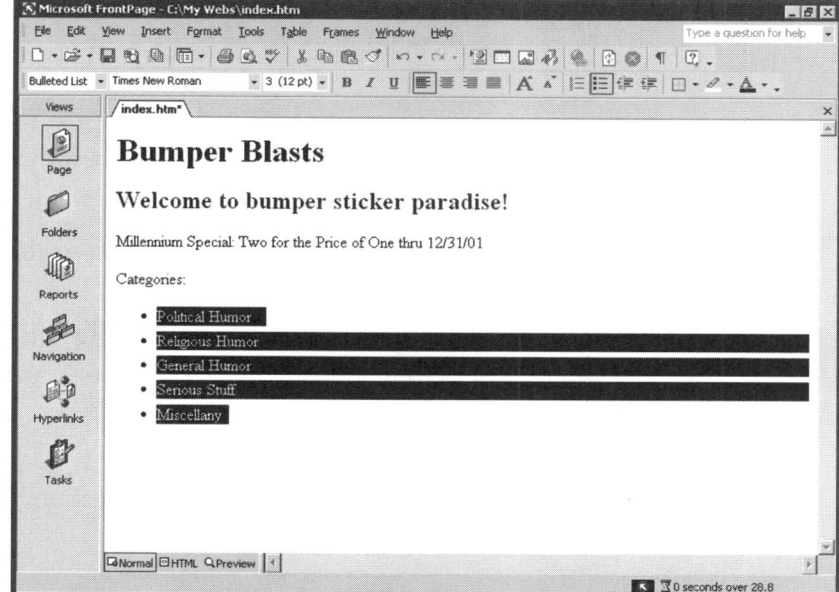

Figure 2.20

A little space between paragraphs never hurts.

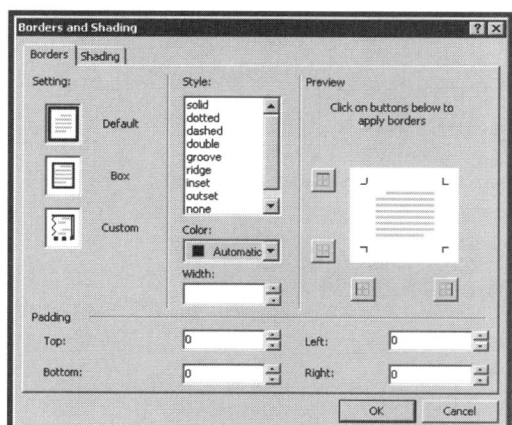

Figure 2.21

Borders and shading can enhance your site as long as you don't overuse them.

3. Under Setting, select Default to apply the standard border, Box to add the border to all four sides, or Custom to select three or fewer sides. If you select Custom, click on the border buttons in the Preview area to choose the sides to which you want to apply borders.

4. Select a style. Try Inset or Outset for that 3D button-like effect, and FrontPage will apply a three-dimensional beveled border.

TIP To remove a border from the selected paragraph, choose the None option in the Style list.

5. Padding refers to the amount of space between the border and the text. Adjust these settings as you see fit.

6. Click on the Shading tab and choose background and foreground colors for your paragraph shading. For the button effect, try a nice gray.

7. Click on OK when you've got it the way you want it. The dialog box closes, and FrontPage shows you the changes (see Figure 2.22).

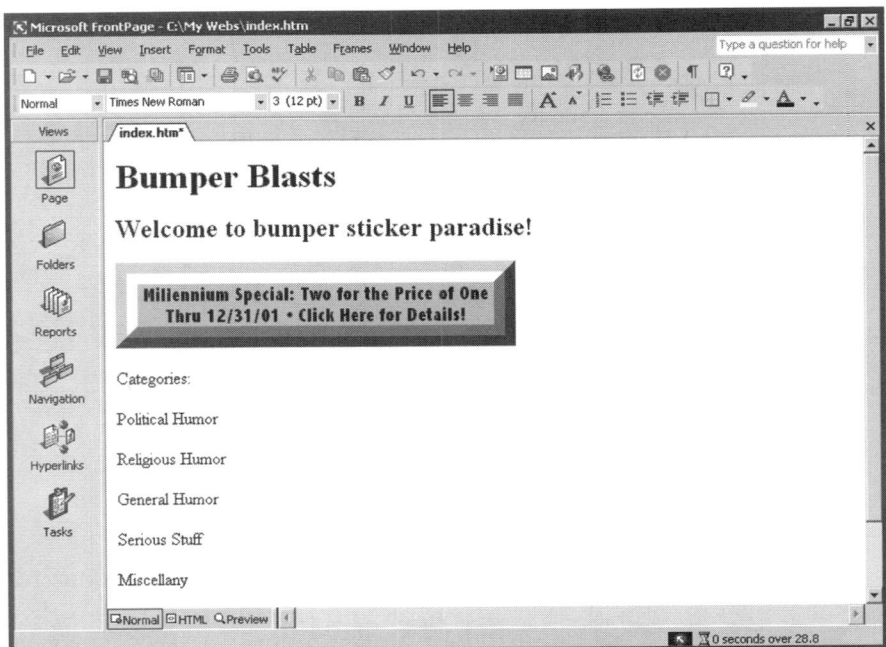

Figure 2.22

You can use 3D border effects to simulate a push button.

What Is Dynamic HTML?

Dynamic HTML (DHTML) gives you the ability to add a bit of animation to your text. If you're familiar with PowerPoint, you've probably used transition effects for your presentations. It's the same idea.

By applying DHTML to a paragraph, you can apply a variety of effects (see Figure 2.23). You can

- **Drop in one word of the paragraph at a time**

- **Spin or fly in the text until it settles into place on the page**

- **Change the font color when you click on or point to a paragraph**

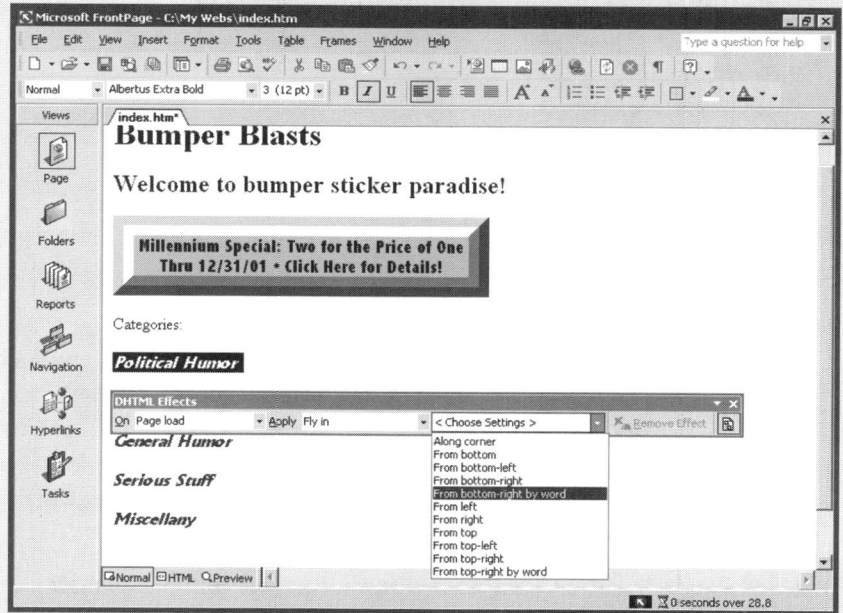

Figure 2.23

Dynamic HTML lets you add animation effects to text.

Dynamic HTML is a Microsoft enhancement to HTML 4.0. It might not work with versions of Internet Explorer or Netscape Navigator older than version 4.0. Results in other browsers might also be unpredictable.

WHAT IS DYNAMIC HTML? *(CONTINUED...)*

If you don't want to be tempted to play with DHTML, leave it disabled and Front-Page won't even make you think about it. To disable DHTML in FrontPage, select Tools, Page Options, then click on the Compatibility tab. Clear the Dynamic HTML check box to disable the use of this feature (see Figure 2.24). Enable it again by selecting the check box. Note that you can control the use of a variety of other "compatibility-sensitive" features from this dialog box as well.

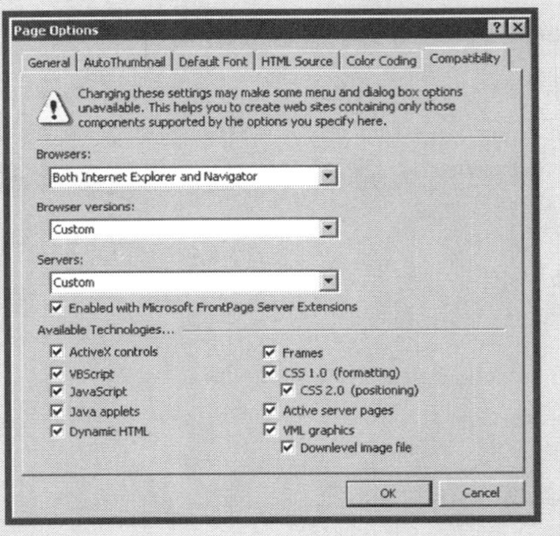

Figure 2.24

If you turn off DHTML, FrontPage won't let you select those options. If you're designing for an audience that might not have current browsers, this is a good idea.

To add DHTML effects to a particular page, open the Format menu and select Dynamic HTML Effects. Once enabled, the DHTML Effects toolbar appears. Select the text and choose your effects from the toolbar. The options are self-explanatory. On Page Load means that the effect will occur when the page first opens in the browser. On Mouse Over means that the effect will occur when the user points to the text with the mouse. You get the idea.

You can experiment on your own with the various options available. Just remember Michael's Design Rule #1: Keep it simple. Lots of special effects can junk up your page, confuse the reader, and sometimes even flake out the browser. They also increase the "overhead" of your page, making it take longer to load in a user's browser (the number one way to lose a visitor's interest quickly).

You can apply DHTML to the basic HTML styles Headings 1-6 and Normal. However, it doesn't work on all styles, like bulleted lists, for example.

Saving Time with the Format Painter

What happens when you decide you like the formatting you just did to one paragraph and you want to apply the same formatting to others? Do you have to go through that whole process for every paragraph? Of course not! Take a shortcut and use the Format Painter. The Format Painter copies multiple text and paragraph formats from one selection and applies them to another. To use the Format Painter, just point and click.

1. Select the text or paragraph with the formatting you want to copy.

2. Click on the Format Painter button once to turn it on (see Figure 2.25).

3. Select the text or paragraph to which you want to apply the formatting. The Format Painter applies the formatting as instructed and turns itself off.

4. To copy the formatting from one selection to several other selections (such as every other paragraph), select the text to copy and

Format Painter button

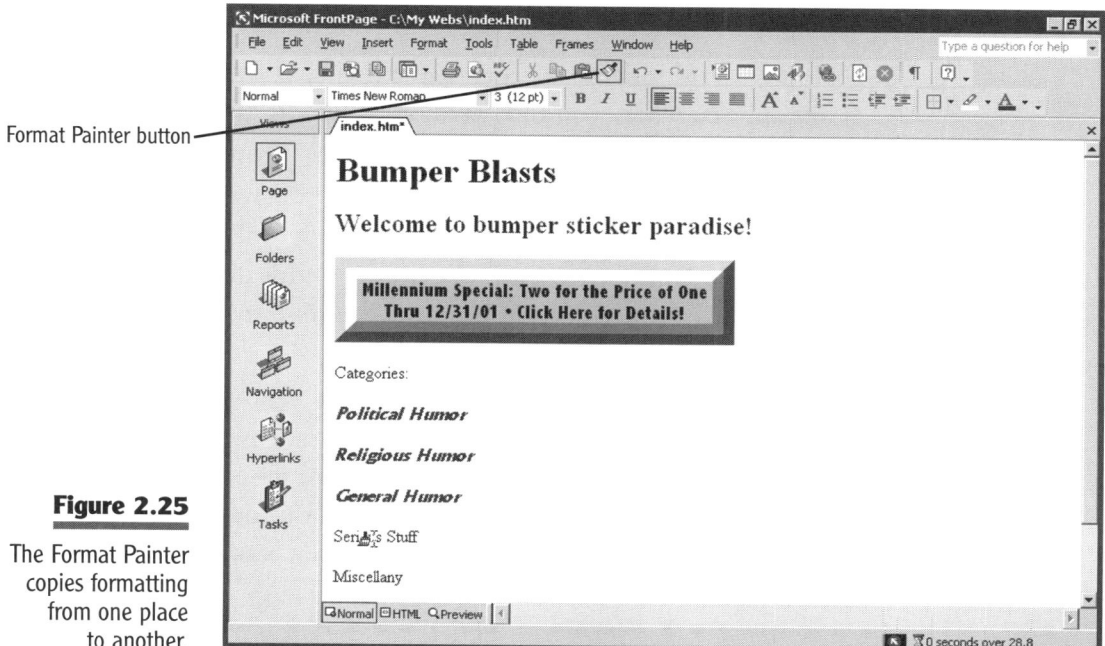

Figure 2.25

The Format Painter copies formatting from one place to another.

then double-click on the Format Painter button. This action tells FrontPage to keep applying the formatting wherever you click until you say stop.

5. To say stop, click on the Format Painter button again or press Esc.

Easy, huh? You don't know how much time that little tool saves me. Oh, and did you know it's also available in Word, Excel, and the other Office XP applications?

Adding a Horizontal Line

Visual dividing lines help keep your page organized and guide the reader to your points of interest. Adding a horizontal line (also called a *rule*) to your page is the quickest means to that end. On the sample page, I'll add a rule above and below my bulleted list to set it off visually. Feel free to follow along.

1. To insert a line above a paragraph, place the cursor to the left of the first character in the paragraph. To place it below the paragraph, place the cursor to the right of the last character.

2. Select Insert, Horizontal Line. A line that spans the width of your page appears where you indicated, as shown in Figure 2.26.

3. Change the appearance of a line by changing its properties. Select the line, then press Alt+Enter to open its Properties dialog box. Here you can set the line's width, height, alignment, and color to your liking. You don't get a Preview area in this dialog box, so you might have to experiment a little to determine the best settings.

 TIP

Using CSS, you can even set the parameters for objects such as horizontal rules or the particulars of the format of an inserted picture by building the parameters into a user-defined style. You only have to set up the details once, then just apply the style anywhere you want it to appear on your Web site. You'll take a quick peek at style sheets before we break for lunch.

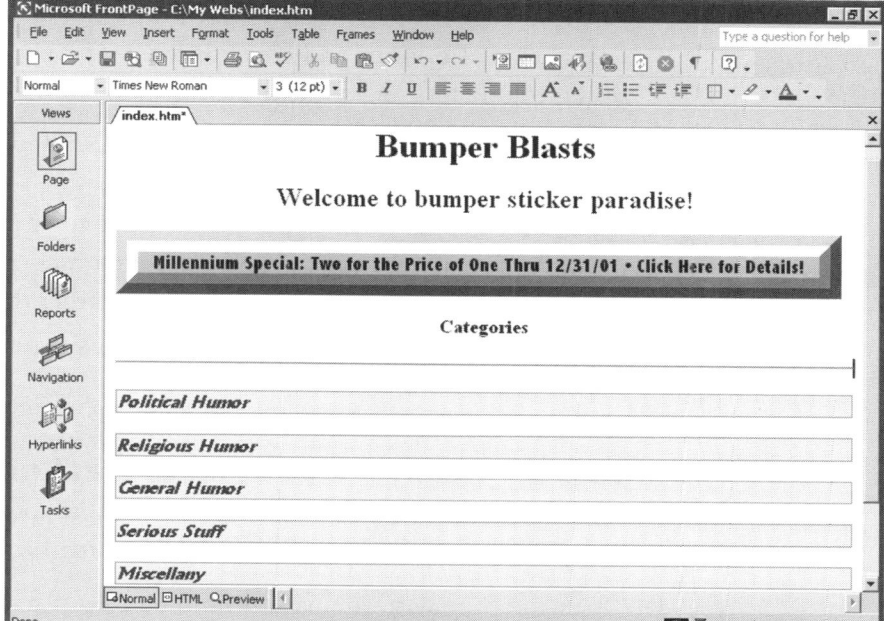

Figure 2.26

A horizontal line gives a visual break to your page, making it easier for visitors to focus on one area at a time.

Adding Colors and Backgrounds

Even with colored text and graphics, your page still might seem like it has too much white space. Unless white is what you want (which is just fine for some designs), the background of your Web pages should be just as attractive as the text and images. As you might suspect by now, it's an easy thing to do.

Adding a Solid-Color Background

A solid-color background is crisp and simple, and it doesn't add a lot of download time to a page. If you want to add a colored background, follow these steps.

1. Open the page with the background you want to change.

2. Right-click on any blank space on the page (not on text or a graphic) to open the shortcut menu.

3. Click on Page Properties. The Page Properties dialog box contains several tabs of options and controls for your page. Click on the Background tab to bring it to the front, as shown in Figure 2.27.

4. Select a color from the Background color palette, which you'll find in the Colors section of the dialog box.

5. Next select a color for the text from the Text color palette. Remember the discussion about legibility and color contrast—make sure that your color choices enhance your Web page rather than detract from it.

6. Click on OK to close the dialog box and see your changes, as shown in Figure 2.28.

Adding a Pattern or Graphical Background

Sometimes a subtle image or pattern in the background is more appropriate for your design. If that's the effect you're looking for, follow these steps.

1. Open the page with the background you want to change.

2. Right-click on any blank space on the page (not on text or a graphic) to open the shortcut menu.

3. Select Page Properties. The dialog box contains several options and controls for your page. Click on the Background tab to bring it to the front.

Figure 2.27

Apply a solid-color background to keep your page less cluttered.

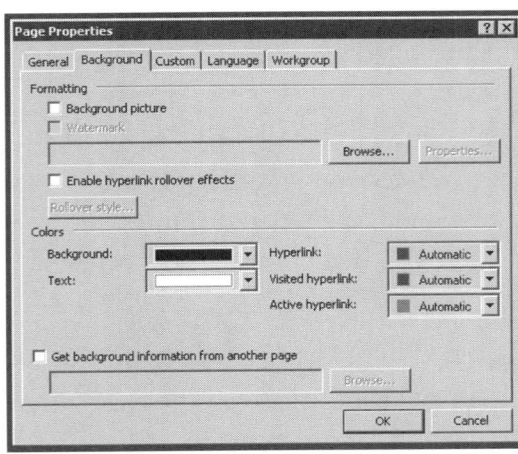

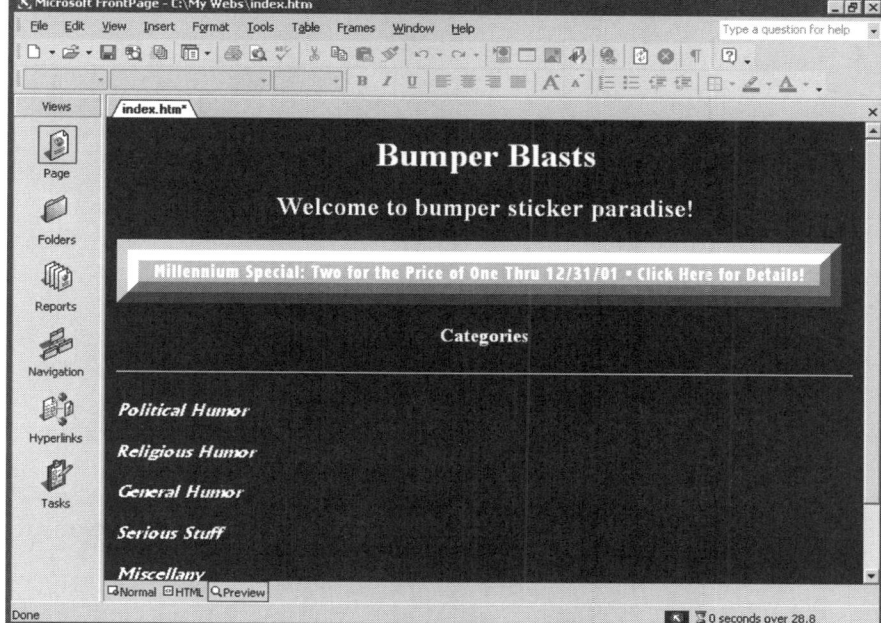

Figure 2.28

White text on a black background has a dramatic effect.

4. You can choose to add a file from your computer, from a Web address, or from the Clip Art Gallery, as in this example. Select Browse and select any file or folder in the list to activate the Open button.

5. Click on the down arrow on the Open button. From the shortcut menu that appears, click on Open from Clip Art. The Select Background dialog box appears, presenting a number of lovely pictures from which to choose (see Figure 2.29).

6. Click on the picture you want (always a tough decision—there are so many good ones) and click on OK. Remember the subtlety factor—busy backgrounds make your text hard to read, so stick with something "quiet." FrontPage enters the path and file name in the edit box.

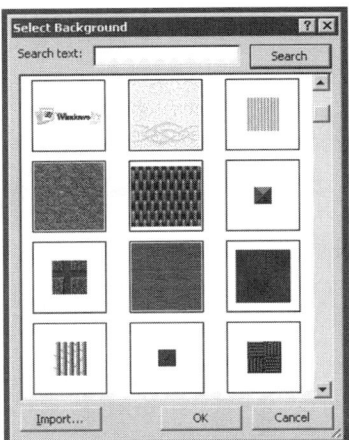

Figure 2.29

Microsoft includes quite a few Web images in the Clip Art Gallery; you might not need to look any further.

7. FrontPage offers a couple of interesting options for your background, including:

   • **Watermark.** When Watermark is selected, your background picture or pattern does not scroll up and down with the text, it remains fixed. Try viewing your background both ways in the Preview window to understand the significance of this effect. The side-by-side examples in Figure 2.30 demonstrate this effect.

   • **Hyperlink rollover.** You can use a "mini-DHTML" effect on your page by telling FrontPage to enable hyperlink rollover effects. In English, this means that when the user points to a hyperlink, the link's color, font, or size changes (see Figure 2.31). The text returns to normal when you move the pointer. Select Rollover Style to choose the rollover font effects. (Keep in mind that if Dynamic HTML is disabled, you won't be able to use this effect.)

8. Click on OK to apply the changes and close the dialog box.

9. To see the changes to your page and to view the effects onscreen, preview the page in your browser by clicking on the Preview in Browser button.

Figure 2.30

A watermark background doesn't scroll; it stays in one place while your text and images move up and down in the browser.

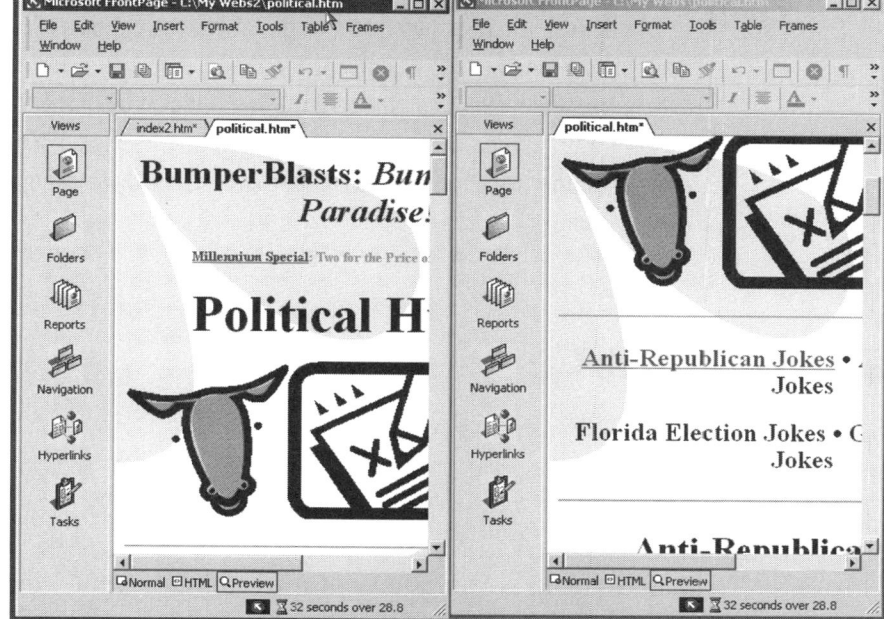

Figure 2.31

Hyperlink rollovers are an easy way to liven up the user's interactivity with your Web site.

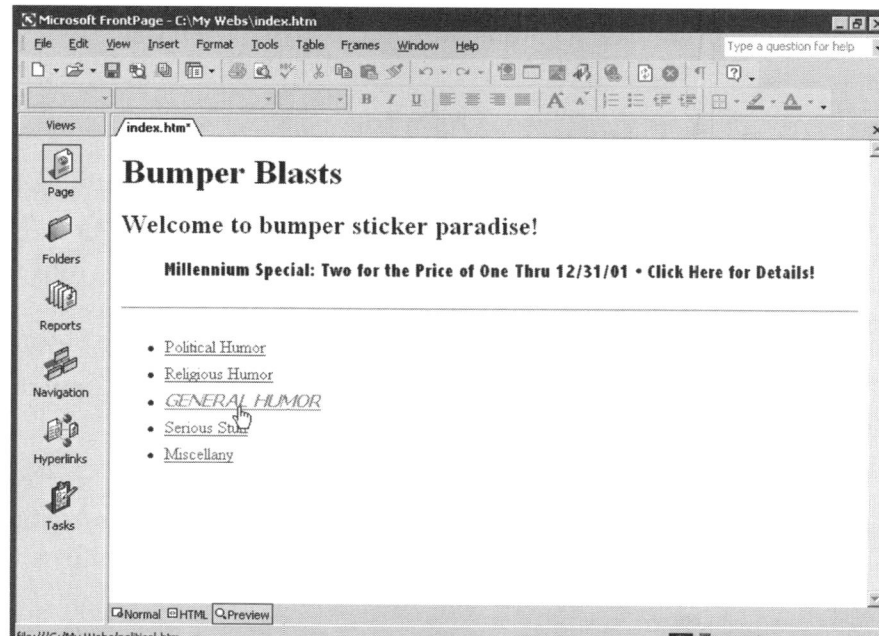

TIP To use the same background settings on all your pages, select Get Background Information from Another Page. Enter the file and path name for the page you want to match. FrontPage mimics all the settings in this dialog box for each page you set. This is an easy way to keep a consistent look from page to page. What's more, if you make changes to the "base" page's background properties, those changes are carried over to the other pages as well.

Take a Break!

You've been sitting for a while now, so you're probably ready to take a quick break. Take the dog for a walk, give your sweetie a peck on the cheek, or check on the kids. Get some more coffee, too. When you're ready to get back to it, I'll be right here.

Before you break for lunch, you'll spend some time working with bulleted and numbered lists and then you'll add some real splash to your Web site by applying a theme that ties together all your headings, text, and backgrounds with one overall look. Go on, I'll wait....

All about Lists

Lists can make a text-heavy page easier to navigate and help your visitors quickly identify areas on your Web site that might be of interest to them. Multilevel lists can work as a content outline for your readers. When you use lists as a pseudo table of contents, with hyperlinks attached to each list item, your visitor can quickly scan a list and go to the area they want to see. In general, lists also help to break up a page visually and give your site more "curb appeal."

Several list styles are available in FrontPage, but the ones you're most likely to use are bullets and numbers. You created a simple bulleted list on your main page last night by selecting the paragraphs and clicking on the Bullets button, but that's just the beginning of what you can do with them.

Working with Bulleted Lists and Collapsible Outlines

Try something a little more complex, since you already did a simple bulleted list. First, you'll need to enter some text for your list. Include both main list items and sublevel items. I've included my main bumper sticker categories and some categories under each of them.

I want to create a three-level bulleted list, with each level set off by a different bullet style. I also want users to see only the top-level items when the page loads, and I want to let them click on a bullet item to expand the list. Sound tricky? Try it yourself.

1. In Normal view, select the entire list and click on the Bullets button on the toolbar. All the selected items are bulleted identically.

2. Select the second- and third-level items and double-click on the Increase Indent button. The selected items indent to the next level and show a new bullet style, as shown in Figure 2.32.

Increase Indent button

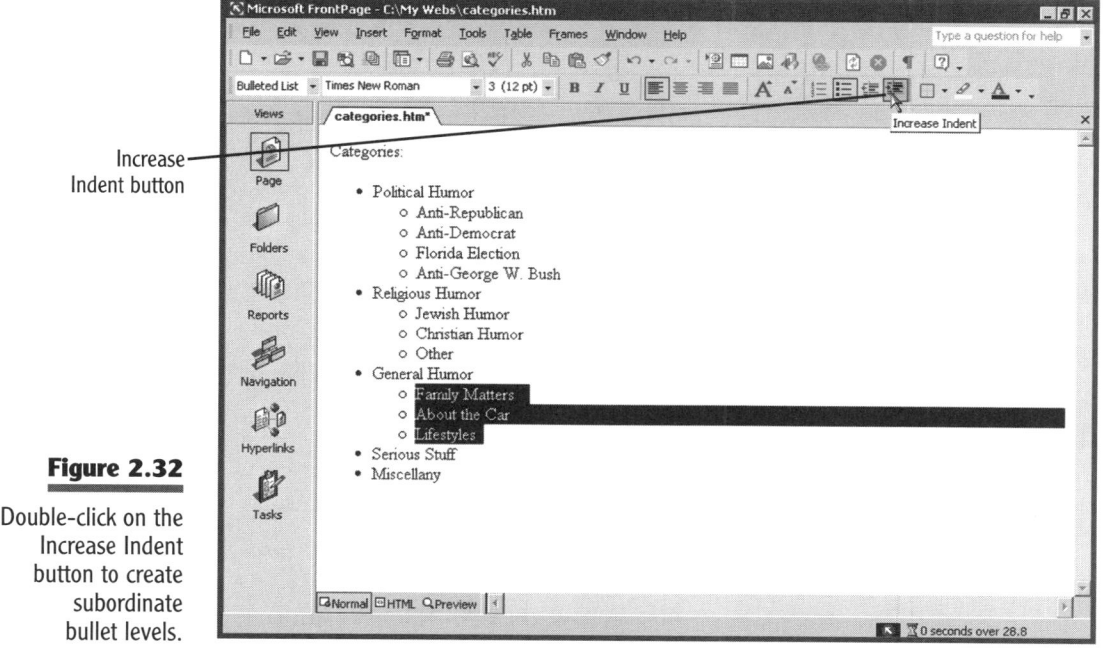

Figure 2.32

Double-click on the Increase Indent button to create subordinate bullet levels.

3. Repeat Step 2 on just the third-level list items to create the third level of bullets.

4. To enable the expand-on-click feature, select the entire list again. Right-click on the selection and select List Properties. The List Properties dialog box opens with the Plain Bullets tab showing.

5. Select the Enable Collapsible Outlines option as well as the option that goes with it, Initially Collapsed. Then, click on OK to close the dialog box.

6. Switch to Preview and check out your list. Click on the main heading that you know has sublevels to reveal the second-level bullets and then do the same for the third level. Your results will look something like Figure 2.33.

TIP

Collapsible outlines might be a cool thing, but only if your visitor knows about them. They aren't underlined like hyperlinks, so you might need to give them another visual or textual clue, as shown in Figure 2.33.

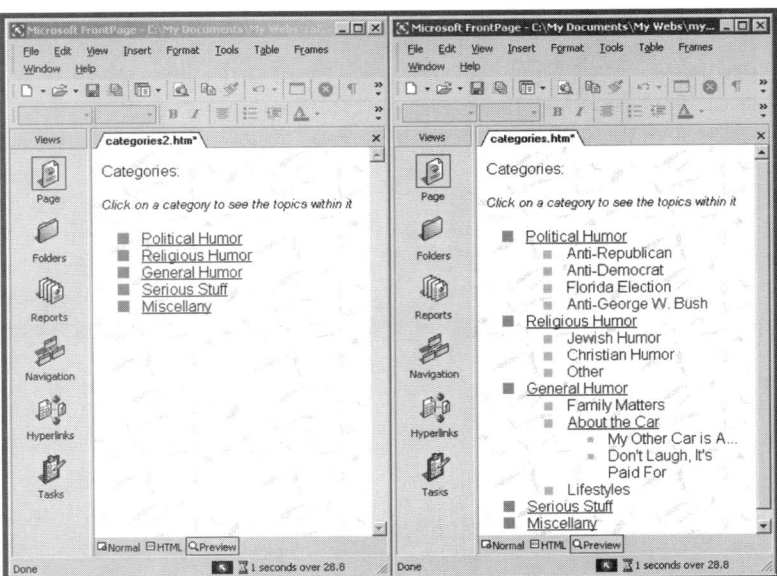

Figure 2.33

Collapsible outlines are one good way to conserve valuable screen real estate. The outline doesn't clutter up the page unless it's expanded.

Pretty slick! You can see now how collapsible lists can come in handy. Incorporate some graphic bullets, hyperlinks, bookmarks, and forward and back buttons, and you have a nice navigational tool for your visitors. (Don't worry; by the end of the weekend, you'll know how to do all that.)

NOTE You can even use collapsible outlines to expand a list to something more detailed, like a descriptive paragraph of text or a table of numbers. Use the same formatting steps given previously, handling the table or text as just another list item. One place where this would be handy is in an online product catalog. Click once to see a description of the item, and click again to see the price, available sizes and colors, and shipping details. You get the picture.

USING PICTURES AS BULLETS

A popular design technique is to replace regular bullets with small graphics or pictures. This adds some visual interest to your page and gives you a little more opportunity for artistic expression.

The procedure for creating graphic bullets starts with the same six steps given previously. When you've accomplished that, delve deeper into the List Properties dialog box using these steps.

1. In Normal view, right-click on a top-level bullet item.

2. Select List Properties from the shortcut menu.

3. Click on the Picture Bullets tab to bring it to the front.

4. Select Specify Picture to enable the feature, and type the picture's path and file name in the edit box (or use Browse to import a file from your computer, the Clip Art Gallery, or the Internet).

5. Click on OK. The graphic is applied to all bulleted items at that level (see Figure 2.34).

USING PICTURES AS BULLETS (CONTINUED...)

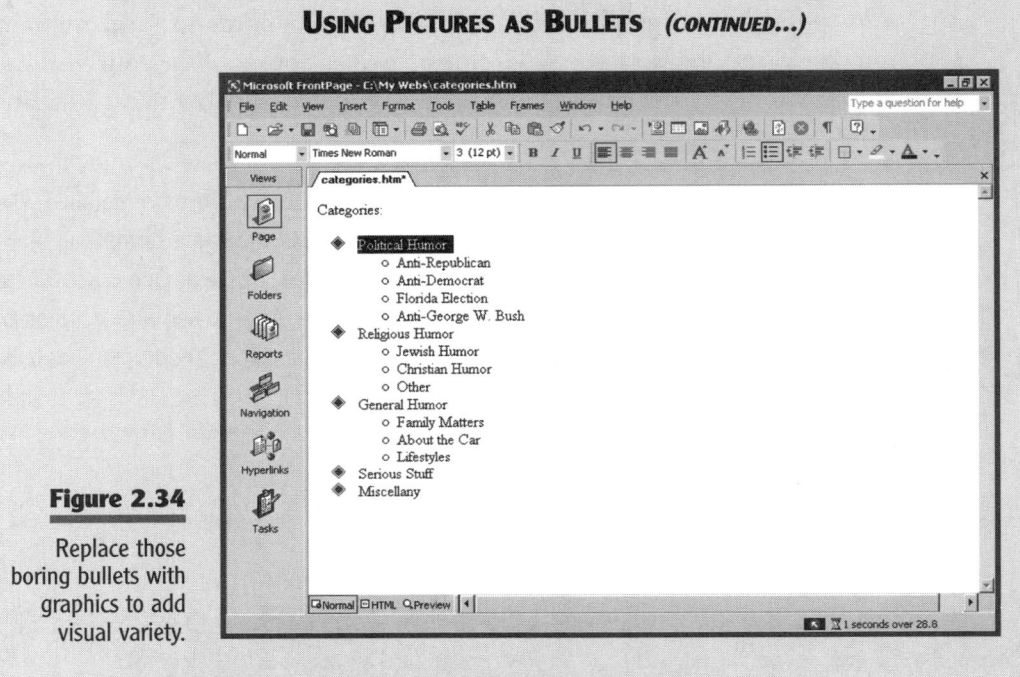

Figure 2.34

Replace those boring bullets with graphics to add visual variety.

6. **Repeat steps 1 through 5 for each level of your list.**

Keep in mind that most graphic images designed to be used as bullets are small—usually about 5 × 5 pixels. If you want to use an image of your own, be sure to resize it before you import it. Otherwise, each of your graphic bullets will appear as a full-sized image.

Using Numbered Lists

Numbered lists can be helpful in a variety of situations. You can use them to give users step-by-step instructions or visual cues for the number of items in a lengthy list, or to give structured multilevel outline format to legal documentation posted online. To create a quick numbered list, just select the paragraphs you want to number and click on the Numbering button on the toolbar.

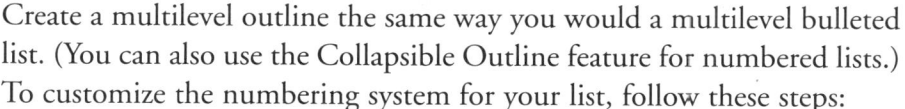

Create a multilevel outline the same way you would a multilevel bulleted list. (You can also use the Collapsible Outline feature for numbered lists.) To customize the numbering system for your list, follow these steps:

1. In Normal view, select the entire list and click on the Numbering button on the toolbar. All the selected items are numbered sequentially.

2. Select the second- and third-level items and double-click on the Increase Indent button. The selected items indent to the next level and are numbered sequentially at that level. The top-level numbers renumber themselves accordingly, as shown in Figure 2.35.

3. Repeat Step 2 on just the third-level list items to create the third level of numbering.

4. To enable the expand-on-click feature, select the entire list again. Right-click on the selection and select List Properties. The List Properties dialog box opens with the Numbers tab showing.

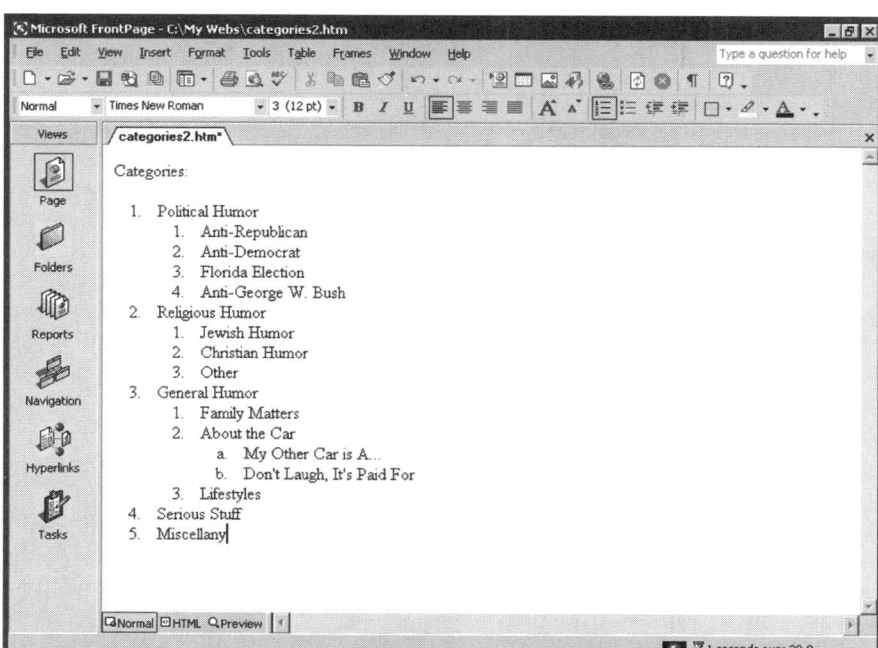

Figure 2.35

Create a multilevel outline using FrontPage's numbered list format.

5. Select the Enable Collapsible Outlines option and the option that goes with it, Initially Collapsed. Then, click on OK to close the dialog box.

6. Switch to Preview and check out your list. Click on the main heading that you know has sublevels to reveal the second-level bullets and then do the same for the third level.

7. To use a different numbering style on a sublevel, right-click on a list item at the level you want to reformat and select List Properties. The List Properties dialog box opens with the Numbers tab showing.

8. Select the numbering style to use for that level (for example, letters or Roman numerals), as shown in Figure 2.36. Click on OK to close the dialog box.

9. Repeat steps 7 and 8 for each sublevel of your list.

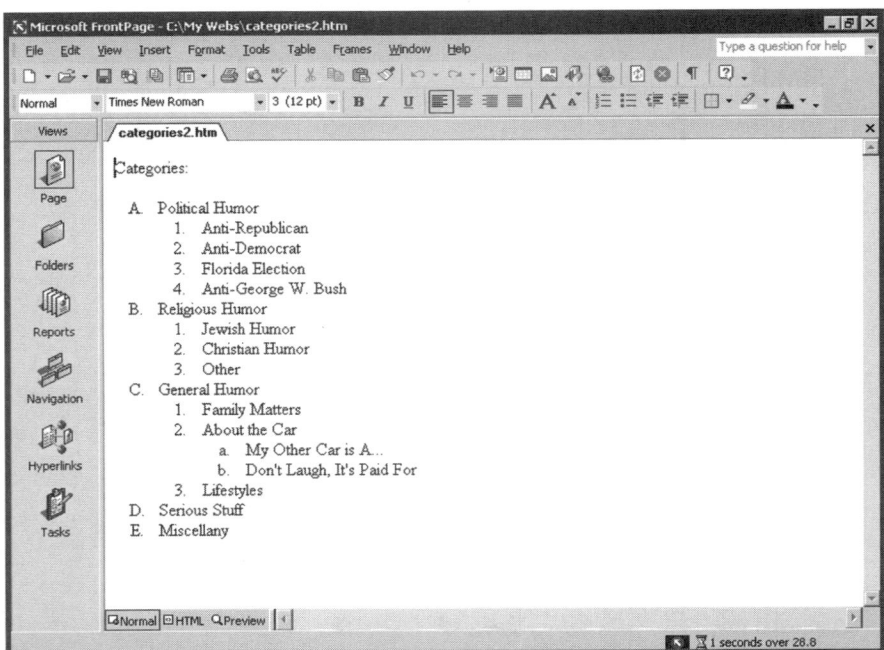

Figure 2.36

Apply a different number style to each list level to create a formal outline.

Working with Other Lists

FrontPage also supports some other types of lists, but their usage is rare. In fact, of the three, most browsers only support one. You'll find these list types on the Other tab of the List Properties dialog box.

- **Definition list**. This style is convenient for presenting a list of terms and their definitions. Terms are displayed flush left and the definitions are block-intended, as shown in Figure 2.37.

- **Directory list**. Use this style to present a sequence of short terms without bullets or numbering. Most browsers ignore the style. You can create the same effect by selecting the list items and clicking on the Increase Indent button.

- **Menu list**. This list presents an unordered list of short entries. You tell me the difference between that and a directory list—I'm stumped. Most browsers also ignore this style, so I guess it doesn't matter.

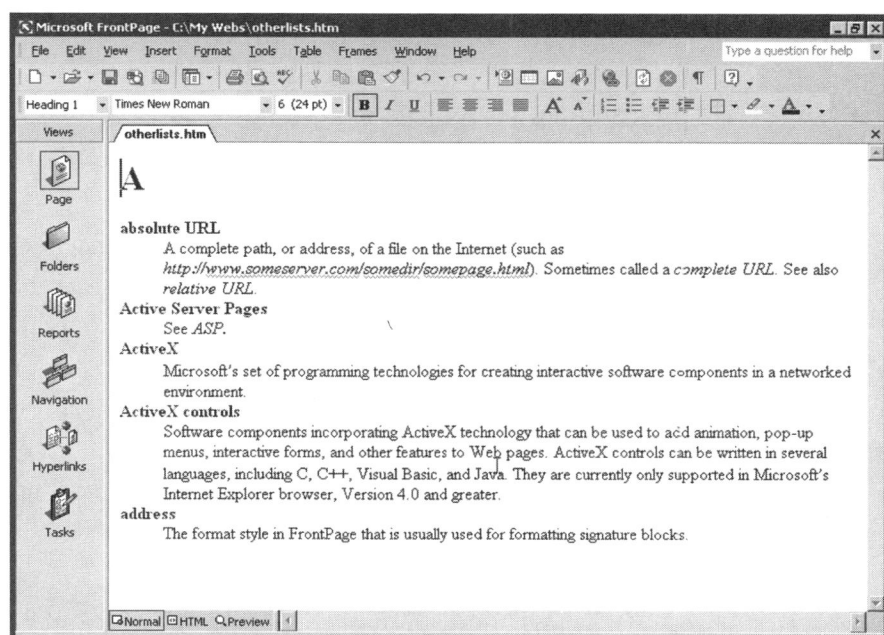

Figure 2.37

A definition list can come in handy when you have a list of terms and lengthy descriptions that accompany them.

 **NOTE** The exact appearance of any list depends on your visitor's browser. It also depends on whether you've added a theme to your Web site.

Getting a Cohesive Look with Themes

All these formatting tools are great for a few lines of text or a few Web pages at a time, but it sure is a lot of work to format entire Webs one line at a time! Wouldn't it be nice if you could apply a whole battery of formatting at one time—background patterns, bullet styles, and even fonts? You can. Apply a theme with a couple of clicks, and presto! It's done.

Applying a Theme

A theme includes a plethora of built-in page and paragraph formats, all tied together in a professionally designed color and graphic scheme. Themes can go a long way in helping you convey your message to visitors (see Figure 2.38). Use a playful theme such as Loose Gesture or Citrus Punch for a festive feel. The Kids theme is perfect for Web sites designed for children, and Chalkboard is great for a school or classroom page. Automotive would be great for a car collector's Web site.

You can apply themes to an entire Web site or just to individual pages. Mix and match themes depending on each page's content, or use just one for a cohesive look across all pages. By default, each of FrontPage's built-in themes applies formatting to the following items:

- Backgrounds
- Paragraph styles, including colors and fonts, and Cascading Style Sheets (CSS)
- Page banners
- Lists
- Navigational buttons (Home, Top, Back, Next, and so on)
- Horizontal lines

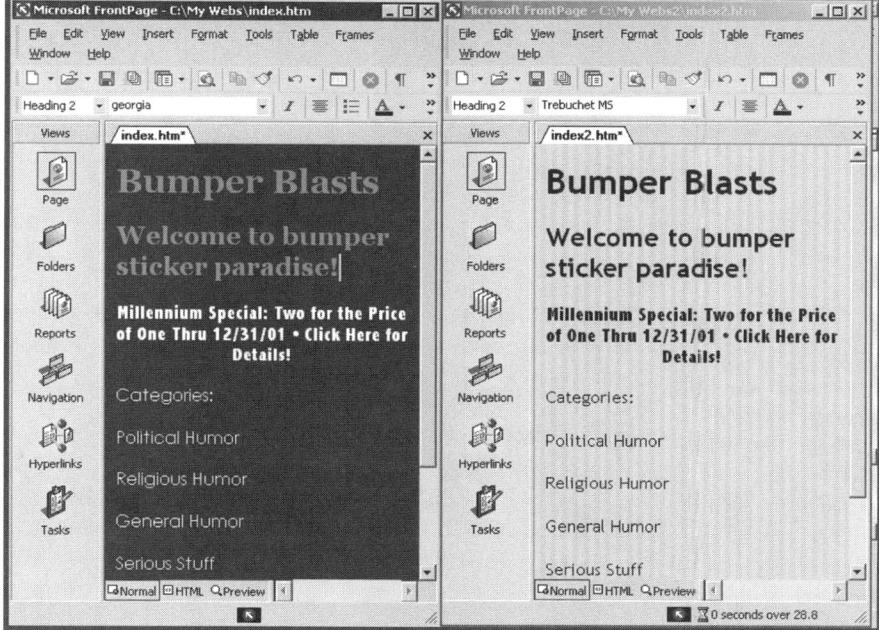

Figure 2.38

Themes can dramatically change your Web site and the message you want to convey. Here is the same text with two different themes applied.

It's truly amazing the difference a theme can make, both in the appearance of your Web site and the time it takes you to design it. To apply a theme, open your Web and follow these steps.

1. From Normal view, select Format, Theme. The Themes dialog box opens with a list of available themes on the left and a large preview area on the right, as shown in Figure 2.39.

TIP

To apply a theme to more than one page but not the entire Web, select the desired pages in Folders view and then open the Themes dialog box.

2. At the top of the dialog box, choose whether you want to apply the theme to all pages or just the selected page(s).

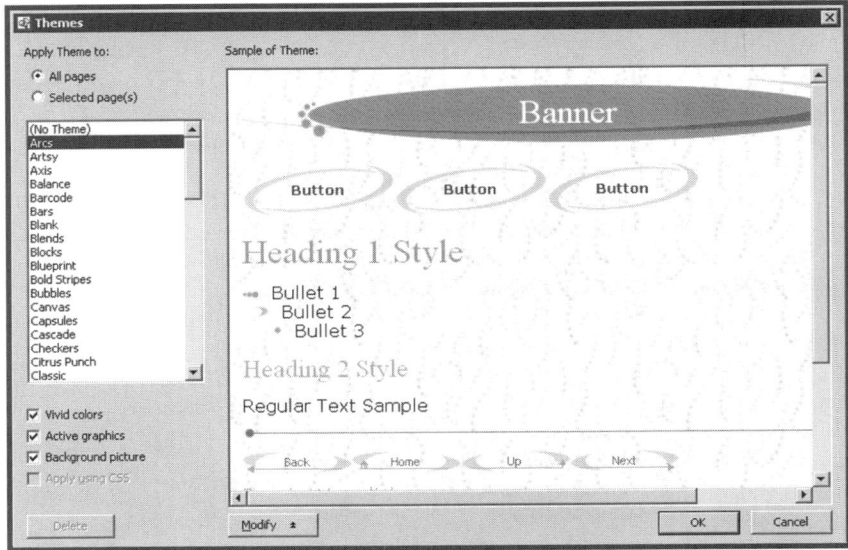

Figure 2.39

Use the preview area to sample various themes until you find one you like.

3. Click on various themes to see how they look in the preview area. Most of their names give you an idea of the concept. Tabs and Folders has that manila envelope look and feel. Technology uses buttons that look like computer boards. Sweets uses lollipops and candy canes.

4. If you're designing for high-end users who are likely to have up-to-date browsers, check the Vivid Colors and Active Graphics options in the lower-left corner of the dialog box. Vivid colors enhances the theme's color scheme by using a higher color mix and greater number of colors. Active graphics replaces plain buttons and navigation bars with animated page elements, such as hover buttons. Remember that not all browsers support these features.

5. After you've made your selections, click on OK to apply the theme. Use Preview or click on the Preview in Browser button to inspect the impact the new theme has on your Web, as shown in Figure 2.40.

If you don't like the theme you've chosen, follow these same steps to change to a new theme. To completely remove a theme from your site or page, click on No Theme at the top of the list of themes.

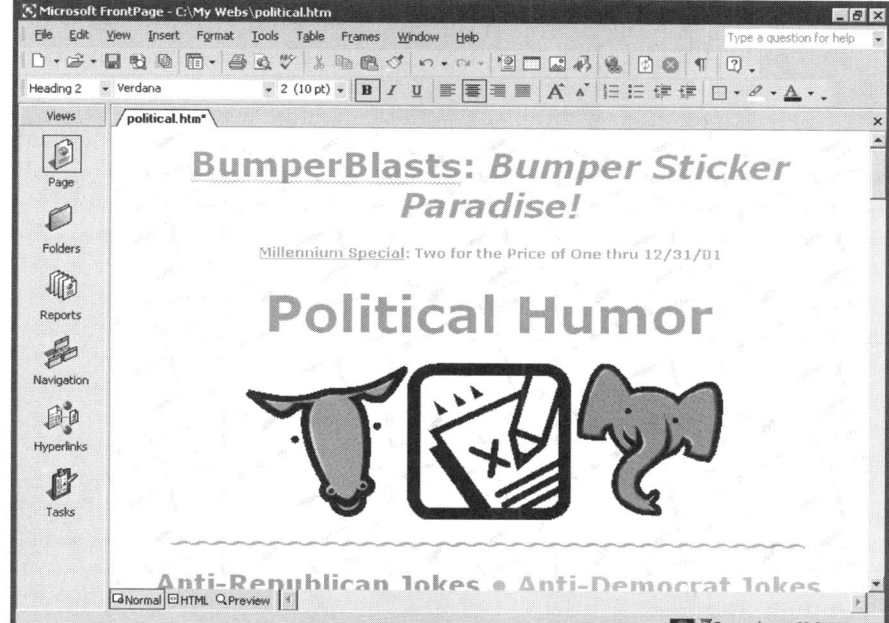

Figure 2.40

Like a well-orchestrated symphony, a theme applies all the right instruments to make beautiful music.

Modifying a Theme

Sometimes you'll find that a theme is *almost* what you want, but not quite. Fortunately, you don't have to bag the idea altogether. Instead, you can customize the theme and save it with a new name. You then can make a variety of changes and adjustments to it. You can remove the background pattern and just use a solid color, substitute your own graphics for bullets and navigational buttons, or change the fonts and colors of text styles. Modifying a theme takes a little time to figure out, but it can be worth the effort. You only have to do it once to create a personalized theme you can use for all your pages (or all your Web sites, if you have more than one). To customize a theme, follow these steps.

1. Select Format, Theme to open the Themes dialog box.

2. Click on the Modify button. FrontPage reveals three new settings buttons: Colors, Graphics, and Text, as shown in Figure 2.41.

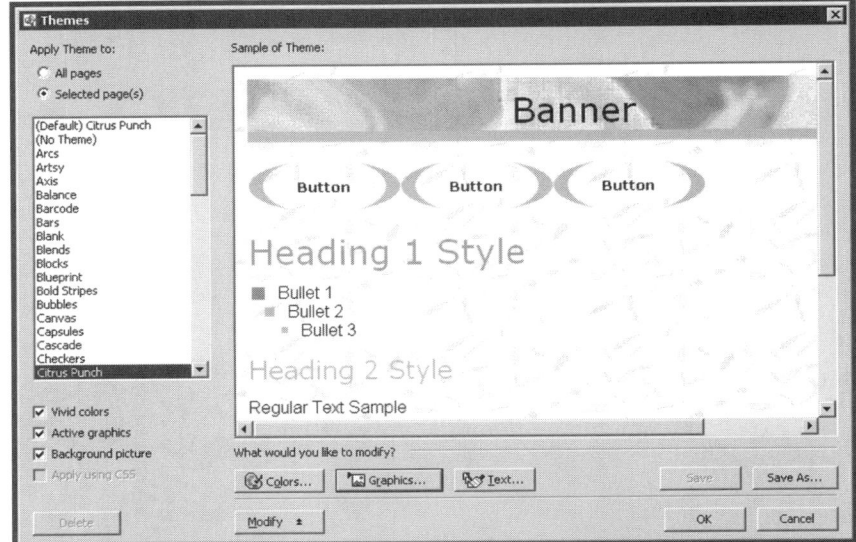

Figure 2.41

You can customize a theme to incorporate your own graphics and color preferences.

3. Click on Colors to apply a different color scheme but keep the theme's graphics intact. You can only apply a new overall color scheme, not customize individual styles. Click on the various color schemes until you find one you like. On the Color Wheel tab, you can adjust the brightness and the colors used. To change the color of individual theme elements (such as background or heading colors), click on the Custom tab. Click on OK after you've applied the new scheme.

4. Click on Graphics to use different graphics in your theme. Most often you'll want to change the background graphic, but you can also insert your own button graphics, bullets, and horizontal lines. To change an individual item, select it from the Item drop-down menu and then enter your changes.

5. Click on Text to apply new fonts to your Normal (Body) and Heading styles. Select an item from the Item list and click on a new font.

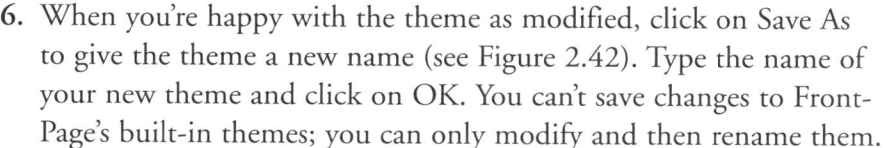

6. When you're happy with the theme as modified, click on Save As to give the theme a new name (see Figure 2.42). Type the name of your new theme and click on OK. You can't save changes to Front-Page's built-in themes; you can only modify and then rename them.

Figure 2.42

Modify an existing theme to your heart's content and then save it with a new name so that you can use it again.

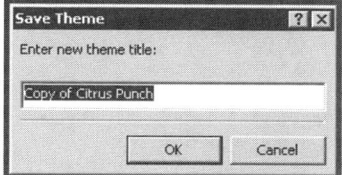

STYLE SHEETS AND CSS

You've probably heard about a new feature in FrontPage 2002 called *Cascading Style Sheets*, or CSS for short. A CSS gives you a great deal more control over your Web site's appearance, and allows you to create additional special effects. Each CSS defines styles you can apply to your pages or text items. Use them to create non-standard styles that you can apply to any item in your Web site. Following are just a few of the items you can add to a CSS.

- **Font.** Apply attributes such as All Caps or Italic as part of a heading style.

- **Paragraph.** Customize the indentation, line spacing, and spacing before or after a paragraph.

- **Borders and shading.** Add special effects, such as boxes, to your text.

- **Positioning.** Control attributes like text wrap and layering of graphic elements.

Covering CSS in detail would take an entire book in itself, and they can be tricky to implement until you really understand what you're doing. You might not want to use style sheets, depending on how large a site you plan. For small sites, style sheets might be more trouble than they're worth, but if you're planning a larger site—or if your site begins to grow larger than you'd originally anticipated—definitely consider using them.

STYLE SHEETS AND CSS *(CONTINUED...)*

For a thorough discussion and examples of how to implement Cascading Style Sheets for your pages or Web site, the FrontPage 2002 Help system is a great place to start. Beyond that, author Steve Callihan explains complicated topics better than anyone I know, and his book, *Learn HTML in a Weekend, 3rd Edition* (Prima, 2000), includes an excellent discussion on how to understand and implement CSS (along with other HTML basics, the knowledge of which will certainly come in handy from time to time).

If you're not into buying a whole new book, however, you can always find good tutorials online. Here's a short list of sites that might help:

- http://home.att.net/~knoblock/cookbook/index.html
  Steve Knoblock's Style Sheet Cookbook, which includes a CSS tutorial and a gallery of style examples.

- http://www.htmlhelp.com/reference/css
  An excellent collection of articles on using CSS in your Web pages from Web Design Group (WDG).

- http://www.w3.org/Style/CSS
  This site includes, among other things, the official recommendations for CSS1 and CSS2.

- http://style.webreview.com
  This site features the browser compatibility charts so that you can compare the way different browser versions of Internet Explorer, Netscape Navigator, and Opera support different features of CSS.

What's Next?

Wow! Is it lunchtime already? Just look at all you've accomplished so far today. You created a new Web; imported the page you created last night; applied background patterns, fonts and colors, and bullets and numbers;

and inserted horizontal lines on your pages. You have likely already developed (or at least started on) several of your site's pages. No wonder why your stomach's growling! Go now and take a nice leisurely lunch break. If you need to run a few errands, this might be a good time. Maybe peek ahead in the book to see what's coming up later.

Grab a bite and rest for a while, and then you'll move on to what makes the World Wide Web live up to its name—hyperlinks. Links connect your pages to other parts of your pages, to other pages within your Web site, and to pages on other sites anywhere on the Internet. It is truly a web of information available to visitors with just a few clicks. See you in an hour or two!

Putting the Web in World Wide Web

- All about Hyperlinks
- Working with Bookmarks
- Adding Shared Borders and Navigation (Link) Bars
- Testing Your Work

Before the days of the World Wide Web, Internet users relied on tools such as Gopher and Archie to find the information they needed. There were no cool search engines that spoke to you in plain English, no easy-to-read pages that directed you to the information you wanted to find, and no pretty pictures to entertain you along the way. These old Internet tools were difficult to understand and use, let alone get results with. It's no surprise that the Web has become so popular. It took the phenomenal potential of the Internet out of the hands of the experts and brought it down to a level that the rest of us can understand and use.

Hyperlinks are the guts of the World Wide Web. In fact, they are the whole point of the Web. Rather than digging around like a gopher and not knowing what you'll come up with, hyperlinks let you quickly zoom from one page to another (or from one Web site to another). You can click on what you want to see details about and ignore the rest.

All about Hyperlinks

I don't think I've seen a Web site yet that did not include some kind of hyperlink, except maybe those one-page "billboard" sites. Because hyperlinks are an integral part of the Internet, you need to know how to create, edit, and work with them in detail. In this session, you'll work with three types of hyperlinks, including

⚙ **External links**. Hyperlinks that point to another Web site.

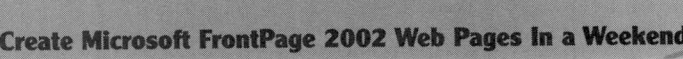

- **Internal links.** Hyperlinks that point to another page in your Web site. Internal links might also include navigation link bars and shared borders.

- **Bookmarks.** Hyperlinks that point to a specific place or object on a page in your Web site (or sometimes on another Web site).

I'll also touch briefly on the most common graphic links: image maps and hotspots—multiple hyperlinks that are built into graphic images.

Text-based links are generally referred to as *hypertext*. Any type of hyperlink, whether text or graphic, points your browser to a different URL (*Universal Resource Locator*), the Web address or path of a particular Web page or site. As Figure 3.1 illustrates, every Web page has a unique URL, just as every home has a unique street address or phone number.

◄ ◄

Hypertext documents are electronic documents that contain links to other documents, allowing nonsequential viewing of large amounts of information. Users can choose their own path through the material by clicking on the link to the topic that interests them. A Web site is a collection of hypertext documents.

◄ ◄

There are two methods for creating hyperlinks. You can create your pages and then add links to the existing pages (within your own Web), or you can create the hyperlink and the new page at the same time. Either method is fine; it just depends on your development style. You'll probably find, in fact, that you do a lot of both.

Figure 3.1

No two Web pages have the same URL.

Address	https://www.fedex.com/cgi-bin/ship_it/interNetShip?us	▼	Go	Links »
Address	http://communities.msn.com/people	▼	Go	Links »
Address	https://www.site-secure.com/cgi-bin/cgig1.exe/fib/SID/GetLogon	▼	Go	Links »

Creating Links to Existing Pages

The easiest links to add are those that connect to pages within your own Web site. To create a link to an existing page in your Web site, follow these steps.

1. In Page view, type the text to be used as the link if it doesn't already exist. Then, select the text. Whatever you select appears underlined on your Web page after you create the link.

TIP You can use the literal URL name to identify the link, or you can use something more descriptive and creative. You've probably seen links handled in a variety of ways. For example:

- Click **here** to download.
- Download a trial version at **www.microsoft.com**.
- Or, more simply: **Download now!**

2. Select the text you just typed (you can select as little or as much of the text as you want) and then right-click to open the shortcut menu (see Figure 3.2).

3. Click on Hyperlink to open the Insert Hyperlink dialog box.

4. You can create the hyperlink in no less than six different ways.

   - Use the Look In drop-down list to navigate to an existing page in your Web site and then use the various navigation buttons to find the file to which you want to link (see Figure 3.3).

   - Click on the Folders button to link to a page that is currently stored on your hard drive or network but which is not yet in your Web folder. Navigate to the file location and click on the file to which you want to link.

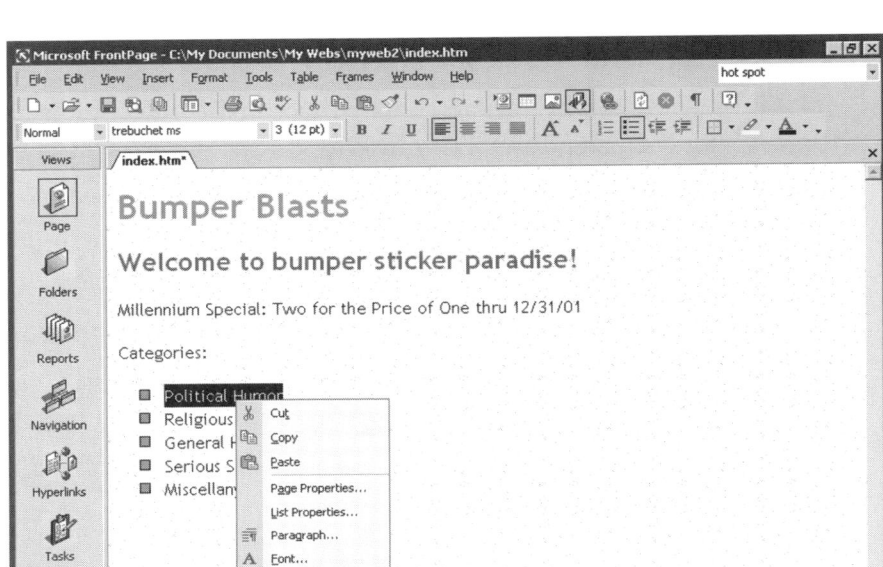

Figure 3.2

Any text or object can become a link by creating a hyperlink.

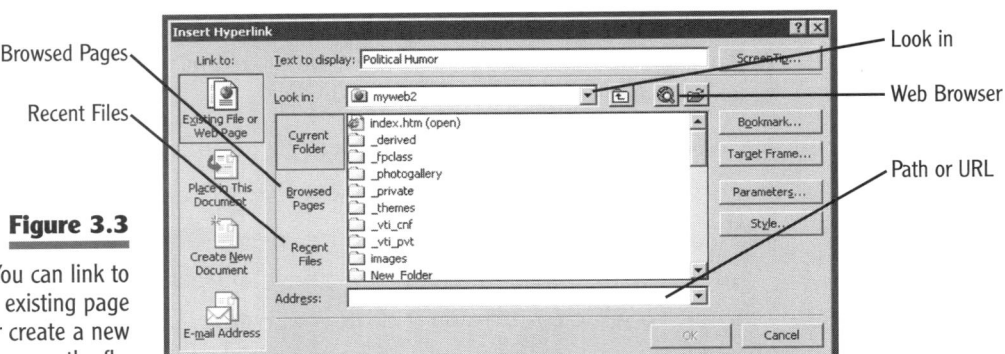

Browsed Pages

Recent Files

Figure 3.3

You can link to an existing page or create a new page on the fly.

Look in

Web Browser

Path or URL

NOTE   If you link to a file you have not yet imported, FrontPage prompts you to import the file the next time you save your work.

- Click on the Web Browser button to link to a page on the Web. When your browser opens, navigate to the Web address and then close the browser.

TIP

If you're linking to the main home page of a Web site, you don't need to enter a specific page or file name. Just type **www.sitename.com** and leave it at that. As you learned this morning, most browsers automatically look for the default or index file if none is specified.

- Click on the Browsed Pages button to see a list of the pages you most recently visited. These might include pages on the Web or on your hard drive.
- Click on Recent Files to grab a file you used not long ago.
- Type the URL or the path and file name directly into the Address text box.

5. When the path for the link appears in the Address text box, make sure that it is complete, as shown in Figure 3.4. External links to other Web pages must begin with http:// followed by the site's URL (such as www.microsoft.com), followed by any subdirectories or specific file names. The complete URL will look something like http://www.microsoft.com/frontpage/sample.html.

Figure 3.4

Do you want to go to the site's home page or a different page within the Web site?

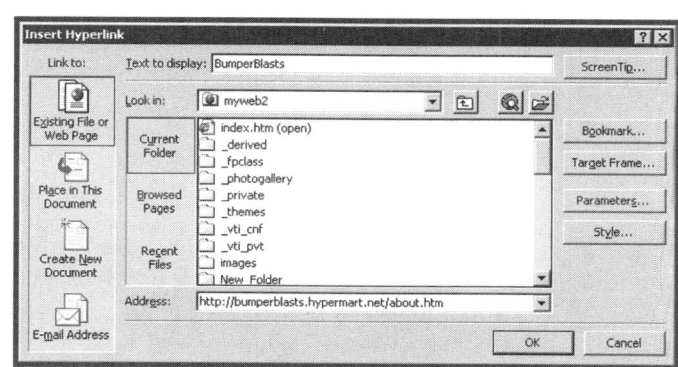

NOTE

Internal links use a normal path name like the ones you've seen in DOS or Windows Explorer. If the file is in a different directory, be sure the full path name is given. For example: images/logo.jpg or about.html.

You don't need the file://c:... garbage that might appear unless you are linking to a file stored on your hard drive or network. Files with this type of path name will only be accessible if your visitor also has direct access to your hard drive or network, which is not likely.

6. Make sure that the Text to Display field shows the text you're using for the link. If it's not right, you can change it here.

7. Click on ScreenTip and add the text you want to appear when the visitor's mouse pointer hovers over the link, then click on OK to close the ScreenTip dialog box.

8. Click on OK again. The Insert Hyperlink dialog box closes.

Presto! You can tell that the link was created because the text is now underlined and colored blue (or whatever color is the default link color for the theme you are using—in my case, it's light green). Figure 3.5 shows the results. If you added ScreenTip text, you'll need to preview the page to test this feature.

Find it...

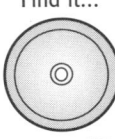

On the CD

If you're linking to a file the user can download, make sure that the file is compressed as small as possible so that the download does not take any longer than necessary. The CD that accompanies this book includes a copy of WinZip, a popular file compression utility that you can use for this purpose.

Creating Links to New Pages

If you don't want to wait until you have all your pages done to create some hyperlinks, you can create the link and ask FrontPage to remind you to add the necessary information later. (The first few steps are the same as in the previous section, "Creating Links to Existing Pages.")

1. In Page view, type the text to be used as the link.

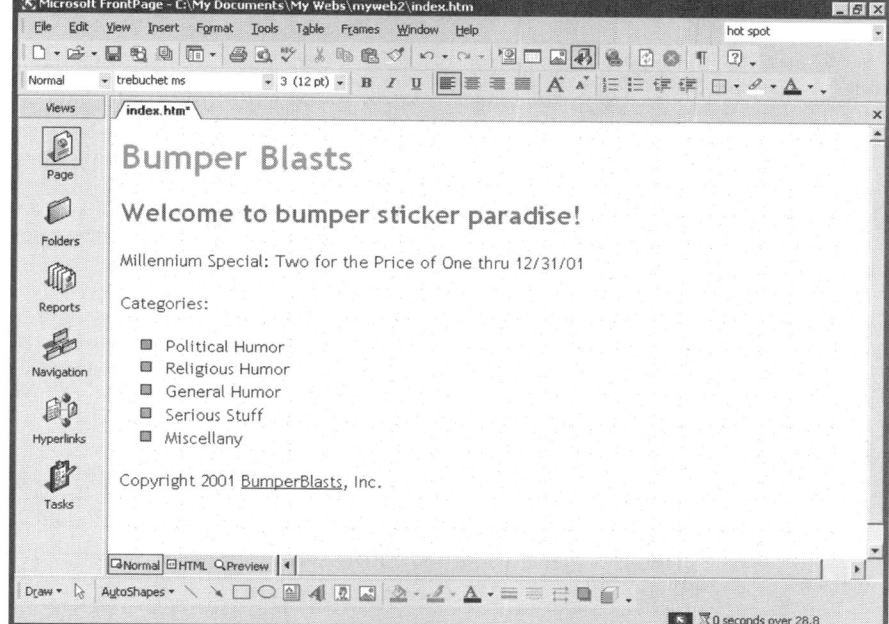

Figure 3.5

Links should be easy to distinguish from other elements on your page.

2. Select the text and then right-click to open the shortcut menu.

3. Select Hyperlink to open the Insert Hyperlink dialog box.

4. Click on the Create New Document button. The dialog box changes to include options for creating a new page, as shown in Figure 3.6.

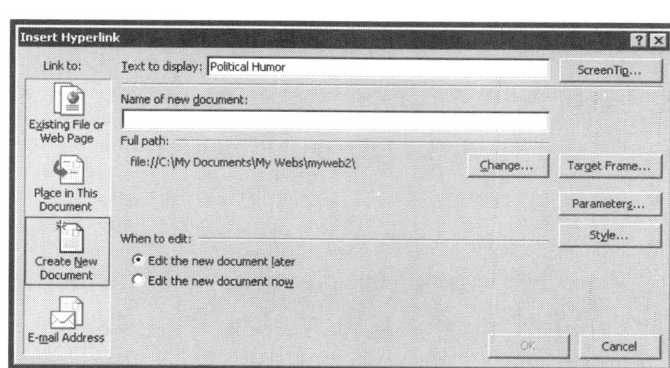

Figure 3.6

FrontPage lets you link to a page that doesn't exist yet, as long as you remember to create it later.

5. In the When to Edit area, select the Edit the New Document Later option.

6. Give the page a name, click on Change, navigate to the appropriate location to control where the file is stored, and then click on Save. FrontPage creates the hyperlink on your existing page.

That's it! Adding your collection of linkage to the millions has never been easier.

To edit your page later, go to the Folders view and double-click on the saved page. The requested page will open, but it will be blank. You can then edit the page as you would any other.

TIP You can attach a hyperlink to any selectable object, including an image or a table—virtually anything on a page the user can point to or click on, except background images.

Creating E-Mail Links

In addition to Web page links, you can create links that enable the visitor to contact you via e-mail. When clicked, a mailto: hyperlink opens a blank e-mail message in your visitor's e-mail software. The message will already be addressed to you. All the user has to do is type the message and click on Send. To create an e-mail link, follow these steps.

1. In Page view, type the text to be used as the link.

2. Select the text and then right-click to open the shortcut menu.

3. Select Hyperlink to open the Insert Hyperlink dialog box.

4. Click on the E-Mail Address button. The dialog box changes to include options appropriate for an e-mail link (see Figure 3.7).

5. Type the e-mail address in the E-Mail Address field. FrontPage automatically inserts the mailto: code. (If you've used the address before in the Web site, you can click on it in the Recently Used E-Mail Addresses list.)

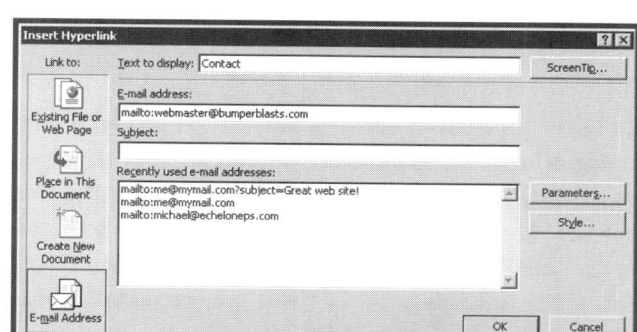

Figure 3.7

A mailto: hyperlink opens a new message in your visitor's e-mail program.

6. Add a ScreenTip and change the text label if you want, then click on OK to close the dialog box. Your link is added to the page, just like that.

TIP

You can add a subject line to the message link (see Figure 3.8) by adding the "syntax" ?subject=*subject* to the edit box so that the link resembles the following: mailto:me@mymail.com?subject=Great web site!

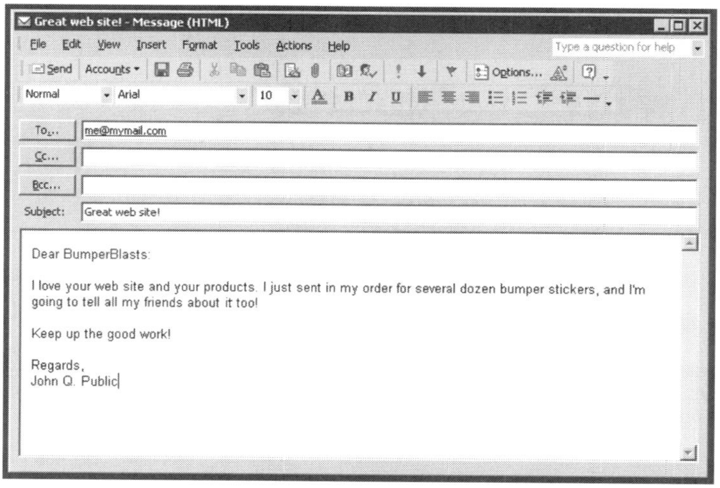

Figure 3.8

Unless the sender manually edits the subject line, you'll automatically know where this message originated.

ALIASES: E-MAIL INCOGNITO

It's always a good idea to give your visitors a way to get in touch with you, especially if you're running a business Web site. If you're worried about giving out your private e-mail address, ask your Web Host if it offers free e-mail aliases. An *alias* is an e-mail address that has no Inbox of its own, but instead works as a forwarding address. A common alias you'll see on the Internet is webmaster@domain.com. Most often, the Webmaster address actually points to the e-mail address of the person who is in charge of managing the Web site.

You can sign up for free e-mail aliases from hundreds of online services as well. Here are just a few to check out.

- http://www.hotmail.com
- http://www.yahoo.com
- http://www.iname.com

I always think of an e-mail alias as something like having a post office box number. Your street address might change, but your PO box doesn't. You can move anywhere and you'll still get your mail (as long as you go pick it up, of course). If I change my e-mail address, or if someone else takes over my site's management, the alias can be redirected to the new e-mail address.

Working with Bookmarks

The hyperlinks you worked with a few minutes ago take you from page to page and from Web site to Web site. If you want to move to a specific location within the Web site, you'll need to use a bookmark. *Bookmarks* are URLs that direct the user to an exact location on a page. Bookmarks help you move quickly to the information you're looking for without wading through irrelevant material. Like other hyperlinks, a bookmark takes two to tango—the link to the bookmark and the bookmark tag itself.

One typical use of bookmarks is to create "thumb tabs" at the top of a page (see Figure 3.9). Want to see the Florida Election jokes under the Political Humor category? You could scroll halfway down a long page, or you could click once on the Florida Election Jokes bookmark and be there instantly.

Defining a Bookmark

Before you can create a link to a bookmark, you must have a bookmark to link to, *n'est ce pas*? To define a bookmark on a page, follow these steps.

1. In Page view, select the text or object that you want to link. You can select an entire line, just a word, or even a graphic. Headings and subheadings, for example, are usually likely candidates for bookmarking.

2. Select Insert, Bookmark. The Bookmark dialog box opens (see Figure 3.10).

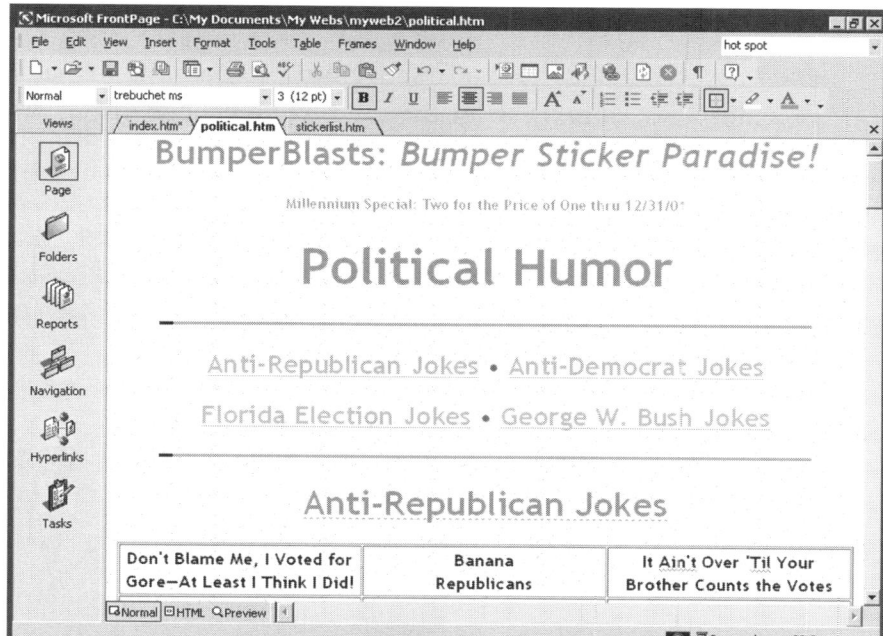

Figure 3.9

Use bookmarks to save your visitors time when they're perusing your Web site.

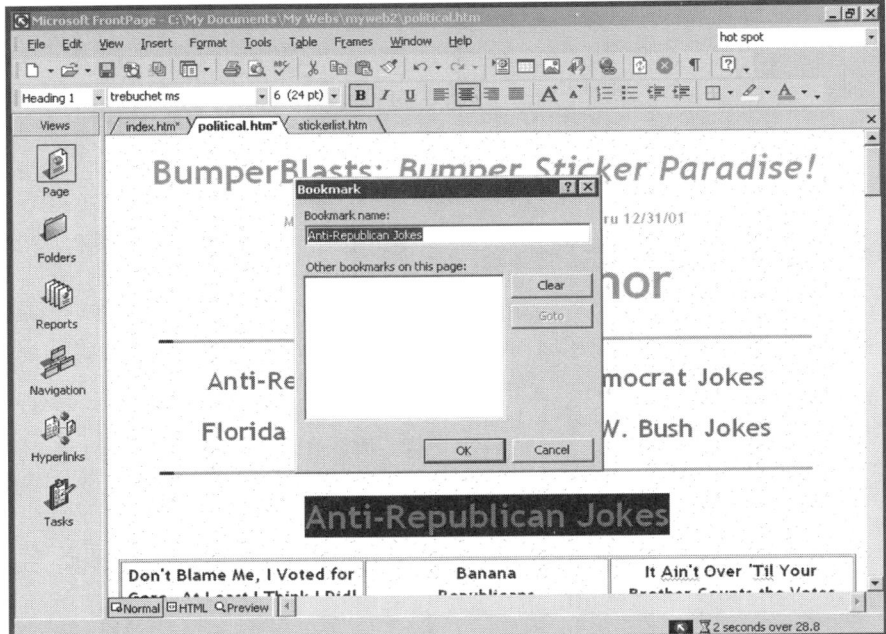

Figure 3.10

FrontPage suggests
a name for the
bookmark.

3. Give your bookmark a brief but meaningful name. Click on OK to close the dialog box and create the bookmark.

TIP

Bookmarks are invisible to the reader; therefore, they don't have to make sense to a reader, but they should make sense to you. If you have many bookmarks on a page, it might become difficult to remember what's what. FrontPage suggests your entire selection as the name—use it if you want.

In Page view, your bookmark appears as a dotted underline (see Figure 3.11). In Preview or in the browser, however, you won't see the dotted underline.

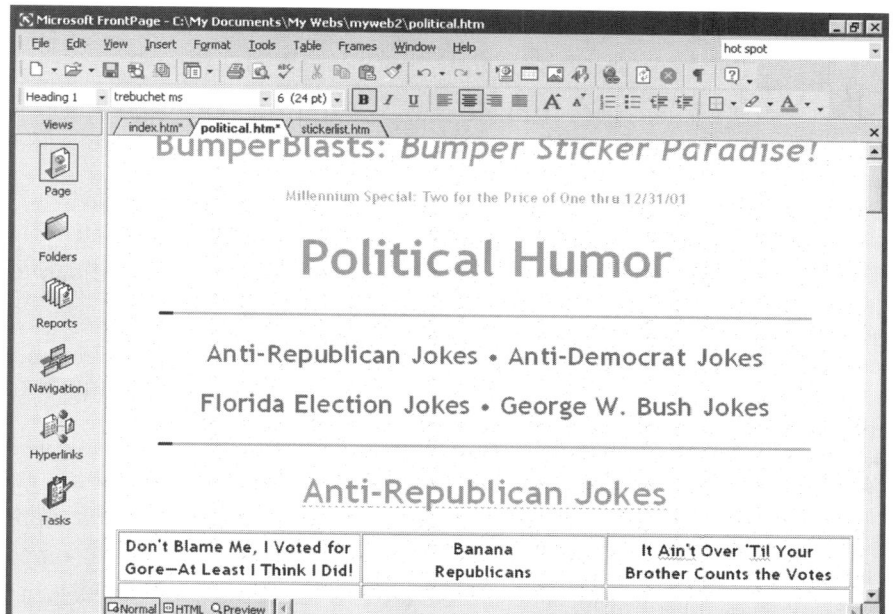

TIP

If you take a peek at the HTML code behind the link, you'll see something like this:

```
<a name="help">How can we help you?</a>
```

The `<a name="x">` tag is what to look for when you're trying to decipher the bookmarks on someone else's pages.

Linking to a Bookmark

You can link to a bookmark from any spot on any Web page. It is just another URL, after all. Ready to try it? It's just like creating any other hyperlink.

1. In Page view, type or select the text or object that will serve as the link.

2. Right-click on your selection and choose Hyperlink from the shortcut menu.

3. Select the file that contains the bookmark, just as you did in the "Creating Links to Existing Pages" section.

4. Click on the Bookmark button. In the Select Place in Document dialog box that appears (see Figure 3.12), select the bookmark you want to target. FrontPage adds a #, plus the name of the bookmark, to the URL text box, so you end up with guestbook.html#help.

5. Click on OK to close the dialog box. The new bookmark link looks like any other hyperlink, underlined and blue (by default, anyway).

TIP

A few automatic bookmark codes are built into HTML. For example, selecting a bookmark coded #top automatically takes you to the top of the current page, even if there's no bookmark defined there. This is handy when you have a long page. You can give the reader a ride back to the top and save them the trouble of scrolling.

In this evening's session, you'll learn about tables. Using a table to organize and align many bookmarks or links is an easy way to keep long lists neat and tidy.

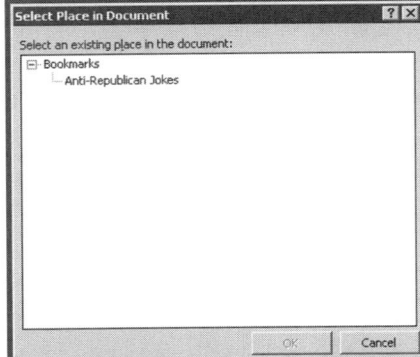

Figure 3.12

You can have a number of bookmarks on the same page.

GRAPHIC LINKS AND IMAGE MAPS

You've seen them—those big flashy graphics that splash across your browser when you land on a particular Web site. There is no text, just a picture. If you were confused at first, you probably quickly realized that you could click on the image itself and go somewhere. Is that a hyperlink? Yes, of course it is. It's just well-disguised as a hotspot on an image map. A *hotspot* is a hyperlink attached to a graphic on a Web page. An *image map* is a graphic that has one or more hotspots.

Although they are much easier to make than they used to be, you still need special software to work on image maps. The details of creating elaborate image maps are beyond the scope of this book. On the other hand, FrontPage gives you some limited hotspot capabilities, and that might very well be all you ever need. To create a hotspot on a graphic, follow these steps.

1. In Page view, select the graphic you want to use. The Pictures toolbar opens. (If it doesn't, right-click on the toolbar area and choose Pictures from the list of available toolbars.)

2. Click on the Hotspot button that corresponds to the shape you want for the hotspot—rectangular, circular, or polygon-shaped (see Figure 3.13).

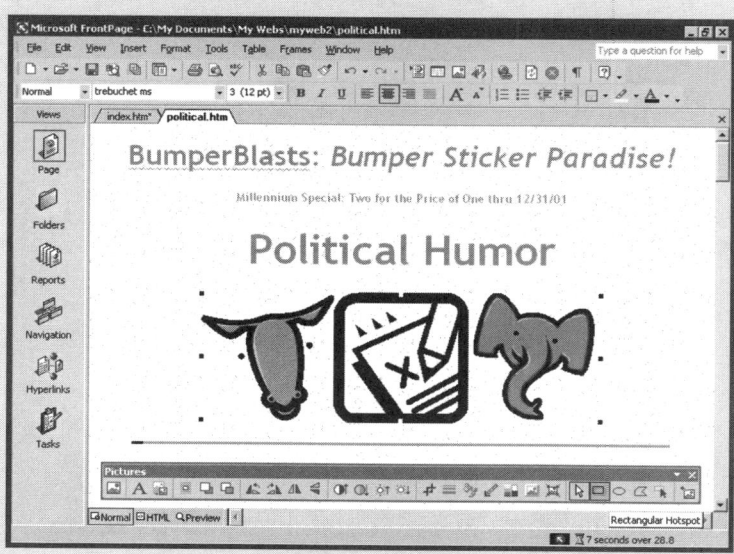

Figure 3.13

You can create simple hotspots for your image files.

GRAPHIC LINKS AND IMAGE MAPS *(CONTINUED...)*

3. **Draw the shape on the graphic where you want the hotspot to be. For polygons, click where you want the polygon to start, click on the location for each corner of the polygon, and then double-click to complete the drawing. When the shape is complete, the Insert Hyperlink dialog box opens, as shown in Figure 3.14.**

4. **Use the normal navigation methods to locate and enter the URL of the link, including any bookmarks if appropriate.**

5. **Click on OK to close the dialog box and create the hotspot.**

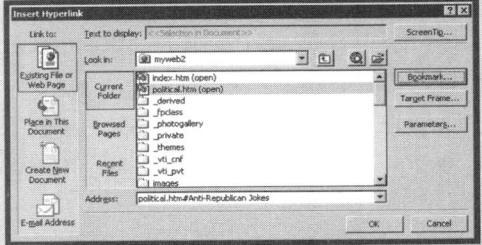

Figure 3.14

Usually, a hotspot sends the user to another page in the Web site.

To test your hotspot, switch to Preview view and point to the hotspot. The pointer changes to a pointing finger, indicating the presence of a link (see Figure 3.15). Click on the link to make sure that it operates as intended.

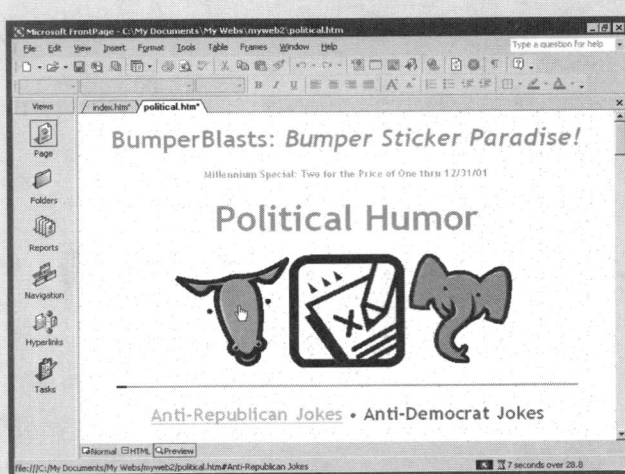

Figure 3.15

Click on the hotspot to go to the link described, just as you would on a text link.

Take a Break!

Well, that was fun. Ready for a stretch? Take a stroll out to the mailbox—maybe there's a letter from an old friend (or maybe just Ed McMahon) waiting to be read. When you come back, you'll wrap up the daylight hours with some more advanced kinds of links: shared borders and navigation bars. These features help you add an easy-to-follow mapping system to your Web site so that your visitors don't get lost. See you in a few! (Don't eat too many of those cookies; it's almost time for dinner.)

Adding Shared Borders and Navigation (Link) Bars

A relatively recent development in Web design is the use of shared borders. Each page's shared border is slightly different in content but maintains a similar look and feel.

◄ ◄

A *shared border* is an area down or across the edge of a page that is reserved for boilerplate information common to all or some of the pages in a Web site.

◄ ◄

On these particular borders, you see a group of buttons (or hyperlinks). The buttons are clearly links to other pages in the Web site, all nicely listed and grouped together for easy access. Although they work similarly, there's no clear dividing line on a shared border as there is in a framed Web site (and no clumsy invisible pages to keep track of).

You can use shared borders to add a common header or footer (like the copyright information shown in Figure 3.16), to include your company logo and contact information in the same place on every page, to add a navigation system to your Web site, or simply to add a bit more flair to your pages. You can even add a graphic in the border as a background image or pattern.

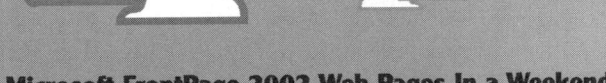

Shared border

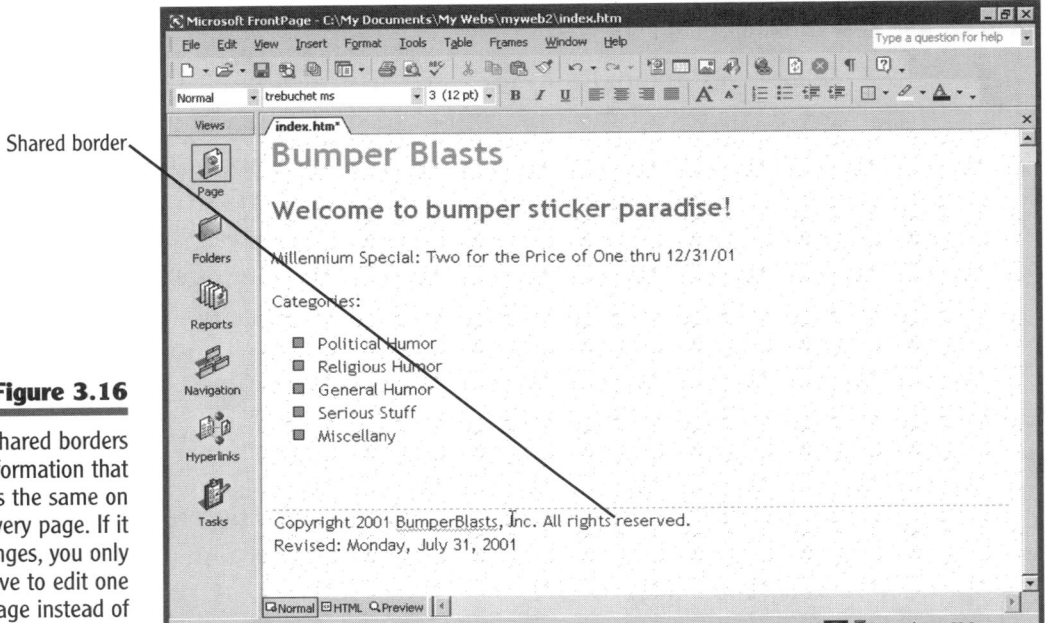

Figure 3.16

Use shared borders
for information that
is the same on
every page. If it
changes, you only
have to edit one
page instead of
all of them.

Link bars, as shown in Figure 3.17, move the reader through your Web site. A link bar can easily guide the reader forward and backward within a group of pages on a similar topic, from one topic to the next, back to the beginning, and so on. The best part is that FrontPage keeps track of the "you are here" point automatically and updates the items in the border as the user moves from page to page.

BUZZ WORD

◄ ◄

Link bars are structured groups of buttons or text links that move visitors through your Web site.

◄ ◄

Navigation link bar

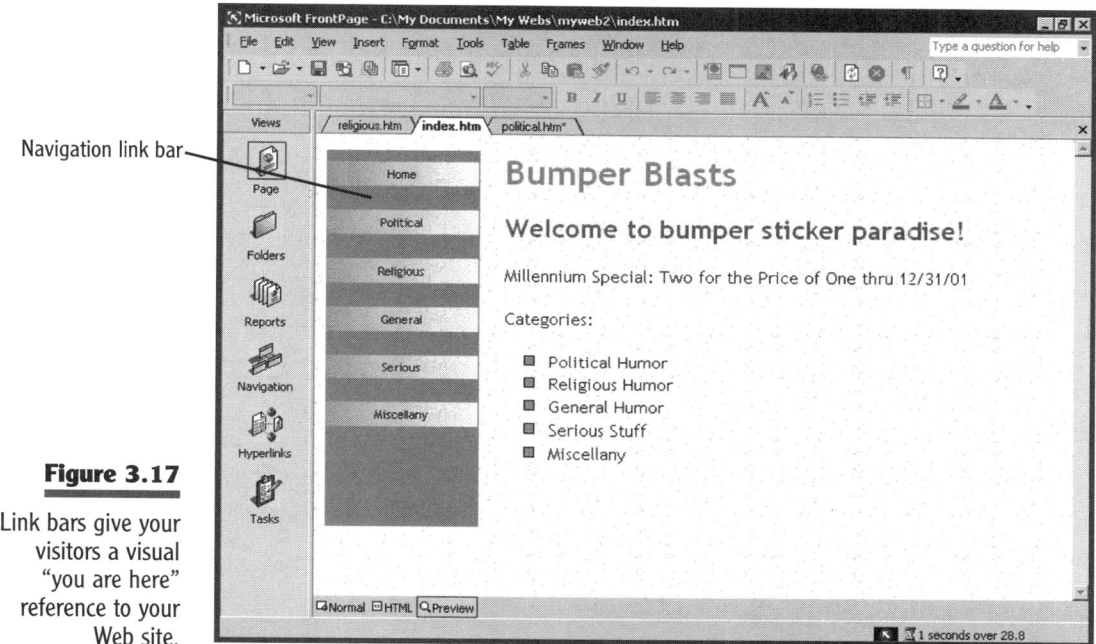

Figure 3.17

Link bars give your visitors a visual "you are here" reference to your Web site.

Organizing Your Pages in Navigation View

Before you can implement shared borders or link bars, you need to tell FrontPage how you want your Web site to be structured. You can click and drag pages around in the Navigation view, creating an organizational chart of sorts.

1. Click on the Navigation view button on the Views bar. FrontPage reveals an open canvas with a single page icon (your index or home page) showing, as shown in Figure 3.18.

2. Think of your Web site in terms of a corporate organization chart. The home page, at the top of the chart, is the company president. All other pages are of some subordinate level below the president. When you're ready to create your navigational structure, click on the Folder List button on the toolbar to reveal the list of files in your Web site.

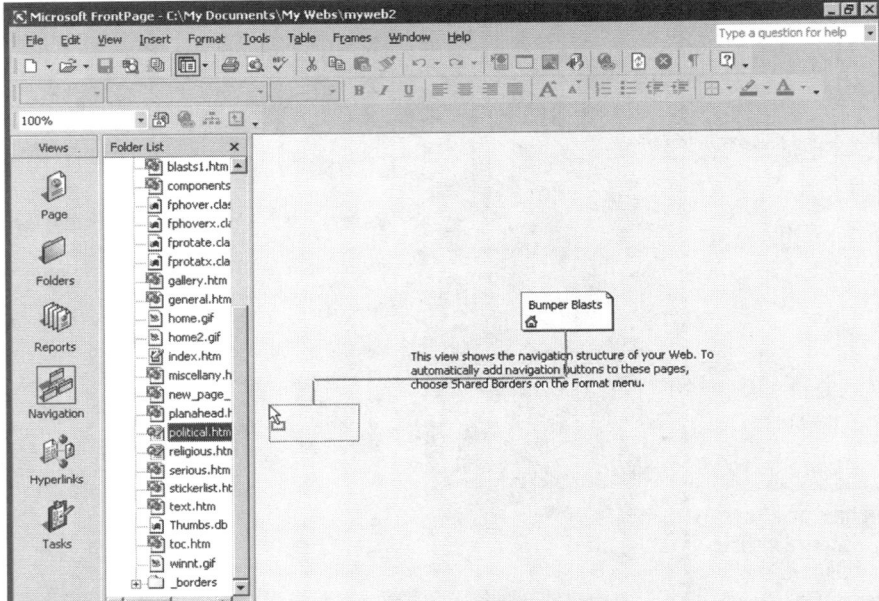

Figure 3.18

Drag pages from the Folder List to create your navigational structure.

3. Click on one of your second-level (vice-presidential, if you will) files in the Folder List and drag it just below the home page icon. When you get close to the icon, a connector appears (see Figure 3.19).

4. Release the mouse button when the page is correctly positioned below the home page. FrontPage adds the page to the navigation structure.

5. Continue dragging your second-level pages. The leftmost pages will be listed first in the link bar. When you've completed the second-level structure, do the same with the third and any additional levels. (Alternatively, you can build one branch or "department" at a time. It just depends on your preference.)

Connector

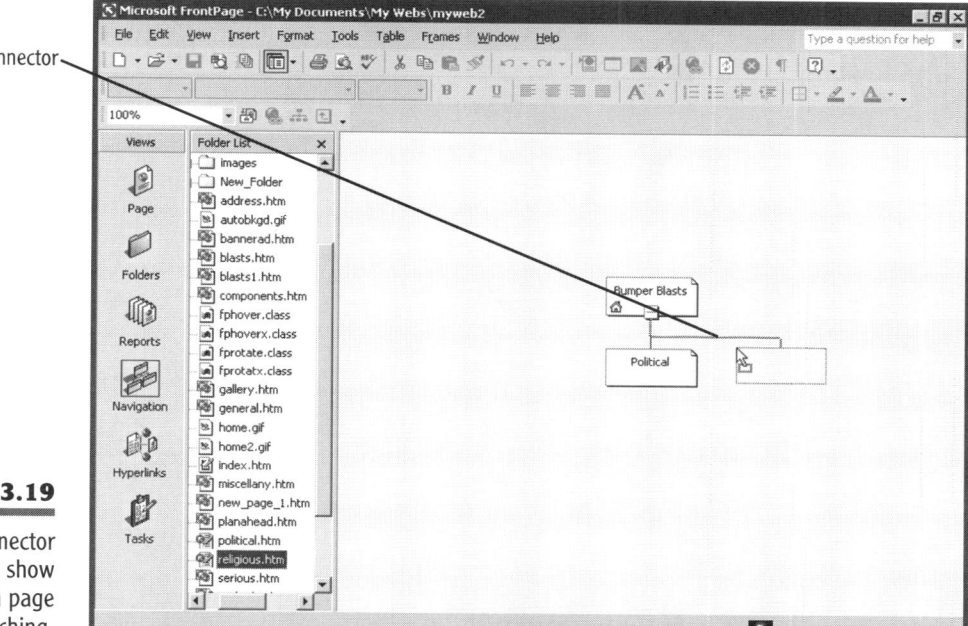

Figure 3.19

The connector appears to show you which page you're approaching.

TIP

If the canvas begins to get too cluttered, you can collapse branches by clicking on the − button. Click the + button to expand the branch again. You also can flip the orientation of the organizational chart from horizontal to vertical by clicking on the Portrait/Landscape button on the Navigation toolbar.

6. There might be some instances in which you need a page in the navigational structure for organizational purposes, but you don't necessarily want it to appear as a link on the link bars. If so, right-click on the file icon and select Included in Navigation Bars on the shortcut menu to remove the check mark. FrontPage disables the page and changes its icon to gray, as shown in Figure 3.20. (It also disables any subordinate pages from appearing in the navigation bars.) You can still access these pages using normal hyperlink procedures; they merely won't have automatic links built into the navigation bar.

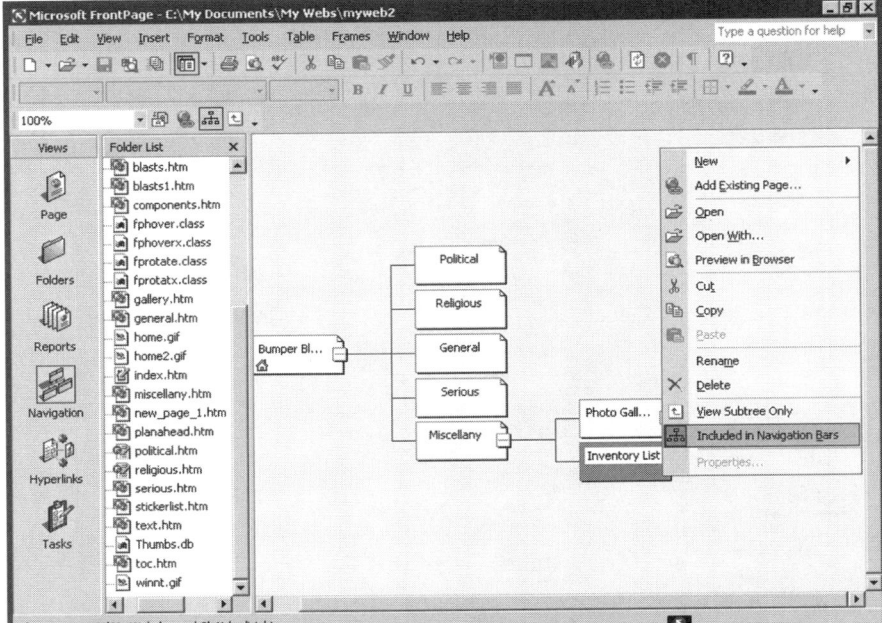

Figure 3.20

You probably don't want pages you use for internal purposes to appear in the navigation bar, because the reader doesn't need (or shouldn't have access to) the information.

7. When you're satisfied with the organizational structure, print a hard copy for later reference. (You'll need it in just a moment.)

Formatting Shared Borders

The next step toward building the navigation bar is to tell FrontPage the type of information to include on each page. Here's where the shared borders feature comes into play. I'm also going to use this feature to add a footer of legal stuff to every page on my site. I'll start there—it's a little less complicated.

1. Click on the Folders button on the Views bar. FrontPage presents your collection of pages and files.

2. Select Format, Shared Borders. The Shared Borders dialog box opens (see Figure 3.21). The small preview area in the dialog box gives you a basic idea of what to expect with each selection.

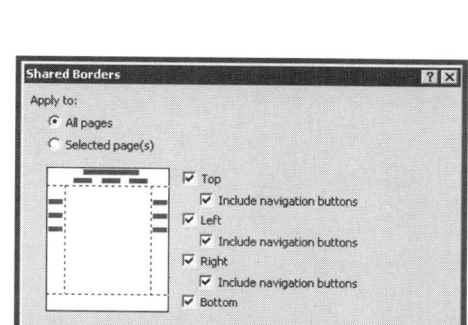

Figure 3.21

You can have shared borders on all four sides if you really want them, but don't forget to leave room for your content!

3. To add a footer to the entire Web site, select All Pages and then put a check mark in the Bottom check box. (You might have to check the box more than once to make the check mark appear.) Don't change any other items that might be selected or partially dimmed. Click on OK to close the dialog box.

4. Double-click on any Web page in the file list. It opens in Page view. Scroll to the bottom of the page and notice the section separated by a thin border. That's the shared border area. Use this area to insert your boilerplate text or objects (see Figure 3.22).

5. Type, format, and arrange the footer text as you want it to appear. Insert tables, graphics, or whatever you want. When you're finished, click on Preview to check the results.

6. Open another page and notice that it contains the same footer text. You now have a running footer that appears at the shared bottom border of every page.

7. To add a link bar on the left, right, or top of every page, repeat this same process, selecting the appropriate check box for the border you want to include. You can customize the type of navigation links included on groups or individual pages, but you must enable the shared border on a page before it will appear.

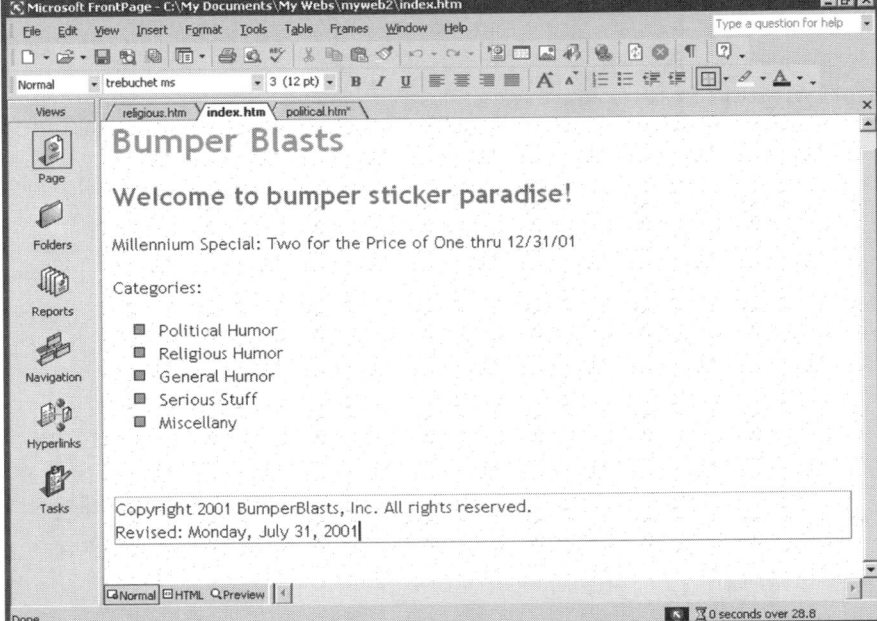

Figure 3.22

The bottom shared border is a good place for your Web site's legal notices.

NOTE

You also have the option to display your navigation links in a variety of text formats or as buttons that coordinate with your chosen theme (see Figure 3.23). To access these options, right-click on the navigation buttons and choose Link Bar Properties. The Link Bar Properties dialog box appears. Click on the Style tab to choose different buttons. Scroll all the way down the list to see the available options for a text-based link bar. FrontPage uses buttons that coordinate with the overall look of the theme, and inserts text labels on the buttons. You might need to experiment with the various settings in this dialog box for best results. Some buttons take up more room on the page than they really should, eating up precious real estate on the main portion of your page. They do enhance your site, though.

Link bar with text links

Link bar with theme buttons

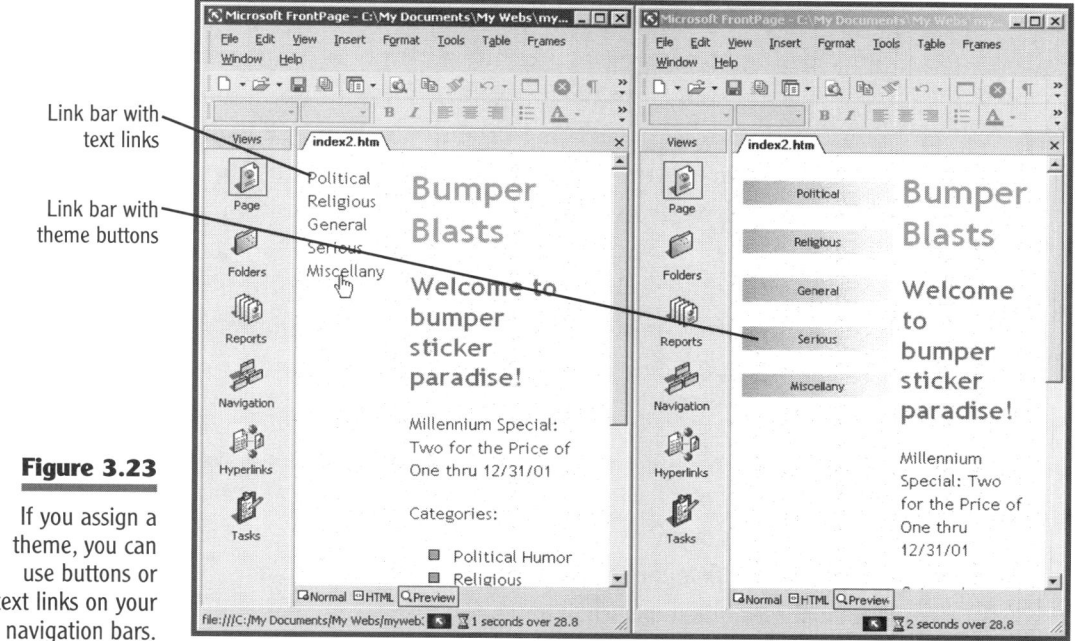

Figure 3.23

If you assign a theme, you can use buttons or text links on your navigation bars.

Configuring Link Bars

With your navigational structure in mind, think about how you want folks to be able to navigate your Web pages. You might want a different set of links for each level of your site. For example, on your home page, you might want to show links only to the second-level pages. On the second-level pages, you might want to show not only links to the other pages on that level (using Forward and Back links), but to all the subordinate or "child" pages under that branch of the structure. Perhaps throw in an Up link back to the next highest level and a Home link back to the main page as well. Before diving in, take a moment to examine the Link Bar Properties dialog box.

1. In Page view, open any page you've designated to have a navigation bar and then right-click on the text in the shared border area.

2. Select Link Bar Properties from the shortcut menu. When the dialog box opens, it presents a variety of configurations for that page's navigation bar, as well as a legend explaining the meanings of the various symbols in the dialog box (see Figure 3.24). When you click on the Style tab, you'll find a list of formatting styles for themed pages or plain-text link bars, along with options for showing the links in vertical or horizontal format and for indicating (as in the Theme Properties dialog box from this morning) whether to use vivid colors and/or active graphics in the link bar. The thumbnail (or miniature) of a site structure changes depending on which options you select.

NOTE Here's another place where you might want to experiment with the various settings on different levels of your Web site structure. Even with the legend onscreen and your Navigation view printout in hand, it might be difficult to determine exactly what you'll get without seeing it in the actual pages.

3. Select an option or two and then click on OK to implement the changes. Notice which page links appear with each setting.

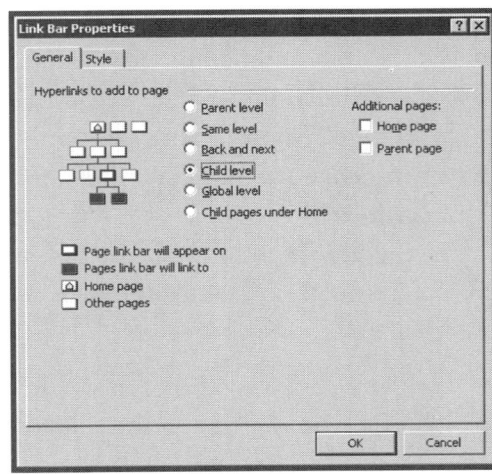

Figure 3.24

FrontPage helps you decide which set of pages to include on the link bar.

4. Repeat steps 1 through 3 a few times until you're comfortable with the impact of each variation.

5. When you're ready, select one of the pages you've designated to share borders and assign the navigation properties you want.

6. Repeat Step 5 to customize settings for individual pages, if necessary. See Figure 3.25 for the results.

Assuming you survived all that unscathed, you're ready to take a break from creating and check out what you've accomplished today.

Testing Your Work

No matter how hard you try, no one is perfect. It's entirely possible that you've made some typing errors in a few of those many links you've recently added to your Web site. Fortunately, FrontPage is forgiving and makes it easy to check for errors and verify the integrity of your links. (This is one of my favorite features because I'm a lousy typist.)

Figure 3.25

A well-designed Web site won't let your visitors get lost among the plethora of pages.

Navigating Hyperlinks in FrontPage

The most obvious way to check whether your links work properly is to click on them. Using FrontPage's Preview view, you can breeze through your Web site to admire your work and find out what's not working like it should. To navigate your hyperlinks from within FrontPage, follow these steps:

1. From Page view, open your home page (index.htm*) file and then click on the Preview tab. Your home page appears in the FrontPage browser.

TIP You can check links from the Normal view tab by pressing Ctrl and clicking on the link.

2. Click on any internal link on your home page. Your browser should take you to the intended destination. If it does, keep clicking on links. Test as many as you can find. Don't worry about external hyperlinks for now; you'll check them next.

TIP Remember that the Preview browser does not include a Back button, so if you get stuck somewhere and can't get back, either right-click on the page and choose Back from the shortcut menu, or just click on the Normal tab to go back to the home page and start over.

3. If you find a link that doesn't work as expected, you can fix it on the fly. Switch back to Normal view, right-click on the link, and select Hyperlink Properties again to investigate the problem (see Figure 3.26). Note that this applies only to regular hyperlinks, not those on the navigation bar. To repair those links, you'll need to work with the navigational structure of your site, as discussed earlier in the "Organizing Your Pages in Navigation View" section.

4. Edit the link as needed, close the dialog box, and then click on the Preview tab again to retest the link.

Mistyped domain name

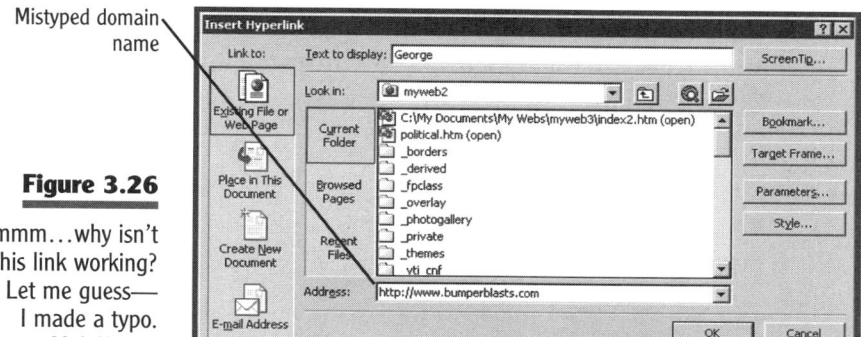

Figure 3.26

Hmmm...why isn't this link working? Let me guess— I made a typo. Me? Never!

5. Save all your files to the hard drive before you run the automated link verification test. Save your work and let FrontPage import any files requested. Close the Web, but don't exit FrontPage.

TIP

After you've saved your pages, you can also test your links by opening the home page, clicking on the Preview in Browser button on the Standard toolbar, and navigating through your pages in a real browser.

Verifying Links

One of FrontPage's collections of Web site management tools is the Broken Hyperlink report feature. Start the report and sit back while FrontPage checks each link in your Web site for you.

NOTE

You must be connected to the Internet or network server to run this report (assuming you have included some external links in your Web site).

1. Reopen your Web by selecting File, Recent Webs, and then selecting the Web name from the list that appears.

2. Select View, Reports, Broken Hyperlinks. FrontPage asks whether you want to verify the hyperlinks in your site. Sure, why not? Click on Yes and let FrontPage run the verification process. When the test is finished, FrontPage displays the report as a list of all your links in table format. The Status column indicates those links that are known problems, those that are OK, and (if applicable) those that have not yet been verified.

NOTE If you have many links (and/or a slow connection), this might take a few moments. As FrontPage verifies each link, it changes the status to OK or Broken. When the test is finished, you might have a rather lengthy list. Don't panic. Most often, one wrong URL can cause errors on several pages at one time (see Figure 3.27). Fix it once, and they will all be correct.

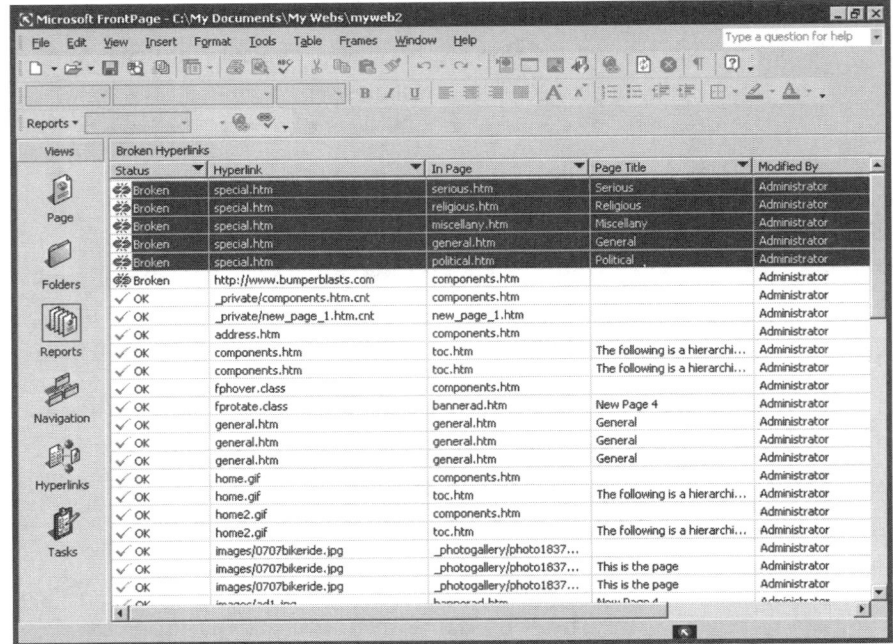

Figure 3.27

Often the same link causes a problem in more than one page.

3. To fix a broken link, double-click on the link in the Reports view. The Edit Hyperlink dialog box opens. You can choose to fix the link by editing the page on which it is found or by editing the URL in the dialog box. If you edit the URL, you have the option of applying the changes to all the affected pages, or just one (see Figure 3.28). After you've repaired a link, the FrontPage report reads Edited.

4. When you've finished the manual repair process, run the verification test again. FrontPage started it automatically last time; this time you'll need to get it going, so click on the Verify Hyperlinks button on the Reports toolbar. When the Verify Hyperlinks dialog box appears, choose whichever option you want. Your best bet is always Verify All Hyperlinks—you never know when a page might disappear from the linked site without your knowing, truly a case of "here one minute, gone the next." Keep repeating the verification process until all the links check out. If one remains stubborn and just won't verify, consider eliminating it and/or replacing it with one that's more cooperative.

What's Next?

At this point, you have enough of a Web site to consider it publishable. It now has several pages, graphics, lists, and most important, lots of links. It's nicely decorated, too. You could post it now and leave it at that.

Figure 3.28

Which method to use? Try repairing the URL first. If it still doesn't work, edit the page to change or eliminate the link.

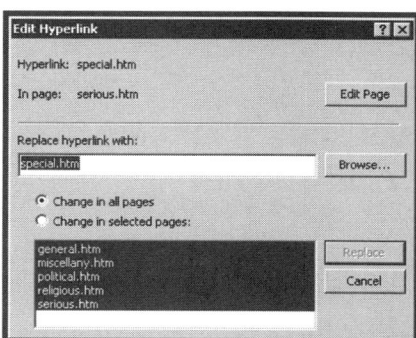

However, why limit yourself to just a basic Web site? FrontPage leveled the playing field between professional developers and the rest of us by making it easy to build in advanced features and special effects, so why not take advantage of it? Tonight after dinner, you'll work with two common features of more sophisticated Web sites, tables and frames. Tables help you organize information on a page neatly and efficiently. Frames are an advanced method of building a navigational structure into your Web site (useful for a large site with lots of information).

Go have a nice dinner with your family or friends and relax for a while. Tuck the kids in and come back for a few more hours of fabulous Front-Page fun. (Okay, so that was corny. Bear with me. I get a little crazy when I'm hungry.)

Working with Tables and Frames

I f all you're interested in is a simple Web site with a few graphics and a couple of links, your job is done. However, if you're up to the challenge of building a more sophisticated site, stay tuned. In tonight's session, you'll learn how to take your site to the next level by implementing tables and frames.

Tables Are Your Friends

You're probably familiar with tables in general. You know that tables come in handy when you need to organize information in a Word document, for example. What you might not know is that FrontPage makes it easy to add tables to your Web pages.

The first time I tried to design a table for a Web site (in the days before Microsoft FrontPage), it took me hours—and it wasn't a complicated table. Writing the HTML code by hand was a chore, and keeping track of all the rows and columns nearly drove me nuts. Boy, was I delighted to find the great table design features in FrontPage! Now you can create tables in a snap. You can use tables to:

- Organize text and graphics on your page in rows and columns
- Line up links or buttons
- Give your pages a multiple-column layout (like a newspaper)
- Display more than one page at a time

You can create the table and then fill it in, or you can convert existing text to a table. In addition, FrontPage includes some friendly table-based templates to get you started with multicolumn layouts.

FIND IT ▶
ONLINE
The popular shareware Web site Tucows (The Ultimate Collection of Winsock Software) uses a table-based design to organize the data for the hundreds of shareware applications available on its site. For some superb examples of table usage, visit http://www.tucows.com. It's also a great place to poke around for Web tools and utilities.

On the Bumper Blasts Web site, I'll create a simple table to organize the major links on the home page. Next, I'll pull in some text from Word and Excel documents and create a table on the fly. Then, I'll show you how to format your tables, add or remove rows and columns, split and merge cells and tables, and even add headings or captions. You'll have this table thing down in nothing flat. Given my early table design experiences, I envy you.

Creating a New Table

Start by creating a simple table to use as a navigational tool. (I'm putting it on my index page. You can put your table wherever you want.)

1. In Page view, open the file you want to edit. Click on the Normal tab to ensure that you're in editing mode.

2. Create a new paragraph at the point where the table will be inserted.

3. Click on the Insert Table button on the toolbar. The Table palette appears, enabling you to tell FrontPage how many rows and columns to include in your table (see Figure 4.1).

4. Select the box that represents the number of rows and columns you want in the table. I have six major topics, so I'll need two rows and three columns (or three rows and two columns, or six rows and one column, or whatever). Your empty table appears at the insertion point, as shown in Figure 4.2. You can see the outline of the table and its individual cells.

Insert Table button

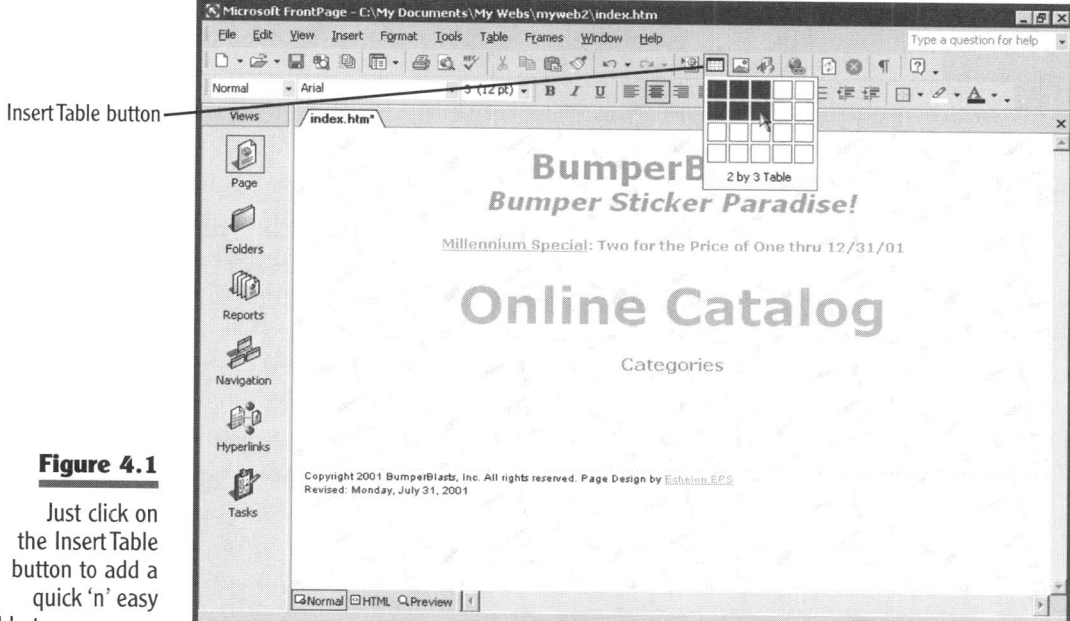

Figure 4.1

Just click on
the Insert Table
button to add a
quick 'n' easy
table to your page.

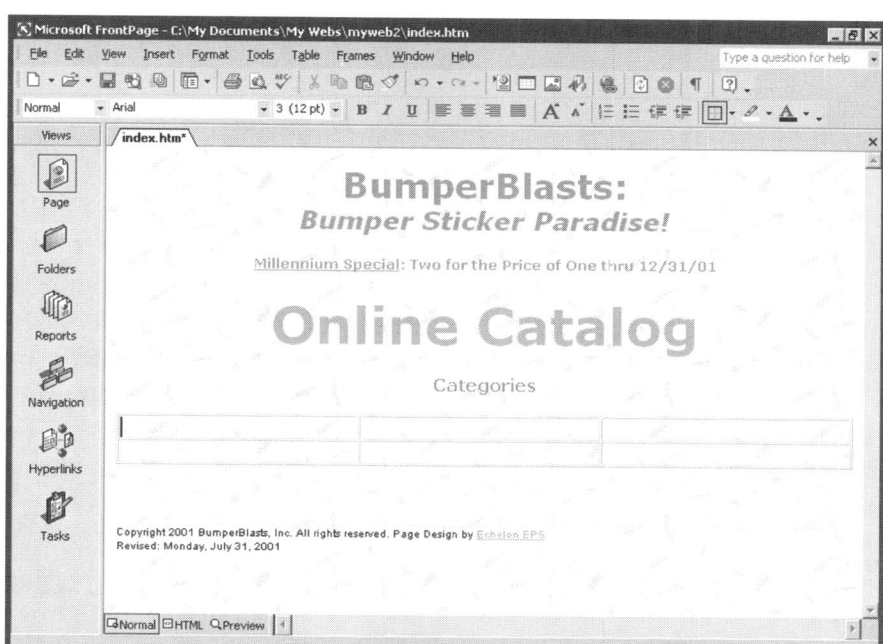

Figure 4.2

FrontPage creates
a table based on
the number of
rows and columns
you selected
from the palette.

Now just fill in the cells with the text for each of your Web site's main areas. You can insert text and/or graphics in each table cell and link to each object as usual.

Converting Text to a Table

You might organize some information as a list, but decide later it might work better as a table. No problem; it's easy to make changes. To convert existing text to a table, follow these steps.

1. In Page view, open the page you want to edit. Click on the Normal tab to ensure that you're in editing mode.

2. Select the text you want to convert to a table.

3. Select Table, Convert, Text To Table. The Convert Text To Table dialog box opens (see Figure 4.3).

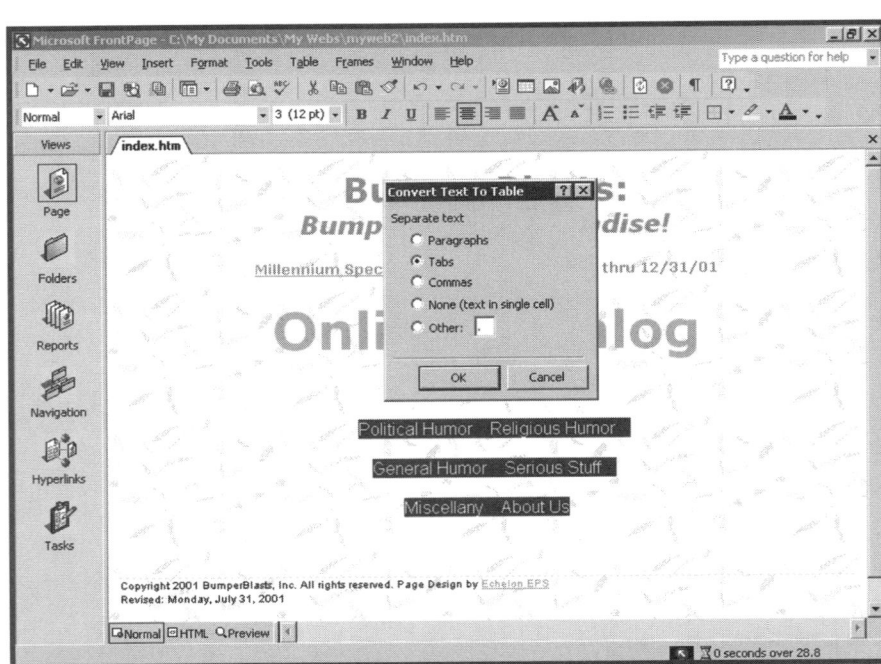

Figure 4.3

Sometimes it's faster to convert existing text, rather than type in new information.

4. If the text for your table is a simple list of short paragraphs, select Paragraphs to separate the text into individual table cells. If you have text with tabs (as shown in Figure 4.3), select Tabs.

5. Click on OK. FrontPage draws the table as you requested and adds the default border style.

TIP

Turn the tables, as they say: Change an existing table back to text by selecting the entire table and then choosing Table, Convert, Table To Text.

Importing Data from Excel or Word to a Table

So far, tables have been a breeze. But what if you want to do something like import spreadsheet data into a Web page? Or maybe you have a table created in Word that you want to use. Don't worry, it's still easy. It just takes a few more steps to get there.

Importing Microsoft Excel Data

Don't waste your time retyping all those numbers on your Web page when you have perfectly good data already available. To import data from Excel as a Web page table, follow these steps.

1. In Page view, open the file you want to edit. Click on the Normal tab to ensure that you're in editing mode.

2. Place the insertion point where the table will be inserted and create a new paragraph.

3. Open Excel and open the worksheet that contains the data (see Figure 4.4).

4. Select the cells you want to copy to your Web page and then click on the Copy button on the toolbar. Your data will be on the Windows Clipboard, ready for pasting.

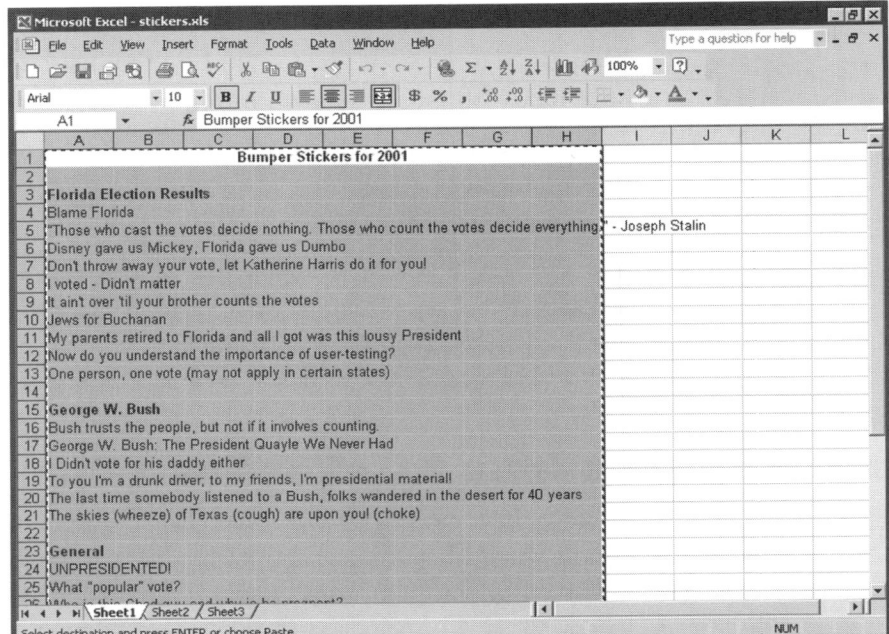

Figure 4.4

Copying data from Excel can save you time.

5. Switch back to FrontPage, click on the insertion point, and click on the Paste button on the toolbar. FrontPage inserts the copied data, as shown in Figure 4.5. (It won't pick up some of your worksheet's formatting properties, but you can fix that in a minute.)

NOTE   The data you've inserted is static. It is not linked to the original spreadsheet and thus won't be updated if you change the spreadsheet. You can insert a dynamic spreadsheet that links directly to Excel using the Office Spreadsheet component. Keep in mind that these components are not visible in some browsers, including Netscape 4.0 and older. For more information on working with this component, open FrontPage's Help system and type **add an office spreadsheet component** in the Answer Wizard.

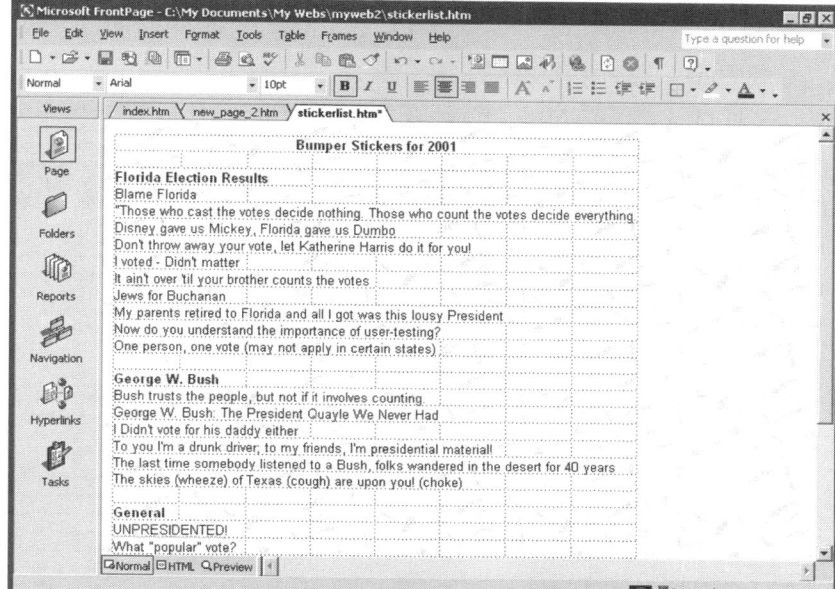

Figure 4.5

This table needs some cleaning up, but it beats starting from scratch.

Copying a Table from Microsoft Word

Maybe you've used Word to create tables in word processing documents, and now you want to use that same information on your Web page. To import data from Word as a Web page table, follow these steps.

1. In Page view, open the file you want to edit. Click on the Normal tab to ensure that you're in editing mode.

2. Place the insertion point where the table will be inserted and create a new paragraph.

3. Open Word and open the document that contains the table.

4. Select the table or the portion of the table that you want to copy to your Web page and then click on the Copy button on the toolbar. Your table will be on the Windows Clipboard, ready for pasting.

5. Switch back to FrontPage, click on the insertion point, and click on the Paste button on the toolbar. FrontPage inserts the table at the place you indicated, as shown in Figure 4.6.

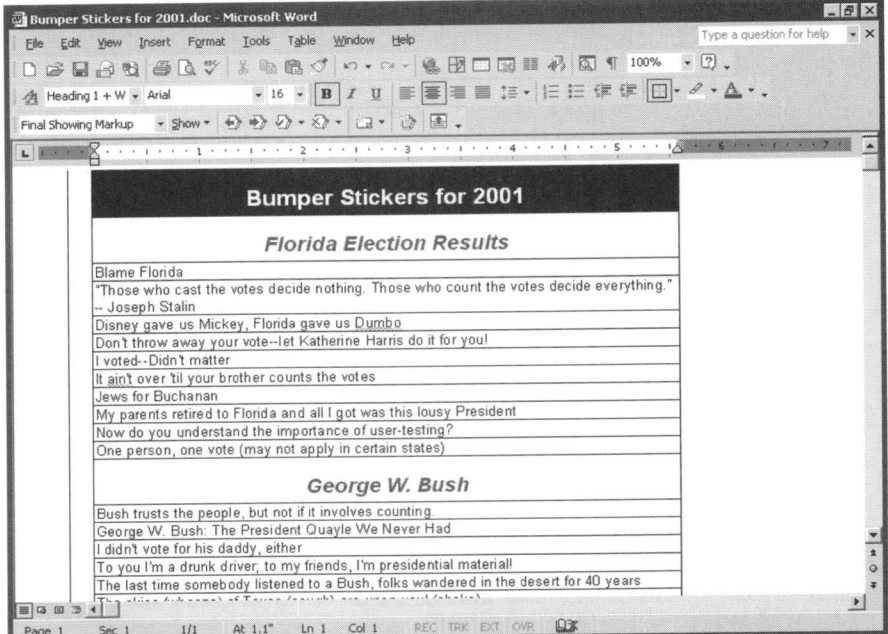

Figure 4.6

Word tables can
be copied or
inserted into your
Web pages.

TIP

If you have a complex table that includes merged cells, special formatting, and so on, you might want to save yourself some formatting work in FrontPage. To more closely match the original formatting of your Word table, select Insert, File and choose the Word document in the Select File dialog box. When you click on OK, FrontPage inserts the document, with the table designed more closely to the way you intended.

BUZZ WORD

Cell *padding* is the amount of space between the inside border of a cell and the outer edge of the text. It's easy to confuse cell padding with cell spacing. Cell *spacing* is the amount of space between the outside borders of two cells, rows, or columns.

Editing and Formatting a Table

Now that you have your table inserted, it probably needs a little sprucing up. FrontPage has a generous array of table formatting tools. You'll find many ways to control the appearance of your table. You can

- Add or change the borders
- Control the table's foreground and background color
- Change the alignment of the table and the amount of space it uses on the page
- Determine how much space or padding to use between the cell borders and the text within the cells
- Add or delete columns and rows
- Merge cells together
- Split cells or the entire table into pieces
- Format the first row or column into headings so that it looks different

Adding Rows and Columns

As you work with your table, you might decide you need more space for text or data. You might want to add more rows or columns. To add a row or column to your existing table, follow these steps.

1. In Normal view, click in the cell next to where you want to make the addition. The addition you're about to make will be relative to the position of the insertion point.

2. Select Table, Insert, Rows or Columns. The Insert Rows or Columns dialog box opens (see Figure 4.7).

3. To insert a row, click on Rows, press Tab, and then type the number of rows to insert. In the Location section, indicate whether you want to insert the row(s) above or below the insertion point. Click on OK.

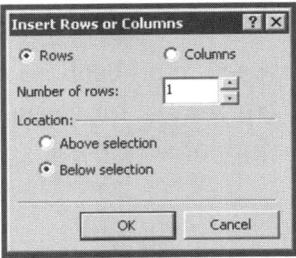

Figure 4.7

Insert a new row or
column anytime,
anywhere.

4. To insert a column, click on Columns, press Tab, and then type
the number of columns to insert. In the Location section, indicate
whether you want to insert the column(s) to the left or right of the
insertion point. Click on OK.

NOTE   Use the shortcut menu to add a new row or column quickly. Select a cell next to where
you want to make the insertion and then right-click to open the shortcut menu and
select Insert Row or Insert Column (see Figure 4.8). By default, the Insert Row command
adds a row above the selection; the Insert Column command adds a column to the left
of the selection. If you select more than one row or column, FrontPage inserts the same
number of rows or columns as you selected.

Merging and Splitting Cells and Tables

The ability to split and merge cells in a table gives you a great deal of
design flexibility for your pages. Consider how you might design a product
catalog. You could create a table with a picture of the product, a description, price, and dimensions for each item in separate cells. Figure 4.9
shows a table with split and merged cells. The following steps enable you
to combine merging and splitting procedures to produce a table similar to
the one shown in Figure 4.9.

1. In Normal view, click on Insert Table on the toolbar and insert a
blank table with four rows and three columns.

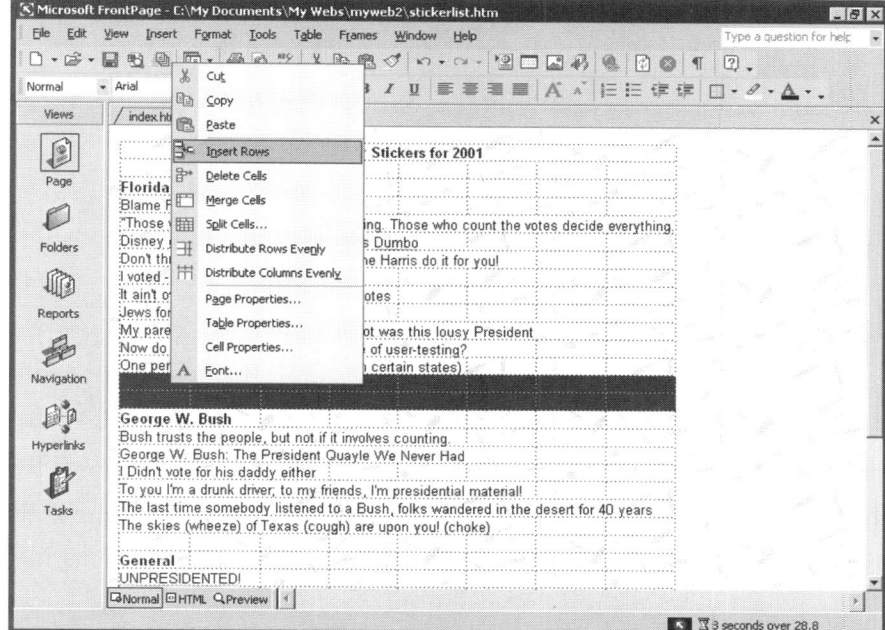

Figure 4.8

It's easy to insert rows or columns into your table.

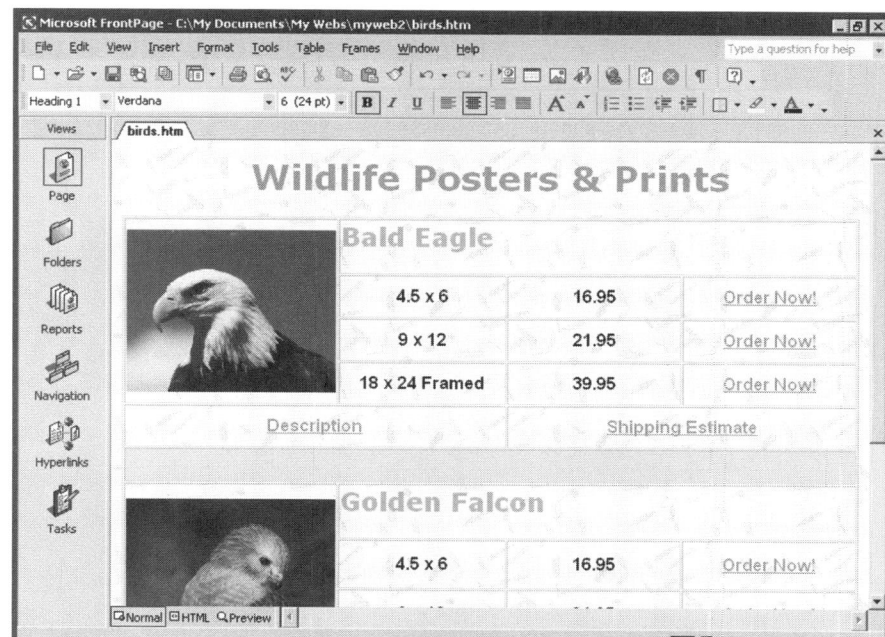

Figure 4.9

Use a table with split and merged cells to create an online catalog like this one.

2. Select the first three cells in the first column. Right-click on the selection and select Merge Cells from the shortcut menu. The three selected cells merge into one cell that is three rows high (see Figure 4.10).

3. Select the bottom row of the table (point to its vertical border to grab the whole row). Right-click on the selection and select Merge Cells from the shortcut menu. The bottom row is now one cell that spans the width of the table.

4. Right-click in the third cell in the second column and select Split Cells from the shortcut menu. The Split Cells dialog box appears (see Figure 4.11).

5. Make sure that Split into Columns is selected and set the number of columns to 2. Click on OK to perform the split.

6. Select the last row of the table again. Select Table, Split Cells. (You might need to expand the menu.) In the Split Cells dialog box, tell FrontPage to split the cell into 2 rows.

7. Click on OK. The original row now has an identical twin.

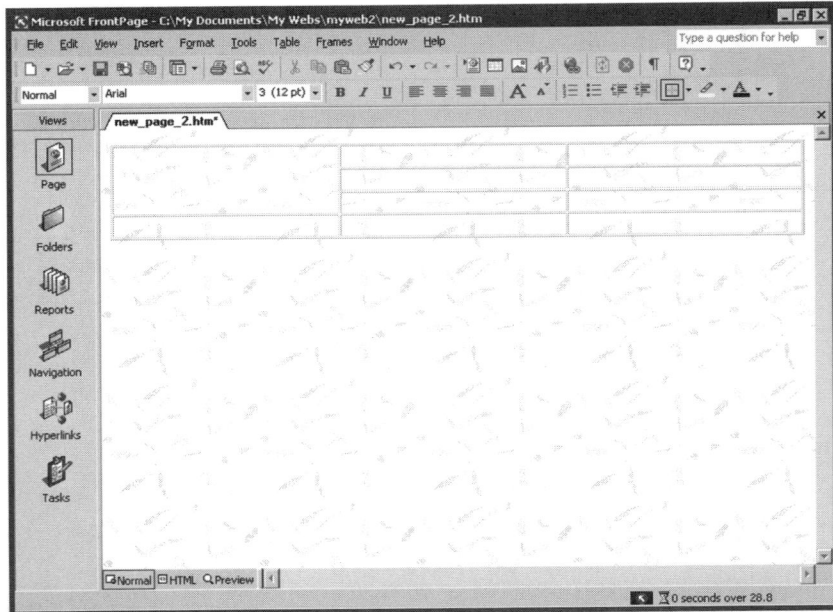

Figure 4.10

Merge cells together to design more creative table layouts.

Figure 4.11

No table design is set in stone, thanks to FrontPage's flexible editing features.

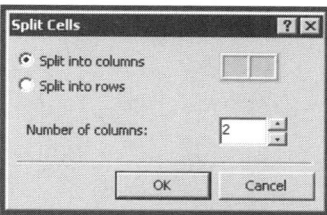

8. Place the cursor anywhere in the next-to-last row, then choose Table, Split Table. (You might need to expand the Table menu to access this command.) FrontPage splits the table in two and inserts a new paragraph between the two tables. You can split a table at any row, but you can't split it between two columns. The results of your work should resemble Figure 4.12.

9. For your purposes here, you don't really need to split the table. I just wanted you to know how to do so in case you ever need to do it. Go ahead and undo the split by pressing Ctrl+Z.

How'd it go? Hey, not bad for a rookie!

Figure 4.12

This is a table with merged and split cells that was then split into two pieces. Looks harder than it is, doesn't it?

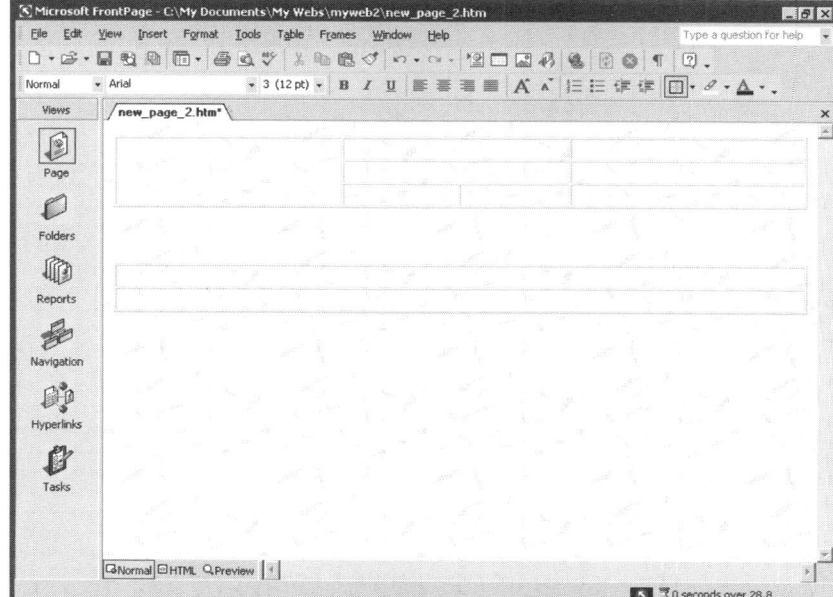

Deleting Rows, Columns, and Cells

If you added rows, columns, or cells that you no longer need, just get rid of them! To delete a table row, column, or cell, follow these steps.

1. Click in an extraneous cell and then select Table, Select. A submenu appears (see Figure 4.13).

2. Choose the command appropriate for what you want to delete: the entire table, the entire row or column, or the individual cell. (For this example, select Table to get rid of these two extra rows you no longer need. FrontPage highlights the selection.

3. Select Table, Delete Cells, and the cells are removed. Figure 4.14 shows the results.

Before you go on, make sure that you've completed the table content as much as you can, including any graphics and hyperlinks. You can always add to it later, but a nearly completed table is easier to format.

Formatting Borders, Backgrounds, and Foregrounds

By default, your table uses the same colors as your Web page's default background and text. With a few simple steps, you can change the table's border style as well as the colors used for the background, foreground, and the spacing around and within cells. You can even use a graphic for the background.

Figure 4.13

You'll need to use the Select menu to be sure that you're selecting the right cells after merging and splitting a few times.

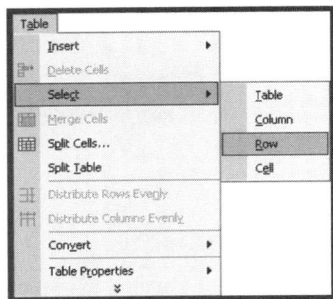

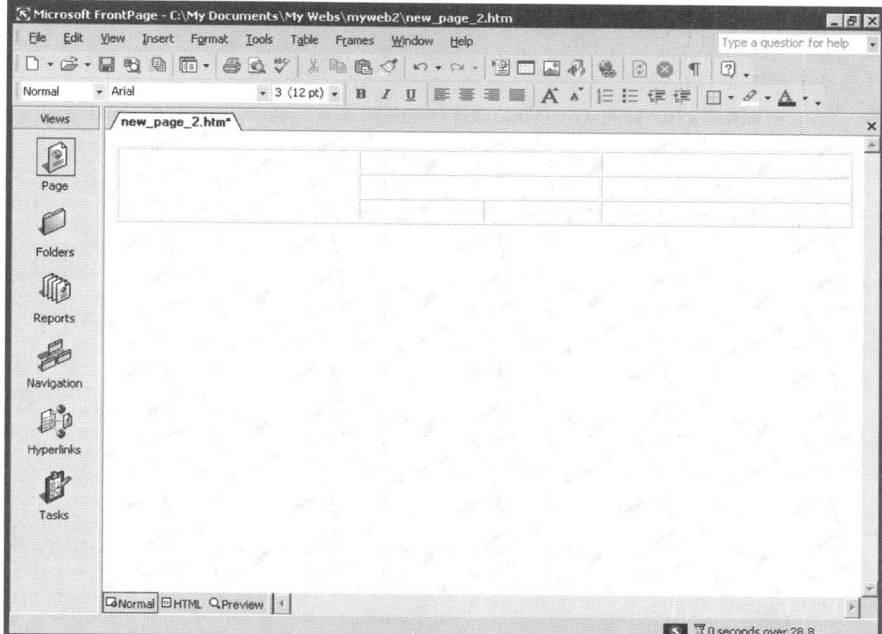

Figure 4.14

Now add text and graphics, and you're all set!

 **NOTE** Some of FrontPage's table formatting options are not compatible with some browsers. For example, some older versions of Netscape Navigator do not support graphic backgrounds in tables.

You can make your tables stand out on a page, or you can make them virtually invisible to the visitor. To change the look of your table, follow these steps.

1. Click anywhere in the table and then choose Table, Select, Table. This ensures that the entire table receives the same treatment.

2. Select Format, Borders and Shading. The Borders and Shading dialog box opens, as shown in Figure 4.15.

3. On the Borders tab, select Box to add or change the border on all four sides of the table.

YOU CAN'T ALWAYS GET WHAT YOU WANT

Selecting the cells you want in a table can be tricky, especially after you've split and merged cells. The original rows and columns might have been manipulated in such a way that it's not always clear to FrontPage (or you) which cells belong in which row or column. Here are a few tips for selecting cells in a table.

- To select an entire row or column, point to the border at the start of the row or column until the pointer changes to a small black arrow, and then click to confirm the selection.

- If your selection area includes merged or split cells, the highlighted results may or may not be what you expected. Use the Select commands on the Table menu to see how FrontPage responds to the Select command from any given cell.

- To select an individual cell, use Alt+click.

- To select more than one row, column, or cell, use Shift+click (or simply click and drag).

- To select non-adjacent items (every other row, for example), use Ctrl+click.

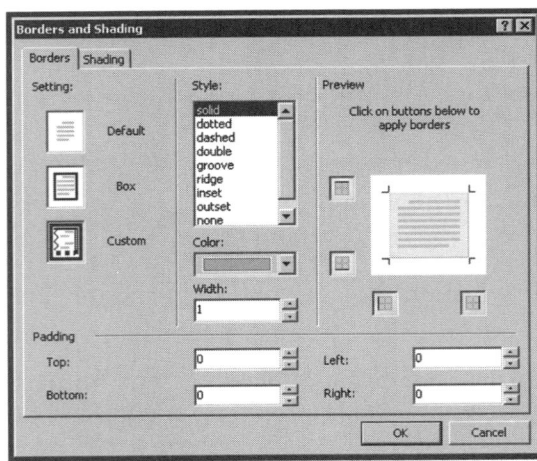

Figure 4.15

You can add a border to all four sides or to just a few.

TIP

For no border, select None. For borders on three or fewer sides, select Custom, and then use the Preview area to select which borders to include.

4. Select a border style. Use the spin button to adjust the border to the desired width.

5. Select a color for the border from the drop-down palette.

6. Now determine how much spacing the cells should have. In the Padding area, click in the Top box and enter a number. (The number represents *pixels*, or screen dots.) For now, enter 5. Press the Tab key and enter the same number for the Bottom, Left, and Right padding. This tells FrontPage to add 5 pixels of space between the inside border and the cell's content, as shown in Figure 4.16.

7. Click on OK to see your progress thus far.

8. Select the entire table. Select Format, Borders and Shading. Click on the Shading tab in the dialog box. The Shading options move to the front, as shown in Figure 4.17.

9. In the Fill area, select a color for the background from the palette. The background is the fill color of the cells.

Figure 4.16

You can control the amount of space between the inside border and the cell's content by using padding.

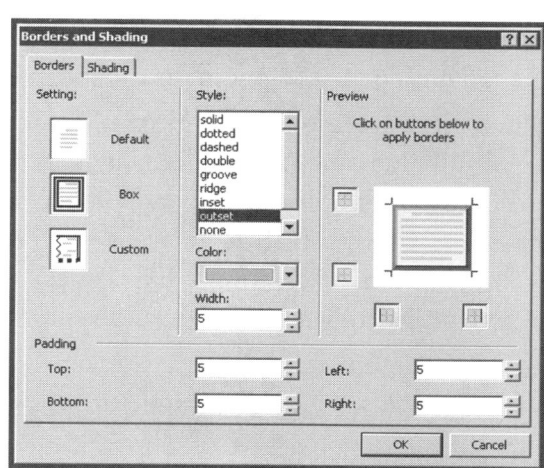

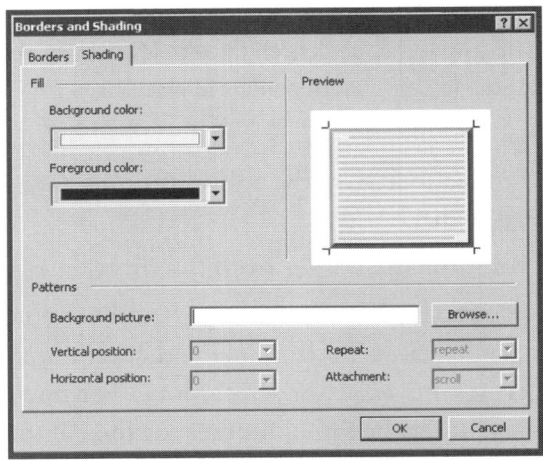

Figure 4.17

Control the table's
foreground and
background colors
with the Shading
settings.

10. Select a color for the foreground. The foreground color affects the color of the text in the cells, as well as the "front" face of a three-dimensional border (such as Groove or Inset).

11. Click on OK to see your progress.

12. Select the entire table. Select Format, Borders and Shading. Click on the Shading tab in the dialog box.

13. To use a graphic as the cell background, select the Background Picture text box under Patterns. Type or navigate to the image file so that its full path or URL appears in the text box.

14. You might want to tell FrontPage how to align and handle the graphic. Align the graphic in the middle by selecting Center from the Vertical Position drop-down list and Center from the Horizontal Position drop-down list. If the image is small enough, it can be tiled or repeated in the background. Experiment with the Repeat and Attachment lists to get the effect you want.

15. Click on OK to close the dialog box. Check your work by previewing the page. Your table should resemble the one shown in Figure 4.18.

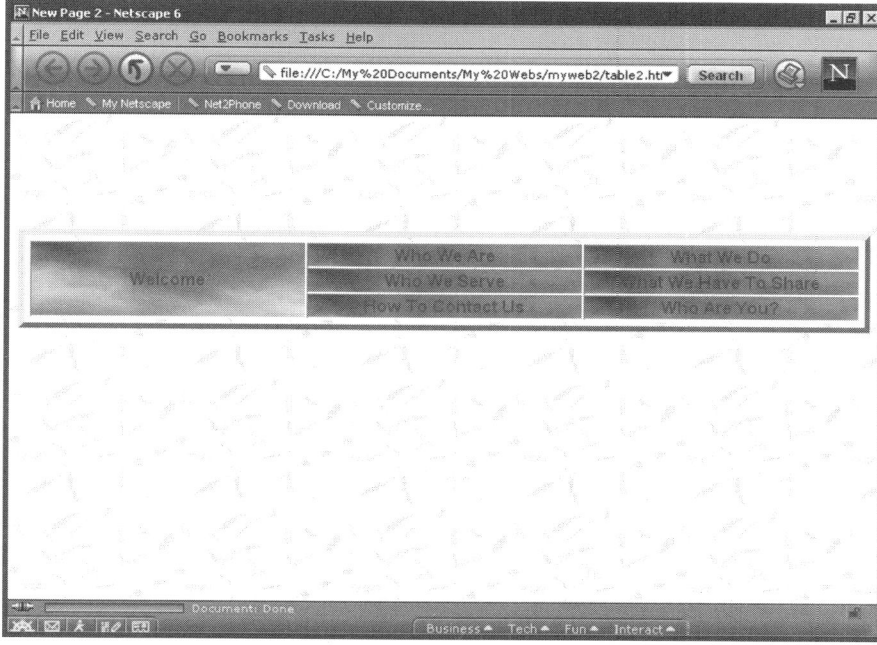

Figure 4.18

Add a patterned background to set the table off from the page.

 TIP

To apply the same steps to individual rows, columns, or cells, use the Table, Select submenu to grab the right cells. This comes in handy when you want to give your individual cell borders a different style than the overall table border.

Controlling Table Size, Alignment, and Position

By default, your table fills the width of the page. If you change the size of your FrontPage or browser window, the table columns automatically resize themselves proportionately across the page, as shown in Figure 4.19. You can change the way your table fits on the page using the following steps.

1. Select the entire table and then select Format, Properties. The Table Properties dialog box opens (see Figure 4.20).

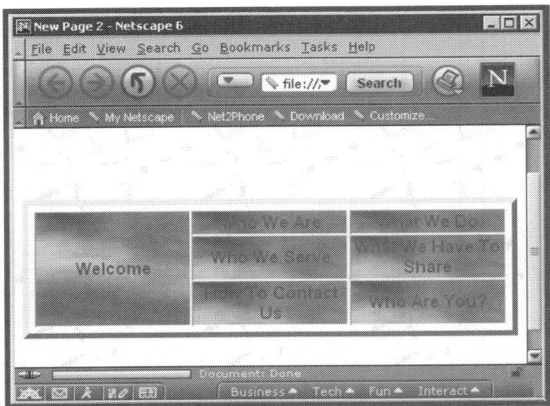

Figure 4.19

By default, tables automatically adjust their column size to fit the page.

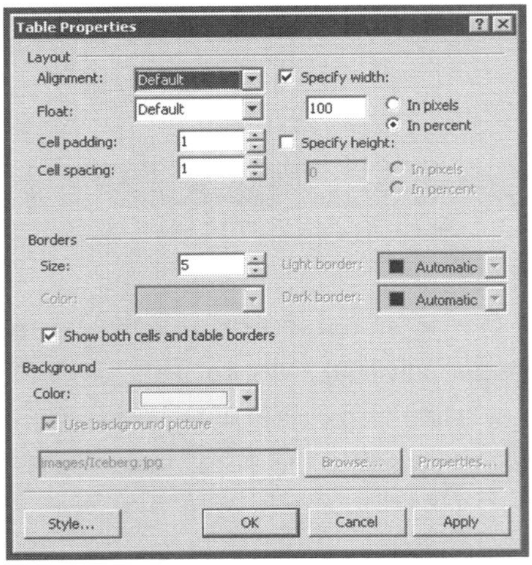

Figure 4.20

You'll find even more ways to customize your table in the Table Properties dialog box.

2. Set an exact width for the table by selecting the Specify Width check box. Type a number in the box and then select In Pixels. To make the table a specific width in relation to the overall page width, select In Percent.

3. To specify an overall height for the table, select the Specify Height check box and follow the instructions in Step 2.

◀ ◀

A *pixel* is a unit of measurement, short for picture element. A pixel identifies a "point" in a graphic. One pixel equals one "dot" on the computer's display screen. The number of pixels does not determine the size of an image, but only the resolution of the image. The size of the image (whether printed or displayed) is determined by the *DPI* (dots per inch) combined with its pixel dimensions, such as 300 × 400.

◀ ◀

4. Choose an alignment to control the position of the table on the page (left, right, centered, justified, or default).

5. Float controls how adjacent text flows around the table. The Default setting actually means none. Select Left or Right to allow text to wrap around the table, as shown in Figure 4.21.

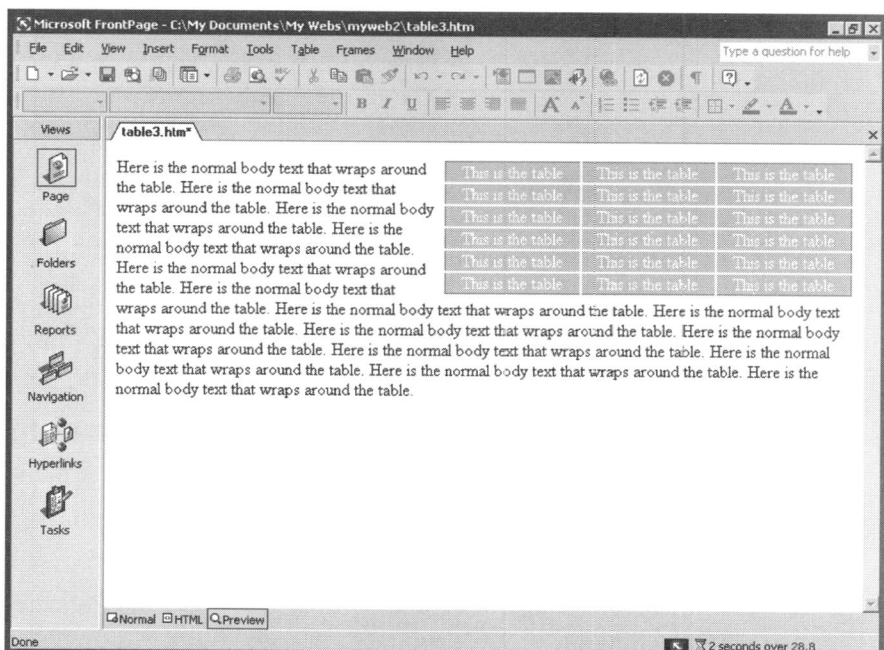

Figure 4.21

Use Float to wrap text around a table or graphic.

NOTE The Float and Alignment settings work hand in hand; changing one option might automatically change the other.

6. To add more space between cells (as opposed to padding within a cell), adjust the number next to Cell Spacing.

Experiment with these settings until you get the effect you want.

Controlling Row Height and Column Width

When FrontPage inserts a new table for you, it assumes that you want all the columns and rows to be the same size. However, FrontPage also allows you to adjust the size of individual rows and columns. You can also set a default size for the entire table. There are three quick ways to make these adjustments within a table.

✪ Point to the border to the right of the column or below the row you want to adjust. The pointer changes to a double-headed arrow. Click and drag the border to the desired new width or height, as shown in Figure 4.22.

✪ Right-click on the row or column you want to change and select Cell Properties. This opens the Cell Properties dialog box. Select In Pixels and enter the specific dimensions.

✪ Right-click on the table and select Distribute Rows Evenly or Distribute Columns Evenly to restore the cells to identical sizes.

Formatting Row and Column Headings

Sometimes you want the first row or column of a table to stand out as the headings that identify the information in the table. To create a header row from existing text in a table, follow these steps.

1. Click in the first row of the table and then select Table, Select, Row.
2. Select Format, Properties. The Cell Properties dialog box opens.

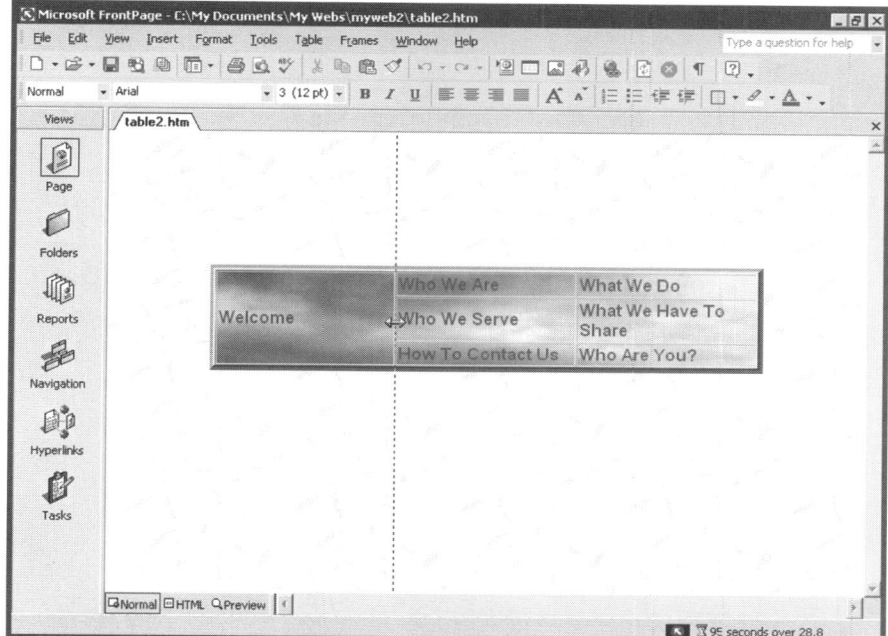

Figure 4.22

Just drag a column
border to change
the column width.

3. Select the Header Cell check box.

4. Click on OK to close the dialog box. FrontPage formats the row a
   little differently than the others. By default, the heading text is bold.

TIP

The steps are identical for creating a header for columns, except that, obviously, you
select the first column rather than the first row.

From here, you can make more formatting changes: center the headings,
change the font size or color, or add background shading. Figure 4.23
shows one such example.

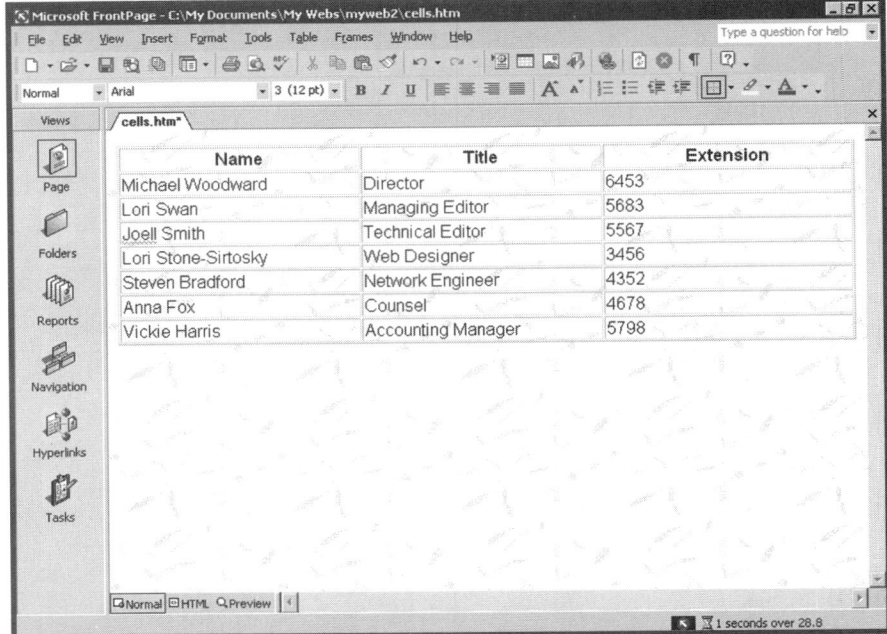

Figure 4.23

Row and column
headings give
your tables a
polished look.

Adding Captions

A table caption identifies your table. Unless you say otherwise, a table caption appears centered above the table, outside the border. To add a caption, follow these steps.

1. Click anywhere in the table and then select Table, Insert, Caption. An empty paragraph and blinking cursor appear above the table, outside the border.

2. Type the text for the caption. Add a graphic, if you want. No matter how you resize or realign the table, the caption remains intact, nicely centered across the width of the table, as shown in Figure 4.24.

3. To show the caption below the table rather than above it, right-click inside the caption and select Caption Properties from the shortcut menu. The Caption Properties dialog box opens.

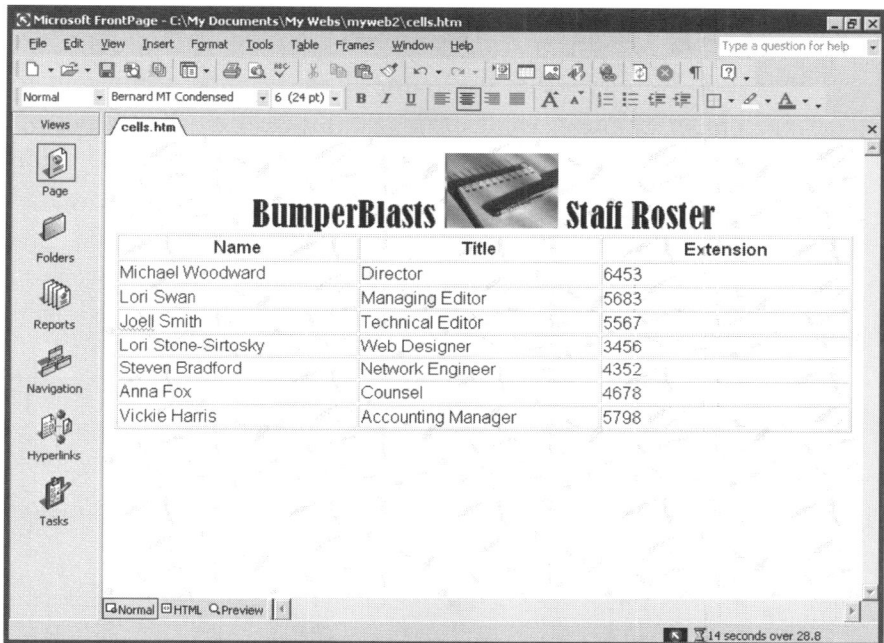

Figure 4.24

You can use table
captions for much
more than just an
identifying label.

4. Select Bottom of Table and press Enter. The dialog box closes, and
   the caption moves to the bottom of the table.

5. After further consideration, the caption looks better at the top,
   don't you think? Select Edit, Undo to erase the change you just
   made. The caption returns to the top of the table.

Take a Break!

You probably zipped through that section in no time, but it's still a good
idea to take a short break now to absorb what you've learned. While you
trot to the kitchen for a refill, think about the world of design options
available to you. When you come back, you'll tackle frames, another
optional but useful page layout option. Frames help you organize your
Web site into "windows" within a browser, letting visitors scroll through
one part of the page while the rest remains static.

Designing with Frames

Web sites that use frames have become popular in recent years because they make navigation easy for visitors. You can display several framed pages in one browser window, or even embed a frameset within another page. This makes design tactics more flexible. Use frames to display navigation bars or logos—the possibilities are endless. Keep in mind, however, that some older browsers don't support frames, so think about your audience before you take the plunge.

◄ ◄

A *frame* allows multiple HTML documents to be displayed at the same time in separate frame windows within a browser.

◄ ◄

Frames work a little like shared borders in that you can use them to display a running header or footer or a navigation bar. They're a lot more powerful than that, however. Each frame window contains a different page. You can move around within one frame window, scrolling, clicking, even opening new pages or Web sites, while the other windows within the frame stay put.

Figure 4.25 shows a variation of the original Bumper Blasts layout using a simple frame. On the left, you see a narrow column containing a button bar designating the major topics of the Web site; on the right is the main informational page. Notice that each window has a scroll bar so that visitors can scroll to see more content in either window if it doesn't all fit within the confines of their browser window.

What you're actually seeing here is three pages, not just two. Every frame consists of at least three pages:

✿ The frames page is the page that "contains" the other embedded pages (the frameset). This page is invisible to the visitor.

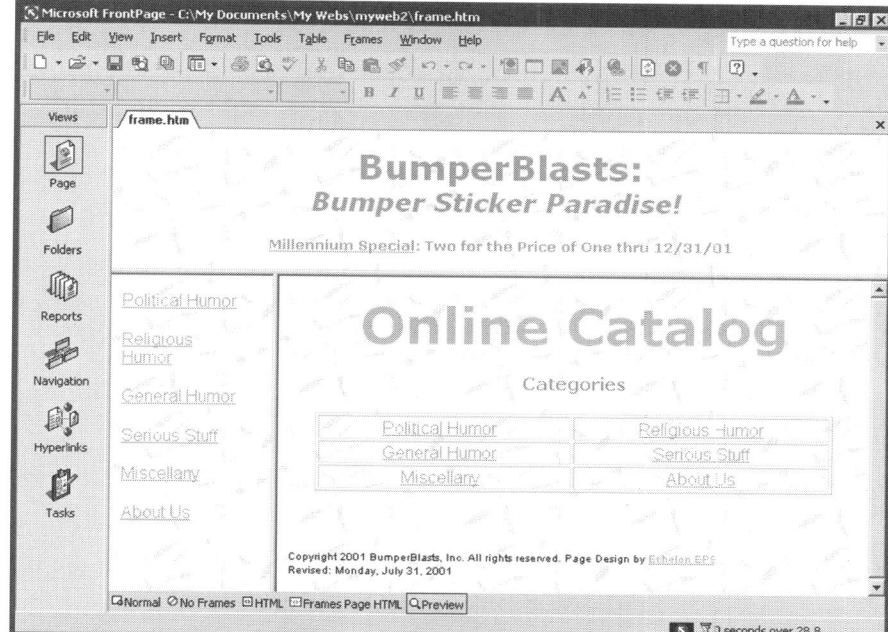

Figure 4.25

Click on a button on the left to display a page on the right. Scroll down either window to see more.

○ Two or more different content pages, one for each window of the frame.

◄ ◄
The foundation for a frame is the *frameset*, a Web page that contains the HTML codes (defined within a FRAMESET tag) defining the layout for a framed Web site. If you use frames on your entire Web site, the page containing the frameset should be your default index page.
◄ ◄

If you have more than two windows in your frame, then you'll have that many more pages included as part of the frame. You can even embed or nest frames within frames, but why complicate a nice, clean layout just because you can?

Preparing the Frame Content

Before you create the frame itself, decide what type of frame you want to use and how many windows it should have. To look at some common frame layouts, switch to Page view and then select File, New, Page or Web. When the Task Pane appears, select Page Templates. When the Page Templates dialog box appears, click on the Frames Pages tab. Click once on each of the available frame templates and check out their description and layout preview. You'll begin to see possibilities for your own pages. As you study the templates, consider these issues before creating frames.

- Do you want a window across the top or bottom that displays an overall header or footer for your Web site?

- Will two side-by-side windows be enough to display the information?

- Should the windows work independently of one another, or will one serve as a (static) navigational tool and the other as the (dynamic) main display area?

- Shared borders and navigation bars might not work as expected. Carefully consider when and where to use them on your frame's content pages, if at all. You might need to choose which to use, frames or shared borders. They can often produce the same effect. Shared borders can be less hassle; frames are more flexible.

If you're concerned about visitors with older browsers (and you probably should be), be sure to read the sidebar in this section, "Frames Support for Older Browsers."

Click on Cancel when you're done perusing the templates. (Don't actually open a new frame yet.)

When you've decided on a layout, you can design your content pages accordingly. As you're designing them, keep in mind where in the frame the page will appear and how its content will affect the layout. If you're going for a basic two-window design like the example, you know that the left "table of contents" window is narrow. You don't want this window to

FRAMES SUPPORT FOR OLDER BROWSERS

Visitors using a browser older than Internet Explorer 3.0 or Netscape Navigator 2.0 cannot view framed Web pages. What's more, some browsers that do support frames allow the user to disable their use. Until the day all the masses are using frames-friendly browsers, you'll want to consider adding "no-frames" support to your frame-based Web site. The no-frames page is actually a fourth "page" that should be considered a vital part of every frame unless you're certain the vast majority of your target audience will only be using frames-friendly browsers.

To support these older browsers, you need to design an alternate page that can appear in place of the frames page. If it's simple enough you can use your same main content page, as long as that page contains links to your other pages. Other-wise, the visitor will be stuck after he clicks past the first page, and he'll have to step back out of the page using the browser's Back button.

When you're working with frames, FrontPage adds two additional tabs to the types of page views available. No Frames view shows you what visitors will see if their browser does not support frames, and Frames Page HTML helps you sort out the complex HTML code required for the frameset architecture by keeping it separate from the rest of the code (such as the style info and page content).

If you're really slick, you can use the FrontPage component called Include Page to automatically display the contents of an existing page, in its entirety, in your no-frames support page. See the Sunday Morning session, "Putting the Power of Components to Work," for more information on working with the Include component.

take up a lot of screen real estate, and you don't want the visitor to have to scroll too much on this side of the frame. Keep any such pages as short and clean as possible.

Running the Frame Wizard

After you develop your frame content pages, as well as the no-frames support page, you can begin setting up the frame. So that you don't mess up your Web currently in progress, start with a fresh Web. You can import the files back into the original site, or vice versa, later. After that's done, you'll step through the Frames Wizard, an important tool that takes all the pain out of creating a framed page (or most of it, anyway).

1. Close any open Webs and then click on View, Task Pane. On the Task pane, click on Web Site Templates. The Web Site Templates dialog box opens, as shown in Figure 4.26.

2. Specify the location of the new Web in the Options area of the dialog box.

3. You don't need a bunch of extra pages here. Click on the Empty Web template and then click on OK. FrontPage creates the new Web and opens it in a separate window.

4. Switch to Page view if you're not already there, and then open the Task pane again and click on Page Templates. The Page Templates dialog box opens.

5. Click on the Frames Pages tab to reveal the available frame templates, as shown in Figure 4.27. Click on the template style you want to use and then click on OK. For the example, I'm choosing the Banner and Contents template. FrontPage creates your frame "skeleton" and displays two command buttons in each frame window.

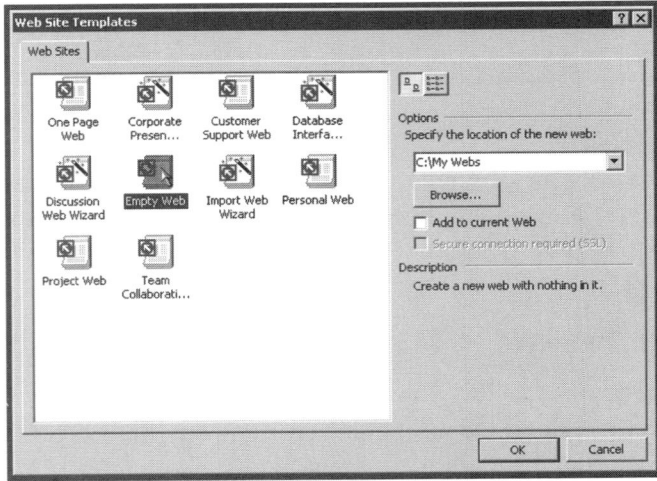

Figure 4.26

Start a frames-based Web from the Empty Web template.

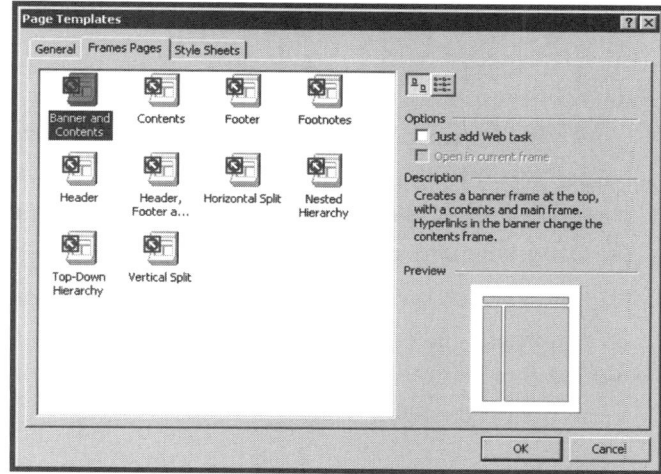

Figure 4.27

A wide range of Frames Pages templates are available in FrontPage.

6. Import the content pages you developed from your original Web by selecting File, Import. Select the files via the Add Files to Import dialog box, as you learned this morning. Don't forget to import any graphics, subfolders, or other items included on your content pages. You can select all the files from the previous Web site by clicking on the first file, holding Shift, and then clicking on the last file. Select non-contiguous files by holding down the Ctrl key as you click on files.

NOTE To use frames on the opening page of your Web site, your frame skeleton (or container) page must use the default home page file name (index.* or default.*). If one of your content pages already uses that name, rename it by selecting Modify in the Import dialog box and entering the new file name. When you save the frames page, name it index.html, or whatever your server requires. If you're not sure, use index.htm. (You can always change it later.)

For the sake of clarity, it might behoove you to name these files based on their targeted positions. Name the page for the left-side frame left.htm and name the main window page main.htm, for example.

7. Now tell FrontPage where the pages should go. In the left window, click on the Set Initial Page button. In the dialog box, select the file to include in the left side of the frame (the window called Content). If you're following the example, that would be the page named left.htm. Click on OK. If you haven't created your content pages yet and would rather create a new page on the fly, click on the New Page button instead.

8. Repeat Step 7 for the right-side window (the window called Main). Both content pages should now be showing in the frame windows. Notice that there are some extra tabs at the bottom of the screen in the FrontPage editing view.

   - **No Frames.** Click on this tab to see how your frames page looks in a browser that doesn't support frames. Right now, it should be empty except for a line that reminds the visitor, "This page uses frames, but your browser doesn't support them." (See Figure 4.28.)

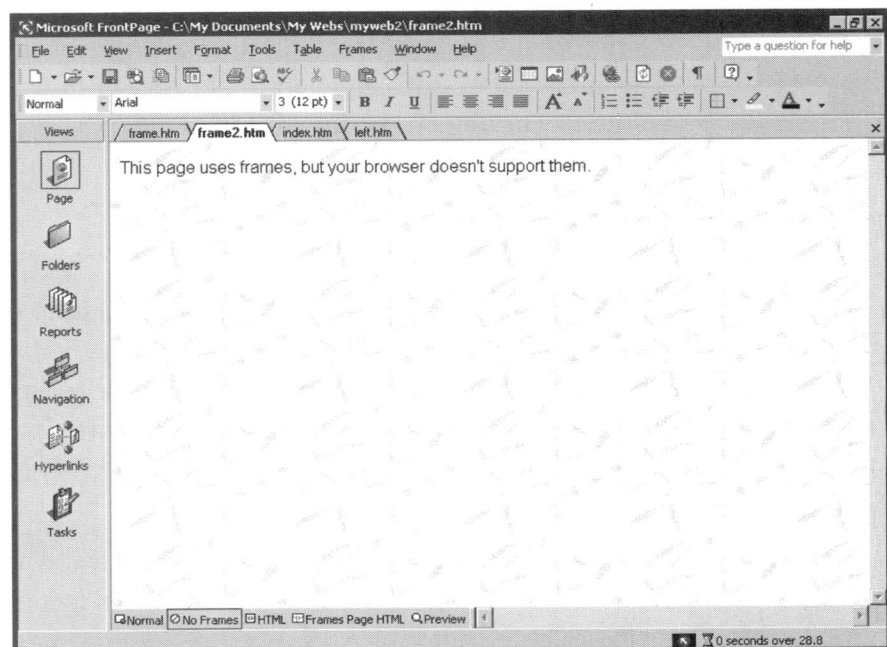

Figure 4.28

Unless you add content to the No Frames window, visitors whose browsers don't support frames will be left out in the cold.

- **Frames Page HTML.** Use this tab to view and edit the frames page code (good luck!). It's nice that FrontPage keeps track of the frame coding when you do need to work with it manually. If you're the inquisitive type, studying the code on this page will give you a much better understanding of how frames are constructed from a technical aspect.

9. To add your no-frames support page, click on the No Frames tab. Delete the existing line of text and select Insert, File. Then, choose the file to display, or design the page right then and there if you want.

> This is not really a page unto itself, just an alternate view of the framed page. Each view is hidden from the other. Your visitors will see either the frames page or the no-frames page. There won't be a separate file to name and save for the no-frames support text.

10. When you're finished, preview the page to see your frame (see Figure 4.29). If there are problems or if the frame doesn't work as expected, it's likely due to some frame-related settings you need to adjust. You'll do that in a moment.

> You can only view the No Frames page in editing mode, or in a browser that does not support frames. You won't be able to see it in FrontPage's Preview view or in any browser that supports frames by default.

That's about the size of it. Frames can be a little tricky, but they're not too confusing.

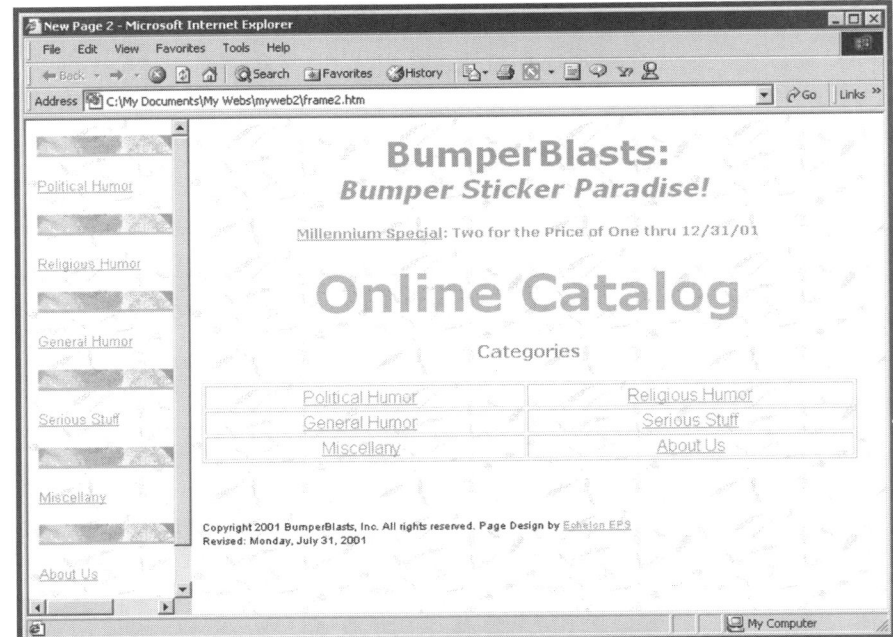

Figure 4.29

This simple two-pane design is only the beginning of what you can do with frames.

Adding Inline Frames to Existing Pages

Occasionally, you'll want to use a frame within another page. One common reason is to display the contents of another Web page. Consider a simple example. To take a resource list one step beyond a simple list of links, you can use inline frames to give your visitors direct access to the referenced site—without having them leave *your* site! Keeping your visitors around can be important, especially for a commercial site. Typical links don't accomplish that very well.

Unlike the Include component (which you'll learn more about on Sunday morning), an inline frame can include any Web page, even those from a subweb or from another Web site entirely. Inline frames also differ from Includes because you can control the size and shape of the frame, whereas an included page takes up the entire width of the page or window into which it is inserted. You can even embed an inline frame in a table. Inline frames are still on the new side, but as they become more widely used, you'll be amazed at the creative possibilities.

To try one on for size, follow these steps.

1. Open or create the page that will "host" the inline frame.

2. Place the cursor at the point on the page at which you want the frame to start.

3. Click on Insert, Inline Frame. The new frame appears with the default width and height of 300 × 150 pixels.

4. Follow the directions in Step 7 from the last exercise to tell Front-Page which page to display in the frame. It can be any page from anywhere—any old page at all (see Figure 4.30).

5. Plug in the initial page information like you did in Step 7 of the previous exercise. Click on the Set Initial Page button, then select or create the file to include and click on OK.

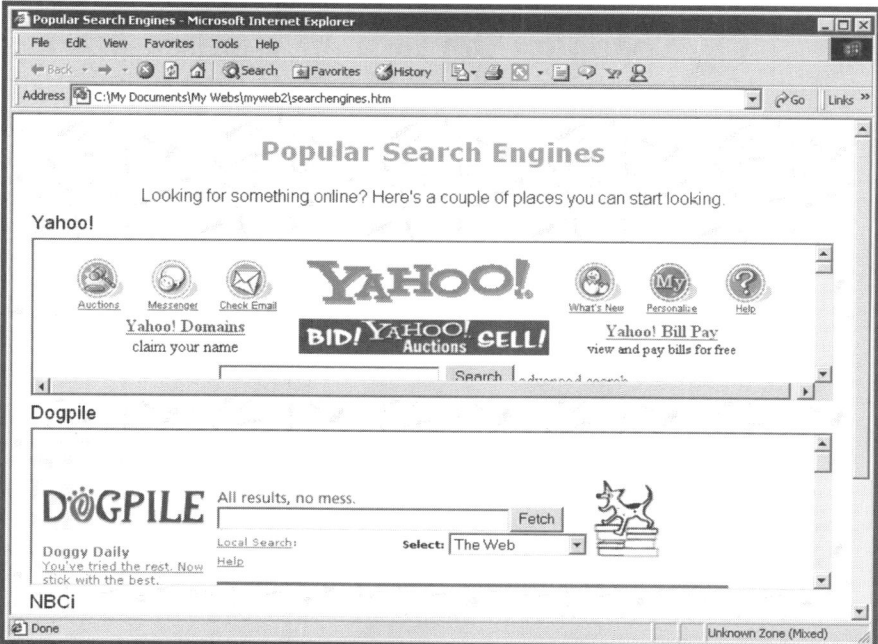

Figure 4.30

An inline frame gives you even more content and design flexibility.

6. You can control a number of options for your new frame. To get to the controls, point to the top edge of the frame and watch for the cursor to change to a left-pointing arrow. When that happens, double-click anywhere inside the inline frame. The Inline Frame Properties dialog box opens.

7. In this dialog box, you can change the initial page that is displayed, turn scroll bars on or off, set the top and left margins for the frame, and provide alternate text for browsers that can't display inline frames. Make the necessary changes and click on OK. All done! (For more details on editing these controls, read on.)

Editing Frames

You can rework a frameset layout any way you choose. You can delete, remove, or resize frame windows; substitute different content pages; and even add nested frames (frames within frames). Take a quick look at how to accomplish these feats. Most of these controls also apply to inline frames.

Changing the Initial Page in a Frame Window

Just as your index or home page automatically appears when the user types your domain name in his browser, each window of a frame automatically displays a default initial page until the user clicks on a link to see something new. If you want a different initial page to display in one of your frame windows, follow these steps.

1. Right-click in the frame and then select Frame Properties from the shortcut menu. The Frame Properties dialog box opens, as shown in Figure 4.31.

2. In the Initial Page text box, type or navigate to the new page so that the path and file name or URL of the page appear in the text box.

3. Click on OK. The frames page reappears with the replacement page in place.

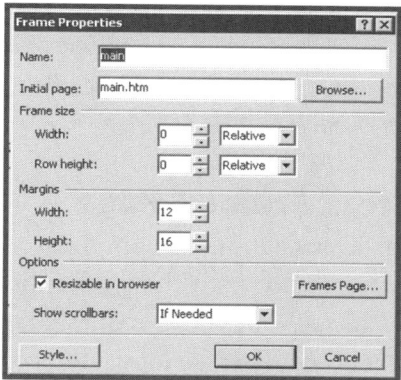

Figure 4.31

You can change which page displays in a frame window in the Frame Properties dialog box.

Adjusting Frame Properties and Settings

You can control a number of details to bend a frameset to your will, thanks to your friend the Frame Properties dialog box (refer back to Figure 4.31). You can control

⚙ The width and height of the individual frame window.

⚙ Showing or hiding borders between frames.

⚙ Whether visitors can resize the frames pages in their browsers by dragging on a border.

⚙ Spacing between frames (essentially, the width of the border). Click on the Frames Page button, then click on the Frames tab to bring it to the front. Adjust the width of the border by increasing or decreasing the Frames Spacing value.

⚙ The margins inside each frame window (the space between the edge of the frame and the start of the content within it).

⚙ Whether scroll bars should appear. If the framed page includes more content than will fit in the allotted space, you should make scroll bars available. If you're sure it will all fit regardless of your visitor's setup, it's okay to turn scroll bars off for a cleaner look.

TIP For details on these controls (as well as a detailed overview of designing and working with frames), read the information contained in FrontPage's Help system.

Creating a Link to a Framed Page

If you're using frames as a navigational method for your Web site, you need to tell FrontPage what to do when the visitor clicks on a link in the navigation window. Should it open the requested page in the main window, the footer, or a new browser window altogether?

The frame window you want to use to display a page is called the target. Each target has a different name. You use the target name to tell FrontPage where to open the page. To set a target for a hyperlink, follow these steps.

BUZZ WORD When creating a link to display a page within a frame, the window in which you want a particular page to appear is called the *target*.

1. Right-click on the hyperlink and select Hyperlink Properties from the shortcut menu. The Insert Hyperlink dialog box opens.

2. Click on the Target Frame button. The Target Frame dialog box appears (see Figure 4.32). Here you'll see a small diagram of your frames page, along with a list of common targets available.

3. Click on a window in the Current Frames Page diagram. Notice that the content of the Target Setting text box changes. To display a page in the left frame window, click in the left pane of the diagram. To display it in the right window, click in the right pane. No matter how many windows you have in your frame, they will all be available in this dialog box.

Figure 4.32

You can tell FrontPage to open a page in the current window, a different window in the frame, or even in a whole new browser window.

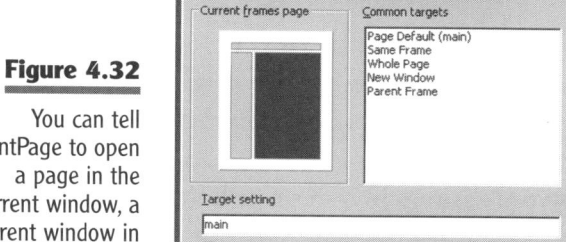

You'll notice some additional targets in the Common Targets area of the dialog box. These predefined targets are understood by all frames-friendly browsers. Here's what they mean.

- **Same Frame**. Open the linked page in the same frame window the current page uses. Leave the other frame windows in the frameset as they are. The HTML code that appears in the Target Setting text box is _self.

- **Whole Page**. Close the current frameset and all its windows. In its place, open the linked page in the full browser window. The HTML code is _top.

- **New Window**. Leave this current frameset and its windows as they are. Open the linked page in a new instance of the browser. The HTML code is _blank.

- **Parent Frame**. (For nested frames only.) Close the current nested frameset and all its windows. Open the linked page in the next highest frameset. The HTML code is _parent.

4. Select your target window and click on OK. You'll return to the Edit Hyperlink dialog box. Click on OK again to see the changes.

What's Next?

Now, wasn't that worth sticking around for? As you now know, tables and frames are powerful design tools you can employ to give your Web site a professional, easy-to-use interface. Tables help you include a lot of information on your pages, and frames help you include many pages in your Web site without losing your visitors in a maze of links and bookmarks.

Well, it's getting late—save your work and close FrontPage. Tomorrow morning's session is "Putting the Power of Components to Work." You'll really start to feel like a pro when you learn how to add features such as hit counters, hover buttons, and search forms. If you think those features sound hard to pull off, you'll be pleasantly surprised. But that's tomorrow, and tomorrow is another day. ¡Hasta mañana!

Putting the Power of Components to Work

- ✿ Adding a Hit Counter
- ✿ Inserting Automatic Web Content
- ✿ Creating a Hover Button
- ✿ Adding a Search Form
- ✿ Creating a Table of Contents

You had a big day yesterday, especially if you finished all the Saturday sessions. If you didn't get everything done on Saturday, that's okay. You can always go back later and cover any material you might have missed.

You have a lot to cover this morning, so if you haven't had breakfast yet, go get that bowl of cereal, have some toast and jam, or boil an egg. You have to stoke the furnace if you want to have the energy. Go ahead and pour that second (or third) cup of coffee, if that's what you need to get a jumpstart in the morning.

In this morning's session, you'll learn how to put FrontPage 2002's components to work for you. The term *component* in FrontPage is actually short for *WebBot component*. FrontPage's components allow you to easily add many features to your FrontPage Web pages that otherwise only experts at HTML coding could manage to do.

◄ ◄
A **WebBot** (derived from "robot"), as the term implies, automates the execution of what would otherwise be complex Web page features.
◄ ◄

FrontPage 2002 has more components than you'll have time to tackle this morning. This morning's session covers several of the most useful components, including

- Comment
- Photo Gallery
- Automatic Content Bots
- Hit Counter
- Hover Button
- Include Page
- Date and Time (Timestamp)
- Scheduled Picture or Include Page
- Search Form
- Table of Contents
- Banner Ad Manager

If this seems like a long list, don't worry—the Search Form, Table of Contents, and Banner Ad Manager components are optional for this session. Also, most components are not difficult to implement. So, depending on your learning style and speed, you should be able to learn how to use many of these useful components before the morning's over.

Before you begin, you'll need to open your FrontPage Web and create a new blank page if you don't already have one. Save your initial blank page as components.htm, in your local Web folder (C:\My Webs, or any other FrontPage Web in which you want to work) for this session. Some of the components require that the page be saved before the component can be previewed in a browser.

 **NOTE** The files listed in your Folder List might not match what you see in the figure illustrations. You might have added files and folders to your Web during previous sessions that aren't shown in the figure illustrations for this session.

Adding Comments

You can add comments that won't be displayed when your Web page is opened in a Web browser window. However, the comments are visible to anyone who looks at the page source in a browser. Comments are also visible in various views in FrontPage. They are displayed in a different font color in FrontPage's Normal view. Comments are also visible if you view the page in HTML view. So even though they won't appear in a Web browser's window, you shouldn't put anything in a comment that you wouldn't want others to see.

You might want to include comments as notes to yourself. Then, if you don't work on a page for a while, you'll be able to read your own notes to remind yourself how you've set up the page. Comments can also be handy if you're working as part of a workgroup or if someone needs to complete your work later.

To insert a comment into your FrontPage 2002 Web page, follow these steps.

1. Select Insert, Comment.
2. Type your comment in the Comment box (see Figure 5.1). Click on OK.

Notice that your comment text is in purple, to set it apart from regular body text. It is also prefaced by the word "Comment."

If you click on the HTML tab, you can see the actual code that FrontPage inserts into your page when you add a comment. The codes, <!-- and -->, are the standard HTML codes used for inserting comments

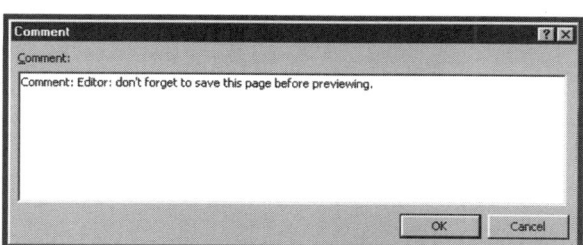

Figure 5.1

Inserting a FrontPage comment is easy.

ADDING HTML COMMENTS

You can add a regular HTML comment to your FrontPage Web page. Open the HTML view, click the mouse where you want to add the comment, and then type your comment bracketed within the HTML "comment" codes (<!-- *Type your comment here.*-->). Unlike a FrontPage comment, a regular HTML comment won't show up in FrontPage's Normal view. You can view HTML comments in the HTML view, or by viewing the page source in a Web browser (View, Source in Internet Explorer; View, Page Source in Netscape Navigator).

---

into HTML pages. They are used here to keep the WebBot codes from being displayed in a browser, in addition to indicating a comment.

Adding a Hit Counter

One of the most commonly asked questions from Web publishing neophytes is, "How do I add a hit counter?" Without FrontPage, you'd have to run a CGI script on your server to add a hit counter. Most Web Hosts provide hit counter scripts that you can use. Some even let you run your own custom scripts, but it's best to leave that for the experts. Other providers won't let you run custom hit counter scripts at all.

◄ ◄

BUZZ WORD A *hit counter*, as the name implies, counts the number of *hits* to a Web page. Each visit to a Web page is a hit (even your own).

◄ ◄

FrontPage 2002 makes adding a hit counter a snap. There is no need to contact your server administrator or create your own scripts. FrontPage 2002 can do it all for you. To add a hit counter in FrontPage 2002, follow these steps.

1. Click the mouse where you want to insert the counter, and then select Insert, Web Component. The Insert Web Component dialog box opens (see Figure 5.2).

TIP

You'll become very familiar with the Insert Web Component dialog box this morning. Take a moment to poke around in the various categories to get a taste of what's to come. Notice that Microsoft has even thought to include a direct link to the Web right there so that you can look for and install new components that might come along after FrontPage hits the shelves.

2. Click on Hit Counter, then select the counter style from the options presented. Click on Finish. FrontPage opens the Hit Counter Properties dialog box.

3. If you want to start the hit counter at a number other than 1, select the first check box (Reset Counter To) and type the number you want the counter to start with in the box to the right.

4. Select the second check box (Fixed Number of Digits). Type the number of digits you want to appear in the box to the right. If you type 4 for the number of digits, then the number for your hit counter will be displayed as 0055, for instance, instead of as 55.

5. Click on OK. You'll see "[Hit Counter]" inserted in your page.

Figure 5.2

The Insert Web Component dialog box lets you choose what kind of hit counter you want to add to your page.

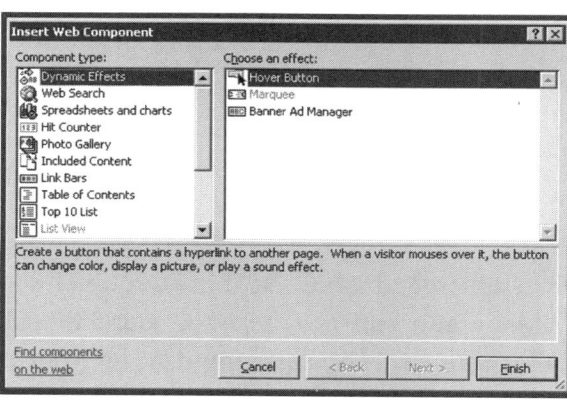

Before you can actually see your hit counter, you need to save and then publish your page. (If you already saved the page at the start of this session, just press Ctrl+S to resave it.) To be able to publish your page, you'll need to have either a Web space account on a FrontPage Web server (with the FrontPage 2000 or 2002 server extensions installed) or a personal Web server on your local hard drive.

If you already have an account on a FrontPage Web server, publish your Web to your Web server as you normally would. When your Web is published, FrontPage provides a link you can click to preview your site. For information on finding a FrontPage Web Presence Provider and publishing your pages to a FrontPage server, see Appendix A, "Publishing Your FrontPage 2002 Web Pages."

NOTE You can also install a personal Web server on your local hard drive. This allows you to publish and preview your FrontPage Web locally, before publishing to a remote server on the Web. For instructions on installing Microsoft Personal Web Server (PWS) and the FrontPage server extensions, see Appendix E, "Implementing Special Features."

To preview components.htm (if that's what you've named the page), click on the link provided at the end of the publishing process. Type the file name (components.htm) at the end of the URL in the address box (http://myserver.com/components.htm, for instance) and press Enter to see your components page. Or, you can open your Web that's on your server in FrontPage 2002, double-click on components.htm in the Folder List to open it, and then click on the Preview tab. (You can also select File, Preview in Browser.)

Formatting Your Hit Counter

Most Web designers add some text above a counter, such as "You're visitor number." Many also add text below a counter, such as "since July 1, 1999." (Substitute the actual starting date for your counter.) To center

CREATING YOUR OWN CUSTOM COUNTER

If you don't like any of the counter styles that come with Front-Page 2002, create your own! Use a graphics program to create an image including the numbers 0, 1, 2, 3, 4, 5, 6, 7, 8, and 9. Space the numbers equally. If your image editor has rulers, use them to make sure that every number takes up an equal amount of space. (Don't forget that space also has to be added in before the 0 and after the 9.) Choose whatever font face and color you want to use and add other special effects, such as a drop shadow or a 3D effect. For best results, you probably don't want the graphic to be any wider than about 100–150 pixels. You might need to experiment with the size to get just the look you want.

Save your hit counter graphic in the FrontPage Web folder that contains the page in which you want to use your custom counter. Next, in the Hit Counter Properties dialog box for your counter, select the Custom Picture radio button and type the name of your new counter graphic in the box to the right. Click on OK. Then, publish your Web to see what your new counter looks like. (If your numbers don't line up exactly, you might need to go back to your image editor and reposition the numbers in your counter graphic.)

the text and hit counter, select the two lines of text and the counter. Then, click on the Center tool on the Formatting toolbar.

Take a look at Figure 5.3 to see what a hit counter looks like in a Web browser published to a FrontPage Web server. (This hit counter uses the first counter style, with the number of digits set to five.)

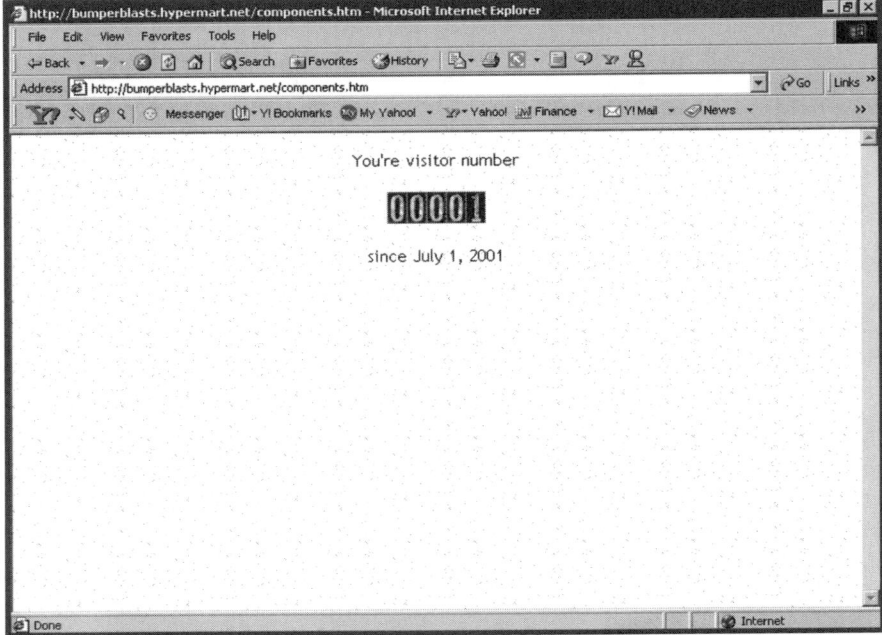

Designing a Photo Gallery

New to FrontPage 2002 is the Photo Gallery, and wow, is it a great time saver! The Photo Gallery component inserts a nicely formatted, dynamic display for your favorite photos. You could also use the Photo Gallery to create an online catalog if you're developing an e-commerce site.

1. Click on Insert, Component to open the Web Component Properties dialog box again. When you click on Photo Gallery, FrontPage displays a preview of the available templates for your gallery. Deciding which format you like best can be difficult—they're all nice. Fortunately, you can change your mind later without losing any work. For this example, I chose the Vertical layout.

2. Pick a format you want to try and click on Finish. The Photo Gallery Properties dialog box opens, but most of the options are grayed out (see Figure 5.4).

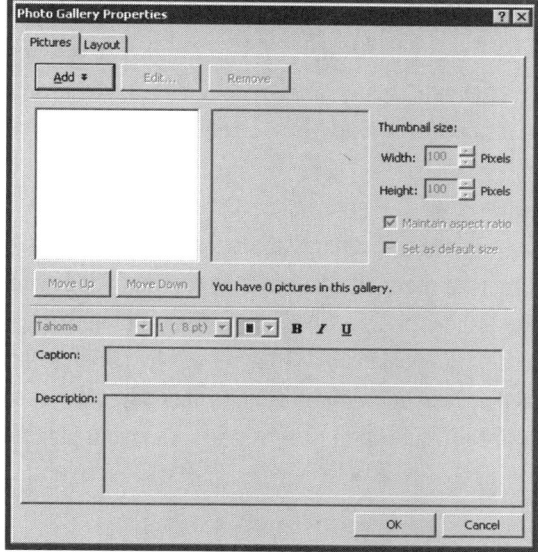

Figure 5.4

Add as many photos to the gallery as you want. They don't even have to be photos, for that matter—any graphic file will do.

3. Now it's time to tell FrontPage which photos you want in your gallery. You can import graphics files from your hard drive or the Web, or you can create them on the fly from your scanner or digital camera. I'll demonstrate using existing files for this example, so click on Add and then choose Pictures from Files. The File Open dialog box opens.

4. Navigate to and select the desired file, then click on Open. FrontPage adds the selected photo to the file list. Add as many photos as you want for your gallery, from as many different locations as you want. All the photos you choose will appear in the file list in the order selected.

5. Decide in what order you want the pictures to appear. (The pictures will appear in the gallery in the same order as they appear on the file list.) Click on a file name and click on Move Up or Move Down to change the order.

6. The default size for the thumbnail is 100 × 65 pixels, which is somewhere around the size of a postage stamp onscreen, depending on your visitor's display settings. If you have a reason to change the thumbnail size go ahead, but I recommend leaving it as is.

◄ ◄

A *thumbnail* is a miniature version of a larger original. When loading several photos on a page, it's best to keep them all small so that the page loads into your visitor's browser quickly. The Photo Gallery page actually shows only thumbnails of your pictures at first. Your visitor can see a larger version of any photo by clicking on it. The term originates from precomputer days, when editors would manually draw a small sketch of a page (often about the size of your thumbnail) as part of a layout plan for a book or magazine.

◄ ◄

7. If a photo isn't quite right as is, you can tweak it a bit right there in the dialog box. Click on Edit to get to the controls. In the Edit Picture dialog box, you can resize, crop, and even rotate the photos (see Figure 5.5). If you need to work on more than one photo, click on the Previous or Next buttons to cycle through the list of files in the Photo Gallery Properties dialog box. Click on OK when you're finished editing photos.

■ ■

For best results, your photos should all be the same dimensions; otherwise, the thumbnails might look distorted unless you set specific dimensions for each thumbnail (which is a pain, but doable).

■ ■

8. Click on the first photo on the list, then give the photo a caption (title) and a description. Whatever you type here will be shown in the Photo Gallery. Repeat this for each photo in the list. You can even format the caption text as you see fit—change the font or give it a new color.

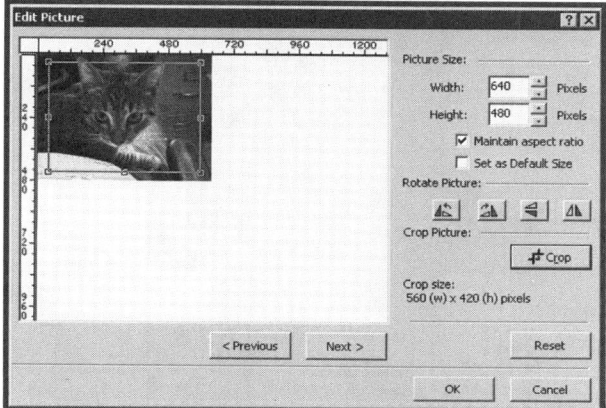

Figure 5.5

"I'm ready for my close-up, Mister Woodward."

Not all of the gallery templates include designs that use captions, so you might not see this option.

9. Click on OK to generate the Photo Gallery. In a moment, the gallery will appear on the page, as shown in Figure 5.6.

10. To edit the Photo Gallery, right-click anywhere on it and choose Photo Gallery Properties from the shortcut menu. Click on the Layout tab to choose a different page design.

11. Tweak all settings as needed, and then click on OK. FrontPage regenerates the gallery and displays it on your page again.

12. Don't forget to preview the Photo Gallery in a browser to make sure that it looks the way you want it to. (I'll tell you up front that Netscape sometimes stumbles on this component.) Test the individual photos to make sure that they look okay when the visitor clicks on them.

Like I said, pretty cool stuff for such little effort! No wonder Bill Gates is the world's wealthiest man.

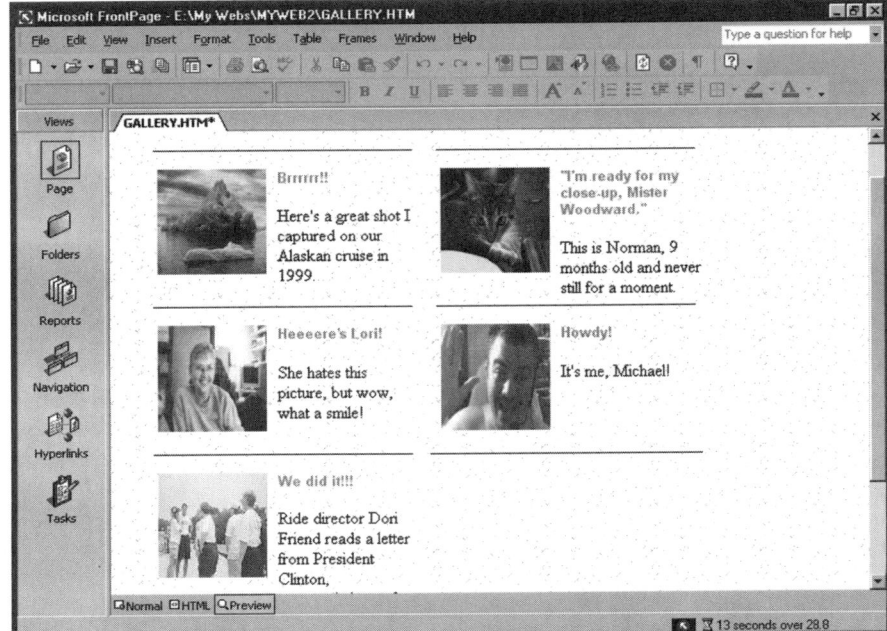

Figure 5.6

Do you know how long it would have taken me to set this whole thing up myself? FrontPage Web components are wonderful!

Inserting Automatic Web Content

Another new member of the bot family is the Automatic Web Content component. Want to show current weather conditions where you are every time a visitor stops by? Or, maybe you want to give your visitor an instantly accessible place to initiate a Web search. These are but two of the items available in this category. Most of these components pull data directly from one of Microsoft's commercial Web sites, such a bCentral (for business) or MSN (for general public). The complete list of automatic content components (as of this writing) includes

- ✪ bCentral Banner Network
- ✪ bCentral FastCounter (an alternative to your homegrown version we discussed previously)
- ✪ Look up a stock quote (on MSN)

- Search the Web (on MSN)
- Insert a weather forecast (from MSNBC)

No doubt that as Office XP becomes the new standard, new components will become available because more people will be demanding variety. Still, this is more than enough for starters. Let's try one, shall we? I think I'd like to show the current temperature in my city (Indianapolis) on my site, just for kicks.

 **NOTE**   This component requires an Internet connection to set it up. If you do not yet have a dial-up service set up, you'll have to skip this procedure for now. You can come back to it later.

1. Click the mouse where you want to insert the component, and then select Insert, Web Component. The Web Component dialog box opens.

2. Click on MSNBC Components (or whichever one is appropriate for your needs).

3. Click on Insert a Weather Forecast, then click on Finish. The Insert a Weather Forecast Properties Wizard opens, as shown in Figure 5.7. (This may take a moment and might require you to connect to the Internet.)

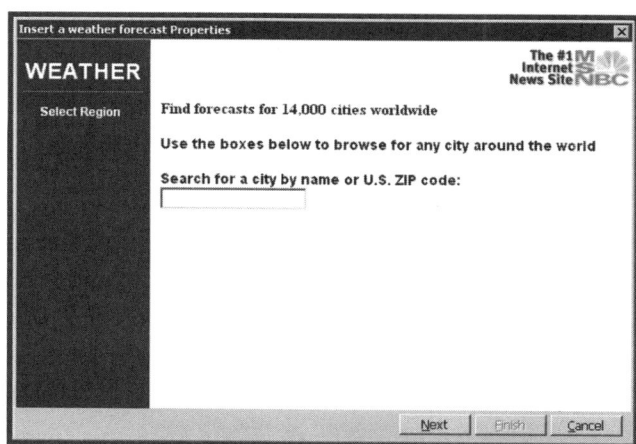

Figure 5.7

The weather component only works for cities in the United States.

4. Enter the ZIP code for the city for which you want to display the forecast, and then click on Next. The wizard displays a list of cities within that ZIP code. (In some cases, there might only be one.)

5. Click on the appropriate city and click on Finish. FrontPage inserts the component into your page.

6. Click on Preview to see how the weather component looks on your page. It should resemble the one shown in Figure 5.8.

Creating a Hover Button

I'm sure you've run across buttons in Web pages that change colors, display alternate images, or emit sound effects when the mouse is passed over them. You probably thought, "I'd sure like to put some of those in my Web pages," but then immediately decided that only professional Web programmers could figure out how to do it. Not so! Using FrontPage's Hover Button component, anyone can easily add dynamic buttons to Web pages.

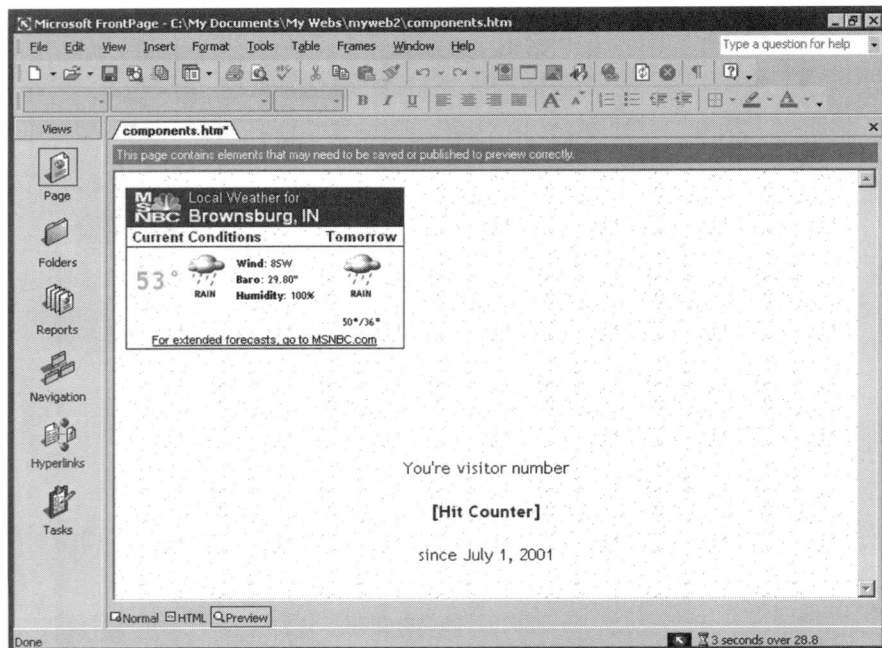

Figure 5.8

The weather forecast component is a cool little gadget to display, especially on a page about your hometown or company's headquarters.

◄ ◄

A *hover button* comes to life when the mouse hovers (or passes) over it. The Hover Button component actually inserts a Java applet into your page, to which you can assign various properties, such as visual and sound effects. In addition, a hover button usually specifies a hypertext link to activate when the button is clicked.

◄ ◄

For this example, you'll be creating a text-based hover button. When the mouse passes over the button, a Glow effect displays behind the button text. To add a hover button to your page, follow these steps.

1. Click the mouse where you want to insert the hover button, and then select Insert, Web Component. The Insert Web Component dialog box opens. Click on the Dynamic Effects component type (if it is not already selected) and choose Hover Button. Click on Finish to open the Hover Button Properties dialog box, as shown in Figure 5.9.

2. In the Button Text box, type the text you want to include on your button. For instance, you might type My Home Page if you're creating a button that loops back to your home page.

3. To select a font for your text, click on the Font button. The Font dialog box opens (see Figure 5.10).

4. For this example, leave the font setting (MS Sans Serif) as it is, but select Bold for the font style and 24 for the size. To select a color for your text, click on the Color box. (Try the bright yellow color.) Click on OK.

Figure 5.9

In the Hover Button Properties dialog box, you can specify the text, effect, colors, and size for your button.

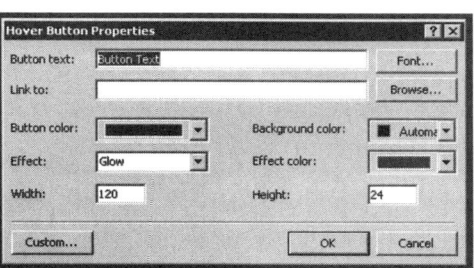

Figure 5.10

In the Font dialog box, you can specify the font, style, size, and color for the button's text.

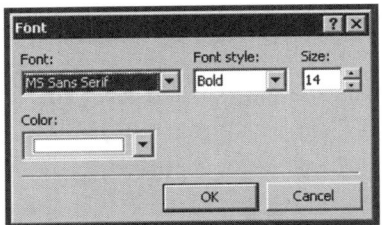

5. In the Link To box back in the Hover Button Properties dialog box, type the URL of the file to which your button will link when clicked. For this example, type the file name of any other file (an HTML, JPG, or GIF file) saved in the same folder as components.htm. Or, you can leave the Link To box blank, if you want. You could also type the full URL of any page out on the Web that you want to link to (http://www.microsoft.com/frontpage, for example). For information on using the Link To box's Browse button to link to a file located elsewhere in your Web, or to create a mailto: link, see the section titled, "Selecting Hover Button Hyperlinks Using the Browse Button."

◆ ◆

CAUTION Hover buttons are Java applets, so file names (and other URLs) are case sensitive. If a file name is listed in the Folder List as MyFile.htm, for example, you need to type it exactly as it appears (and *not* as myfile.htm).

◆ ◆

6. To change the color of your button, click on the Button color box. For this example, leave the color set to navy blue.

7. To change the effect you want to use, click on the Effect box. For this example, leave Glow set as the effect. (After creating and previewing your hover button, feel free to try out any of the other effects, such as Bevel In or Bevel Out.)

8. To change the color of the effect, click on the Effect Color box. For this example, leave the effect color set to blue.

9. Because you increased the size of the font, you'll need to also increase the dimensions of the button. Type 200 as the width and 40 as the height. Click on OK, and the hover button will be added to your page (see Figure 5.11).

Previewing Your Hover Button

You must save your file to preview your hover button. Save your file by pressing Ctrl+S. Then, click on the Preview tab to preview your hover button. Try out the hover button by passing the mouse over it (see Figure 5.12). If you added a link to the hover button, click on the link to jump to the linked page.

NOTE The Glow effect doesn't show up very well in this book. Just take my word for it, or try it out for yourself!

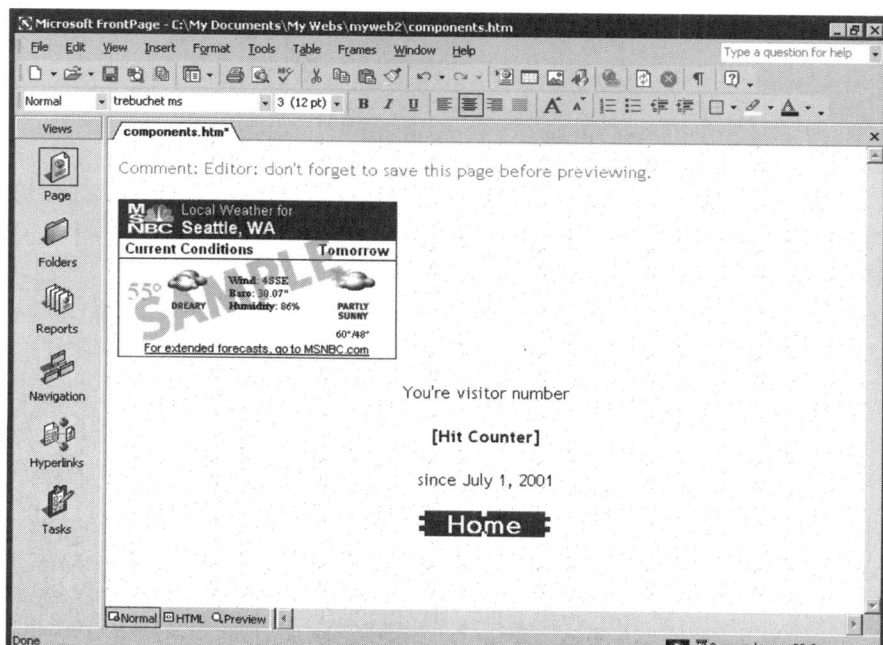

Figure 5.11

The hover button is added to the page.

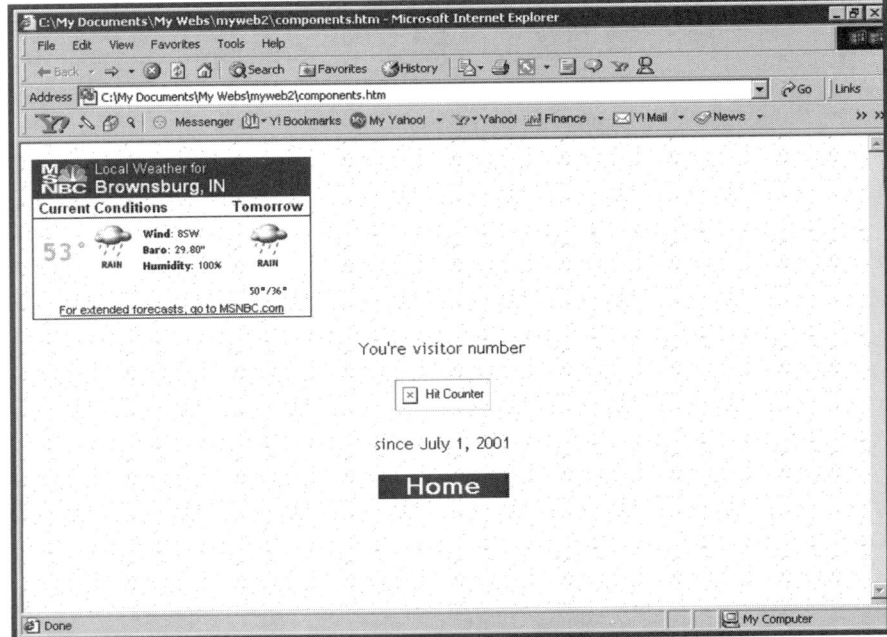

Figure 5.12

The glow effect activates when the mouse passes over the hover button.

To edit the properties of your hover button in Normal view, double-click on the hover button object.

Selecting Hover Button Hyperlinks Using the Browse Button

In the previous section, you typed a file name in the Link To box for your hover button hyperlink, or you just left it blank. To learn other ways you can link files or pages to your hover button, double-click on your hover button to open the Hover Button Properties dialog box. Then, click on the Browse button (next to the Link To box). In the Select Hover Button Hyperlink dialog box, you can choose to

○ Link to a file within the currently open FrontPage Web

○ Link to a file on the Web

- Link to a page located elsewhere on your computer
- Link to your e-mail address
- Create a new page and link to it
- Link to a bookmark or a frame target

To link to a file or page in an open Web, just locate and click on the file to which you want to link. To link to a file or page already published on the Internet, click on the small globe button to the right of the Look In list. Connect to the Internet (if necessary) and then use your browser to browse to the URL that you want to use. When you close your browser, the URL to which you last browsed will be inserted into the URL box.

To link to a file or page located on your local computer but outside your open Web, click on the second icon to the right of the URL box. In the Select File dialog box, browse to and click on the file to which you want to link. When you resave your page, FrontPage automatically prompts you to resave the file within your open Web.

To create an e-mail link, click on the third button to the right of the URL box. Type your e-mail address and click on OK. This allows someone to click on the hover button to send you an e-mail message.

To create a new page and then link your hover button to it, click on the fourth button to the right of the URL box. Double-click on the Normal Page template (or any other template you want to use) to open a new page. Close the Hover Button Properties dialog box. Create and save your new page. Reopen the page where your hover button is located (components.htm, for example). Double-click on the hover button to edit its properties. You'll see that the name of your new page has been inserted into the Link To box.

The Browse button also lets you specify a bookmark or a frame target for your link. To link to a bookmark within the page to which you're linking, first select the page, then click on Bookmark and select the bookmark to which you want to link from the dialog box. To link to a frame target, select the pencil button to the right of the Target Frame box.

Adding Sound to Your Hover Button

You can add a sound effect to your hover button that plays when the mouse moves over or clicks on it. However, because hover buttons are actually Java applets, you are limited to using only one type of sound file: 8-bit, 8000 Hz, mono, u-law *.au sound files. To add an *.au sound effect to your hover button, follow these steps.

1. In the Hover Button Properties dialog box, click on the Custom button.

2. If you have a compatible *.au file, click on the Browse button (next to On Click). If the *.au file is outside your Web, click on the second icon to the right of the URL box to browse for it.

3. To select an *.au sound file that will play when the mouse is passed over the button, click on the Browse button next to the On Hover box.

4. Click on OK.

Using Images in Hover Buttons

You don't have to stick to creating text-only hover buttons. You can specify image files for both your button and the button's hover effect. The primary advantage of using images for your hover buttons is that you can use any font you have installed for creating your button text. You can also use other effects, such as drop shadows, gradient fills, patterns, and 3D effects.

If you don't already have an image you want to use, you'll need to first create the image in an image editor. After you've created and saved the image you want to use, follow these steps to include it in your hover button:

1. In the Hover Button Properties dialog box, click on the Custom button.

2. Click on the Browse button to the right of the Button box to select the image file you want to use for your button. (Click on the

second button to the right of the URL box to browse your computer's files, if the image file is not in one of your Web's folders.)

3. Click on the Browse button to the right of the On Hover box to select the image file you want to use for your button's hover effect. Click on OK.

4. Delete any text that is displayed in the Button text box (otherwise, it'll be displayed over your images).

5. In the Width and Height boxes, type the width and height (in pixels) of your images. Click on OK. Figure 5.13 shows an example of an image-based hover button as it appears in Internet Explorer 5.0, with the mouse cursor not yet passing over the button. Figure 5.14 shows the same hover button, but this time with the mouse cursor passing over it. If you've assigned any sound effects, they'll also play when you pass the mouse over or click on the hover button.

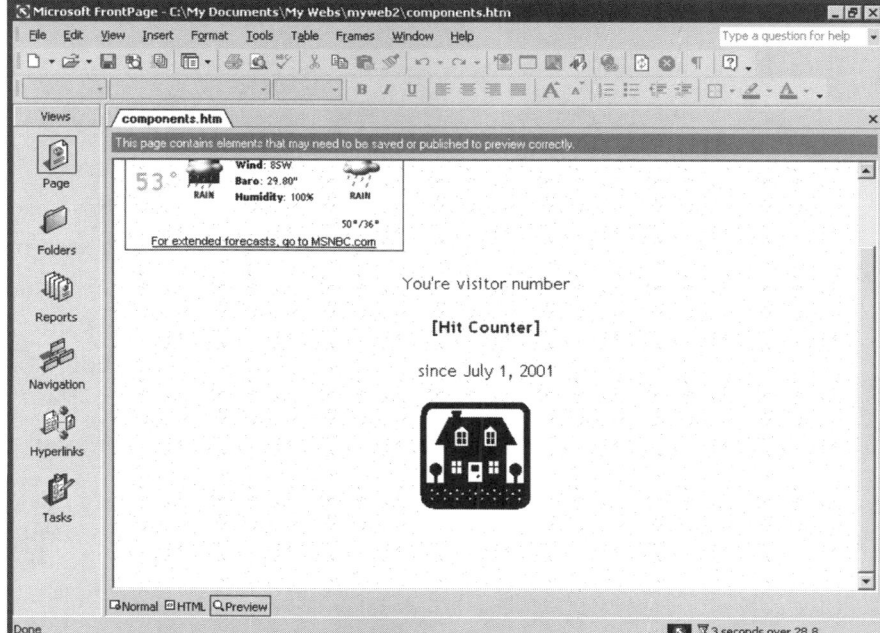

Figure 5.13

When previewing an image-based hover button in a Java-enabled browser, the first image is displayed before the mouse cursor passes over the button.

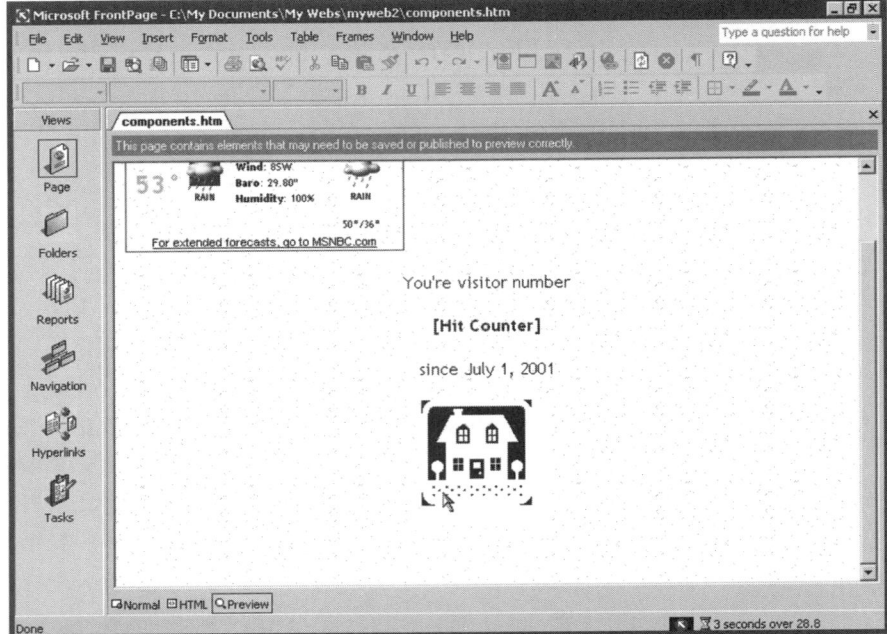

Figure 5.14

When the mouse cursor passes over an image-based hover button, the second image is displayed.

Take a Break!

So far this morning, you've learned to add comments, hit counters, and hover buttons to your pages. Feel free at this point to get up and take a break. If you haven't had your breakfast yet, go ahead and fix yourself a bite. You've got lots more to do today, so you don't want to short yourself on energy. If the morning has stretched on toward noon, break for lunch. The rest of this session is optional, so feel free to skip ahead at this point to the Sunday Afternoon session, "Finalizing and Maintaining Your Pages."

However, if the morning is still young and you're ready to go, I'll see you back here in ten minutes or so. In the next section, you'll learn how to use more of FrontPage 2002's handy components.

Using Include Pages

You might want to repeat information on many different pages, or on all your pages. You can create a separate page that includes the information you want to use repeatedly and then use FrontPage 2002's Include Page component to easily add it to your pages. This can save you time; rather than searching for and replacing the same piece of text on several pages, it's much easier to edit it once. The changes will be applied to any page on which the included page appears. I use includes often for things like copyright notices.

Creating an Include Page

An include page is just a regular Web page that is included in another page. For this example, you'll create a separate page that will hold your address block—your name, e-mail address, URL, and any other information you want to include at the bottom of your pages. To create this page, open a new blank page and follow these steps.

1. To add a separator above your address section, insert a horizontal line. Select Insert, Horizontal Line. (To edit the properties of your horizontal line, double-click on the line.)

2. From the Style list on the Formatting toolbar, select Address. Type your name. Because you've applied the Address format style, the text should be in italics. Don't add a hard return (by pressing the Enter key). Instead, press Shift+Enter to add a line break (sometimes called a soft return). This adds a single space, rather than a double space, between the lines.

3. Add a link to your e-mail address. Type **E-Mail:** followed by a space, and then type your e-mail address. Select your e-mail address with the mouse. Select Insert, Hyperlink. Click on the E-Mail Address button, then type your e-mail address in the E-Mail Address field and click on OK. Click on OK again, and FrontPage adds the e-mail link to your address block, as shown in Figure 5.15. Add another line break (Shift+Enter).

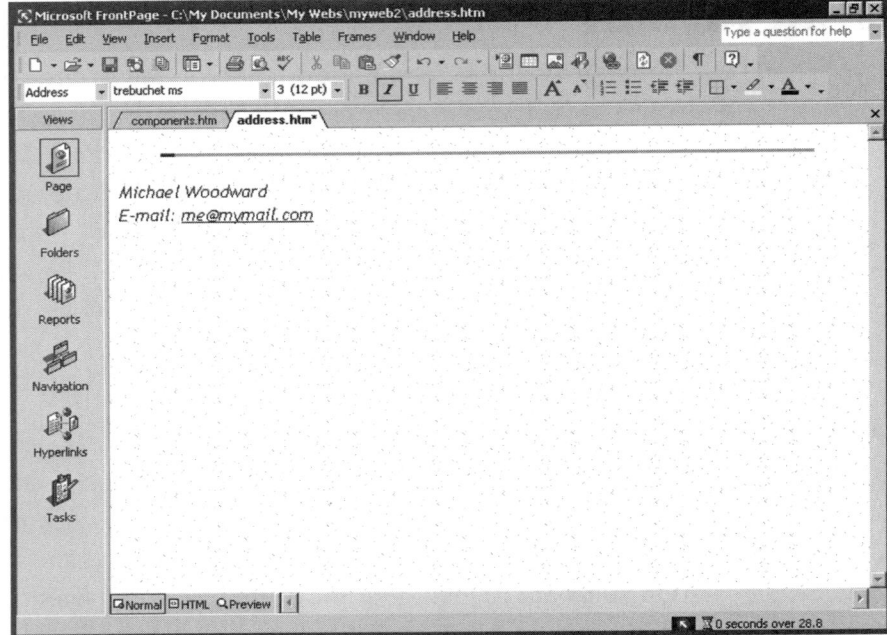

Figure 5.15

Having all
this information
contained on one
page makes
updating it a
no-brainer.

NOTE Some browsers, including some earlier versions of Internet Explorer, can't handle e-mail links. To allow for those browsers, it is a good idea to always include your actual e-mail address as your linked text, instead of using something like "Click here to e-mail me." That way, even if a browser won't handle mailto: links, visitors to your site can still contact you using their regular e-mail client.

4. On the next line, add the URL for your home page, if you have one. Type **Home Page:** followed by a space, and then select Insert, Hyperlink. Following http://, type the rest of your home page's URL and click on OK. Press the space bar once and then add another line break (see Figure 5.16).

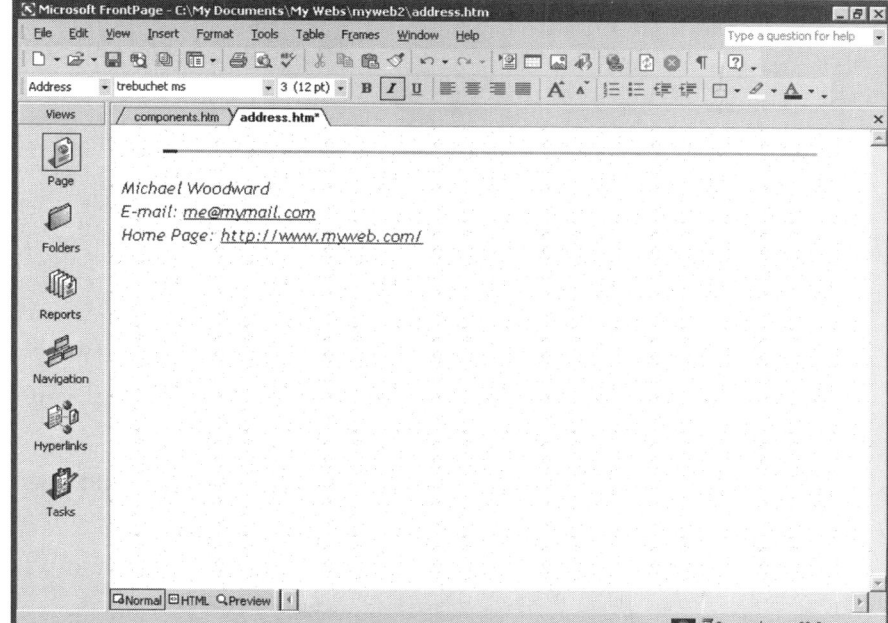

Figure 5.16

Add a name,
e-mail address, and
home page URL to
the address section.

5. Type anything else you want to include, such as your address, phone number, and so on. Add line breaks, rather than hard returns, at the end of each line.

6. Save your file as address.htm.

Adding the Date and Time

Including the date and time when a page was last updated can be helpful to visitors to your site. This is also called a *timestamp*. If you regularly update your page, a timestamp will tell visitors that the info on your page is the latest and the greatest. Manually updating your timestamp at the bottom of every page that you edit or update, however, can be a royal pain, to say the least. The trick here is to use FrontPage 2002's Date and Time component to add the date and time to your address page. Then you only need to include this page at the bottom of all your other pages, and they will automatically be stamped with the date and time when you last made changes to them. To add a date and timestamp to your address section, follow these steps.

1. If you haven't done so already, add a line break at the end of the last line you added to your address section.

2. Type **Last Updated:** followed by a space, and then select Insert, Date and Time.

3. In the Date and Time dialog box, leave the first radio button (Date This Page Was Last Edited) selected (see Figure 5.17).

4. From the Date Format list, select the format you want to use to display the date.

5. From the Time Format list, select the format you want to use to display the time.

6. Click on OK to apply your date and timestamp (see Figure 5.18). Press Ctrl+S to resave address.htm.

Including Your Address Page on Other Pages

Now, all you have to do is include your address page (address.htm) at the bottom of any other page you create. You should never have to create an address section again for any of your pages. They will be automatically stamped with the new date and time whenever you make update changes to them. Follow these steps to insert address.htm at the bottom of components.htm.

1. In the Folder List, double-click on components.htm to open it.

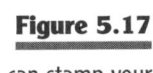

Figure 5.17

You can stamp your page with the date and time when the page was last edited or updated.

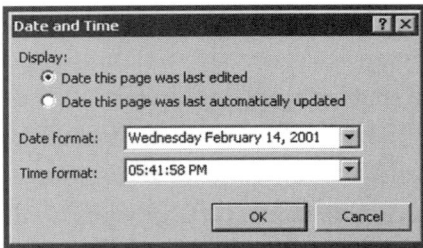

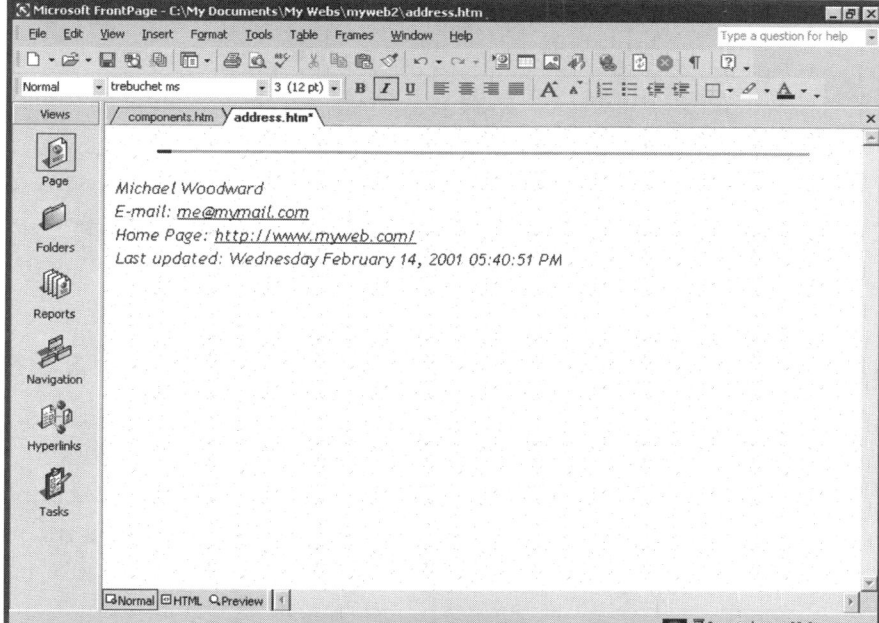

Figure 5.18

The date and timestamp have been added to the address section.

2. To include your address page at the bottom of your components page, place your cursor at the bottom of the page and select Insert, Web Component. The Insert Web Component dialog box appears. Select Included Content from the Component Types box, and then click on Page on the right side of the dialog box.

3. In the Include Page Properties dialog box, type **address.htm**, as shown in Figure 5.19. Alternatively, you can click on the Browse button to select the file. Click on OK.

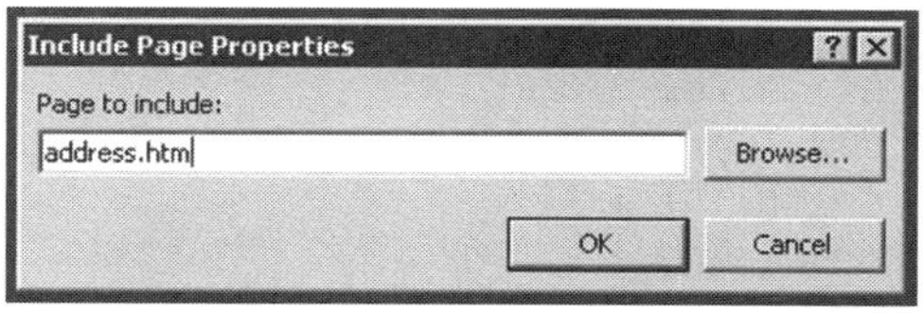

Figure 5.19

The page, address.htm, will be included at the cursor location in the current page.

As shown in Figure 5.20, your address page should now be included at the bottom of components.htm. Now, whenever you make any editing changes to the page, the date and timestamp will update automatically.

You can add your include page to any other page you create in your Web, even if your include page and the page where you want to add it are not in the same folder. Then, whenever you update your include page, all the pages where it has been included will also be automatically updated.

Scheduling Pictures or Include Pages

Using either the Scheduled Picture or the Scheduled Include Page component, you can schedule the display of a picture or page so that it will only be displayed during a specified period. For example, you could create a picture or an include page that is tied to a particular holiday, such as Christmas. Then, you could schedule that picture or page so that it would

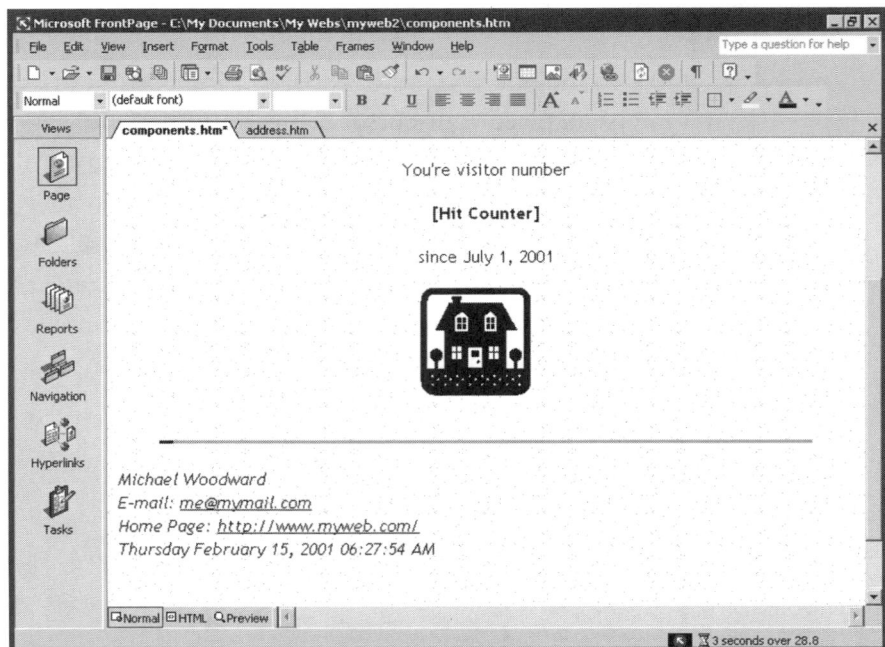

Figure 5.20

The address page (address.htm) has been included at the bottom of the current page (components.htm).

be displayed from December 15 to December 25, but not before or after. You could create other pictures or include pages that would be displayed leading up to and on other holidays, such as Valentine's Day, Easter, the 4th of July, Halloween, or Thanksgiving. You could also schedule pictures and pages that would display only on the birthdays of friends, relatives, or associates. You could even use this feature to schedule articles, press releases, announcements, and so on. Another idea would be to create include pages that contain agendas or calendars keyed to specific months or weeks. You would only need to update, save, and publish the pages, and they would be displayed automatically during their relevant periods. To schedule pictures or include pages, perform the following steps.

1. Open or create a page in which you want to insert a scheduled picture or include page. In Normal view, click on the place where you want to insert it.

2. Select Insert, Web Component, and then click on Included Content. Select either Picture Based on Schedule or Page Based on Schedule (see Figure 5.21).

3. Type the file name (or relative URL) of a picture or include page you want to schedule in the During the Scheduled Time text box. You can also use the Browse button to select a picture or include page.

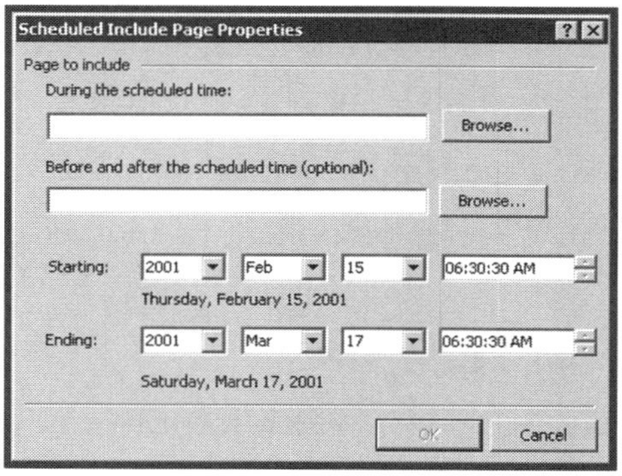

Figure 5.21

The only difference between the Scheduled Picture and Scheduled Include Page Properties dialog boxes is that you specify pictures in one and pages in the other.

TIP If the file to be scheduled is in the same folder as the page in which it will be displayed, you only need to type the file name. If it is in a different folder, you'll need to type the file's relative URL. If you're hazy on using relative URLs, use the Browse button to select a picture or include page, and FrontPage will insert the relative URL for you.

4. Optionally, you can type the file name (or relative URL) of a picture or include page you want to display before and after the scheduled time in the second text box. You can also use the Browse button to select a picture or include page.

5. In the Starting section, choose when you want the schedule period for the picture or include page to start. (The default is the current year, month, day, and time.)

6. In the Ending section, choose when you want the schedule period for the picture or include page to end. (The default is one month from the current year, month, day, and time.)

7. Click on OK to insert the scheduled picture or include page.

Adding a Search Form

One of the handier features you can add to your Web site is a search form that allows visitors to do a keyword search of your site. It's easy! The only requirement is that your Web server must have the FrontPage server extensions installed for your account. There are two ways to set up a search form for your Web site. You can set up the search form by:

○ Using the Search Page template
○ Adding the Search Form component to another page

Using the Search Page Template

This is the easiest way to add a search form to your site. Create a new page, using the Search Page template. Then, edit the page to add your

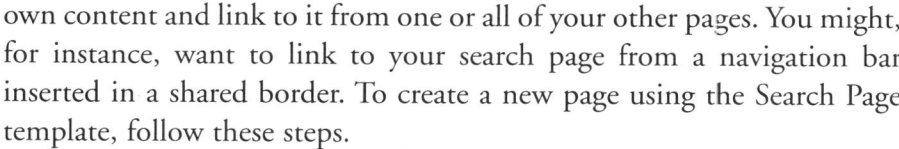

own content and link to it from one or all of your other pages. You might, for instance, want to link to your search page from a navigation bar inserted in a shared border. To create a new page using the Search Page template, follow these steps.

1. Select File, New, Page or Web, then click on Page Templates. The Page Templates dialog box opens.

2. Under the General tab, scroll down until you see the Search Page template, as shown in Figure 5.22. Double-click on it to open it (see Figure 5.23).

Edit the page to add your own heading, graphics, and other information. Edit the page properties to create your own title. Edit the author info at the bottom of the page or, if you want, go ahead and add the include page (address.htm) that you created earlier. When you're satisfied, save your new file (as search.htm, for example).

Adding the Search Form Component to another Page

You might already have created a page to which you want to add a search form. It's easy using the Search Form component. For this example, if

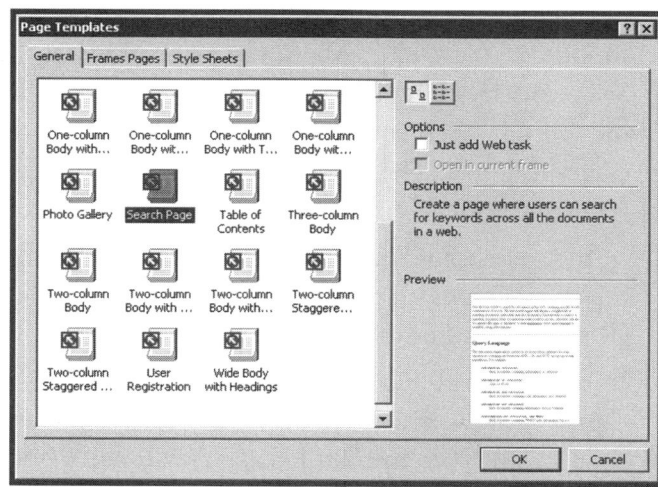

Figure 5.22

Select the Search Page template to create a new page with a ready-made search form.

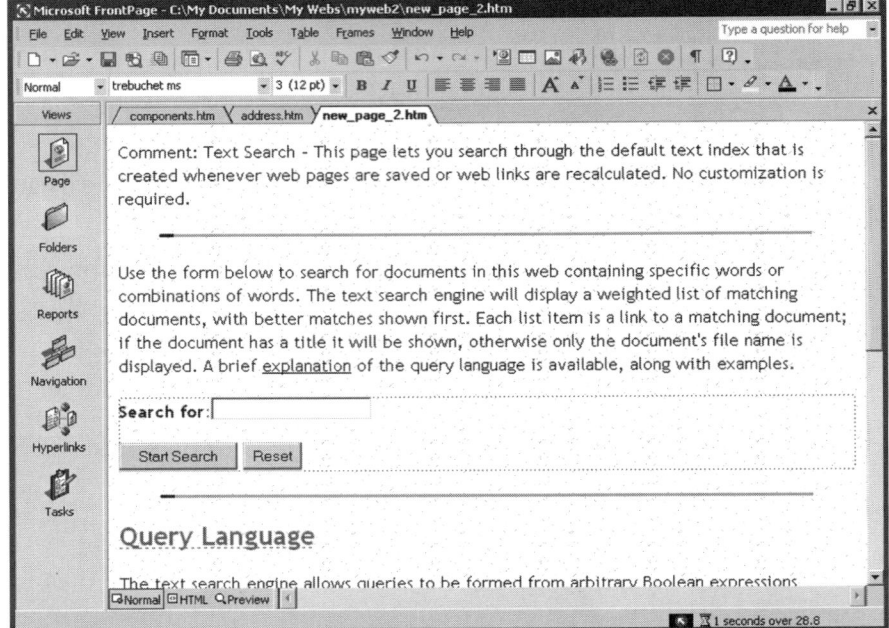

Figure 5.23

A new page with a search form is opened in FrontPage.

component.htm is not displayed, double-click on it in the Folder List to bring it to the front. To add a search form to component.htm (or any other page), follow these steps.

1. In Normal view, click where you want to insert the search form. Select Insert, Component, and then click on Web Search. Choose the Current Web component (probably the only one listed) and click on Finish. The Search Form Properties dialog box opens (see Figure 5.24).

2. In the Search Form Properties tab, you can specify the input label, the character width of the input box, and the labels for the start and clear buttons. For this example, leave all the settings as they are.

3. In the Search Results tab, shown in Figure 5.25, the Display Options check boxes let you specify how you want the search results to be presented. If left clear, only file names will be listed.

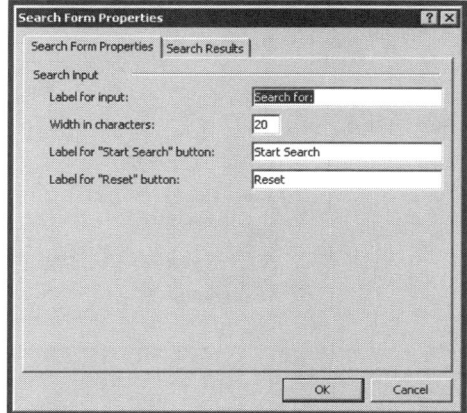

Figure 5.24

The Search Form Properties dialog box lets you alter the look and feel of your search form.

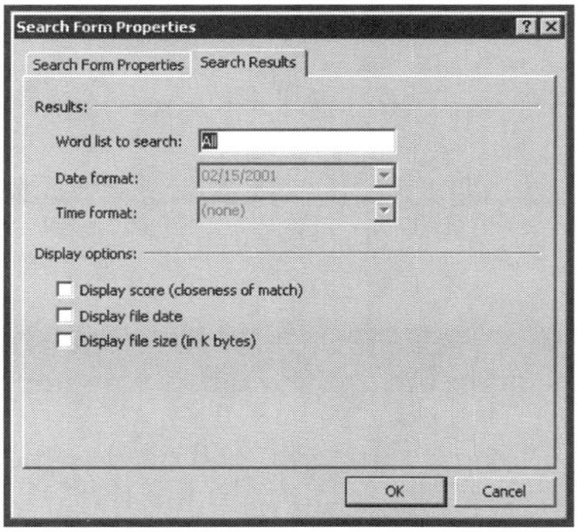

Figure 5.25

The Search Results tab lets you specify how you want search results to be presented.

Check the appropriate box if you also want to display the match score, file date, or file size. For this example, leave all the settings as they are and click on OK. A search component is added to your page (see Figure 5.26).

TIP

You can center the search form on the page by selecting the entire component and clicking on Center on the toolbar.

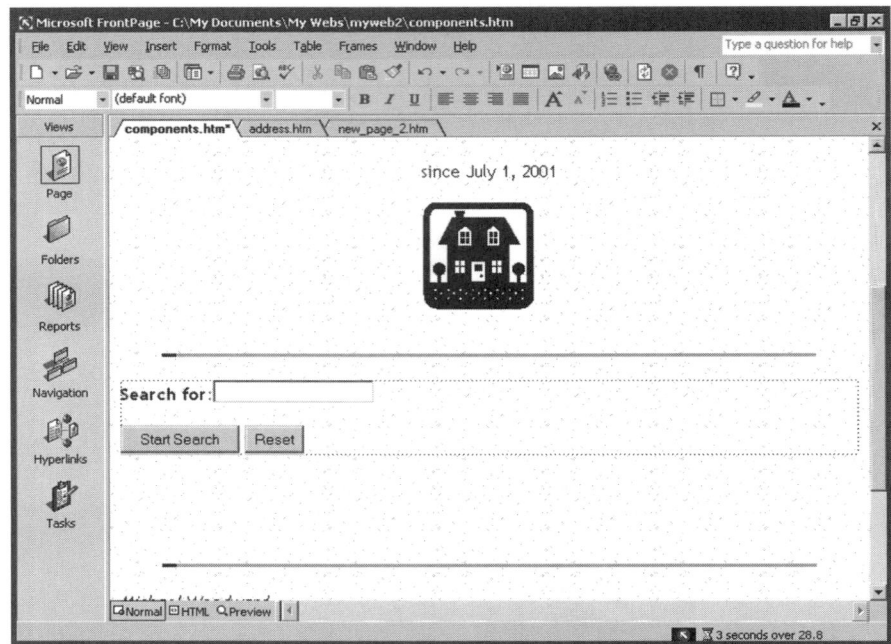

Figure 5.26

A search form
has been added
to the page.

4. To check out what your search form will look like when displayed in a browser, click on the Preview tab (see Figure 5.27).

To actually test your search form, you will need to publish it to a server with the FrontPage server extensions running. If you have installed a Personal Web Server (PWS) on your computer, you will be able to check out your search form locally, before publishing your Web to a FrontPage server on the Web. (For instructions for installing a PWS, see Appendix E, "Implementing Special Features.") Here are some quick pointers on what else you can do with the Search Form component.

❖ Double-click on the Search Form component in Normal view to re-edit its properties. Change the input and button labels to give your search form a different look and feel. (That way, it won't look like every other FrontPage search form on the Web.)

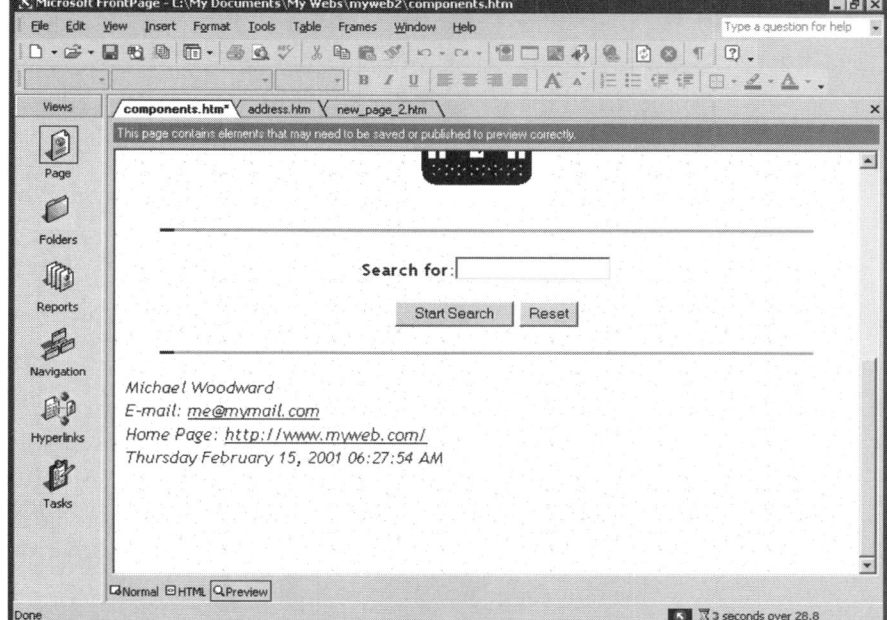

Figure 5.27

Use Preview to show the search form.

○ In the Search Results tab, always leave All as the word list to search, unless you're creating a search form for a discussion group. (To limit the search for a discussion group, replace All with the name of the discussion group folder.)

○ FrontPage 2002 automatically generates an index of the words included in your Web. As you save new pages, new words are continually added to the index. However, when you delete a page or remove material from a page, the index entries for those pages are not removed from the search index. To create a new search index with outdated entries removed, click on Tools, Recalculate Hyperlinks. (If you have many pages in your Web, this can take a couple of minutes, so be patient.)

Creating a Table of Contents

Another feature seen on many Web sites is a table of contents that provides links to all the pages in the site. Using FrontPage 2002's Table of Contents component makes adding a table of contents to your Web a snap.

The Table of Contents component can create a table of contents of every page in your Web, of all pages linked to from your default home page (index.htm or default.htm, for example), or of only pages linked to from any other page you might specify. For this example, you will create a table of contents of all pages to which your default home page links. Before creating a table of contents, you might need to do a little setup work.

- Your default home page (index.htm or default.htm, for example) should have hyperlinks from it to other pages in your Web. If not, you'll need to edit your default home page to add some hyperlinks to it. (If the pages you're linking to don't exist yet, go ahead and create them first.)

- Because page titles are used to create the table of contents entries, make sure that descriptive titles have been created for all the pages that will be listed in the table of contents. Right-click on any page, select Page Properties, and then type a descriptive title in the Title box.

- To see how the Table of Contents component can present a hierarchical listing of all pages branching off your default home page, you should have at least one link on your default home page that links to another page.

As with the search form, there are two ways to create a table of contents. You can create a table of contents by:

- Using the Table of Contents template
- Adding the Table of Contents component to another page

Using the Table of Contents Template

If you've done the prep work detailed in the previous section, here's all you have to do to create a new page using the Table of Contents template.

1. Select File, New, Page or Web, then click on Page Templates. The Page Templates dialog box opens.

2. In the General tab, scroll down until you see the Table of Contents template. Double-click on it to open it. A new page is created with the Table of Contents template, as shown in Figure 5.28.

3. To edit the properties of the Table of Contents component (under "Table of Contents Heading Page"), double-click on it. The Table of Contents Properties dialog box appears (see Figure 5.29).

4. The name of your default home page is automatically displayed in the Page URL for Starting Point of Table box. For this example, just leave this option as it is. If you want to create a table of contents branching off a different page, type its file name or relative URL (or use the Browse button to select it).

Figure 5.28

A new page created with the Table of Contents template

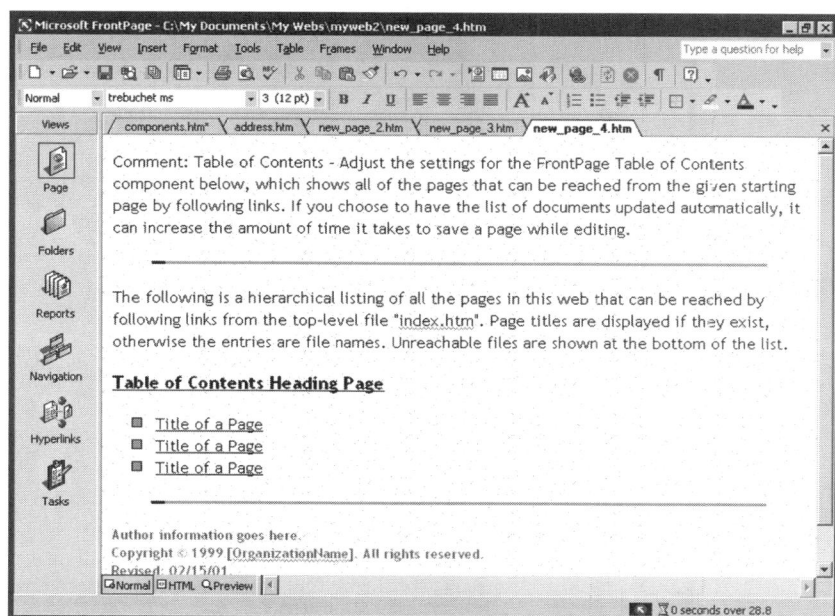

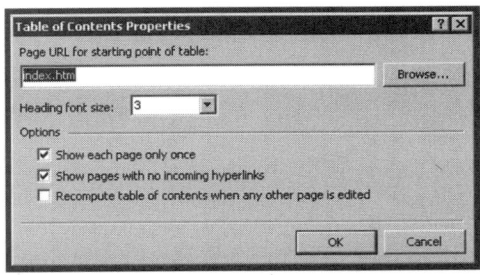

Figure 5.29

You determine what your table of contents will display by editing its properties.

5. For this example, clear both the first check box (Show Each Page Only Once) and the second check box (Show Pages with No Incoming Hyperlinks). Click on OK.

6. Save your table of contents page (as toc.htm, for example).

7. To see how your table of contents will look, you need to preview it in your browser. Click on File, Preview in Browser, and double-click on the browser you want to use. In Figure 5.30, I've used Internet Explorer to preview my table of contents page.

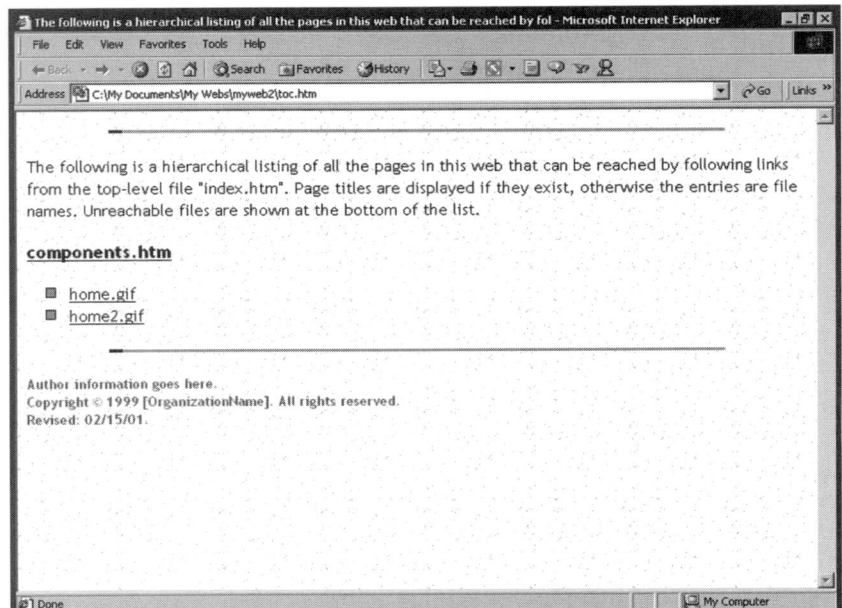

Figure 5.30

This table of contents is pretty basic right now, but I can always edit it later as I add more pages to my site.

TABLE OF CONTENTS CHECK BOX OPTIONS

In the Table of Contents Properties dialog box, you control what will be included in your table of contents by selecting or clearing any of the Options check boxes.

- Selecting the Show Each Page Only Once check box includes a linked page only the first time it appears in the table of contents.

- Selecting the Show Pages with No Incoming Hyperlinks check box includes all pages in your Web, regardless of whether any other pages link to them.

- Selecting the Recompute Table of Contents When Any Other Page is Edited check box creates a dynamic table of contents that changes as your site changes.

Because the links from your default home page will be different, your table of contents won't look exactly like what's shown in Figure 5.30. The basic layout, however, should be the same. Enhance the page by adding a top-level heading (Heading 1) and any other relevant text, adding a background color or image, or applying a theme before publishing.

Adding the Table of Contents Component to another Page

You don't have to use the Table of Contents template to create a table of contents. You might prefer using the Table of Contents component to insert a table of contents into a page you've already created. To do so, simply follow these steps.

1. In Normal view, click where you want to insert the table of contents. Select Insert, Web Component, then click on Table of Contents. Choose the For This Web Site option and click on Finish. The Table of Contents Properties dialog box appears.

2. Make any changes you want in the Table of Contents Properties dialog box. I'd recommend clearing any of the check boxes that are checked. (See the sidebar, "Table of Contents Check Box Options,"

in the previous section for descriptions of the check box options.) Click on OK.

3. Save your page and then preview it in your browser.

Using the Banner Ad Manager Component

The Banner Ad Manager component allows you to insert a revolving banner ad (or any other set of images) in your page. You can link your banner ad to any other page, or you can use it as a way of inserting slide shows into your page.

Before you start to use the Banner Ad Manager component, either create the images you are going to use or decide what images you already have that you want to use. The images, ideally, should all be the same dimensions (make a note of the width and height). To use the Banner Ad Manager, perform the following steps.

1. Position the mouse cursor where you want to insert the banner ad. (Banner ads are usually displayed at the top of a page.) Select Insert, Web Component, and then choose Dynamic Effects from the Component Types box. On the right-hand side of the dialog box, choose Banner Ad Manager. The Banner Ad Manager Properties dialog box opens.

2. Type the dimensions of your banner ad images in the Width and Height boxes.

3. From the Transition Effect list, you can select a transition. For this example, leave the Dissolve transition selected.

4. In the Show Each Picture for (Seconds) text box, type the number of seconds you want each image to be displayed. For this example, leave 5 as the number of seconds.

5. In the Link To box, type the URL of the page to which you want your banner ad to link. For example, to link the banner ad to Microsoft's FrontPage site, type http://www.microsoft.com/frontpage.

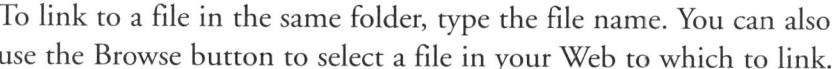

To link to a file in the same folder, type the file name. You can also use the Browse button to select a file in your Web to which to link.

6. Click on the Add button to add the first banner image. Select the banner image you want to add. (If the image you want to use is outside your Web, click on the second icon to the right of the URL box to select it.)

7. Repeat Step 6 for each additional image you want to add (see Figure 5.31). Click on OK when you're finished.

8. Click on the Center icon on the Formatting toolbar to center your banner ad. Save your page.

Figure 5.32 shows an example of a banner ad displayed in Internet Explorer.

What's Next?

If you've made it all the way through this session, you've covered a lot of ground. You should have at least a basic understanding of how to add comments, hit counters, hover buttons, include pages, scheduled pictures, scheduled include pages, timestamps, search forms, tables of contents, and banner ads to your FrontPage pages. If you've got any time left this morning, feel free to experiment further with any of the components covered in this session.

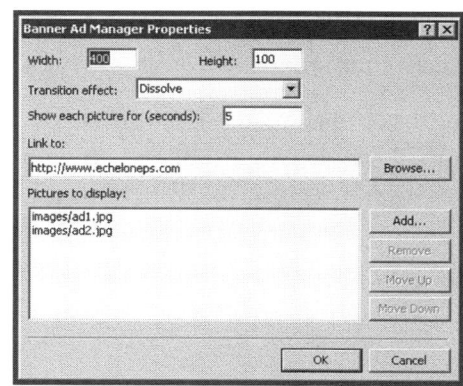

Figure 5.31

Two images are added to the Banner Ad Manager.

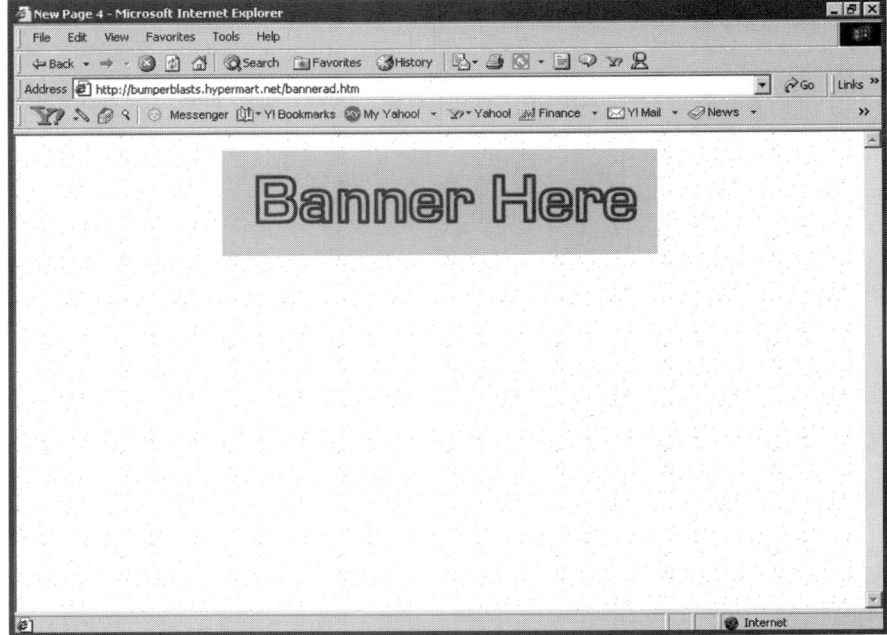

Figure 5.32

You need to publish a banner ad to a FrontPage server before you can preview it in your browser.

There are also a few components that weren't covered in this session, including the Office components (Spreadsheet, PivotTable, and Chart), the Marquee component, the Substitution component, and the Categories component. Feel free to come back later and experiment with these other components. For more information on using the Office Spreadsheet, Office PivotTable, and Office Chart components, click on the Help icon within those components.

Take a break now for lunch. You've got lots more to do in the next session, so get something nourishing. If you feel like it, go for a short walk. (Don't be gone too long, though!) See you back here in an hour or so for the Sunday Afternoon session, "Finalizing and Maintaining Your Pages."

Finalizing and Maintaining Your Pages

- ✪ Saving and Previewing Your Web Site
- ✪ Organizing Files in Your Web Site
- ✪ Working with FrontPage Reports
- ✪ Making Changes to Multiple Pages
- ✪ Completing Web Tasks

Wow, look how far you've come in the last day and a half. You started with only basic knowledge about Web page design, and in less than 48 hours you've graduated to top-notch Web designer.

Now it's time to clean up all those little things you need to do before you actually publish your Web online. In addition to the editing tools you've already discovered, you'll find that FrontPage contains some handy, well-designed tools to make cleanup fast and easy.

Saving and Previewing Your Web Site

When you were learning how to add hyperlinks to your Web site, you spent some time checking your links by viewing pages in Preview, as well as perusing your pages in one or more browsers.

Before I get into the nitty-gritty of site cleanup and management, take a few minutes now to check your entire site using the same methods you learned Saturday morning. Be on the lookout not just for broken links, but also for anything that might seem amiss, including misaligned table text, figures that do not load properly, formatting problems—anything. Take careful notes on what to fix—or better yet, use the Tasks feature to create reminders for each problem. Also, remember these things about your Web site:

- ✿ Don't forget that your main home page must have a specific name—most likely index.html. Check with your Web Host to find out for

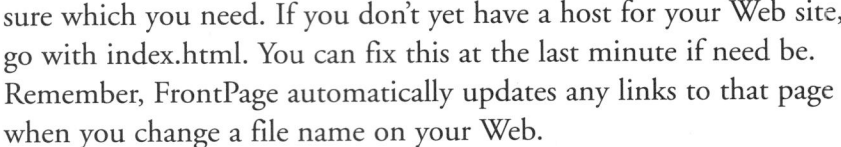

sure which you need. If you don't yet have a host for your Web site, go with index.html. You can fix this at the last minute if need be. Remember, FrontPage automatically updates any links to that page when you change a file name on your Web.

⚙ If you're using frames, the frames page itself must be the default index page.

⚙ Be sure that you've saved all the files. The fastest way to confirm this is to select File, Exit, and then click on Yes or Yes to All when prompted to save your pages and/or graphics.

⚙ Sometimes I find it helpful to publish the Web to another Web folder on my hard drive, or to the personal Web server. I then open that Web in my browser. This technique gives me the ability to see the site from a slightly new perspective. It also helps to identify some problematic links that might not otherwise be obvious—such as those that still point to a file URL on the hard drive rather than within the FrontPage Web site.

Organizing Files in Your Web Site

Even if you're not the details type, you know it's important to keep files reasonably organized on your hard drive. For example, you most likely store your working Office documents in the My Documents folder, your applications in the Program Files folder, system files in your Windows folder, and so on. You know that if you just store files any old place, you eventually end up with such a mess on your computer that it's almost impossible to find anything without extensive searches. (There's nothing more frustrating than the "Now where the heck did I put that blasted thing?" syndrome.)

Along the same lines, it's good to keep your Web files organized logically within the folder structure. By default, FrontPage creates a folder in your Web called Images and stores any imported graphic files there unless you tell it otherwise. FrontPage also creates some folders for its own use. You'll recognize these easily; they have names such as _private, _theme, or _fpclass (see Figure 6.1).

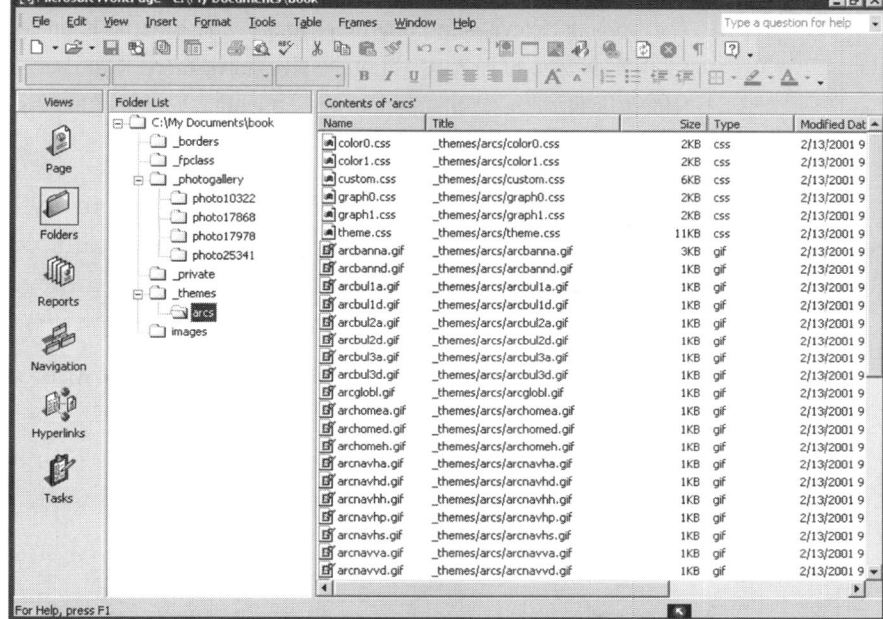

Figure 6.1

This example shows some of the many files FrontPage normally hides by default. Probably a good thing, because the less screen clutter, the better.

> **TIP**
>
> ■
>
> In the course of building your site, FrontPage generates a lot of miscellaneous folders and files it needs to make things happen, such as all the graphics files included in a particular theme (and, boy, are there a ton of those!). So that they don't get in your way or confuse you, however, FrontPage hides these "extra" files by default because there's really nothing you need to do with them, and messing around with them could cause problems. If you want to see what's there, however, you can tell FrontPage to show you all files in the Web site. To toggle this option on or off, choose Tools, Web Settings, then click on the Advanced tab in the Web Settings dialog box. You'll see the Show Hidden Files and Folders check box in the middle of the dialog box under Options. Unless you specifically show, select, and mark these files Don't Publish, FrontPage will publish system files whether they are hidden or not.
>
> ■

NOTE

The _private folder—and any other folder whose name is preceded by an underscore (_)—is hidden to visitors, as are the files stored there. If you need to create more hidden folders or files, create them under the _private folder, or contact your WSP for help.

The more your Web grows, the more important it will be to keep your files neat and tidy. If you have several topics within your Web, and each topic involves several pages, consider storing all those related pages in one folder. To create new folders in your Web, follow these steps.

1. Click on the Folders button on the Views bar to switch to Folders view.

2. Select File, New, Folder. FrontPage creates a new folder. The default name, New_Folder, will be highlighted and ready for you to enter a more logical name, as shown in Figure 6.2.

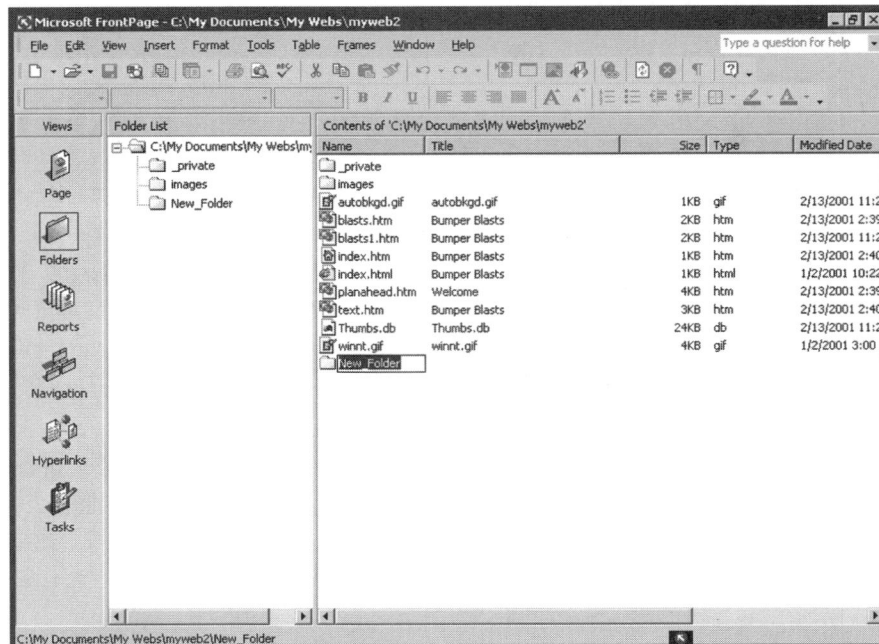

Figure 6.2

Storing related pages in separate folders takes a tad more setup time, but is definitely worth it in the long run.

3. Type the new name for the folder and press Enter. Repeat as needed for as many folders as it takes to do the job.

4. After you've created the folders for your major categories, simply drag all the related files to the appropriate folders. Remember, you can move or copy files and folders from one Web to another by dragging them out of or into the site's Folders view while both Web sites are open in separate FrontPage windows.

Feel free to also create subfolders within those folders. In other words, use whatever organizational system best suits your needs, be it a handful of folders or a detailed multilayer folder structure. (Don't get carried away, though—there is such a thing as too much organization.) See Figure 6.3 for an example.

While you're at it, make sure that all your files have names that make sense to you. When it's time to go back and edit one page of the dozens

Figure 6.3

This Web contains both subfolders and subwebs, making it much easier to manage files for a large—or even medium-sized—Web.

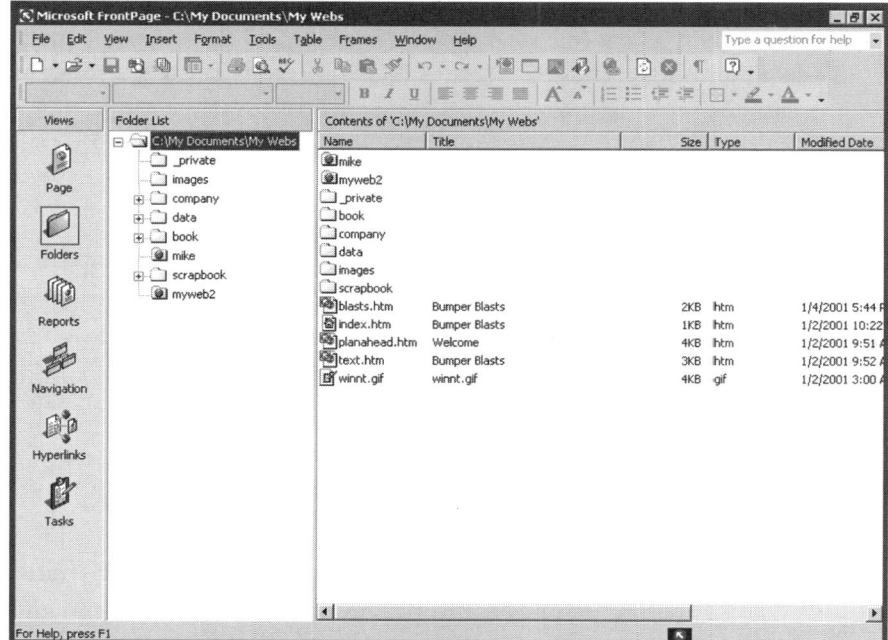

A WEB WITHIN A WEB WITHIN A WEB?

If you're hosting more than one Web site within your domain, you can actually publish each one as a subweb within your main FrontPage Web.

For example, perhaps your small business Web site also is home to your personal Web site. Other than having links to each other and the fact that you maintain both of them, the two sites are unrelated. Thus, you can treat them as separate Web sites but keep the files for both sites under the www.mysite.com umbrella site. Each subweb has its own home page and can use files with the same names as the other site without conflict or confusion.

As your business grows, you might decide to allow your employees to create their own personal Web sites and host them within the company's domain. Using Front-Page's security features, you can give each employee authoring and maintenance rights to his or her pages without compromising the security of the overall site. (See Appendix E, "Implementing Special Features," for more information on site security.)

By storing subwebs within a main Web, you can conveniently publish updates to the entire domain in one fell swoop (perhaps as part of an automated maintenance procedure that runs overnight), or you can update and publish the subwebs individually.

or hundreds of pages in your site, you'll appreciate this advice. Except for the home page, file names are not important to anyone other than you. The browser doesn't care what you name a file as long as you use the correct extension. Your visitors will rarely need to know a specific page's file name as long as the link works properly.

Take a Break!

Your Web site will be ready for posting shortly. Take a short break now before you head into the home stretch. When you come back, you'll tour

the FrontPage reports, which help you keep your site up to date and efficient. Then, you'll learn how to make changes to multiple pages in your Web, and you'll complete the remaining items on your Tasks list. So off you go…come on back when you're ready to wrap things up.

Working with FrontPage Reports

After you're comfortable with your folder and file organization and naming schemes, you're ready to look at what FrontPage has to say about your Web design and structure.

As you learned on Friday evening, the Reports view includes 15 different reports about the contents of your site. Some are informational only, and others provide detailed views you can study. This allows you to streamline and improve the overall effectiveness of your site.

 **NOTE** FrontPage 2002 also includes some high-end reporting tools that help you analyze how and when visitors are using your site. This reporting feature requires you to have direct access to a Web server that supports usage analysis. Because that's not likely to be your situation, I'll spare you the yawns. However, if you are working in that environment, you will be happy to know that the usage reports are just as simple and straightforward as other FrontPage reports.

Generating a Site Summary

To begin working through the various reports, start by clicking on the Reports button on the Views bar. If this is your first time working in the Reports view, the Site Summary report appears first, as shown in Figure 6.4.

The Site Summary lists the overall results of each of the 15 reports at a glance, so you can quickly identify trouble spots.

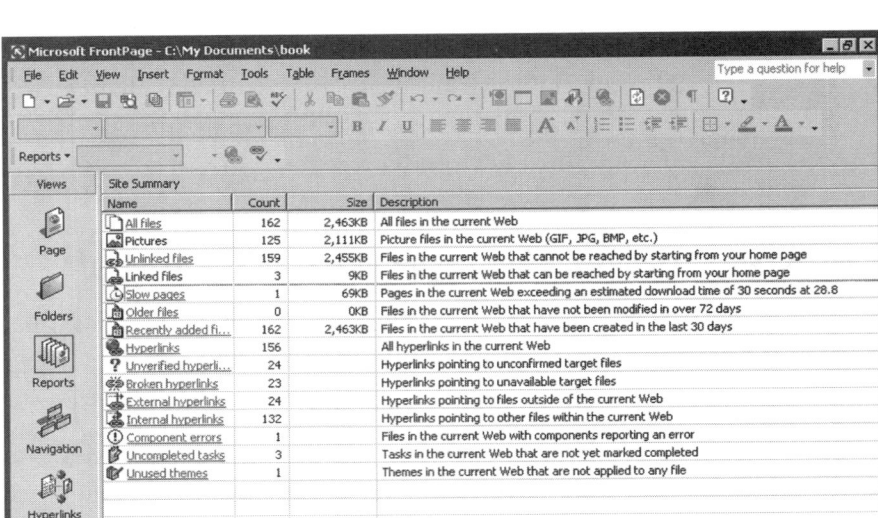

Figure 6.4

The Site Summary is the at-a-glance view of the various FrontPage reports.

TIP

If it doesn't appear by default, open the Reports toolbar while you're working in Reports view. Right-click anywhere on a FrontPage toolbar and select Reporting to toggle it between shown or hidden status. The Reporting toolbar gives you convenient access to the various FrontPage reports via a drop-down list, nicely grouped by topic. It also lets you customize options and values for certain reports. For example, you can define what minimum load time is considered slow for the Slow Pages report. (You can also change these options by selecting Tools, Options, and then clicking on the Reports View tab.)

NOTE

Subsequent returns to Reports view take you back to the last report you viewed onscreen. To reopen the Site Summary, select View, Reports, Site Summary, or just select it from the Reports drop-down list on the toolbar.

Using the FrontPage Reports

To access any report, click on its listing in the Site Summary, or choose a specific report from the View, Reports submenu. The available reports include

- **All Files.** Lists the number and collective size of every file in your Web. Click on the report name to see the details of each file, including
  - The file name
  - The title of the page
  - Where in the Web it is located
  - The file's size
  - What kind of file it is (HTML, graphic, and so on)
  - The date and time is was last modified
  - Who did the updating
  - How many hits that page has received (if your server supports usage analysis)
  - Any additional comments the page creator might have entered during the design process

NOTE In the Site Summary, the total number of files and their collective size will give you an idea of how much storage space your Web will use on the Web server. Keep in mind, however, that by default the report does not include the size of any hidden or system files that FrontPage might have created automatically. To get an even more accurate total size, turn on the hidden files display, as discussed earlier in this session.

- **Pictures.** A subset of the All Files report, this report lists the total number of graphics files (.gif, .jpg, and so on) in your Web site and their collective size. No detailed report is available for just the graphics files, but you can get this information from the All Files report.
- **Unlinked Files.** Lists any files in your Web that cannot be reached by starting from your home page. You might have created a page

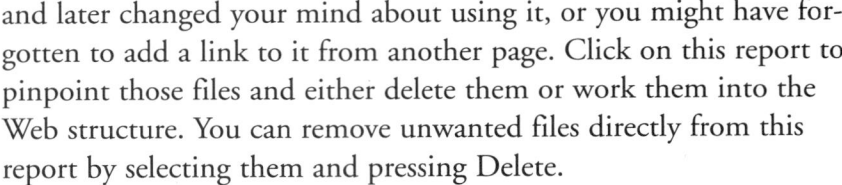

and later changed your mind about using it, or you might have forgotten to add a link to it from another page. Click on this report to pinpoint those files and either delete them or work them into the Web structure. You can remove unwanted files directly from this report by selecting them and pressing Delete.

✿ **Linked Files**. The counterpart to the Unlinked Files report, this report lists the total number of files that *can* be reached via hyperlinks within the Web. No detailed view is available.

✿ **Slow Pages**. Visitors don't like sitting around waiting for pages to load before they can go on. Click on the Slow Pages report to see the full list, and then open each page one by one to see what you might do to speed up the page. Most often, you'll find that many graphics, or even one large graphic, will quickly increase the load time for a page. To avoid this problem, keep the size of your graphics files as small as possible.

You can see the estimated load time of a page while you're editing it. Just check the status bar while you're in Edit view. Near the right end of the status bar, you'll see a small hourglass icon followed by the number of estimated seconds and the default connection (modem) speed to assume. Right-click on the connection speed to select a new speed from the shortcut menu.

✿ **Older Files**. This report lists the number and collective size of the pages in your Web that have not been updated for 30 days. Use this report to keep track of pages that will occasionally need a quick refreshing. (It's a safe bet that a page called "Today's News" that has not been updated for 89 days doesn't really contain today's news—unless of course you're Bill Murray in the movie *Groundhog Day*.) Click on the report to see the details of each file. You can change the number of days since the update using the Reports View tab of the Options dialog box (accessed from the Tools menu).

- **Recently Added Files.** The counterpart to the Older Files report, this report lists any files that have been added to your site within the last several days (2 days, by default). If you recently created a file and now can't remember what you named it, this is a good place to start looking.

- **Hyperlinks.** This report shows a summary of the total number of hyperlinks in your site, including internal and external. Clicking on this report actually opens the Broken Hyperlinks report, which you worked with on Saturday afternoon. Check the individual External Hyperlinks and Internal Hyperlinks reports to see the breakdown.

- **Unverified Hyperlinks.** A subset of the Hyperlinks report, this view shows only links that have not been checked for accuracy. (They may or may not be broken links.) Clicking on the report opens the Broken Hyperlinks report, so you can find out for sure.

- **Broken Hyperlinks.** A subset of the Hyperlinks report, you can use this helpful tool to find errors in your links. Flip back to "Testing Your Work" in Saturday afternoon's session for a detailed explanation of using the Broken Hyperlinks report.

- **External Hyperlinks.** A subset of the Hyperlinks report, this is the total number of links that point to other Web sites. No detailed view is available. Click on the Hyperlinks button on the View bar to check out your hyperlink structure.

- **Internal Hyperlinks.** A subset of the Hyperlinks report, this is the total number of links to pages and bookmarks within your own Web site.

- **Component Errors.** This report lists the total number of files in your Web containing FrontPage components that are not working properly. Click on the report to list and open specific files.

- **Uncompleted Tasks.** This report gives you a quick peek at the status of your Tasks list. Click on the report to switch to the Tasks view. (Later in this session, you'll diligently work on completing those annoying leftover tasks.)

○ **Unused Themes**. You might have changed course midstream in your design process and decided to use a different theme. If so, there might still be files related to the old theme in various folders. Click on the report to eliminate all of them immediately. To see the individual files, open the All Files report and click on the In Folder column header to sort the files by that field. Then, scroll down to the group of files listed under the _themes folder.

NOTE As mentioned previously, you must have the Show Hidden Files option from the All Files report enabled to see hidden files. (Remember, a hidden file is any file in a folder that begins with an underscore.)

As you work your way through each of these reports, fix as many problems as you can. If there is anything you can't or don't want to deal with right away, add it to your Tasks list.

To refresh the Site Summary after you've done some cleanup, press F5. FrontPage recalculates the reports and shows you the updated summary.

Customizing FrontPage Reports

All these various reports are great, and what's even better is that you can tweak most of the reports in one way or another to get just the information you need (assuming that what's there now is not enough).

Sorting by Columns

In most of the detailed reports, you can click on a field's column heading to sort the report's line items by that field. Thus, if you wanted to see which files are the largest ones in your Web, you could follow these steps.

1. Open the All Files report.
2. Click on the Size column heading. FrontPage shows all the files in order from largest to smallest.
3. Click on the heading again to show the list from smallest to largest.

Adjusting Column Order and Width

Just like in most Windows applications, you can make adjustments to columns to better fit the data you want to see on the screen. You can also change the order in which the columns appear. I'll use the All Files report to demonstrate each of these techniques.

1. Open the All Files report. Notice that each column includes a label and a down-pointing arrow.

2. Click on the Name heading and hold down the mouse button. (Avoid that down arrow—we'll get to it momentarily.)

3. Drag the pointer to the right. When you reach the In Folder column, notice that the line between the column headings turns blue (see Figure 6.5). Release the mouse button. The Name column moves toward the right, and the first column of the report becomes Title.

4. To change the column width, point to the line separating the column you want to adjust and the one to its right. The cursor changes into a double-headed arrow.

Figure 6.5

You can adjust the order of the columns in a report by dragging them where you want them.

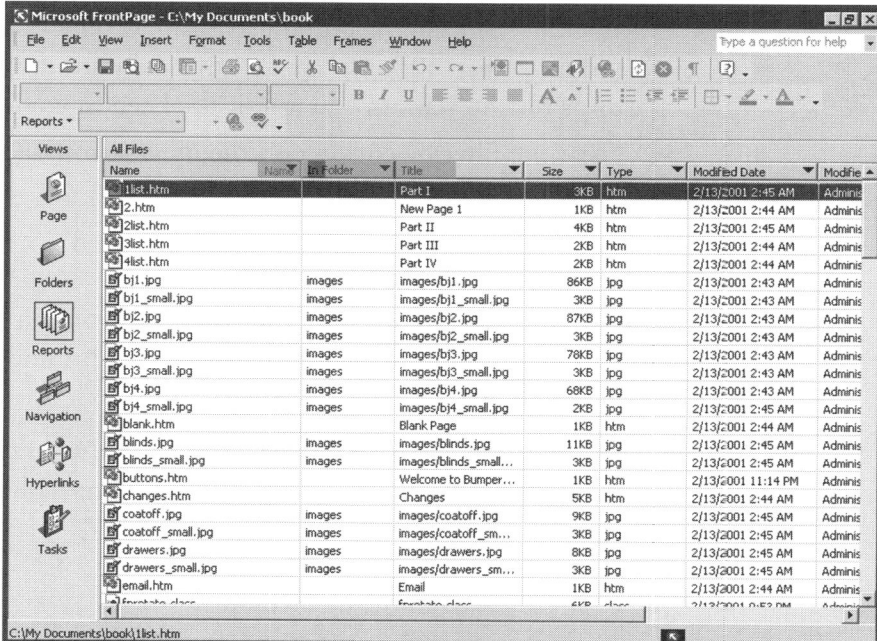

5. Click and drag the heading to the right or left until it is the desired width and release the mouse button.

6. Repeat as needed until all the columns are as wide or as narrow as you need them to be.

Applying a Filter

Sometimes you only want a report for certain file types, those edited on a certain day, or those found in a particular folder. No sweat—FrontPage lets you filter out only those particulars.

1. Open the Recently Added Files report. Adjust the column widths as needed.

2. Click on the down arrow on the far right end of the Type heading. A drop-down list appears, displaying the applicable filters, as shown in Figure 6.6. The filter list is different for each column, but each contains an (All) option, a (Custom) option, and one item for each unique entry in the list. (In other words, the report might contain a dozen .jpg files, but jpg will only be listed once.)

3. Click on jpg. The report adjusts to show only those files in .jpg format. When a filter is applied to a column, the drop-down arrow turns blue to remind you that it has been filtered.

4. Clear the filter by clicking on the down arrow again and choosing (All).

Creating a Custom Filter

What if you want to see only files that are a certain size or larger? Or, maybe you want to see files with both the .htm and .html extensions. If so, you can apply a customized filter to do exactly that.

1. Click on the desired column's down arrow, then choose (Custom) from the list. In this case, I'm using the Type column. The Custom AutoFilter dialog box opens (see Figure 6.7).

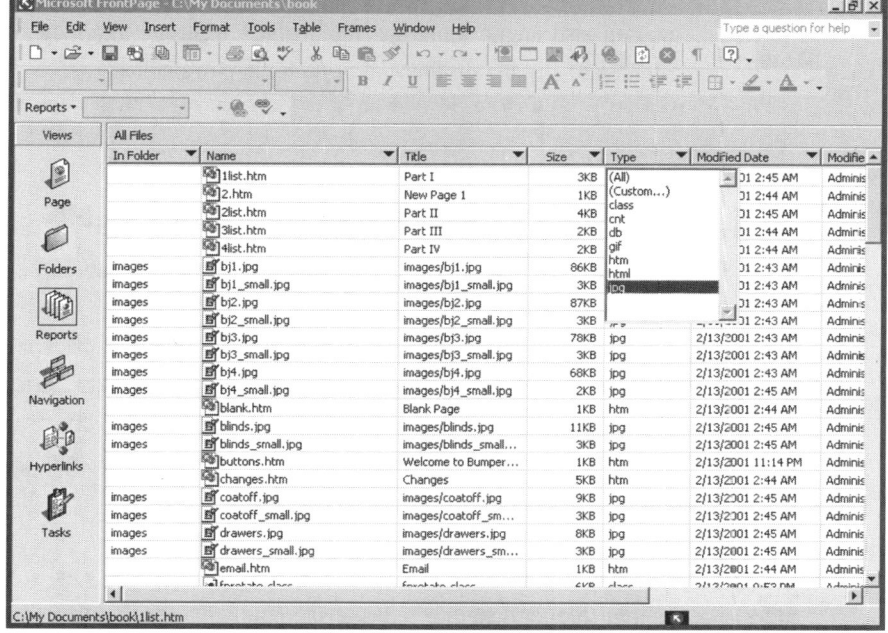

Figure 6.6

Reduce the onscreen clutter by filtering out what you don't need to see.

Figure 6.7

Use a custom filter to define your own list to display.

2. Click on the top-left drop-down list to see the available filter options, including Equal, Does Not Equal, and Is Greater Than.

3. Scroll down the list and click on Contains.

4. Click in the top-right text box and type **htm** (or select it from the list).

5. Click on OK to apply the filter. The dialog box closes, and the filter is applied.

TIP You can also create more specific or more inclusive filters by adding a second set of criteria and clicking on the And or Or option, respectively.

Making Changes to Multiple Pages

Mark my words—there will be a time when you need to make the same change to all or many of the files in your Web. What if your company's name changes or you've misspelled a word that the Spelling Checker doesn't recognize? Imagine opening all those pages individually to search for each occurrence of the text that needs to be changed. Eeek! I shudder at the very thought. Thank goodness for FrontPage's global Find/Replace feature! To make changes to multiple pages, follow these steps.

◄ ◄

The term *global* generally refers to something that applies to an entire Web. For example, a theme is applied *globally* to all pages in your site unless you specify otherwise. Or, a change you make to a style is applied *globally* everywhere the style is used.

◄ ◄

1. Switch to Folders view and then select Edit, Replace. The Find and Replace dialog box opens, as shown in Figure 6.8.

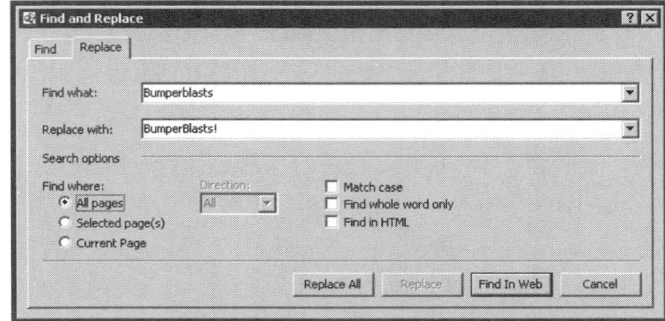

Figure 6.8

FrontPage's global Find and Replace sure beats searching one page at a time.

2. Click in the Find What text box and enter the word or phrase that needs to be changed.

3. Press the Tab key and enter the new word or phrase in the Replace With text box.

4. Under Find Where, select All Pages to search the entire site.

5. Choose any of the following options as necessary:

   - **Match Case**. By default, if you enter "office," FrontPage will find both "office" and "Office." Select Match Case to find text that matches exactly as you enter it.

   - **Find Whole Word Only**. By default, FrontPage will find all occurrences of the text in the Find What box. If you enter "ham," FrontPage will return "ham," "champion," "New Hampshire," and "Birmingham." Select Find Whole Word Only to limit the search to only the word "ham."

   - **Find in HTML**. By default, FrontPage searches only text that appears in Normal view. Select Find in HTML to search the HTML code behind the pages or to change text found on hidden pages. For example, you might want to search the HTML code behind the pages to change all occurrences of heading 1 to heading 2.

6. Click on Find in Web. FrontPage runs the search and returns a list of occurrences it finds, as shown in Figure 6.9.

7. Double-click on the first page listed to make the changes on that page. FrontPage opens the page and highlights the first occurrence of the word on that page, as shown in Figure 6.10.

8. Select Replace to change only that occurrence, Replace All to change all occurrences on that page, or Find Next to skip that occurrence and find the next one. When FrontPage can find no more occurrences, it prompts you to open the next page that contains occurrences of your search, as shown in Figure 6.11.

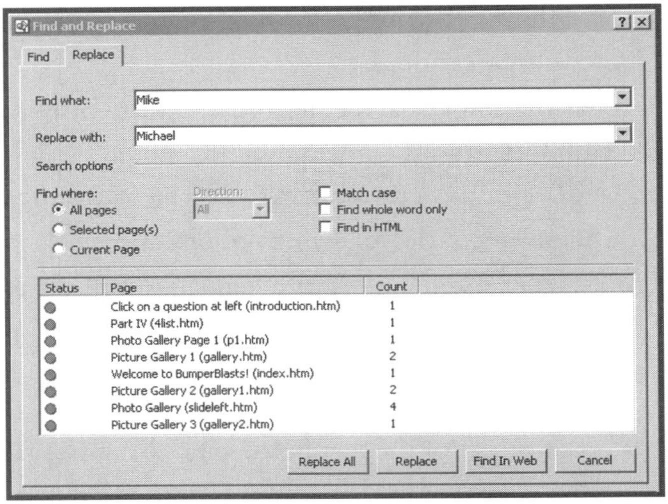

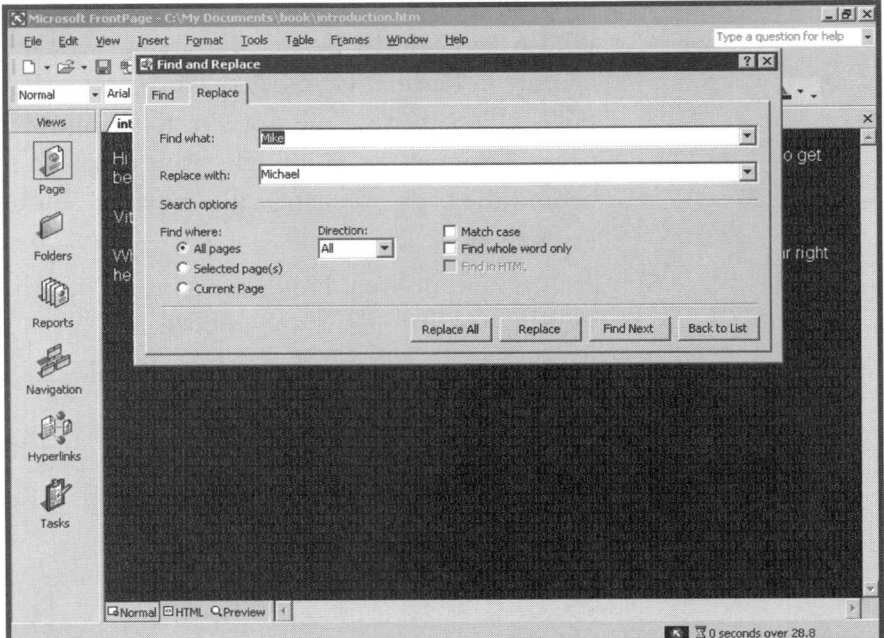

Figure 6.9

FrontPage finds every instance of the word and creates a task for each page you need to edit.

Figure 6.10

This part of the procedure works just like Word's Replace feature.

Figure 6.11

FrontPage prompts
you to go on to the
next page of
replacements.

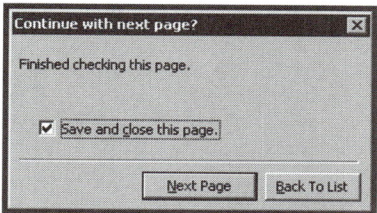

9. Select Next Page to go on, or select Back To List to cancel the
    rest of the search. Eventually, you'll end up back at the Find and
    Replace dialog box.

10. After you've handled changes on each of the pages listed, click
    on Cancel to close the Find and Replace dialog box and end the
    search.

Completing Web Tasks

You're just about finished. You've done the heaviest design work, tested
links, and dumped unwanted files. Now you're ready to put the finishing
touches on your Web. Just whip through the Tasks list and get your ISP
and Web Host information in order (see Appendix A, "Publishing Your
FrontPage 2002 Web Pages"), and you're ready to launch the site.

Depending on your working style, you might reach this point and have
very few to-do items on your Tasks list. If that's the case, you can get them
all squared away in a few minutes. If you're like me, however, there might
still be several hours of work yet to do. Either way, ya gotta do what ya gotta
do. To open the Tasks list and see how scary it looks, then follow these steps.

1. Click on the Tasks button on the Views bar. FrontPage reveals the
    list of tasks remaining to complete (see Figure 6.12). Quickly
    review the list. If there are a lot there, go ahead and take a break
    before you proceed. If you're willing to hang in there just a bit
    longer, go on to Step 2.

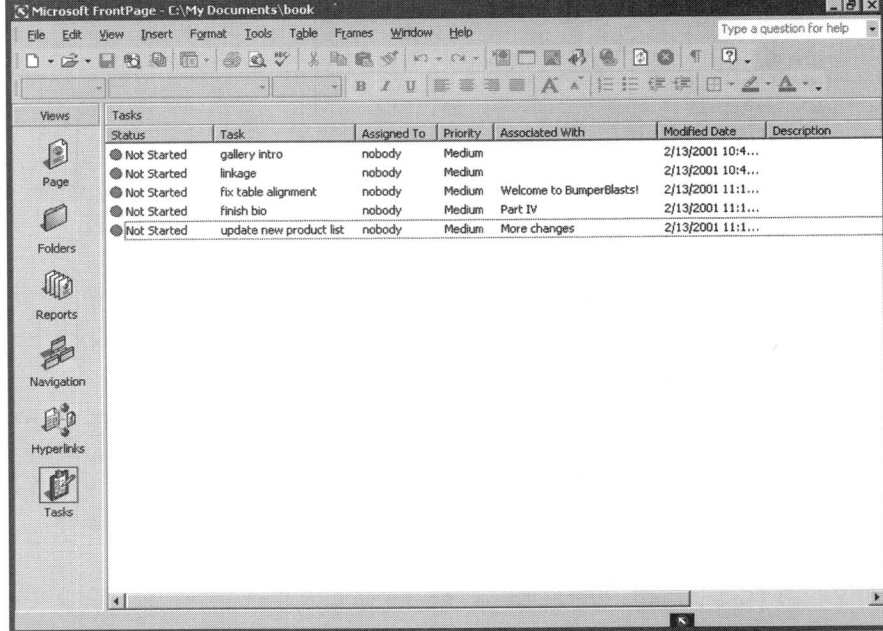

Figure 6.12

For me, adding an item to the Tasks list is the same as choosing the Procrastinate option. I like software that supports my bad habits.

2. Double-click on the first item on the list. The Task Details dialog box opens, as shown in Figure 6.13.

3. The information in the dialog box serves as a reminder for what this task involves. To get to work, click on Start Task. FrontPage sets up whatever you need to finish the task, such as opening a page to edit.

4. After you complete the job, click on Save. When FrontPage prompts you to mark the task as completed, click on Yes (see Figure 6.14).

5. Return to the Tasks view. Notice that the status of the first task now reads Completed. By default, all completed items remain on the Tasks list until you close the Web or refresh the list by pressing F5 (see Figure 6.15).

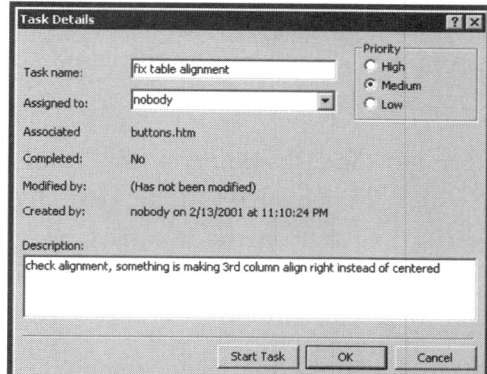

Figure 6.13

Tasks include brief notes to remind you of the task details.

Figure 6.14

You better believe I want you to mark it completed. Now stop pestering me!

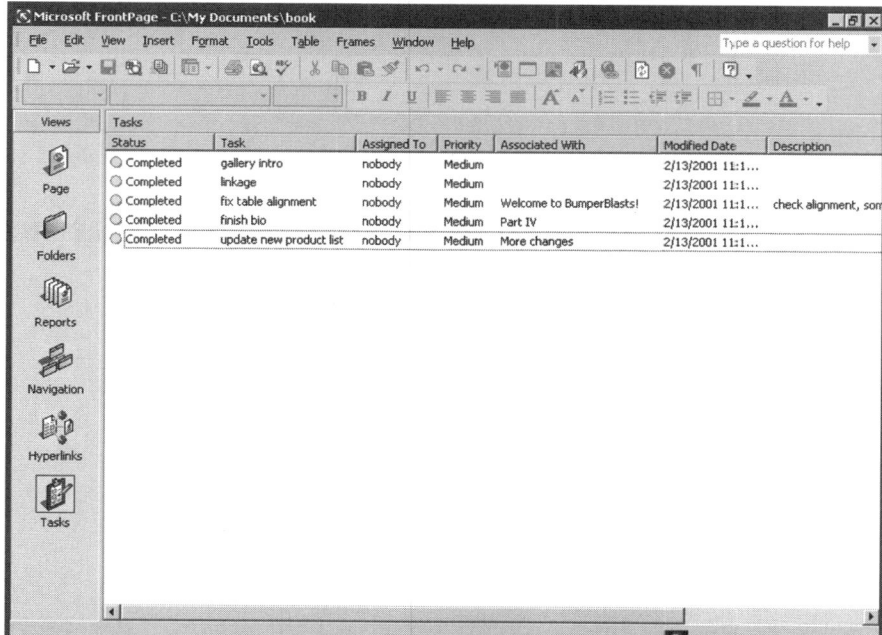

Figure 6.15

You'll get some satisfaction out of completing all the items on the Tasks list.

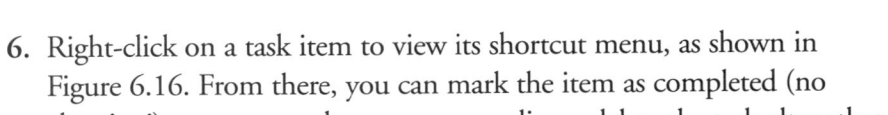

6. Right-click on a task item to view its shortcut menu, as shown in Figure 6.16. From there, you can mark the item as completed (no cheating!), or you can choose to start, edit, or delete the task altogether.

Work your way through the tasks one at a time until you've resolved all the outstanding issues. When that's done, switch back to the Site Summary and press F5 to refresh the report. Check for anything you might have missed on the first pass. When you're satisfied everything is correct, save all your files, close the Web, and exit FrontPage.

Find it...

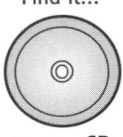

On the CD

The CD that accompanies this book includes several excellent third-party programs and utilities that can help you manage your site more efficiently.

FastStats gives you vital information about your Web site, such as which search engines and keywords are used to access your Web site.

WS_FTP Pro and *CuteFTP* are equally outstanding file transfer utilities for posting your Web pages if your WPP does not support publishing directly from FrontPage.

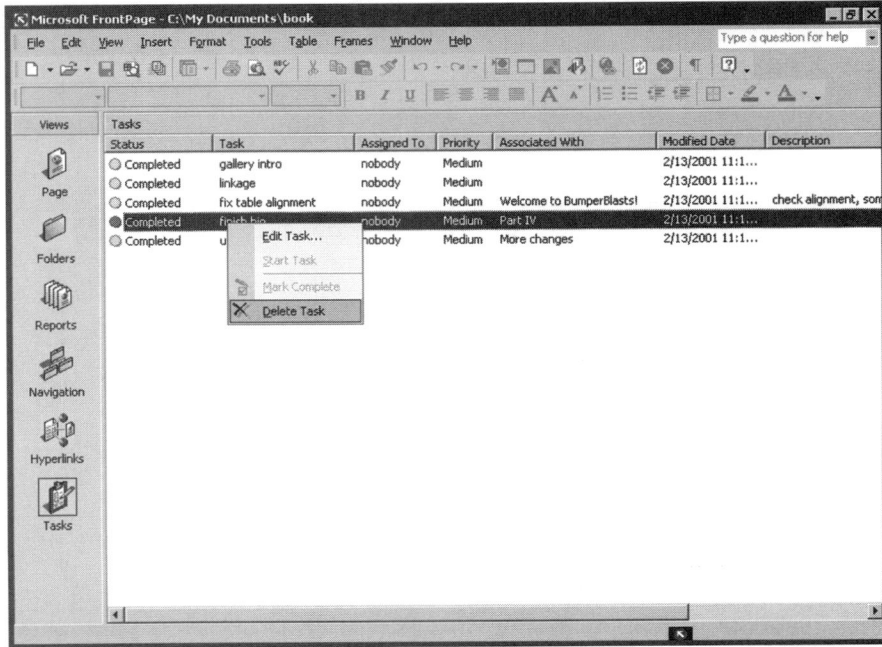

Figure 6.16

Use the shortcut menu to make a quick decision.

What's Next?

All finished? Great! Now stand up, fold one arm over your stomach and one behind your back, bend forward from the waist, and take a bow. Congratulations! Your Web is complete. All that's left to do (for now, anyway) is to post your pages online. It might take you a few days to work out the details of selecting your Internet Service Provider (ISP) and Web Presence Provider (WPP), so I haven't counted it as part of your work this weekend. Rest assured—everything you need to know is covered in Appendix A, "Publishing Your FrontPage 2002 Web Pages." In the remaining appendixes, you'll also find helpful information on things you can do to improve and enhance your Web. You'll learn how to add sound and video, build forms for visitor feedback, promote your site and attract visitors, and much, much more.

As a reward for your hard work, I saved something fun for Sunday night. It's an optional session, but I know you'll want to check it out. Web sites are a great deal more interesting and attractive if your graphics are original, creative, and well done. In our last session together, "Creating Web Art Special Effects," you'll learn how to create, modify, and manipulate graphics for use in your Web site. If you'd rather take the night off and rest up for the upcoming week, that's cool, but be sure to come back to this session some other time.

Bonus Session: Creating Web Art Special Effects

- ✪ Using Fill Effects
- ✪ Working with Layers
- ✪ Creating 3D Effects
- ✪ Creating a Transparent GIF Image
- ✪ Creating 3D Buttons

The clip art included with FrontPage enables you to enhance your FrontPage Web pages. If you want to give your Web site a special look to set it apart, you might want to consider creating your own personalized Web art images. You don't need to be a graphics professional to create attractive and effective Web art for your Web pages. You just need to know how to apply the right tools to get the results you want.

What You Need

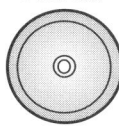

Find it...

On the CD

In this session, you'll be using one of the most popular image editors available on the Windows platform, Paint Shop Pro 7, to learn how to create images using some special effects that are particularly useful for creating graphics for the Web. You can find a fully functional 30-day evaluation version of Paint Shop Pro 7 on the CD-ROM.

FIND IT ▶
ONLINE

If you don't have a CD-ROM drive or access to this book's CD-ROM, you can download the latest version of Paint Shop Pro from Jasc Software's site at http://www.jasc.com (although some procedures to implement features covered in this session might differ in subsequent versions of Paint Shop Pro).

NOTE If you've previously installed Paint Shop Pro 7 and exhausted the trial period (30 days, plus a grace period of another 30 days), you won't be able to install Paint Shop Pro 7 from the CD-ROM. If you want to do the Paint Shop Pro sections of this session, your alternatives are to install Paint Shop Pro 7 on a different computer, download a subsequent version of Paint Shop Pro from Jasc Software's site, or purchase Paint Shop Pro.

All of the examples in this session were created with Small Fonts selected in Windows' display properties. If you have a different setting, your results will look different than what is shown in the figures. In that case, you might just want to adjust the specified font sizes downward (to get the text to fit within the image window, for instance).

If you want your results to look the same as what is shown in the figures, however, you should select Small Fonts in Windows' display properties. If you are not running at 800 × 600 screen resolution, you can select that at the same time. Exit any open programs and then click on Windows' Start button, select Settings, Control Panel, double-click on the Display icon, and click on the Settings tab. Use the Screen Area slider to select 800 by 600 pixels. To select Small Fonts, click on the Advanced button. (If Other is selected, make note of the setting so you can reset it later, if you wish.) From the Font Size list, select Small Fonts, and then click on OK. You'll be prompted to restart Windows to have your new settings take effect.

Running Paint Shop Pro 7

After installing Paint Shop Pro 7 from the CD-ROM (or downloading and installing it from the Web), just follow these steps to run the program.

1. Click on the Start button and then select Programs.

2. Select Jasc Software and then select Paint Shop Pro 7.

3. Click on the Close button to close the Tip of the Day window. Paint Shop Pro's opening window should now be displayed on your screen.

Starting Your Image

For an example of using the different Web art special effects covered in this session, you'll create an example banner image. You can customize this generic banner image later, if you want, and create a more personalized banner image. To begin creating your banner image, start a new image in Paint Shop Pro 7.

1. Select File, New. Type **550** in the Width box and **125** the Height box. Make sure that Pixels is selected as the unit of measure.

2. Click on the Background Color list and select White as the background color, if it isn't already selected.

3. Leave all the other settings as they are: Resolution (72) and Image Type (16.7 Million Colors). Click on OK.

4. Click and drag the Layer palette and the Tool Options palette so that they aren't overlapping your new blank image window (see Figure 7.1).

Figure 7.1

Paint Shop Pro 7 is one of the best image editors available for Windows.

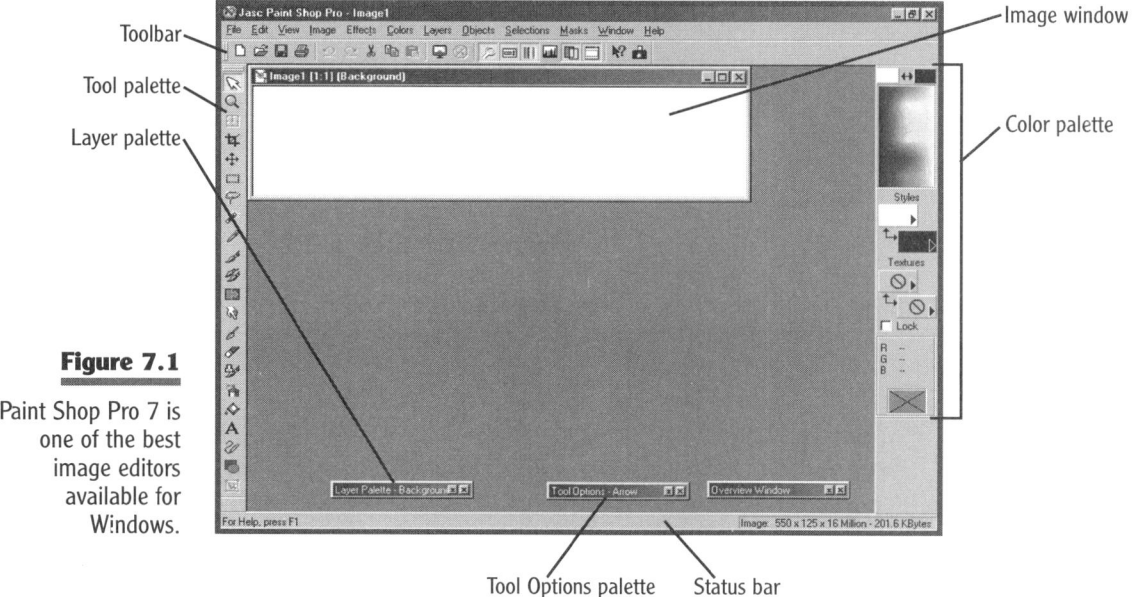

Toolbar
Tool palette
Layer palette
Image window
Color palette
Tool Options palette   Status bar

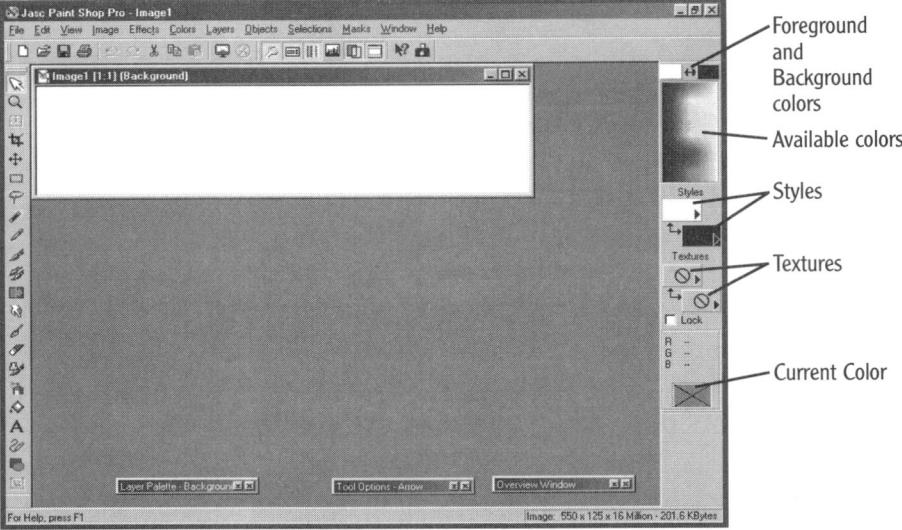

Foreground
and
Background
colors

Available colors

Styles

Textures

Current Color

Figure 7.1
(continued)

Paint Shop Pro 7 is
one of the best
image editors
available for
Windows.

Creating the Banner Text

A banner image is often just a graphical version of your page's title that enables you to select from a much wider range of fonts than is possible using straight HTML. You can also apply many special effects that help your banner graphic stand out from the crowd. For this session's example, you'll create a generic banner graphic, but feel free to customize it later to create a more personalized look.

1. Click on the Text tool (the "A" icon) in the Tool palette and then click in the center of the image window. The Text Entry dialog box opens on the screen.

2. Choose the name and size of the font you want to use. For example, choose Comic Sans MS from the Name menu and choose 72 from the Size menu. Check the Auto Kern check box. If bold is not already selected, click on the B icon to turn on bolding. Make sure that the Floating radio button and the Antialias check box are selected.

3. In the text window, type **My Banner** as the text for the text banner (see Figure 7.2).

NOTE

If you select the Vector radio button rather than the Floating radio button in the Step 2, you won't be able to use any of the painting tools in the Tool palette; they'll be grayed out. You can, however, save an image using vector text objects as a bitmap (a JPEG image, for example) and then reopening it in Paint Shop Pro 7. You then can use any of the painting tools to apply fills or other painting effects to the text.

Next, you need to set the color for your text. To do that, follow these steps.

1. Under Styles, click on the arrow in the Stroke box and click on the null icon (the circle with the strike through it) to specify that your text will not have a border (or stroke).

2. Under Styles, click on the arrow in the Fill box and click on the paintbrush icon to choose to fill your text with a solid color. (You can also choose from the gradient, pattern, or null fill options. You'll learn how to use the gradient and pattern fill options later.)

3. Under Textures, click on the arrow in both the Stroke and Fill boxes and click on the null icon to turn off applying any textures to your text.

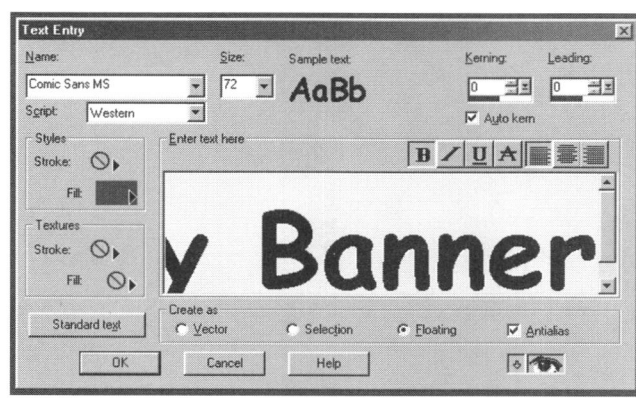

Figure 7.2

In the Text Entry dialog box, you can specify the font, size, color, and content of a text object.

4. Next, under Styles, click inside the Fill box to open the Color dialog box. Choose a color you want to use as the fill for your text. For example, click on the brick red color (third color from the left in the first row of Basic Colors; see Figure 7.3). Click on OK.

5. Click on OK to close the Text Entry dialog box. Click and drag the text object to position it in the center of the window, as shown in Figure 7.4.

If you chose a font other than Comic Sans MS, be aware that different fonts may have different character widths. You might need to adjust the font size down or up to make your text fit nicely inside the image window. If you need to adjust the font size, just press the Delete key to delete your text object, re-click the Flood Fill tool inside of the image window, and then change the font size. Repeat this procedure until you get the exact size you want.

NOTE Many of the effects covered in this session require that the color depth of your image be 16.7 million colors. If you find that an effect option is grayed out, select Colors, Increase Color Depth to see whether the 16 Million Colors option is available. If it is, click on it.

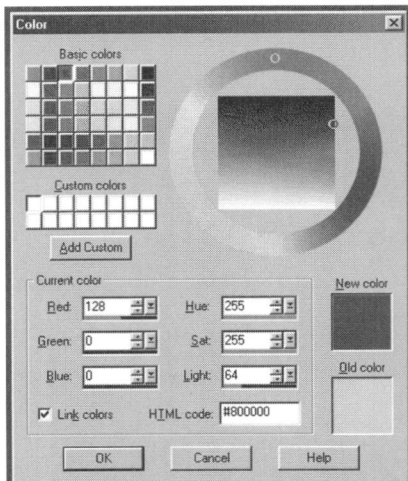

Figure 7.3

Select a brick red color as the text's fill color.

Figure 7.4

The text object, "My Banner," is positioned in the center of the image window.

NOTE Notice that the background color at the top of the Color palette has changed to match the fill color (brick red) that you selected for your text. If you had selected a color for the stroke, the foreground color would have also changed to match. You might see these color assignments change, however, as you select different tools (such as the Flood Fill tool), because these characteristics are set individually for each tool that uses the Styles and Textures settings. To lock in specific settings that will stay constant across different tools, you can check the Lock check box. For this session's examples, however, leave it unchecked.

Using Fill Effects

You can use a variety of different fill effects to add color and pizzazz to your banner graphic. These include solid color, texture, pattern, and a variety of different gradient fills.

NOTE

Three minimized tool palettes are displayed when you first run Paint Shop Pro: the Tool Options palette, the Layer palette, and the Overview window. In the following section, you'll make extensive use of the Tool Options palette. If that palette's minimized title bar is not visible in your work area, you might need to turn on its display. Select View, Toolbars, and then make sure that the Tool Options Palette check box is checked.

Using Solid Color Fills

A solid color fill, as its name implies, fills an area with a solid color. To fill your text with a different solid fill color, follow these steps.

1. Click on the Flood Fill tool (the paint bucket icon) in the Tool palette.

2. In the Styles section of the Color palette, click on the arrow in the first box and select a solid fill style. Next, click inside that same box and select a color to use for the fill. For example, select the lighter lime-green color in the Basic Colors section. (It's the third color down in the sixth column.) Click on OK.

3. Expand the Tool Options palette by passing the mouse pointer over its minimized title bar. If it's not already selected, choose Normal as the Blend mode and None as the Match mode. Set the Opacity value at 100 (see Figure 7.5).

4. Now, click the mouse inside any of the letters in your banner text. All the letters of your banner text are now filled with the lime-green color you selected as your foreground fill color style (see Figure 7.6).

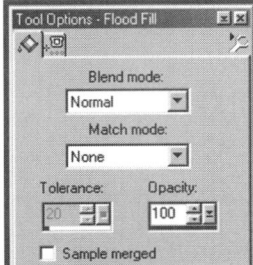

Figure 7.5

Specify the characteristics of your fill in the Tool Options palette.

Solid fill

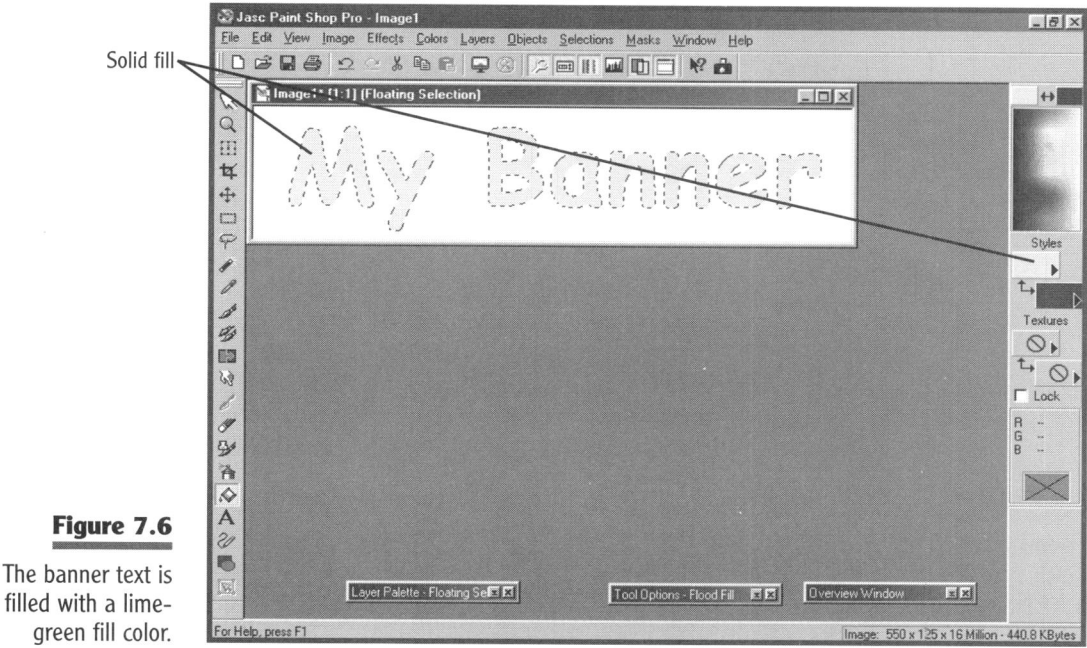

Figure 7.6

The banner text is filled with a lime-green fill color.

As long as you select a Match mode of None, the fill will be applied to all the letters of your selected text object. To fill only a single letter while leaving all the letters selected, just choose a Match mode other than None. To try this out, follow these steps.

1. With the Flood Fill tool still selected, select RGB Value as the Match mode in the Tool Options palette.

2. Click in the first Styles box and select a different color (the navy blue color, five down in the third column, for example). Click on OK.

3. Click inside the letter "M" in your banner text. This time, only the first letter is filled with the fill color you selected. That's because it is only filling that specific color area, rather than the entire selection (see Figure 7.7).

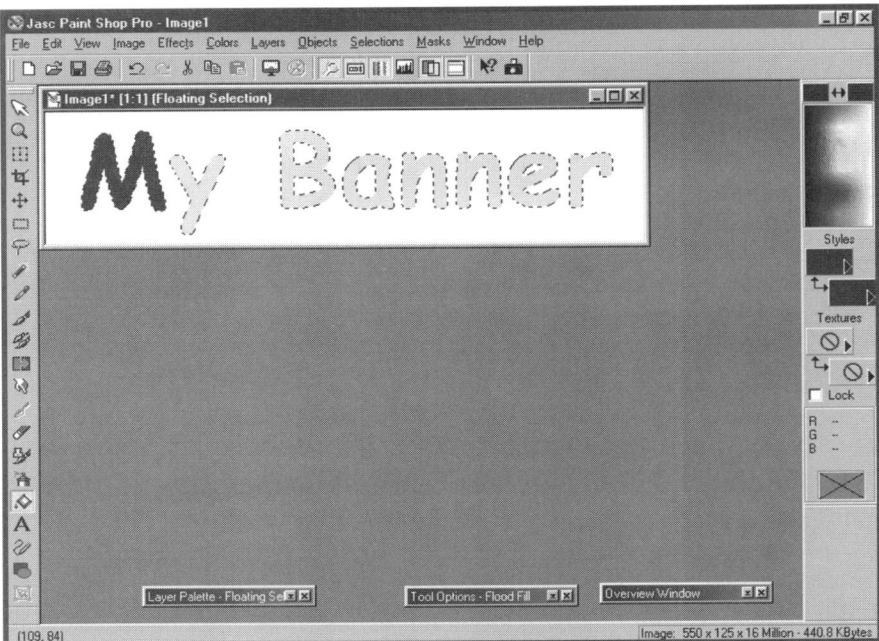

Figure 7.7

Only the first letter of the selected text is filled with the new fill color.

TIP

Clicking in a letter fills it with the color you selected as the foreground fill. If you've also selected a color for the background fill (in the second box under Styles), right-clicking inside a letter fills it with that color.

The Tool Options palette for the Flood Fill tool offers many additional Blend mode and Match mode options that you can use to define how the Flood Fill tool will fill your text or other objects. The Blend modes, as their name implies, control how the color pixels of your fill blend with the underlying color pixels. The Match modes, on the other hand, control what actually gets filled. A Match mode of None, as you've seen, fills the entire selection with the fill, whereas RGB Value fills a specific color area. Feel free to experiment with some of the other Blend and Match modes to see what they do.

There are two other settings in the Tool Options palette for the Flood Fill tool that you haven't done anything with yet: the Tolerance and Opacity controls. Increasing the Tolerance setting increases the range within which a fill operates—for instance, if you've specified an RGB Value match mode, increasing the Tolerance value includes a wider tonal range of the underlying color in the fill. This can be helpful if the underlying color that you want to fill is textured or otherwise not flat. Increasing the Opacity setting, on the other hand, decreases how much of the underlying color shows through your fill color.

Using Textures

Paint Shop Pro 7 provides a variety of different textures that you can combine with your solid colors and other fills. To experiment with different textures, follow these steps.

1. With the Flood Fill tool still selected, click on the arrow in the first box under Textures (in the Color palette). Click on the texture icon (the left icon), instead of the null icon.

2. Click on that same box to open the Texture dialog box. Click on the currently selected texture (see Figure 7.8).

3. Click on one of the textures to select it (the Gravel texture, for example). Click on OK.

4. Under Styles in the Color palette, click on the first box and select a new foreground fill color (the blue-green color, fourth down in the third column, for example). Remember, if you don't select a color that is different than the earlier fill color you applied, the texture won't show up. Click on OK.

5. Click inside the letter "y" in your text banner. Your selected fill color is now combined with the texture you just selected, as shown in Figure 7.9.

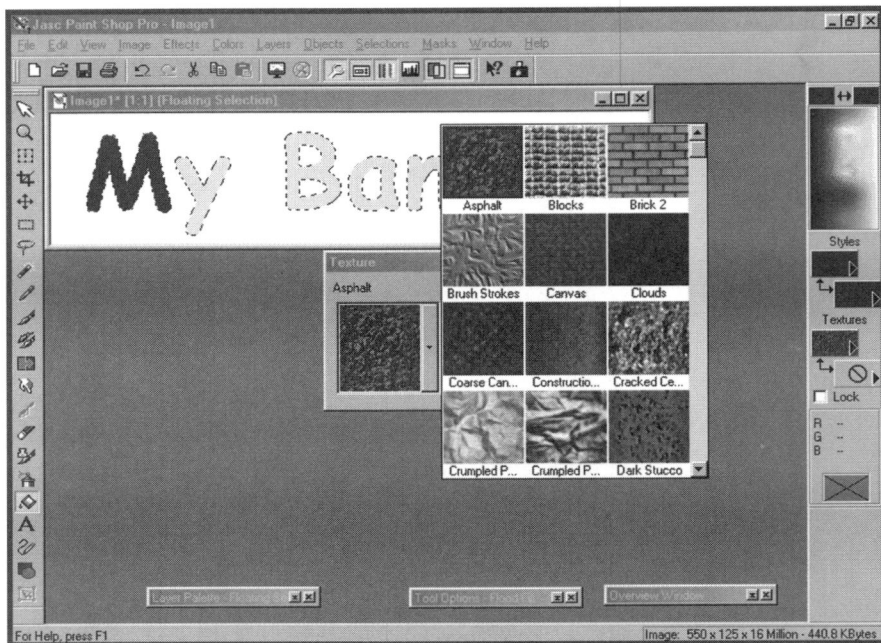

Figure 7.8

Paint Shop Pro 7 provides a broad range of textures that you can use in your fills.

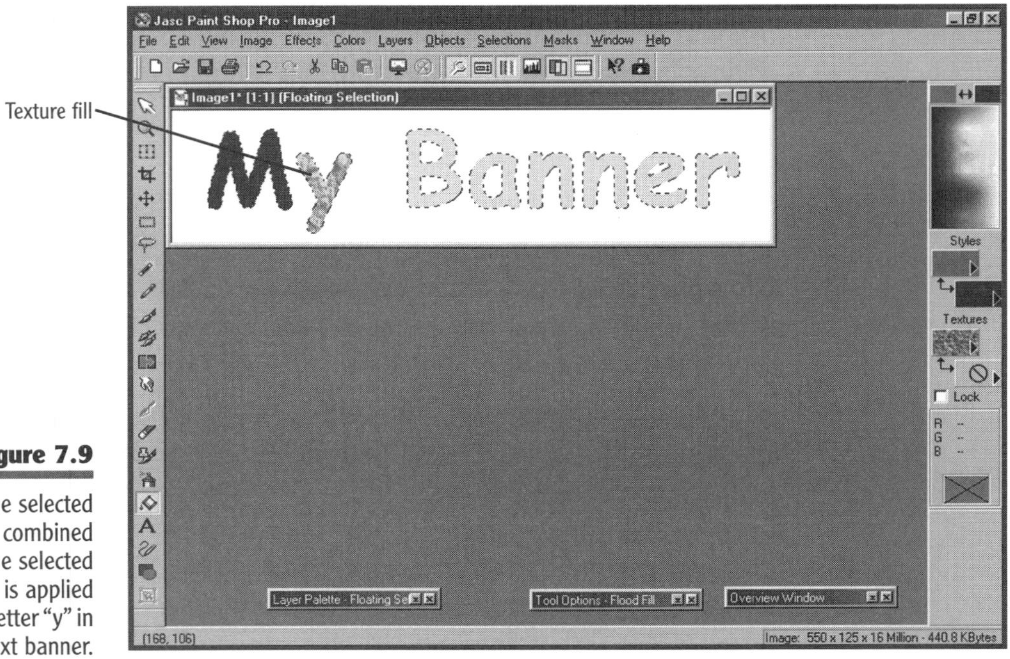

Texture fill

Figure 7.9

The selected texture, combined with the selected fill color, is applied to the letter "y" in the text banner.

Using Pattern Fills

With a pattern fill, you can fill an area with a pattern based on a selected image file. Paint Shop Pro 7 includes a variety of different pattern fills that you can apply to your images. To apply a pattern fill, follow these steps.

1. In the Color palette, click on the arrow in the first Textures box and choose the null value to turn off the texture fill.

2. Click on the arrow in the first Styles box and choose the Pattern value (third from the left).

3. Click on that same box to open the Pattern dialog box. Click on the selected pattern to display the available patterns (see Figure 7.10).

4. Click on any pattern that you want to use (the Grainy pattern, for instance). Leave the other settings as they are. Click on OK.

5. Click inside the letter "B" in your text banner. The pattern you selected now fills the letter, as shown in Figure 7.11.

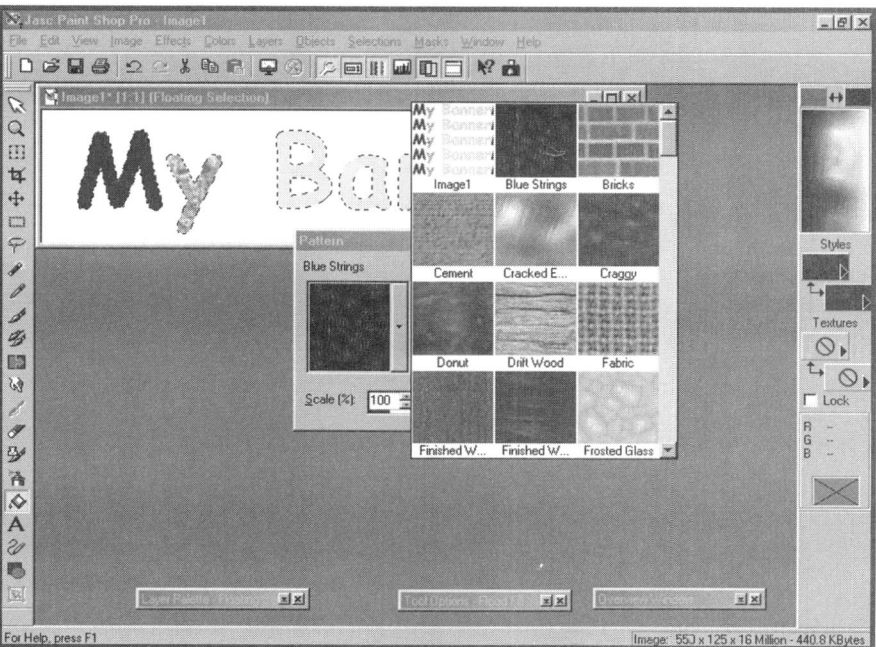

Figure 7.10

Paint Shop Pro provides a variety of different patterns that can be used as fills.

Pattern fill

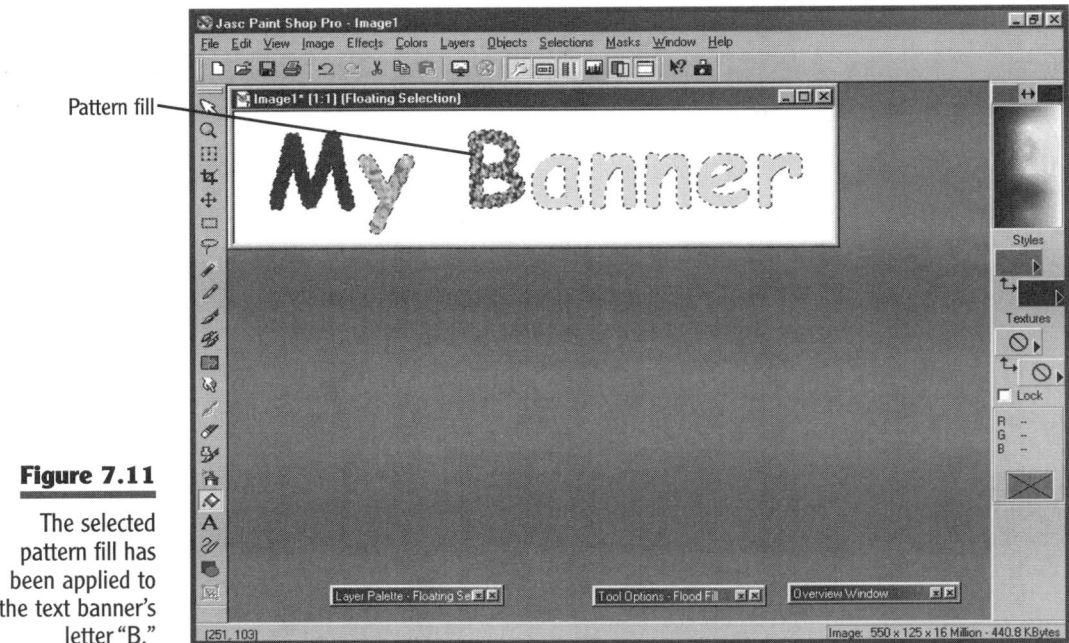

Figure 7.11

The selected pattern fill has been applied to the text banner's letter "B."

You're not limited to only using the pattern images provided with Paint Shop Pro. Many background images that you can use are available on the Web. There are two ways to make additional pattern images available. The first way is simply to open an image you want to use as a pattern in Paint Shop Pro 7. Any image that is open in Paint Shop Pro 7 will be automatically available, along with the other pattern images.

If you want a particular pattern image to be permanently displayed along with the other pattern images, regardless of whether it is open in Paint Shop Pro 7, just open the background image and then resave it as a BMP image (select Windows or OS/2 Bitmap (*.bmp) from the Save as Type menu) in the folder where Paint Shop Pro stores its patterns (\Program Files\Jasc Software Inc\Paint Shop Pro 7\Patterns). It will then be displayed along with the other pattern image files.

You can also specify alternative paths where pattern images can be found. In the Pattern dialog box, just click on the Edit Paths button. For example, there are pattern images in BMP format available in the Windows folder—just click on the Browse button to the right of the second text box, click on the Windows folder, and then click on OK. To also include any BMP files that might be present in subfolders under the Windows folder, click on the Use Sub Folders check box and then click on OK. Now, when you access the list of patterns in the Pattern dialog box, any BMP files included in the Windows folder or any of its subfolders will be displayed along with the other pattern files.

TIP

Paint Shop Pro 7 also has a nifty feature that lets you create your own seamless background patterns. Just open an image that includes an area you want to use as a background pattern, choose the Selection tool from the Tool palette (the sixth tool down), draw a rectangle around the area you want to use, and then choose Selections, Convert to Seamless Pattern.

Using Gradient Fills

A *gradient fill* blends two or more colors into a single fill effect. You can use several kinds of gradient fill effects, including linear, rectangular, sunburst, and radial. In a linear gradient, the colors are blended in a single direction (either left to right, up and down, or at an angle). The other three gradient effects blend their colors in various manners from the inside to the outside of the fill area. For your example banner graphic, you'll be using a linear gradient fill to fill the remaining letters in the banner text.

1. With the Flood Fill tool still selected, click on the arrow in the first Styles box and choose the Gradient value.

2. At the top of the Color palette, click on the first of the two side-by-side color boxes and select a foreground color to use in your gradient fill. (For example, select the bright red color, which is the first color in the first column of Basic Colors.) Click on OK.

3. Next, click on the second of the two side-by-side color boxes and select a background color to use in your gradient fill. (For example, select the bright yellow color, which is the second color in the first column of Basic Colors.) Click on OK.

4. Now, click on the first Styles box to open the Gradient dialog box. Click on the selected gradient to display the available gradients (see Figure 7.12). For now, just click on the currently highlighted gradient (Foreground-Background) to reselect it.

5. The only problem is that you want the yellow color to be at the top and the red color to be at the bottom of your gradient fill. No problem! Just check the Invert Gradient check box and the colors in your gradient will be inverted.

6. In the Style area of the Gradient dialog box, you can choose from the four different types of gradient fills. For now, just leave the linear gradient option (the top option) selected. Click on OK.

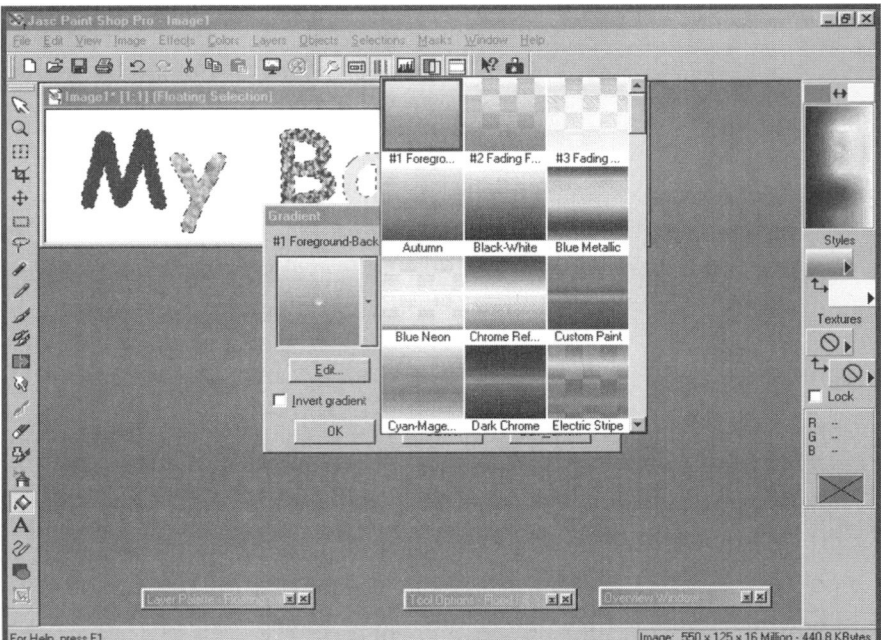

Figure 7.12

Paint Shop Pro 7 offers a number of preset gradient fills that you can use.

7. In the Tool Options palette, make sure that the Match mode is set to RGB Value. Now click inside each of the remaining letters ("anner") in your text object to fill them with the specified gradient fill (see Figure 7.13).

You've just scratched the surface of working with gradient fills. In the Gradient dialog box, you can change the angle of your gradient fill, specify a repeat value, and edit the selected gradient. You can also save your own custom gradients so that you can use them later.

TIP

If you decide you don't like the results of a particular effect, you can use Paint Shop Pro 7's Undo feature to walk back through your previous steps. Just select Edit and the particular Undo step that is presented. Alternatively, you can press Ctrl+Z to do this. There is no limit to how many steps you can undo. If you want to walk back through all the steps involved in creating your image, you can do it. You can also redo an undone step. Just select Edit and the particular Redo step that is presented.

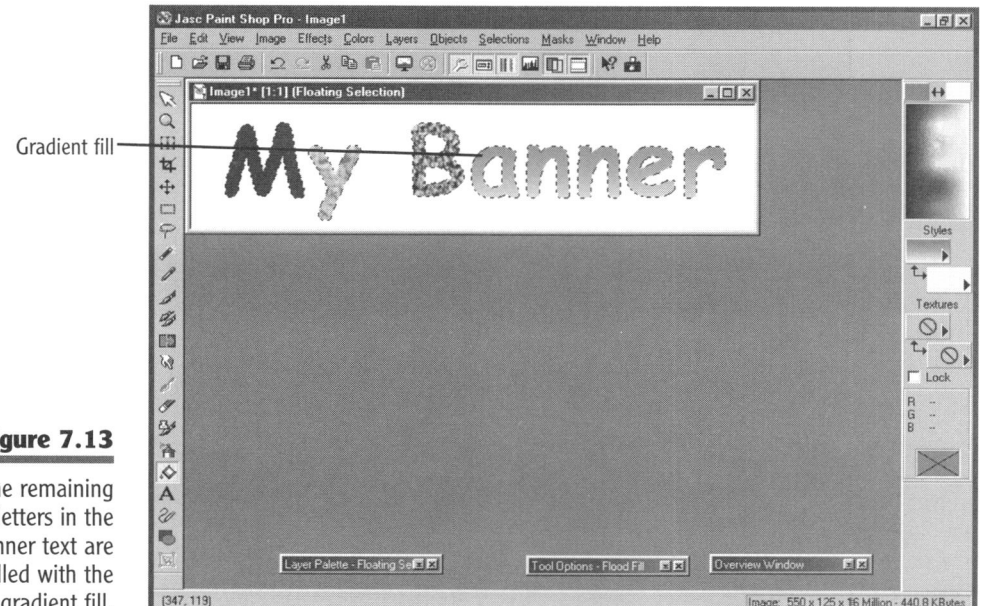

Figure 7.13

The remaining letters in the banner text are filled with the linear gradient fill.

Gradient fill

Working with Layers

Paint Shop Pro 7 lets you work in multiple layers when creating an image. This lets you assign a color, pattern, or other effect to your image's background layer, while assigning a text object to a separate layer, for example. This can be handy when you're creating images that use antialiased text or other blending effects (such as a Drop Shadow effect) that you want to display transparently against an HTML file's background image or color. By placing your background and your text object on separate layers, you can easily change the color of the background layer of your image to match an HTML file's background color or image, without having to recreate your text object.

NOTE The following steps use a floating palette, the Layer palette. When you install Paint Shop Pro 7, the Layer palette bar is displayed by default in the work area. If the Layer palette isn't displayed, just select View, Toolbars, and make sure that the Layer Palette option is checked.

If you pass the mouse over the Layer palette's minimized title bar, you'll notice that your image currently has one layer, the Background layer, while your text object is a floating selection on top of that layer (see Figure 7.14).

In the following steps, you'll add a new layer to your image, with your text object as a floating object on top of the new layer.

1. With the Layer palette unrolled, click on the Background layer bar so that it is highlighted (rather than the Floating Selection bar).

Figure 7.14

The Layer palette shows the layers and floating selections present in the image.

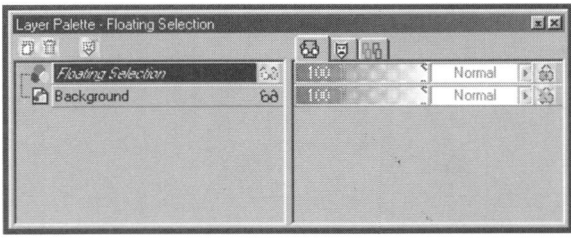

2. Click on the Create Layer icon (the first icon in the upper-left corner of the palette). In the Layer Properties dialog box, leave all the options as they are: Name (Layer2), Blend mode (Normal), Opacity (100), Group (0). Leave the Lock Transparency option unchecked, and leave all other check boxes checked, as shown in Figure 7.15. Click on OK.

3. Now if you pass the mouse over the Layer palette bar to unroll it, you'll notice that a new layer, Layer2, has been added between your text object (the floating selection) and the background layer (see Figure 7.16).

4. In the Layer palette, click on the Floating Selection bar to reselect it. (If you don't do this, you won't be able to make further changes to your text object.)

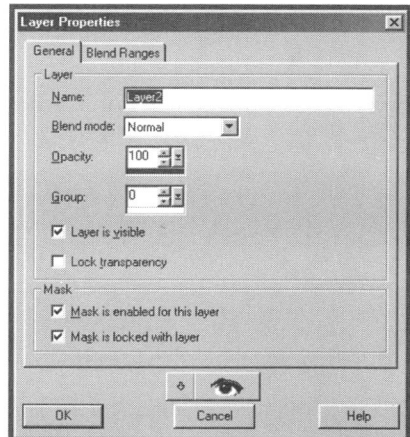

Figure 7.15

The Layer Properties dialog box defines the properties for a new layer.

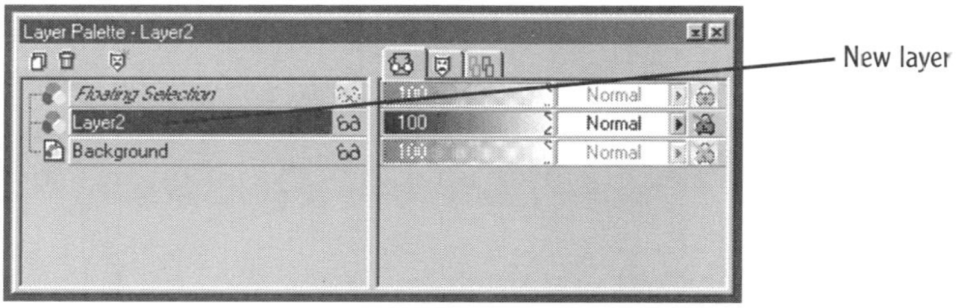

Figure 7.16

A new layer has been added between the Background layer and the text object (Floating Selection).

You won't be doing anything right now with the new layer, but a little later on, when you're creating a transparent GIF image, you'll see one of the benefits of working with separate layers, rather than having everything in your image on a single layer.

In the Layer palette, you can delete any layer, other than the Background layer, by first selecting it and then clicking on the Delete Layer icon (the icon that looks like a garbage can). Don't do that now, however—just remember it in case you need to delete a layer at some point in the future.

Creating 3D Effects

Paint Shop Pro 7 includes quite a few different effects that you can use to give your text object more of a 3D look. In this section, you'll be using several of the more useful ones.

Using the Inner Bevel Effect

Paint Shop Pro 7's Inner Bevel effect is a good way to add some 3D emphasis to your text object. To apply the Inner Bevel effect, just follow these steps.

1. Your text object should still be selected. Select Effects, 3D Effects, Inner Bevel.

2. To see the available bevel forms, click on the Bevel box (see Figure 7.17). Select the rounded bevel form (the second one in the first row).

3. Set the following values: Width (5), Smoothness (35), Depth (5), Ambience (0), Shininess (0), Color (White), Angle (315), Intensity (55), and Elevation (30). Click on the Proof button (the eye icon) to proof the effect. (Move the Inner Bevel dialog box out of the way so that you can see your text object, as shown in Figure 7.18). If you like what you see, click on OK. (You might need to move the dialog box back up if the OK button isn't showing.)

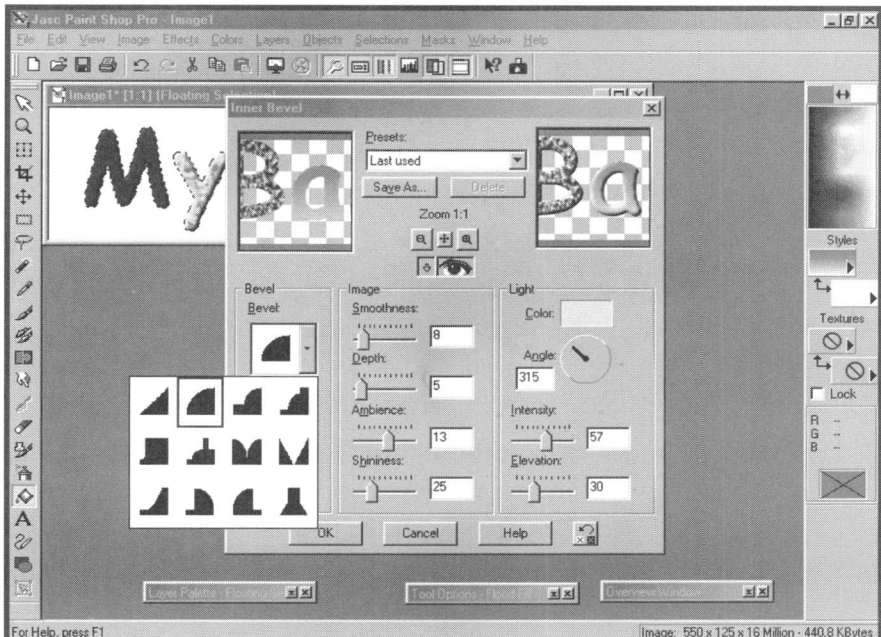

Figure 7.17

When using the Inner Bevel effect, you can choose from 12 different bevels forms.

Proof button

Figure 7.18

The Inner Bevel effect can help give your object even more of a 3D look.

Using the Cutout Effect

The Cutout effect is another of Paint Shop Pro 7's 3D effects. You don't need to stick to just a single effect—you can combine more than one effect to get different and varying effects. To apply a cutout effect to your text, just follow these steps.

1. Your text object should still be selected. Select Effects, 3D Effects, Cutout. The Cutout dialog box appears.

2. First, uncheck the Fill Interior with Color check box. Notice that the fill effects you created earlier are now showing through the cutout effect shown in the preview window.

3. Click on the Shadow Color box and choose a different color for the cutout shadow. For example, choose the lighter yellow color, second down in the sixth column of the Basic Colors. Click on OK.

4. Set the Vertical and Horizontal Offset values to 5. Set the Opacity value to 80. Set the Blur value to 5, as shown in Figure 7.19.

5. To proof what your cutout effect will look like if applied to your text object, just click on the eye icon. You might have to move the Cutout dialog box out of the way to see your text object. Click on OK.

Figure 7.19

The Cutout effect is another way to give your text and other objects more of a 3D look.

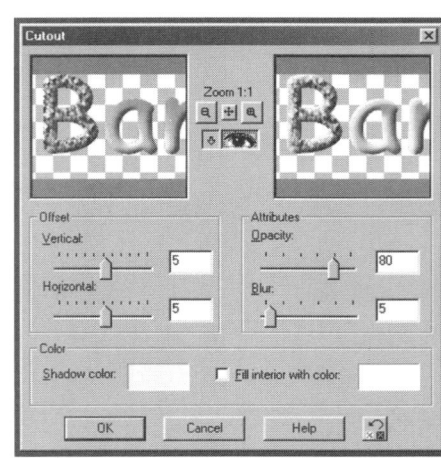

TIP

■ ■
To automatically proof your changes while creating them, just click on the down arrow
to the left of the eye icon.
■ ■

Creating a Drop Shadow Effect

Using a Drop Shadow effect can be a great way to set off your text object
from the background and give it a 3D look. To add a drop shadow to
your "My Banner" text object, just follow these steps.

1. The "My Banner" text should still be selected. Select Effects, 3D
   Effects, Drop Shadow.

2. In the Drop Shadow dialog box, click on the Color box to select
   the color you want to use for the drop shadow. For example,
   choose the reddish-brown color, which is the second color over in
   the first row. Click on OK.

3. Set both the Vertical Offset and Horizontal Offset to 6, the
   Opacity value to 70, and the Blur value to 10. Click on the eye
   icon to proof your settings (see Figure 7.20). Click on OK.

Figure 7.20

A Drop Shadow
effect can really
help to set off your
text object from
your image's
background.

Saving Your Image as a Paint Shop Pro 7 Image

To preserve the layers in an image so that you can edit their contents later, you need to save your image as a Paint Shop Pro 7 image. If you save your image as a GIF or JPEG image, the layers will be collapsed to a single layer. To save your image as a Paint Shop Pro 7 (*.psp) file, follow these steps.

1. Select File, Save. If Paint Shop Pro 7's Images folder is not already selected, click in the Save In box, click on your hard drive's icon (C:), and then navigate to the Program Files, Jasc Software Inc, Paint Shop Pro 7, Images folder.

2. Type **mybanner** as the image name and click on the Save button.

If you later reopen the image, all the characteristics it had when you saved it will be preserved, including layers, selected areas, and so on.

Take a Break!

This is a good place to take a quick break, if you think you need it. Get up and shake your arms and legs to loosen up and get the circulation flowing. Grab a snack or something to drink if you're hungry or thirsty. I'll see you back here in five minutes or so, and you'll learn how to create transparent GIF images and optimized color palettes.

Creating a Transparent GIF Image

If you save your image as a GIF (CompuServe Graphics Interchange Format) image, you can set one of the colors in the image to be transparent. This can be especially effective when you're displaying the image against a Web page's background image. The following steps show you how to save your image as a transparent GIF image.

1. Select Colors, Set Palette Transparency.

2. When prompted to reduce the image to a single layer, click on Yes.

3. In the Decrease Color Depth – 256 Colors dialog box, leave Optimized Median Cut selected as the Palette type. For the Reduction method, select Error Diffusion. Select the Reduce Color Bleeding check box. Leave the other two check box options unchecked, as shown in Figure 7.21. Click on OK.

4. You're now presented with the Set Palette Transparency dialog box. To assign the actual color of the image's background as the transparent color, click the mouse inside the image's background. Make sure that you click away from the drop shadow. The R, G, and B values displayed next to the cursor should all be 255, denoting that the underlying color is pure white, as shown in Figure 7.22. Click on OK.

5. To check out your transparent color, select Colors, View Palette Transparency. Notice that the area that will be transparent is now displayed in a checkerboard pattern (see Figure 7.23).

6. To turn off display of the palette transparency, just select Colors, View Palette Transparency again.

Figure 7.21

You can create an optimized color palette for your image that includes only colors included in the image.

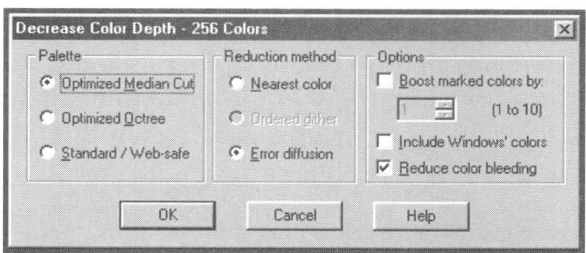

Figure 7.22

Transparent color

The white color in the image's background is set to be transparent.

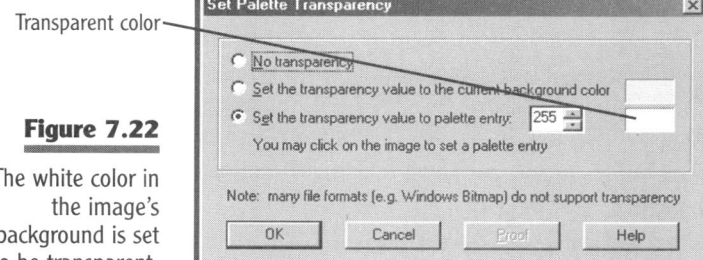

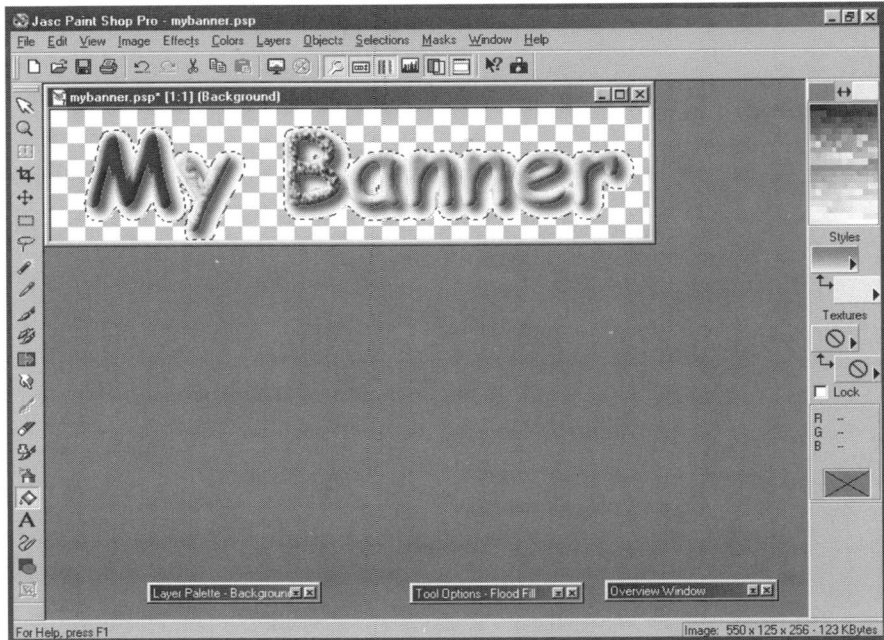

Figure 7.23

When you view
the palette
transparency, it is
displayed in a
checkerboard
pattern.

7. To save your transparent image, select File, Save As. The folder where you previously saved your image should still be selected (Paint Shop Pro 7's Images folder). Select CompuServe Graphics Interchange (*.gif) as the file type. (You'll notice that the file name automatically changes to mybanner.gif.)

8. To also save your image as an interlaced image, click on the Options button. Leave the Version 89a radio button selected and select the Interlaced radio button. Click on OK and then click on the Save button.

 **NOTE** Interlacing causes the image to be displayed progressively as it is still being downloaded. This allows a viewer to see the whole image, just not entirely resolved, while it is still being downloaded.

Now, when you display your image in a Web page, the page's background will show through the transparent area of your image.

Viewing Your Image in FrontPage

If you want to check out how your banner looks in a Web page, just insert it into a page in your FrontPage Web. To see the transparency effect, you'll need to specify a background image for your page. Because the current transparency color for your image is white, you'll need to choose a light background image with a significant amount of white in it.

TIP

If you don't already know which background image you want to use, you can use Paint Shop Pro 7's Browse feature to view thumbnails of all available images in a folder. Just select File, Browse, and then click on any folder that has images you want to browse. If the image you want to use is not a GIF (*.gif) or JPEG (*.jpg) image, just open it in Paint Shop Pro 7 and then resave it as a GIF or JPEG image.

To specify a background image for a non-themed page in FrontPage:

1. Right-click on your page's background and select Page Properties. (Alternatively, you can select File, Properties.) Click on the Background tab.

2. Under Formatting, select the Background Picture check box and then click on the Browse button to choose the background image you want to use.

Figure 7.24 shows a hypothetical FrontPage page with mybanner.gif displayed against a light-colored background image (with white as a significant color).

If you're using a theme to format your page, you can either choose a theme that'll work with your transparent GIF (in this case, one with a light-colored background image with a significant amount of white in it), or

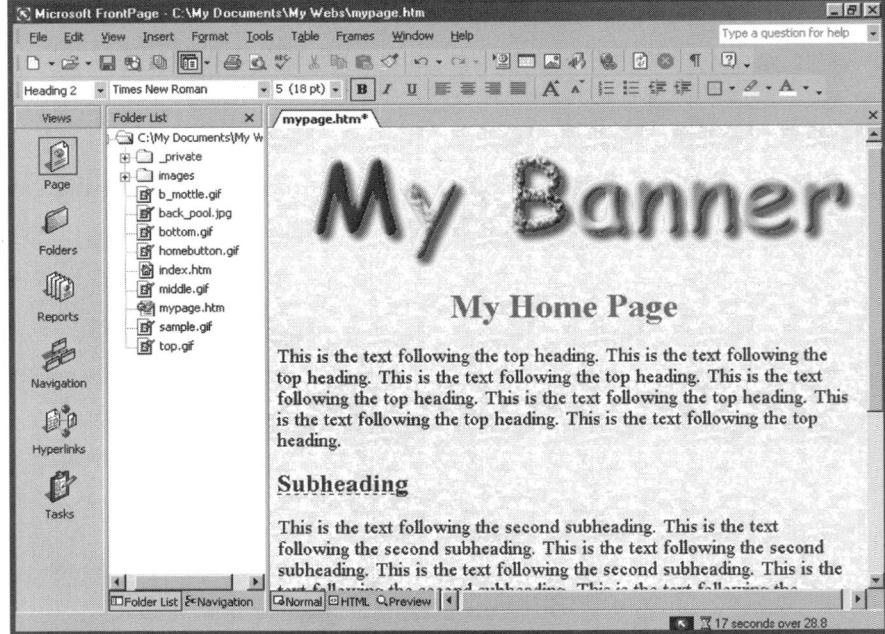

Figure 7.24

The background
image shows
through the
transparent areas
of mybanner.gif.

you can change the current background image in a theme you're already
using. To change the background image in a theme, follow these steps.

1. Select Format, Theme.

2. In the Themes dialog box, click on the Modify button and then
   click on the Graphics button.

3. With Background Picture selected from the Item list, click on
   the Browse button in the Picture tab to select the background
   image you want to use. Click on OK to close the Modify
   Themes dialog box.

4. To make sure that you don't overwrite the original theme, click
   on the Save As button and save your theme with a new name.
   Click on OK to close the Themes dialog box.

Displaying a Transparent GIF against a Non-White Background

If you display mybanner.gif against a non-white background (meaning, a background image without white as a significant color or a background color that is not white), a noticeable halo effect will appear around the banner text. This halo is the area where the Drop Shadow effect blends with the color of your image's background. In this case, it blends from brown (the color of the Drop Shadow effect) to white (the color of the image background). Figure 7.25 shows mybanner.gif displayed against a darker background image, so that you can see what the halo effect looks like.

This halo effect can be a problem not only when using a Drop Shadow effect with a transparent background, but with any effect that blends pixels with the image's background color. Even plain text without any Drop Shadow effect can display a halo effect if antialiasing has been set, because antialiasing smooths out curves and diagonals in a font face by blending pixels at the edge of the font face with the background.

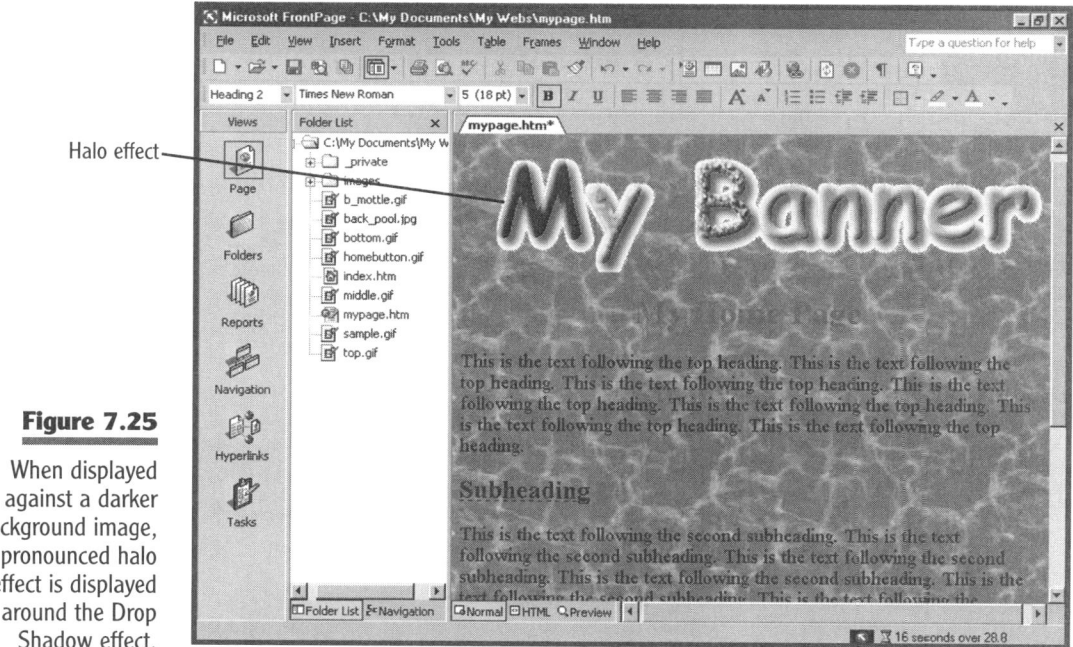

Figure 7.25

When displayed against a darker background image, a pronounced halo effect is displayed around the Drop Shadow effect.

The solution is to match the color of your image's background with the color of your Web page's background. To do that, just follow these steps.

1. First, in Paint Shop Pro 7, close mybanner.gif and reopen the copy of mybanner.psp that you saved earlier. (After selecting the File menu option, you should see mybanner.psp listed at the bottom of the menu—just click on it to open it.)

2. Next, open the background image you want to use in your Web page. You can use the Browse feature (select File, Browse) described earlier to locate a background image you want to use. For example, using the Browse feature, go to Paint Shop Pro's Patterns folder (C:\Program Files\Jasc Software Inc\Paint Shop Pro 7\Patterns).

NOTE Paint Shop Pro 7's pattern files are in BMP format. If you want to use the same image as a background to your Web page, resave it as a GIF or JPEG image.

3. Select the Flood Fill tool from the Tool palette. If the second box under Styles does not already display a solid fill color, click on the box's arrow and select the solid fill option.

4. Select the Dropper tool from the Tool palette and pass the cursor (now shaped like an eye dropper) over the background image. You'll see the color currently located under the cursor displayed in the Current Color box at the bottom of the Color palette.

5. Look for the most common color (or the most neutral color) that is present within the image. When you see the color you want, right-click on it to assign the color as the background fill color. The color is assigned to both the background color box (the second box) at the top of the Color palette and the second color box under Styles.

6. Click back on the title bar of mybanner.psp to reselect it. Choose Selections, Select None. (Before you can apply a fill to the image's background layer, you have to turn off any selections.)

7. Unroll the Layer palette and click on the Background layer to select it. Select the Flood Fill tool from the Tool palette and right-click it in your image's background. The color you assigned earlier with the Dropper tool is applied to the image's background layer, with the text's drop shadow blending with that color (see Figure 7.26).

You now need to set your image's background color as transparent and save your image as a GIF image.

1. Select Colors, Set Palette Transparency to set the color of your image's background as transparent. Click on Yes to reduce the image to a single layer.

2. This is important! In the Decrease Color Depth – 256 Colors dialog box, leave Optimized Median Cut selected, but select Nearest Color as the reduction method. (If you select the Error Diffusion reduction method, your background color might end up getting diffused as more than one color, which you don't want

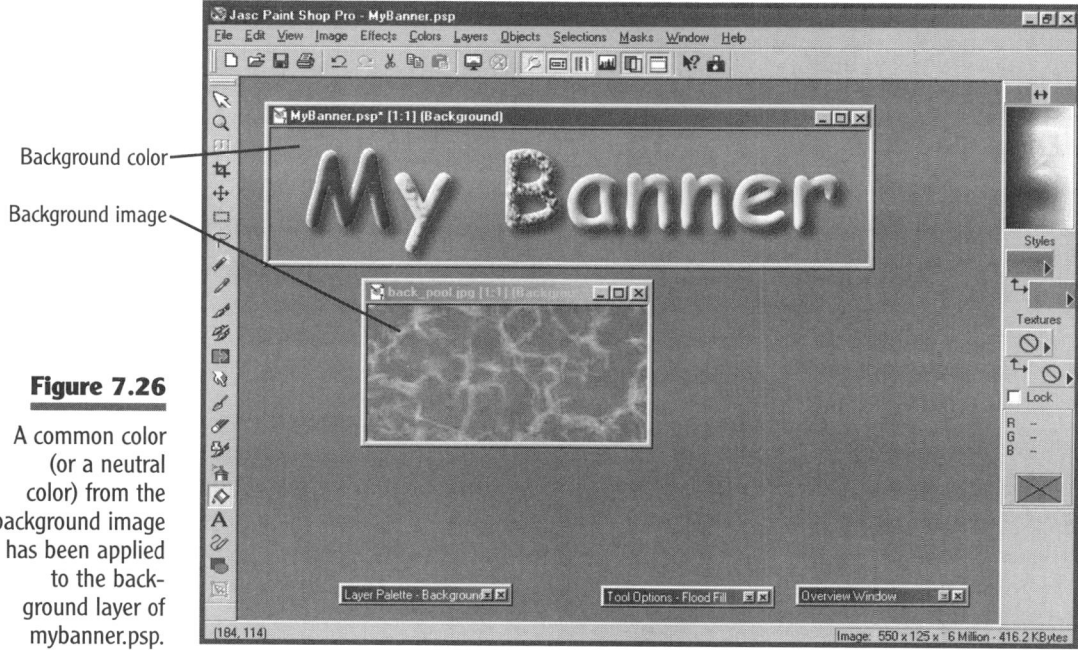

Background color

Background image

Figure 7.26

A common color (or a neutral color) from the background image has been applied to the background layer of mybanner.psp.

because you can only assign one color as transparent. See the Tip on page 273, however, for a workaround.) Click on OK.

3. In the Set Palette Transparency dialog box, click the mouse inside your image's background (but away from the Drop Shadow effect). Click on OK. (If you want to view your image's transparency, select Colors, View Palette Transparency.)

4. To save your image as a GIF image, select File, Save Copy As. Paint Shop Pro 7's Images folder should still be selected. Select CompuServe Graphics Interchange (*.gif) as the file type. If you don't want to save over the earlier copy of your image (with the white background), type a new file name (mybanner2.gif, for instance). Click on Save.

Figure 7.27 shows a hypothetical FrontPage page with mybanner2.gif displayed against the background image that was used to assign its background color. Notice that the Drop Shadow effect no longer has a white halo around it, and it blends seamlessly with the background.

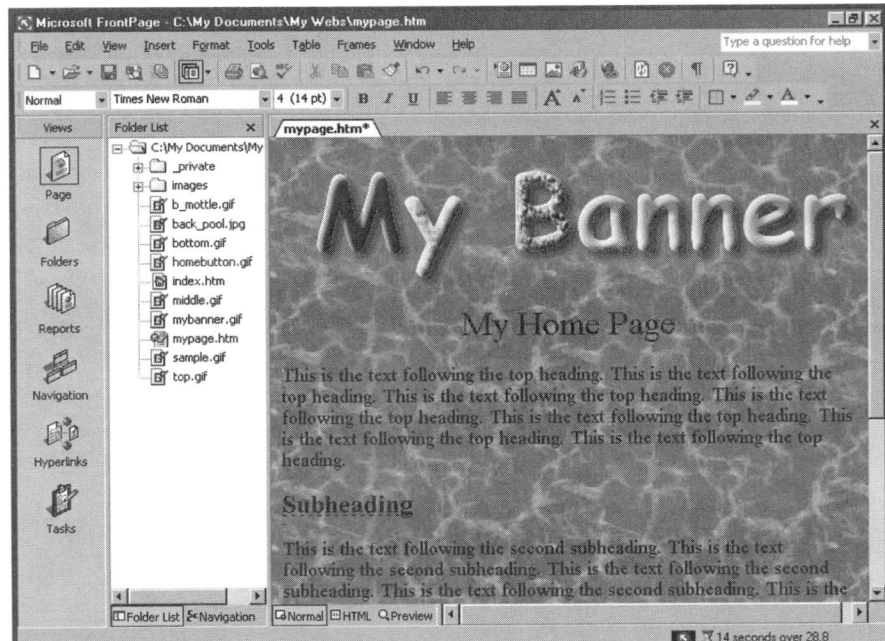

Figure 7.27

With their backgrounds now matched, mybanner.gif's drop shadow blends seamlessly with the Web page's background image.

TIP

As noted in the previous example, if you select Error Diffusion when creating an optimized palette for an image with a colored background, the likely result is that the background color will be diffused into more than one color. The solution to this problem is to refill the image's background using an RGB Value fill, but with the Tolerance value set high enough (at 20, for instance) so that it replaces the multiple shades of color in the background with a single color. Then, just reassign the image's background color as transparent.

Creating 3D Buttons

Paint Shop Pro 7's Buttonize effect lets you create your own 3D buttons. Buttons can be used for individual links or combined to create menus of links.

Starting Your Button

Go ahead and close or minimize any image windows you have open in Paint Shop Pro 7 and then start a new image.

1. Select File, New. Set the Width to 150 and the Height to 75.

2. Leave the other settings as they are: Resolution (72), Background Color (White), and Image Type (16.7 million colors). Click on OK.

Filling the Background with a Pattern Fill

To give your button image a more textured look, you'll be applying a pattern fill to your button's surface. To do this, follow these steps.

1. Select the Flood Fill tool from the Tool palette.

2. Click on the arrow in the first Styles box and select the Pattern value.

3. Click inside the first Styles box to open the Pattern dialog box. Click on the pattern that you want to use. For this example, click on the Stained Wood pattern. Click on OK.

4. Click the mouse inside the image window. The background of the image is filled with the wood grain pattern you just selected.

Resizing Your Image

One trick for creating sharper and smoother text in your Web images is to increase the size of your image, create your text, and then reduce the the size of your image back to what you actually want to use. This can result in smoother diagonals and curves in your fonts. To do this:

1. Select Image, Resize. The Resize dialog box appears.

2. Make sure that the Maintain Aspect Ratio check box is checked. In the Resize Type menu, make sure that Smart Size is selected.

3. Select the Percentage of Original radio button and type **200** in the Width box. The Height box should automatically change to match (see Figure 7.28). Click on OK.

The dimensions (height and width) of your image are doubled, quadrupling the size of your image.

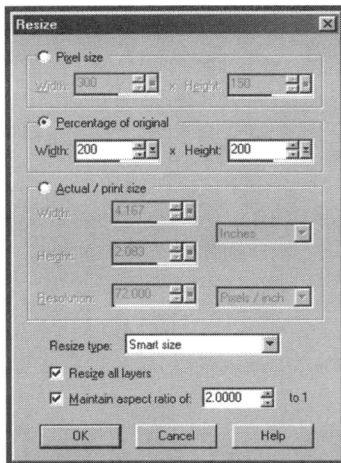

Figure 7.28

You can resize your image to a percentage of the original size.

Applying the Buttonize Effect

You can now apply Paint Shop Pro's Buttonize effect to give your image a 3D (button-like) appearance.

1. First you need to assign the shadow color that will be used to create the Buttonize effect. Click on the second of the two side-by-side color boxes at the top of the Color palette to select a background color. Select the color you want to use. For this example, select the dark brown color, which is the first color in the second column. Click on OK.

2. Select Effects, 3D Effects, Buttonize.

3. In the Buttonize dialog box, set 15 as the Height, 15 as the Width, and 75 as the Opacity (see Figure 7.29). Make sure that the Transparent Edge radio button is selected. To proof what your effect will look like when it is applied to your button, click on the eye icon. Click on OK.

Saving Your Blank Button

You might want to use your blank button later for creating additional buttons. Just select File, Save Copy As. Paint Shop Pro 7's Images folder should still be selected. Type a name for your image: blankbutton, for example. The Paint Shop Pro Image format should still be selected (if not, select it from the menu). Click on Save. Now, whenever you want to create a button using the effect you just created, just open blankbutton.psp.

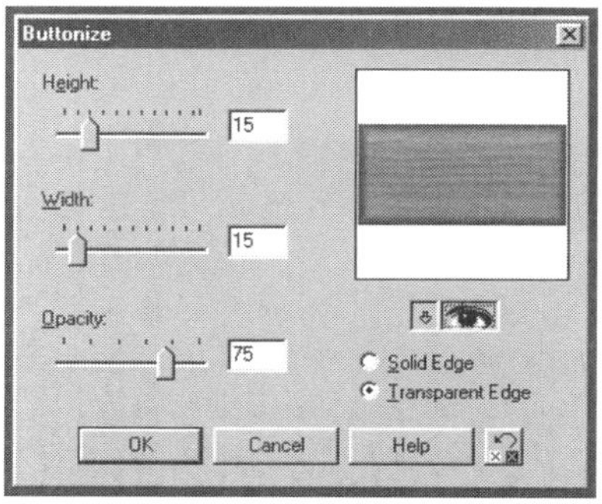

Figure 7.29

The Buttonize effect is applied to the image's wood pattern background, giving it a 3D look.

Adding Text to Your Button

Just a button by itself isn't much use. You need to create a label for the button to identify what it's for. For this example, you'll create a "Home" label, which identifies that the button is to be used to link to your home page.

1. Select the Text tool from the Tool palette and click it inside the button image.

2. For this example, select Arial as the font and type **68** as the font size. If Bold is not already selected, click on the B button to turn on bolding.

3. In the Styles section of the Text Entry dialog box, make sure that the null value is selected in the Stroke box. Make sure that a solid fill is specified in the Fill box.

4. Click inside the same Fill box (under Styles) and select a color for your text. For example, select the lighter lime-green color, which is the third color down in the sixth row. Click on OK.

5. Click inside the text window and delete the text that is there. Type **Home** as your new text. Make sure that the Floating radio button and Antialias check box are selected. Click on OK.

6. Click and drag the mouse to position your text in the middle of your button.

Applying Effects to Your Text

Because you've already run through applying the Pattern, Gradient, Inner Bevel, Cutout, and Drop Shadow effects, I'm not going to specifically spell out how to do that again. Feel free to experiment with applying any or all of those effects to your button's text object. Figure 7.30 shows what the button's text might look like with the Inner Bevel, Cutout, and Drop Shadow effects applied.

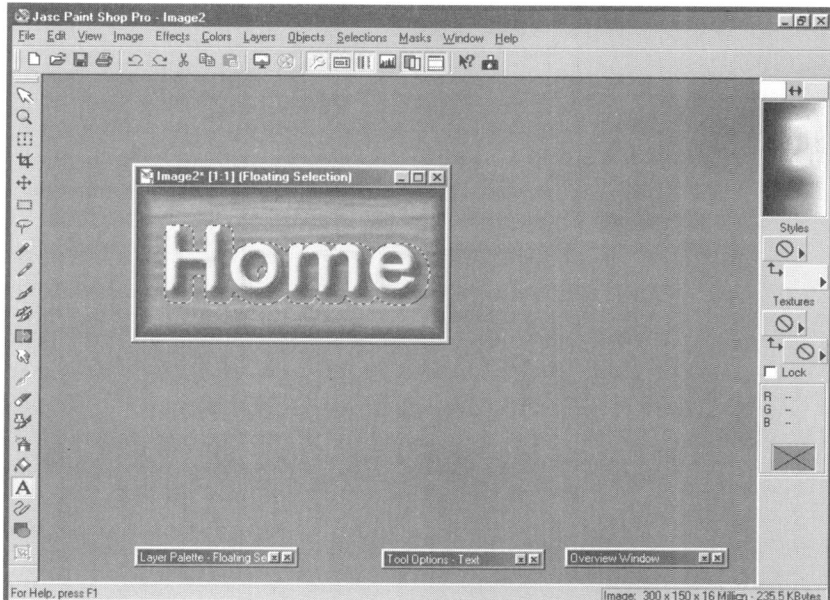

Figure 7.30

By applying different 3D effects to your button's text, you can give it even more of a 3D look.

Reducing the Size of Your Button

After you get the combination of effects that you want to use applied to your button's text, you'll need to reduce the size of your image to the actual size you want your button to be.

1. Select Image, Resize.
2. The Percentage of Original radio button should still be selected, as well as the Maintain Aspect Ratio check box. Type **50** in the Width box to reduce the dimensions of your image by 50 percent. The Height value should automatically change to match. Click on OK.

Saving Your Button

You might want to save your button as a Paint Shop Pro image so that you can come back and work on it later. Just follow the steps shown earlier for saving a copy of your image, but save it this time as mybutton.psp.

Optimizing Your Button

When you specified a transparent color for your banner graphic, you also created an optimized color palette that contained only colors included in the image. Although you won't be specifying a transparent color for your 3D button, you can still create an optimized color palette for it.

1. Select Colors, Decrease Color Depth, Xcolors (4/8 bit).

2. For starters, set 256 as the number of colors in your palette. Select the Optimized Median Cut radio button, the Error Diffusion radio button and the Reduce Color Bleeding check box, as shown in Figure 7.31. Click on OK.

3. Select File, Save As and save your image as a GIF image. Paint Shop Pro 7's Images folder should still be selected. Select CompuServe Graphics Interchange as the file type. Because you might want to create other types of buttons, give the image a name that designates its function, such as homebutton.gif.

Setting up Your Button as a Link in FrontPage

Setting up your new button so that it functions as a link is pretty easy.

1. Insert your button image where you want to display it in your page. Because it will function as a link back to your home page, you might want to place it near the bottom of your page. You could also center it (see Figure 7.32).

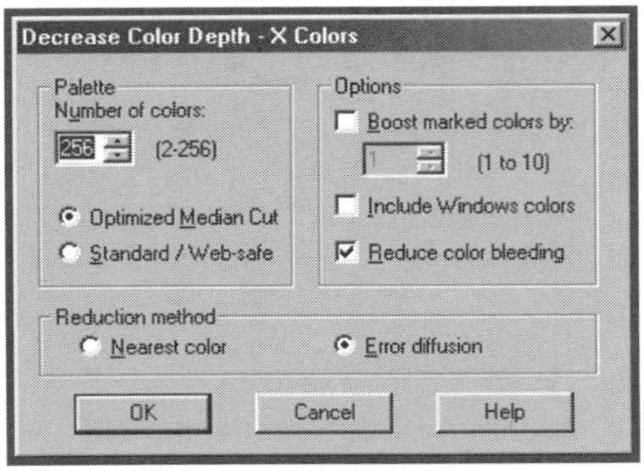

Figure 7.31

Saving your image with an optimized color palette lets you retain image quality while decreasing the file size.

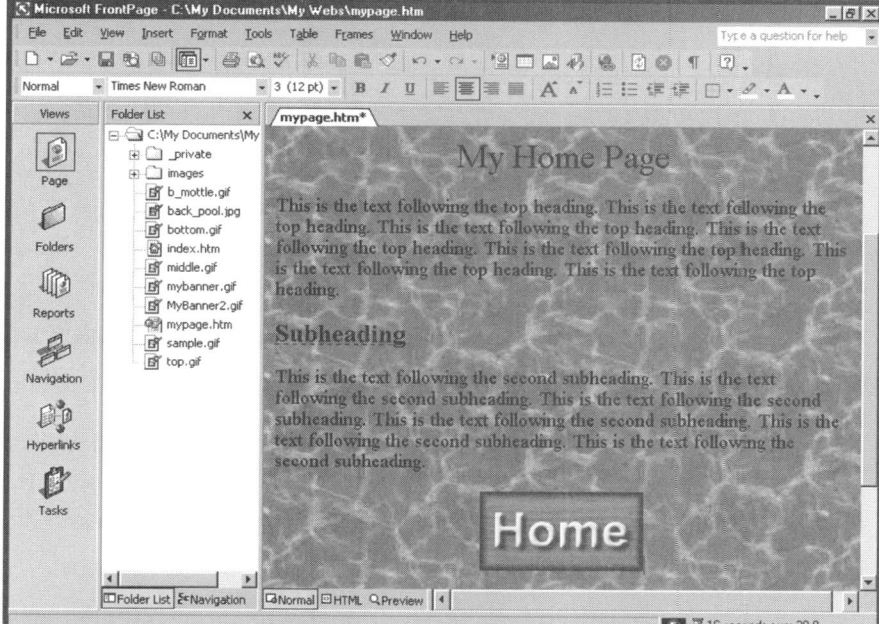

Figure 7.32

The Home button is
inserted into a
FrontPage page.

2. To set up the button image as a link, right-click on the image and select Hyperlink.

3. If the page to be linked is inside your FrontPage Web, just click on its file name in the folder window to assign it to the Address box (see Figure 7.33). If the page to be linked is located out on the World Wide Web (outside your FrontPage Web), just type its address in the Address box (http://www.yourserver.com/yoursite, for example).

4. If your Web page is located inside a frame, you might want to set the Target Frame parameter. Otherwise, the linked page will be displayed in the same frame as the current page. To specify the target for your link, click on the Target Frame button. To have the linked page open in the current browser window, select Whole Page. To have it open in a new browser window, select New Window. You can also target a specific frame by typing its name in the Target Setting box. Click on OK. Click on OK again to close the Insert Hyperlink dialog box.

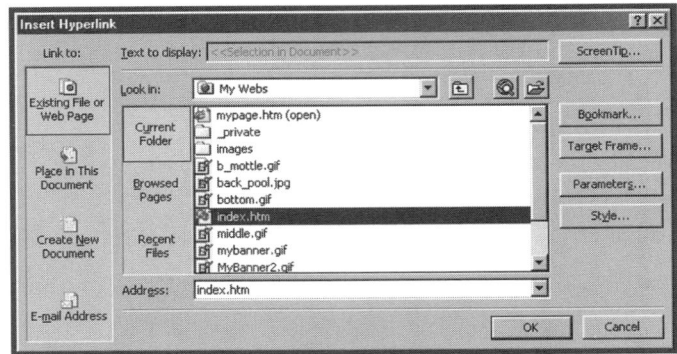

Figure 7.33

You can set the link for an image in the Insert Hyperlink dialog box.

To test your button link, just click on the Preview tab and then click on your button. (If your link is to a page that is out on the Web, you'll be prompted to connect to the Internet.) Click on the Normal tab to return to the page on which you're working.

Saving JPEG Images

So far, in this session you've only saved your Web images as GIF images. There is a reason for that—GIF images that include text will be sharper and clearer than corresponding JPEG images, even though GIF images can't include anywhere near as many colors as JPEG images.

The JPEG image format is best used with photographic images or images that feature a lot of continuous tone areas. If your image also includes a lot of gradients and blends that can't be properly represented in a GIF image, you might also want to save it as a JPEG image, although any text will be somewhat less sharp.

JPEG images use a *lossy* compression method. This means that color information is subtracted from the image to achieve smaller file sizes and can't be recovered after the subtraction has been done. The JPEG format's compression method allows images to retain a high degree of image quality in highly complex images containing many colors, while dramat- ically reducing the file size. (A *lossless* compression method, on the other hand, enables you to undo a compression, but you can't achieve the same level of file size savings as with the lossy method.)

Because JPEG images use a lossy method of compression, always save your original image in an uncompressed format before saving your image as a JPEG with compression turned on. To do this, just save it as a Paint Shop Pro 7 image, or in the native format of any other image editor you might be using. You can also save your image as an uncompressed JPEG (with a compression level of 1 set in Paint Shop Pro 7), although that'll also collapse any layers you've created.

The trick to optimizing your JPEG images is simply to find the optimum compression setting for your image, where you'll achieve the maximum amount of reduction in file size while retaining acceptable image quality. This varies from image to image; the optimum compression setting for one image can differ significantly from what it might be for another image.

In Paint Shop Pro 7, you set the compression setting when you save your image as a JPEG.

1. Select File, Save As. In the Save As dialog box, select the JPEG - JIF Compliant (*.jpg, *.jif, *.jpeg) format.

2. Click on the Options button. The Save Options dialog box appears (see Figure 7.34). Leave the Standard Encoding radio button selected. (Because some earlier browsers are not compatible, it is probably best to avoid selecting the Progressive Encoding option.)

3. Use the slider to select a compression setting for your image, or just type in the compression setting you want. Most images can take a compression setting of at least 30 without significant loss of image quality. How much higher you'll be able to increase the compres- sion setting without unacceptable loss of image quality depends on the particular image.

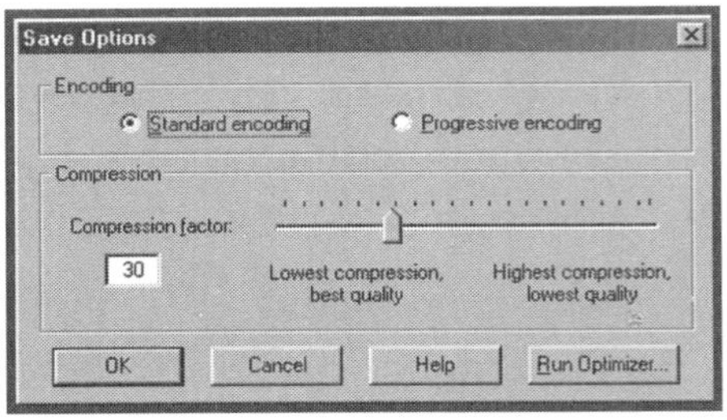

Figure 7.34

To reduce the size of a JPEG image, you need to increase the compression setting (but increase it too much, and you'll get a splotchy image).

Using the Optimizer

While still in the Save Options dialog box, you'll notice the Run Optimizer button in the bottom-right corner of the window. This allows you to run Paint Shop Pro 7's optimizer for finding the best compression level for your JPEG image. To use it, follow these steps.

1. Click on the Run Optimizer button.

2. Experiment with specifying different compression values, comparing the number of bytes saved against the relative quality of the compressed image. Figure 7.35 shows the result of a compression level of 20. At that level, the size of the file is reduced to around 3 kilobytes from an original size of around 12 kilobytes.

3. The Format tab lets you choose between creating a standard and a progressive JPEG. Because some older browsers do not support progressive JPEGs, you might want to stick to saving your JPEGs using the standard option.

4. The Download Times tab shows you the estimated download times at different connection speeds for the image at the selected compression level.

5. When you think you've found the optimum mix of file-size savings and image quality preservation, just click on OK to close the JPEG Optimizer. Click on Save to save your optimized image.

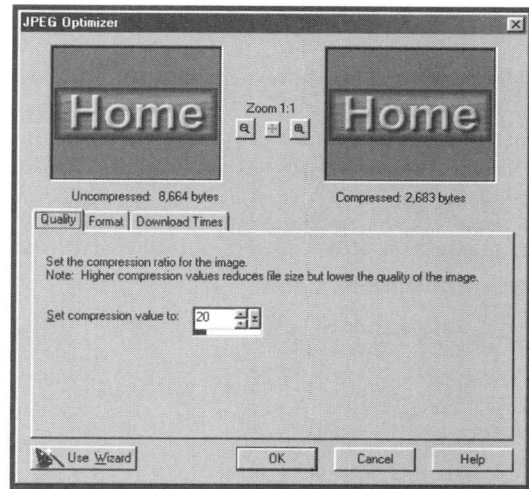

Figure 7.35

Paint Shop Pro 7's JPEG Optimizer makes optimizing your JPEG images a snap.

What's Next?

This is the end of the weekend! If you made it through everything, that's great! If you've skipped any of the sessions, feel free to come back next weekend to finish what you started this weekend. Finishing this session won't turn you into a graphics pro, but you should at least now know some of the tricks that the pros use to create more effective and appealing Web images. To become really proficient takes much longer than a single evening or a single weekend. What you've learned this evening should be a good start, however.

You'll also find additional material in this book's appendixes that you can peruse this weekend, if you've got the time, or you can come back next weekend to tackle them. Among other things, you'll find information in the appendixes to teach you how to:

○ Find a FrontPage Web server and publish your FrontPage pages on the Web

- Add interactive forms to your FrontPage pages
- Add multimedia effects, including sound, animation, and more, to your FrontPage pages
- Optimize your Web pages for the search engines and promote your pages
- Implement special features, such as password protection, inserting Java applets, and more

Publishing Your FrontPage 2002 Web Pages

After you've finished fine-tuning your FrontPage 2002 Web pages and spent some time learning how to create your own personalized Web art images, you're going to want to publish your Web pages on the Internet. Even if you haven't finished your site yet, you might want to experiment with publishing your Web pages anyway.

What You'll Need

Before you can start publishing your FrontPage 2002 Web pages on the Web, you need:

- A dial-up account or other connection to the Internet. This can be a local ISP or it can be a national ISP, such as the Microsoft Network, America Online, or CompuServe.

- A Web presence account, preferably with either the FrontPage 2002 or FrontPage 2000 server extensions installed for your account. Although you can also publish to a server without the FrontPage server extensions installed, you won't be able to include any of the features in your pages that require them.

NOTE If the Web Host you use supports FrontPage 2000 extensions but not FrontPage 2002 extensions, you'll be okay—for the most part. Some features new to FrontPage 2002 won't be supported, but everything else will be just fine. Contact your Web Host to inquire when they will be upgrading their extensions so that you can take full advantage of FrontPage 2002.

Getting on the Internet

You probably already have a dial-up account or other connection to the Internet. If not, however, you'll need to get connected to the Internet to publish your FrontPage 2002 Web pages on the Internet.

When shopping for an ISP, check whether the ISP provides free Web space with the FrontPage 2002 or FrontPage 2000 server extensions enabled. If so, that might save you from having to find a separate FrontPage Web host.

Finding a FrontPage Web Host

Many ISPs these days offer anywhere from two to ten or more megabytes of free Web space along with your dial-up account. Although most ISPs do not offer the FrontPage 2002 or 2000 server extensions, you might be lucky enough to find one that does. Check with your Internet provider to see whether they can enable the server extensions for your account.

If your ISP doesn't support the FrontPage server extensions, check to see whether any ISPs in your area include the FrontPage server extensions in your free Web space allotment. Keep in mind that changing your ISP would also mean changing your e-mail address. To take advantage of FrontPage features that require the server extensions, you'll need to find a separate FrontPage Web Host.

Finding a Free FrontPage Web Host

Yes, there is a free lunch! Some Web Hosts provide free Web space in exchange for the ability to sell pop-up or banner advertising that displays when visitors surf your Web pages. Some free Web Hosts also include the FrontPage server extensions at no extra cost. If you want to experiment with the different FrontPage features that require the server extensions, this can be a great option. Here's a brief listing of some free FrontPage Web Hosts.

FIND IT
ONLINE

- ❖ HyperMart at http://www.hypermart.net
- ❖ Web Provider at http://www.webprovider.com

- ✿ Tripod at http://www.tripod.com
- ✿ Tripod-UK at http://www.tripod.co.uk
- ✿ The DJ Café at http://www.members.djcafe.com
- ✿ Tony-Net at http://www.tony-net.net

NOTE When you're starting out, you might want to use one of the free FrontPage servers to experiment and play around with FrontPage 2002. If so, you need to keep the search engines from indexing your site until you're ready for prime time. You might also decide later that you want to publish your site to a for-pay FrontPage server. For information on how to keep search engines from indexing your site until you're ready to lift the curtain, see Appendix D, "Web Site Promotion Tips and Tricks."

Finding a For-Pay FrontPage Web Host

If you're putting up a business site, planning to get a domain name hosted, requiring more services, or desiring greater space and traffic allowances, you'll want to consider finding a for-pay, rather than free, FrontPage Web Host. To search Microsoft's database of registered Web Hosts, see Microsoft's Web Presence Providers page at http://www.microsoftwpp.com/wppsearch.

TIP You can use Microsoft's list of registered FrontPage Web Hosts to look for a dial-up ISP in your local area that also supports the FrontPage server extensions. Just select your state or province (U.S. or Canadian) from the View by State/Province list and then click on Go. Check any companies listed that are located within your local calling area to see whether they also offer dial-up accounts.

Publishing to a FrontPage Web Server

This section tells you how to publish your Web pages to a Web server with either the FrontPage 2002 or FrontPage 2000 server extensions installed. In most cases, you only need to know the following information to publish your FrontPage Web site to your folders on a FrontPage Web server.

✿ **The URL.** This is provided by your FrontPage Web Host, and is where you will publish your Web pages. This might be something like http://username.servername.net or http://www.servername.net/username. Make sure that you use the exact URL specified by your provider.

✿ **Your user name and password.** Your FrontPage Web Host will provide these to you, usually in an e-mail message. They are case sensitive so when using them, be sure to type them exactly as they appear.

 **NOTE** After you get an account on a Web server that provides the FrontPage 2000 or FrontPage 2002 server extensions, you might need to request that the server extensions be installed for your account. If you're not sure whether the extensions have been installed for your account, check first with your provider before trying to publish your site.

Publishing Your FrontPage 2002 Pages

Do you have an account on a Web server that provides either the FrontPage 2000 or FrontPage 2002 server extensions? Have the server extensions been enabled for your account? If so, you should already have everything you need to start publishing your FrontPage 2002 Web pages. To publish your Web pages to a FrontPage Web server, follow these steps.

1. Select File, Publish Web.

2. **Type** the URL for the FrontPage Web to which you're publishing (see Figure A.1). When publishing to a FrontPage server, always use an HTTP (*Hypertext Transfer Protocol*) URL, such as: http://username.servername.net or http://www.servername. net/username. Click on OK.

3. Enter your account or user name and password in the Enter Network Password dialog box, as shown in Figure A.2. (Remember, user names and passwords are case sensitive.) Click on OK. FrontPage logs you onto the Web server, and the Publish Web dialog box opens.

In the Publish Web dialog box (which has been greatly enhanced over previous versions of FrontPage, I might add!), you see two sets of file lists.

Figure A.1

In the Publish Destination dialog box, specify the URL for the location where you want to publish your FrontPage Web pages.

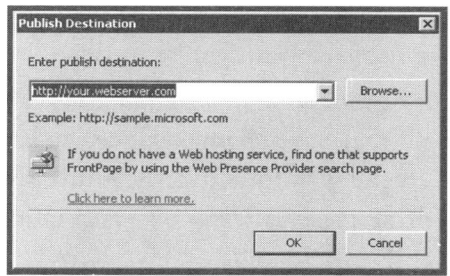

Figure A.2

Check the Save This Password in Your Password List box only if you're the only one who has access to your computer (or if you completely trust anyone and everyone else who does).

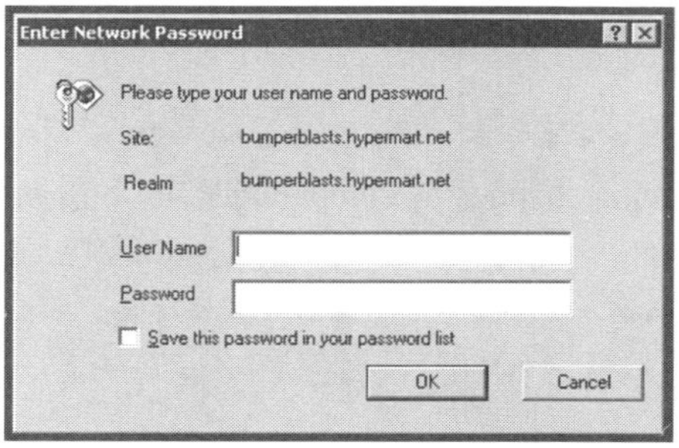

On the left is the list of files on your hard drive that you're about to publish. Any existing pages or files already on the server appear on the right. You can use the shortcut menus to do some quick file management before you publish.

1. In the left pane, right-click on a file name, then choose Don't Publish if you want to prevent FrontPage from uploading that particular file (see Figure A.3).

2. If you only want to upload a few files rather than let FrontPage run through the whole publishing process, select just those files, then right-click and choose Publish Selected Files. The selected files are copied to the server, but FrontPage ignores everything else.

3. If this is not the first time you've published your site, click on Options. The Options dialog box appears. On the Publish tab shown in Figure A.4, you can change the way FrontPage handles the update. Click on OK when you're finished.

   - In the Publish section, click on Changed Pages Only to upload only those pages that have changed since the last time you published your Web site. Or, to reload the entire site, choose All Pages, Overwriting Pages Already on Destination.

   - In the Changes section, you can tell FrontPage how to determine what you mean by "changed" in the Publish section—by comparing the existing Web in its entirety to the one you're about to upload, or by looking at the timestamp of each file and using whichever ones are newest.

CAUTION

◆ ◆

If you choose to determine changes by comparing Webs, be aware that FrontPage will automatically remove files from the server if they don't also exist in the source Web.

◆ ◆

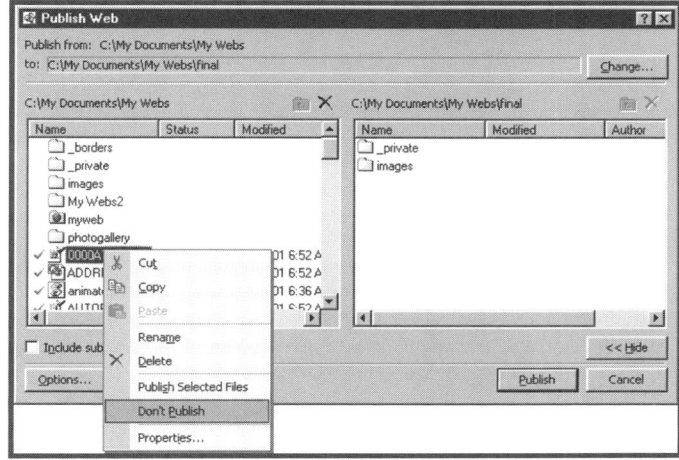

Figure A.3

You can tell FrontPage not to publish a particular page or file that's not yet ready for prime time.

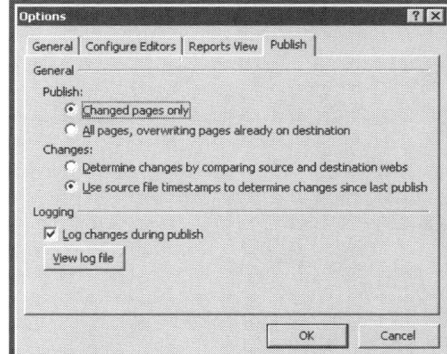

Figure A.4

How do you want FrontPage to deal with the updates?

4. To publish your Web site, click on the Publish button in the Publish Web dialog box. If you're not connected to the Internet, connect when prompted. After you're connected, FrontPage presents a dialog box showing the progress of the upload.

5. When prompted that your Web site was published successfully, you can choose to view your published site or take a peek at the log file, which tracks all the changes that were made (see Figure A.5). Just click on the appropriate link. Otherwise, click on the Done button, as shown in Figure A.6.

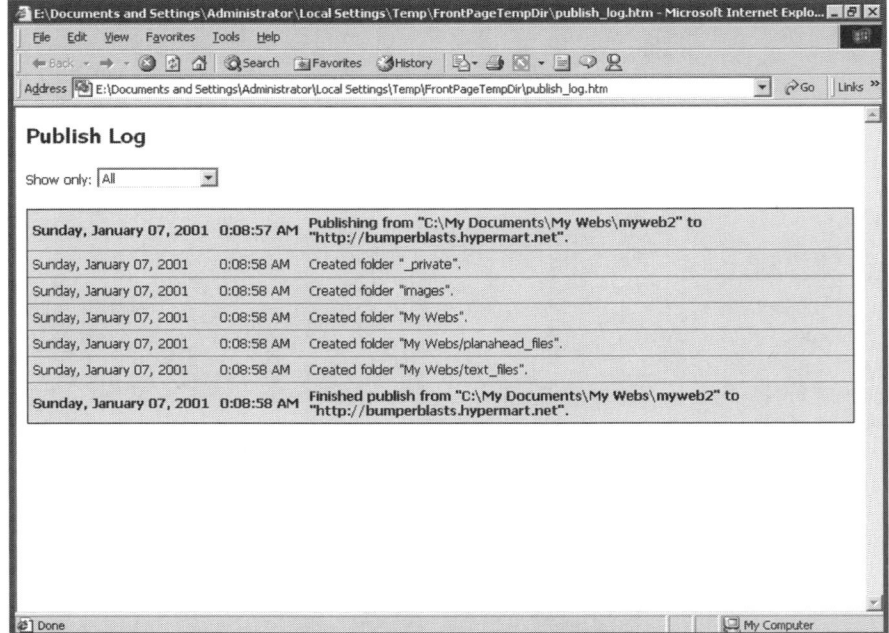

Figure A.5

The Publish Log can help you track the changes FrontPage makes to your Web site.

Figure A.6

Go ahead, take a peek—you know you want to!

NOTE

After you successfully publish your site the first time, FrontPage creates a new item in your Network Places folder. From then on, you can return to that place quickly by clicking on the network folder in the Open Web dialog box.

PUBLISHING TO A FRONTPAGE 2002 WEB SERVER

FrontPage 2002 works just fine publishing to a Web server with the FrontPage 2002 server extensions. A few things, however, won't work if you publish to a server with the FrontPage 2000 server extensions enabled. These include:

- Subwebs nested within other subwebs. (Subwebs nested within the root Web are okay.)
- Database query results (Database Results Wizard).
- Sending form responses to a database.

If your current Web Host doesn't support either the FrontPage 2000 or FrontPage 2002 server extensions and you're not planning to find a provider that does, see the "Publishing to an FTP Server" section in this appendix.

Maintaining Your Site on a FrontPage Web Server

After publishing your Web site to your FrontPage Web server, you can open it directly in FrontPage 2002 if you want. You can add folders, edit or delete files, and so on. To open your remote FrontPage Web site within FrontPage 2002, follow these steps.

1. Select File, Open Web.

2. In the Web Name box, type the URL for your FrontPage Web server folder. (Your FrontPage Web Host will tell you what you need to type here.) Click on Open. (You can also click on the pull-down handle to the right of the Web Name box to select from a list of FrontPage Webs you've opened previously.)

3. In the Enter Network Password dialog box, enter your user name and password. (Your FrontPage Web Host will tell you what your user name and password are.) Check the Save the Password in Your Password List check box if you don't want to have to enter these every time. Click on OK.

4. When your folders in your remote FrontPage Web site appear, click on Open to open the Web in FrontPage 2002.

That's it. You can now do anything in your remote FrontPage Web that you can do in your local FrontPage Web (C:\My Webs, for example). One of the advantages of opening your remote FrontPage Web site in FrontPage 2002 is that you can easily maneuver and browse within your site to test it out. To preview an open page, just select File, Preview in Browser.

CAUTION

◆◆◆

Some people create their Web site entirely on their remote FrontPage Web server. However, if your server crashes or suddenly goes out of business, you might lose everything on your site. Or, if you're like me, sometimes you start making changes to the site, then change your mind halfway through and decide to scrap the whole thing and start over. If you work directly from your server, you have nothing to which to go back.

For these reasons, it is a good idea to make all changes to your FrontPage Web on your local computer, and then publish them to your remote FrontPage server. That way, you only need to republish your site if anything happens to your remote FrontPage server. Just as it's important to back up your computer files often, you should never let your working files be your only files. You will live to regret it at some point—I can almost guarantee it.

◆◆◆

PUBLISHING LOCALLY TO A PERSONAL WEB SERVER

Although most FrontPage 2002 features can be tested out on your local disk-based Web (C:\My Webs, for example), some features won't work until you actually publish your site to a server with the FrontPage 2000 or FrontPage 2002 server extensions installed. To install Microsoft Personal Web Server 4.0 and the FrontPage 2002 server extensions so that you can preview these features on your local hard drive, see Appendix E, "Implementing Special Features." Using this technique is also an excellent way to create a local backup of your site in case something happens to the files on your provider's server.

Publishing to an FTP Server

If the FrontPage 2000 or 2002 server extensions are not available or haven't been installed for your Web presence account, FrontPage 2002's Web Publishing Wizard will transfer your files to your server using FTP. If your Web includes any FrontPage features not supported by an FTP server, you'll be notified when you publish your files.

CAUTION

♦ ♦

If the FrontPage server extensions are available for your Web presence account but have not been installed, do not try to publish your site using FTP. Ask your Web Host to install the FrontPage server extensions for your account and then follow the steps given previously to publish your site using HTTP. You should only use FTP to publish your site if the FrontPage server extensions are not available for your account.

You should *never* publish via FTP to a server that has the FrontPage server extensions installed. Always use HTTP—always make sure that "http://" is at the start of your server's URL when publishing to a FrontPage server.

If you do use FTP to publish to a FrontPage-enabled server, the server extensions might become corrupted, and you might need to have them reinstalled for your account.

♦ ♦

Publishing your files to an FTP server is done pretty much the same way as publishing to a FrontPage server. The only difference is that you publish using the File Transfer Protocol (ftp://) instead of the Hypertext Transfer Protocol (http://). To publish your Web pages to an FTP server, follow these steps.

1. Select File, Publish Web.
2. Type the full "ftp://" URL for the folder to which you want to publish your pages. Be sure to include
   - The server name or your domain name
   - The path on your server to your own folder

- The specific folder (or folder path) to which you want to publish (if you're not publishing to your root folder, which is likely). For example, if your provider's FTP server name is server1.myprovider.net, your personal folder on that server is located at /users/yourname, and the specific subfolder to which you want to publish is /yoursub, then the URL would need to be ftp://server1.myprovider.net/users/yourname/yoursub.

3. To change any of the publishing options, select the Options button.

4. To publish your Web pages, click on the Publish button. If you're not connected to the Internet, just click on Connect when prompted.

5. Type your user name and password, remembering that they are case sensitive. Click on OK.

NOTE If you've previously published your Web site, you might be prompted to overwrite files that have been changed or delete files that are no longer part of your FrontPage Web.

6. Click on the provided link to view your published site, or click on the Done button.

FrontPage 2002 remembers the last URL you used to publish to an FTP server, so the next time you publish to an FTP server (as long as you don't publish to another location), you won't have to retype the full URL. You will have to type your user name and password each time you publish, however.

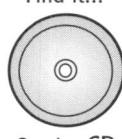

Find it...

On the CD

Many FrontPage users prefer to use a regular FTP program, such as WS_FTP or CuteFTP, for example, when publishing their Web pages to an FTP server. Both programs are included on this book's CD-ROM.

Maintaining Your Site on an FTP Server

You can use FrontPage 2002 to add new folders on an FTP server. This can be handy if you want to publish your FrontPage Web to a subfolder that hasn't been created yet on your FTP server. Doing this for the first time is a two-step process. First, you need to add the URL for your FTP server to FrontPage's list of FTP locations, and then you need to open that URL in FrontPage 2002.

Adding Your FTP Location

To add your FTP server to FrontPage 2002's list of FTP locations, just follow these steps.

1. Select File, Publish Web.
2. Click on the Browse button and then click on the down arrow next to the Look In box. Select the Add/Modify FTP Locations option to display the Add/Modify FTP Locations dialog box (see Figure A.7).
3. In the dialog box, first type the name of your FTP server (for example, ftp://servernumber.providername.net).
4. Select the User radio button, then type your user name and password. Click on the Add button, then click on OK.

You only need to do this once. After the first time, you won't need to do it again to open your FTP location. Follow the steps in the next section to open your FTP location.

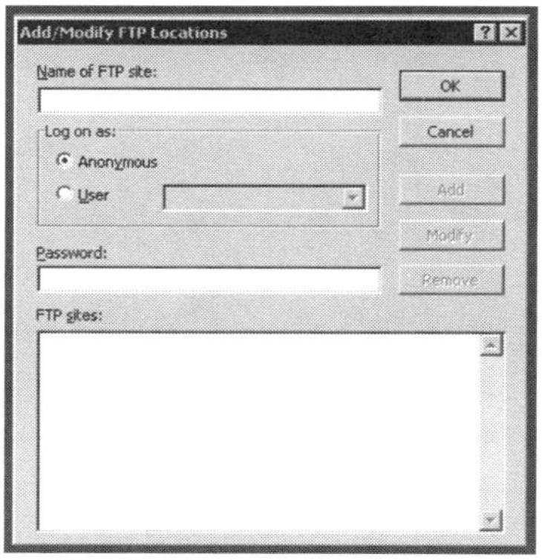

Figure A.7

You can add your FTP location to FrontPage 2002's list of FTP locations so that you won't have to remember the URL, user name, and password each time.

Opening Your FTP Location

To open your FTP server in FrontPage 2002, follow these steps.

1. Select File, Open Web.

2. Click on the down arrow next to the Look In box, then choose the URL for your FTP server (under FTP Locations).

3. You'll need to know which folders lead to your personal folder. (Ask your provider if you don't already know.) Just double-click on the folders that form the path to your personal folder. After you're inside your personal folder, you can add a new folder by clicking on the Create New Folder icon.

What You Can't Publish to an FTP Server

When you publish your Web pages to an FTP server using FrontPage 2002, you won't be able to include a number of features or components that require the FrontPage server extensions. If your Web pages include any of these features, you'll get a message when you try to publish your Web pages. Here are the main features and components that can't be published to an FTP server. (I haven't included *everything* here, just the features or components you are most likely to use.)

- Hit counter
- Form handler
- Discussion group form
- Search form
- Subwebs or virtual servers
- Database Results Wizard
- Cascading Style Sheets
- Custom themes
- Dynamic HTML
- Shared borders

Getting Visitor Feedback with Forms

J ust about any Web site you visit has an area dedicated to user feedback. It might be an informal guest book, a product registration area, a customer service inquiry area, a discussion group, or an online sales catalog. You name it, it's out there. Even with personal Web sites, hearing from visitors is important. Why should your site be any different?

Forms give your visitors the opportunity to talk to you. Just as with paper forms, you can ask a user to fill in blanks, check boxes, choose options, and even write lengthy descriptions.

◀ ◀

A *form* is a grouping of data-entry fields, check boxes, radio buttons, and so on that can be filled out by a visitor to a Web site. The data can be collected by the site manager in a variety of ways, including as a text or HTML file, as a database record, in an e-mail, or to a custom-built application.

◀ ◀

NOTE

Unless you want to deal with ugly stuff like CGI scripts (mini-programs), forms created in FrontPage require that the site be published to a server that has the FrontPage server extensions installed.

The type of form you build depends on the kind of information you want to get back and how you want that information communicated to you. In this appendix, you will:

- Recognize the different types of form fields
- Create new forms using a FrontPage template and the Form Page Wizard
- Set field defaults and data limits
- Determine a way to retrieve the form results
- Create a confirmation page for visitors

Planning a Form

Before you jump in with both feet, take a few minutes to think about the purpose of your form and what kind of information you want to gather from your visitors.

- Do you need contact information such as names, addresses, or e-mail addresses?
- Are visitors registering a product or purchase requiring serial numbers, model numbers, and the like?
- Do you want demographic information such as age or physical characteristics?

You get the idea. Make a list of everything you want to know. You might want to surf the Internet a bit and gather ideas from other forms you find. Remember that forms don't have to be boring. After you design the basics, you can format and edit a form page just like you would any other Web page, even adding graphics and backgrounds.

After you've decided on your questions, consider the layout of the form. Should the layout be in paragraphs, a table, or bulleted lists? The Form Page Wizard uses a combination of all these elements to design a form that best suits your needs. If you don't like the suggested layout, you can always modify it later.

Finally, consider how you want to save the form results or the data that is generated. You can save the results as a Web page, a text file, an e-mail, or data that can be dumped to a database. You can even devise custom scripts to handle the results.

Understanding Form Fields

For each question or data set you want to collect, you need a form field. You will recognize most form fields from your everyday use of application dialog boxes. Forms can incorporate check boxes, option buttons, menus and drop-down lists, push buttons, and a variety of other field types. You'll find these types of fields in any of the forms you generate using the built-in templates or the Form Page Wizard. You can add others as needed. Here's a list of common form fields (see Figure B.1).

BUZZ WORD

◀ ◀

A *form field* is a data entry field on an HTML form. The user makes selections or adds text to a form field, depending on the field type. Common form field types include check boxes, option buttons, text boxes, and drop-down lists.

◀ ◀

- **Option buttons (also called radio buttons).** Use these to present an "either/or" choice to the visitor. There can be many options in one group, but only one can be selected at a time.
- **Check boxes.** Use these for multiple optional selections, such as what topics are of interest to the visitor. The visitor clicks on each desired item to place a check mark in the box.
- **Drop-down lists.** Use these to present a list of choices. The visitor chooses an option by clicking on the desired item on the list. Drop-down lists have the same effect as groups of option buttons, but they save space on the page.
- **Text boxes.** Use a text box for a small amount of text, such as a name or address.

Option button

Drop-down list

Scrolling text box

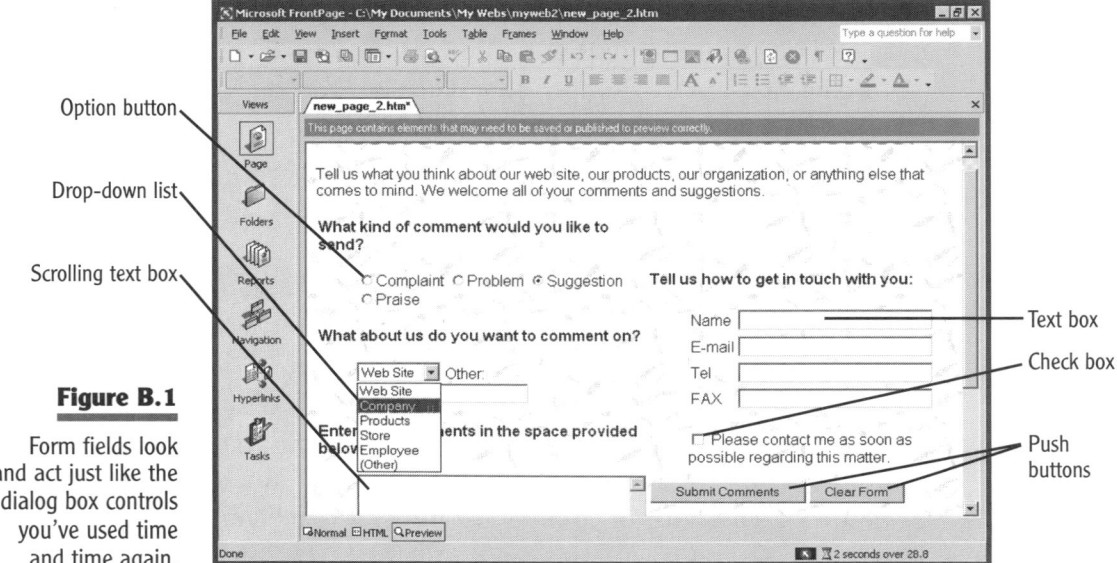

Figure B.1

Form fields look and act just like the dialog box controls you've used time and time again.

Text box

Check box

Push buttons

- 🔘 **Scrolling text boxes**. Use a scrolling text box to accommodate a larger amount of text, such as a comment or description.
- 🔘 **Push buttons**. Use these to let the visitor submit or clear the form, or to run custom scripts, such as one to calculate totals on an order form.

Building a Simple Form

There will always be purists out there who teach you how to build everything from scratch so that you'll learn the rules before you learn how to break them. Although there's certainly merit to that philosophy—and occasional times when it really might be necessary—why go to all that trouble if you don't have to? FrontPage's Form Page Wizard can save you hours of work, and it has several form templates. I don't know about you, but as long as I don't end up creating more work for myself in the long run, I'll take a shortcut any day.

In this appendix, you will create a new form from one of FrontPage's built-in templates and learn how to edit the form to meet your needs. Then, you'll use the Form Page Wizard to set up a custom form.

Creating a Form from a FrontPage Template

FrontPage includes common form styles you're likely to use. You can add one to your Web site with just a few steps.

1. Switch to Page view and then select File, New, Page or Web. Then, click on Page Templates in the Task pane. The Page Templates dialog box opens, as shown in Figure B.2.

2. Review the list of available templates on the General tab and choose one of the available forms, such as Feedback Form. Click on the form you want, then click on OK. FrontPage opens a new page with the skeleton form already prepared for you (see Figure B.3). Scroll down the page to see the types of questions and fields included in the form.

3. From Normal view, edit the headings, text, and background of the form using regular page editing procedures. (You'll learn how to edit the properties of the fields themselves a little later.)

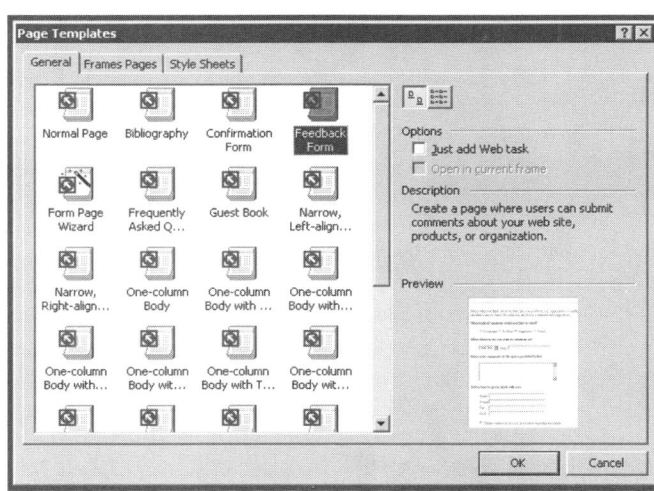

Figure B.2

You can save a lot of form-building time by starting with a form template, such as Feedback Form or Guest Book.

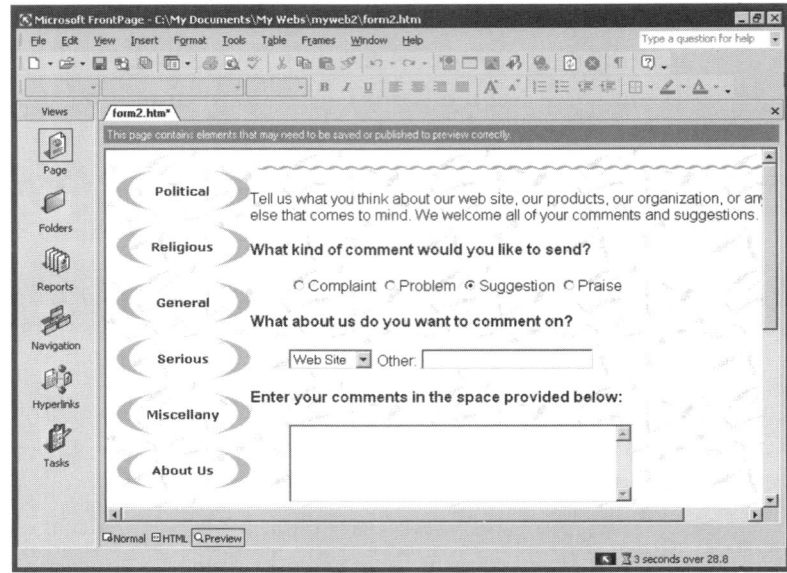

Figure B.3

FrontPage does most of the work for you. It lays out the basic form and even includes default themes and shared borders settings.

4. Add a new field to the form by selecting Insert, Form, and selecting the desired field from the submenu, as shown in Figure B.4.

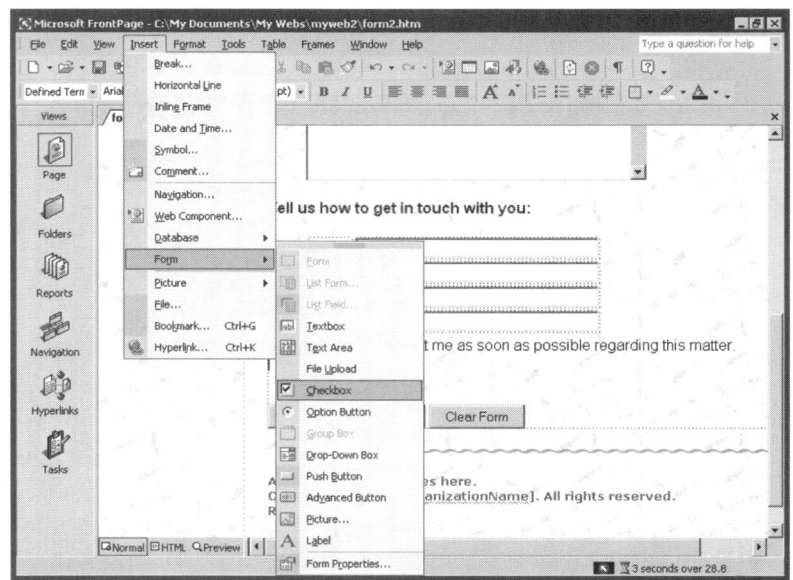

Figure B.4

If the template doesn't have everything you want, you can add your own questions and fields.

Creating a Form Using the Form Page Wizard

If the available templates don't have exactly what you're looking for, you can ask FrontPage to help you design something more specific to your needs. To run the Form Page Wizard, follow these steps.

1. Switch to Page view and then select File, New, Page or Web. Then, click on Page Templates in the Task pane. The Page Templates dialog box opens.

2. Click on Form Page Wizard and then click on OK. The wizard opens with a welcome message explaining the procedure you're about to perform. Read the message and then click on Next. The wizard opens to a blank list that you will use to add questions to your form (see Figure B.5).

3. Click on Add to create the first group of questions. The wizard presents a list of question types. Click on a question type to see a description of the questions included in the group. For example, the contact information group asks users for their name, company affiliation, address, and phone number.

4. Click in the text box if you want to edit the text of the question. You might, for example, change "Please provide the following contact information" to "Please tell us a little about yourself." You can be as creative or as straightforward as you want. Click on Next when you're finished.

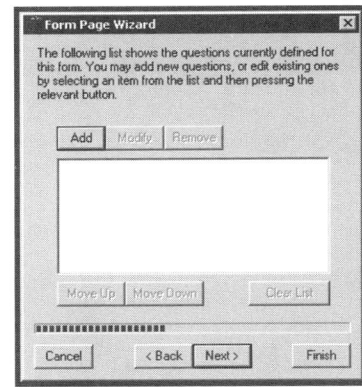

Figure B.5

Build a list of questions for your custom form using the Form Page Wizard.

5. On the next page, the wizard asks you to specify exactly what information you want to include and in what format, such as name, address, e-mail, phone and fax numbers, and so on (see Figure B.6). Check the boxes and options you prefer.

6. Click on Next when you've made your selections. Your completed question appears on the question list, as shown in Figure B.7.

7. Click on Add to add more questions. Repeat steps 4 and 5 for each new question in your form. When you've finished building the list of questions, click on Next. The wizard's Presentation Options page appears (see Figure B.8).

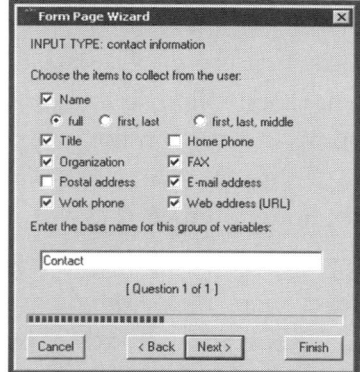

Figure B.6

Some people might not want to give you a lot of information.

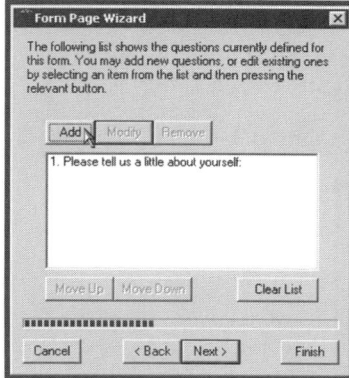

Figure B.7

Add to or edit the list of questions for your form.

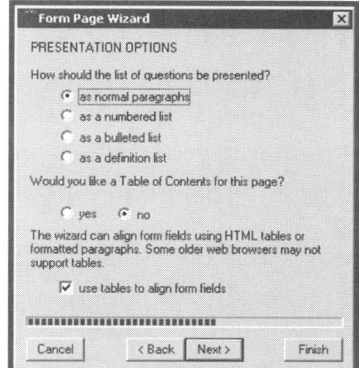

Figure B.8

Now choose how you want your form to be designed.

8. Click on one of the style options to tell the wizard how you want to present the questions.

9. If your form is rather long, you might want to consider adding an automatic table of contents at the top. If so, click on the Yes radio button. FrontPage includes a table of contents at the top of your form, with bookmarks that point to each question on your list.

TIP Click on Back to make changes to your selections before generating the form.

10. If it's okay for FrontPage to format your form using tables, check the Use Tables to Align Form Fields box. Click on Next when you're done.

11. Tell FrontPage what you want it to do with the results that are generated when the visitor submits the form. Give the resulting file a name if prompted. (See "So What Happens to the Results?" later in this appendix for details on handling form results.)

12. Click on Finish when you reach the last page of the wizard (see Figure B.9). FrontPage generates the form and opens it in Normal view for editing.

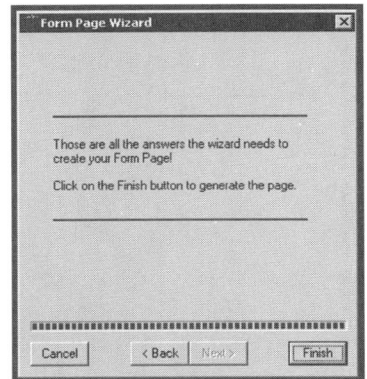

Figure B.9

Click on Finish and
then sit back and
let the wizard work
its magic.

13. Edit the headings, text, and background of the form using regular
    page editing procedures. (You'll learn how to set the properties for
    the form fields themselves in a moment.)

14. Add a new field to the form by selecting Insert, Form, and selecting
    the desired field from the submenu.

Editing Form Field Properties

No matter whether you used a template or the Form Page Wizard, you've
gotten a jump-start on your form. The text is edited and formatted, but
you still need to customize the form fields so that they look and work as
you want. To edit the form properties for any field, follow these steps.

1. Right-click on the field and select Form Field Properties from the
   shortcut menu. The Properties dialog box opens. The available controls and options will vary depending on which type of field you're
   editing. In the example, I'm editing the properties of a drop-down
   list (see Figure B.10). I can add, remove, or modify the items that
   appear in the menu and control the order in which they appear. I
   can also tell FrontPage how many items to initially show on the
   menu (the "height" of the list), whether the user can select more
   than one item, and where in the tab order this field should fall.

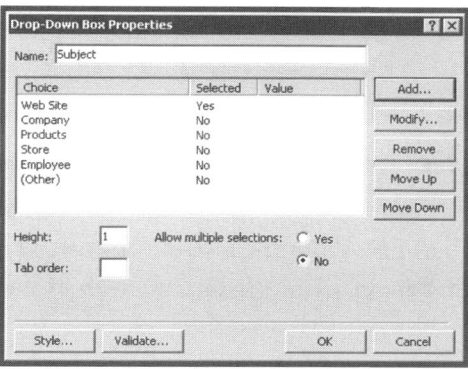

Figure B.10

You can control the look and function of form fields via their Properties settings.

 TIP

When filling in forms, it's often more expedient for the user to move between fields by pressing the Tab key rather than moving from keyboard to mouse to click in the next field. By default, a form's tab order (the order in which the fields are selected as the visitor presses the Tab key) is set according to the order in which the fields were created. (For pages generated by wizards or templates, this usually means the order in which they appear on the page.) To make adjustments, enter a specific number for each field in its Tab Order box. You can test a form's tab order by previewing the page. Click in the first field and then press the Tab key to move from field to field.

2. Edit the properties as desired. Most of the controls are self-explanatory, so I won't go into every nuance of every field type. If you need help with a particular item or option, click on the What's This? button (next to the Close button on the title bar of the dialog box) and then click on the item for which you need help. FrontPage displays a pop-up help balloon that describes the item in question.

3. Click on OK to save the changes and close the dialog box.

4. Switch to Preview view to check the functionality and appearance of your form and its fields.

WHAT IS FIELD VALIDATION?

You've probably already noticed a few things about fields:

- Form fields sometimes include a default answer, so the visitor can skip that question if the answer is already correct.

- Some fields only allow you to add a specific number of characters (like a ten-digit phone number) or numbers in a specific format (such as mm-dd-yyyy for a date field).

- A drop-down list might include a question or prompt as the first list item, such as "Choose your type of operating system." When you click on that item, the text box's drop-down list appears. You can't select the first item (the one that asks the question), but you can select any of the actual items on the list.

All these types of controls are called field validations. The options vary depending on the field type. To set the validations for a field, select Validate in the field's Properties dialog box. The available options for that field appear in the Validation dialog box.

You can experiment with each of these settings to learn what they do and how they control the function and appearance of a field. For detailed instructions, click on the What's This? button or press F1 to open FrontPage Help.

(Just in case you're curious, the validation that controls the drop-down list discussed previously is called Disallow First Item. You'll see it in the Validation dialog box for a drop-down list.)

Don't forget to include a push button so that visitors can submit their form. Make the label read whatever you want—the default is Submit.

So What Happens to the Results?

All these lovely forms are great, but without a way for FrontPage to deliver the results, you're just spinning your wheels, and your visitor's.

The type of form you use will most likely dictate how the results should be handled. If you're creating a guest book, for example, you'll probably want FrontPage to save all your visitors' submissions to a Web page that other visitors can view. You might want customer service inquiries sent as e-mails to your help desk coordinator. Orders from your online customers could be integrated into your order entry system. On the other hand, you might want FrontPage to save a text file for you so that you can use it for some other purpose. To set or change the form-handling options, follow these steps.

1. Right-click anywhere in the form and select Form Properties from the shortcut menu that appears. The Form Properties dialog box opens.

2. Click on Options. The Saving Results dialog box opens with the File Results tab in front, as shown in Figure B.11. Form handling options include the following:

    • **Save to an HTML or text file**. Each submission is added (or *appended*) to the end of an existing file. If you choose to save to an HTML file, you can make that file available for viewing on your Web site. Then, visitors can read what other people have to say and add their own comments. Note that by default, the results file is stored in the _private folder, which makes it invisible to visitors. If you want the page to be seen, move it to

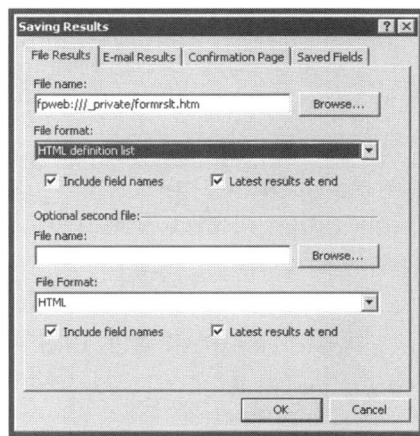

Figure B.11

How do you want to get the information back from your visitors?

another location within your Web folder structure. If it's going to be visible, don't forget to format it to match the rest of your Web site (add shared borders, apply a theme, and so on).

NOTE Your Web server must be running the FrontPage 2000 or 2002 extensions to save each submission to an HTML or text file.

- **Save results to a database**. Each submission is converted to a table and saved as a record in the database on your Web server. FrontPage directly supports Microsoft Access databases, but you can work with any database that accepts data from comma-, tab-, or space-delimited files—including Microsoft Excel.

NOTE Your Web server must be running the FrontPage 2000 or 2002 extensions to save the submissions to a database.

- **Save results using a custom form handler**. For more complex operations, such as commercial shopping sites, you can create custom scripts or programs that run when a form is submitted. The good news is that you don't need the FrontPage extensions for this option. The bad news is that you need to know at least a little about Internet programming languages such as Perl. Talk to your network administrator or the tech support folks at your Web Host for help.

You can find some very helpful ready-made scripts available for downloading from a variety of Web sites that offer Web-building tools. (Some of these scripts are free; some are not.) For starters, try these:

- The Complete Resource for All Web Builders: http://www.reallybig.com

- The Ultimate Webmaster's Resource:
  http://www.htmldirectory.com
- TopHosts.com, the complete Web-hosting resource:
  http://webmaster.tophosts.com

- **Have FrontPage compose and send you an e-mail containing the form results.** To do so, just click on the E-Mail Results tab and enter the requested information. As your traffic grows, so will the volume of mail coming to your Inbox.

NOTE Your Web server must be running the FrontPage 2000 or 2002 extensions to have FrontPage e-mail you the form results.

3. After you've set all the necessary options in the dialog boxes, click on OK to save your changes and return to page-editing mode.

4. Save the page(s). Then, test your form by clicking on Preview in Browser and going through the entire submission process.

TIP Dealing with form results can be a complex matter, especially if you're working with databases. You can use the FrontPage Help system to look up the specifics for the handling option you want to implement.

Sending Visitors a Confirmation

When a visitor submits a form, it's good (and sometimes critical) to acknowledge that the form was successfully submitted. By default (unless you're using a custom script), FrontPage creates a simple confirmation page, but you'll probably want to customize it a little (see Figure B.12). You might want a simple "thanks for your feedback" message, or a more sophisticated reply. For example, if you request the site visitor's name in your form, you can confirm the submission with a friendly greeting like, "Dear Janet, thanks for taking the time to check out our Web site. We appreciate your feedback, and we will address any questions you might have as quickly as possible." You can also display the form results back to visitors, so that they can double-check their entries and correct them if necessary.

TIP

■ ■
For complete details on creating and customizing confirmation pages, look up "Create a confirmation page and assign it to a form" in FrontPage Help.
■ ■

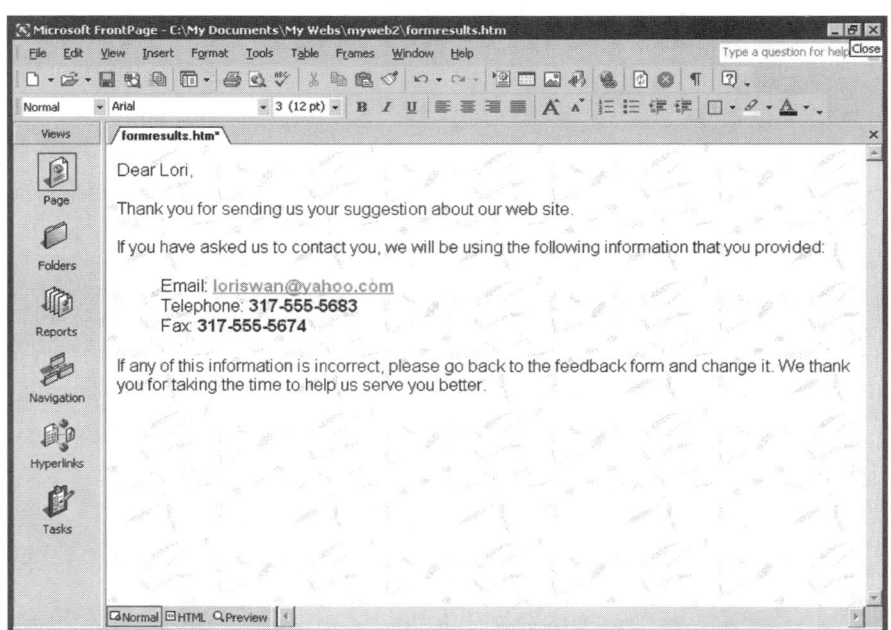

Figure B.12

Let your visitors know you've received their input by including a confirmation page.

Adding
Multimedia

dding the right mix of multimedia effects to your FrontPage Web pages can not only make them more visually and aurally appealing, but more effective as well. Because of the versatility of HTML and the Web, you are not limited merely to static text and images as the content for your Web pages. Many other forms of electronic media can be either linked to or displayed inline. These can include

- GIF animations
- Background and other sounds
- Inline video
- Streaming media (audio, video, and animation)

The following sections cover these different multimedia options. This appendix does not provide exhaustive coverage of these topics. It does, however, include some examples, a few tips here and there, and some pointers for finding further tools and resources on the Internet.

Using GIF Animations

Many GIF animations are available for download from the Internet. A discretely placed GIF animation in the form of an animated image link, for example, can be a great way to add just a dash of dynamite to your page. You insert a GIF animation into your Web page the same way that you insert a regular GIF image. The differences are purely internal. GIF images can include either a single image frame or multiple image frames.

◆◆◆◆◆◆◆◆◆◆◆◆◆◆◆◆◆◆◆◆◆◆◆◆◆◆◆◆◆◆◆◆◆◆◆◆

The copyright status of many GIF animations available on the Internet is not clear. If you use a GIF animation that you don't have permission from the author to use, or that has not been expressly made available by the author for free use by all without restrictions, you could be courting a lawsuit, especially if you are putting up a commercial or business Web site. The safe bet, and the ethically pure route, is to use only GIF animations that you have permission to use or that have been made available by their authors for free use by all without restrictions.

◆◆◆◆◆◆◆◆◆◆◆◆◆◆◆◆◆◆◆◆◆◆◆◆◆◆◆◆◆◆◆◆◆◆◆◆

A few image viewers and editors will play a GIF animation, but generally you have to display a GIF animation in your browser (or FrontPage's Preview window) for it to be played. Most regular image viewers and editors will only display the first frame.

Finding GIF Animations

You don't have to create your own GIF animations to be able to add them to your site. Here are some places on the Web where you can find GIF animations that you can download and use.

- Animation Library at http://www.animationlibrary.com
- Animation Factory at http://www.eclipsed.com
- Rose's Animated Gifs at http://www.wanderers2.com/rose/animate.html

Although you can't create or edit GIF animations in FrontPage, you can view a GIF animation in FrontPage's Preview window.

Creating GIF Animations with Animation Shop 3

The GIF 89a format allows multiple images (or frames) to be included in a single GIF image. When displayed in a browser, the images are then displayed sequentially as a GIF animation. Including GIF animations in your page can be an easy way to add some dynamic movement to your site.

Although you can view GIF animations in your browser, you usually can't view (or create or edit) GIF animations in your image editor. To do that, you generally need to use a special class of software, the GIF animation editor. This section gives you a quick overview of using Animation Shop 3, a GIF animation editor included with Paint Shop Pro 7, to create and edit your own GIF animations.

Creating Your Frame Images

Before you can create a GIF animation, you need to create the individual images that will be the individual frames in your animation. You can do that in any image editor, such as Paint Shop Pro 7. Just save your frame images as regular GIF images (at the size at which you want them to appear). You can also use any sequence of GIF or JPEG images that you have handy, which will create a kind of slide show.

Running Animation Shop 3

If you've already installed Paint Shop Pro 7 from the CD-ROM, then Animation Shop 3 was installed at that time. If you haven't installed Paint Shop Pro 7 yet, you'll need to do that first to be able to run Animation Shop 3.

To run Animation Shop 3, just click on the Start button and then select Programs, Jasc Software, and Animation Shop 3.

Using the Animation Wizard

Animation Shop 3 includes a handy feature, the Animation Wizard, which makes creating your own GIF animations truly a snap. To run and use the Animation Wizard, follow these steps.

1. Select File, Animation Wizard. The first dialog box lets you size your animation based on the first image frame, or you can choose the specific dimensions you want to use (see Figure C.1). Click on Next to go to the next dialog box.

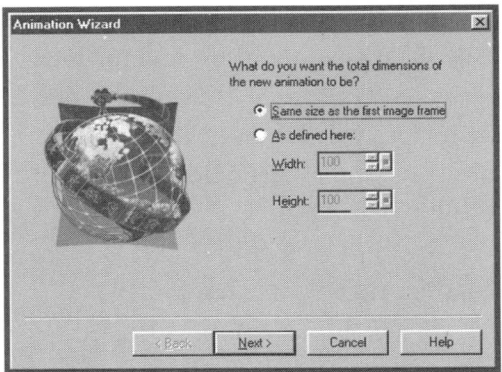

Figure C.1

Specify the dimensions of your animation in Animation Shop 3's initial dialog box.

2. In the next dialog box, you can choose the default canvas color for your animation and whether you want it to be opaque or transparent (see Figure C.2). Click on Next to go to the next dialog box.

3. In the next dialog box, you can choose how your image frames will be positioned within your animation, as well as how the remainder of the animation window will be treated if an image frame doesn't take up the whole window (see Figure C.3). You can also scale your image frames to fit the animation window. The options here are primarily of concern if your animation will be using images of different sizes. Click on Next to go to the next dialog box.

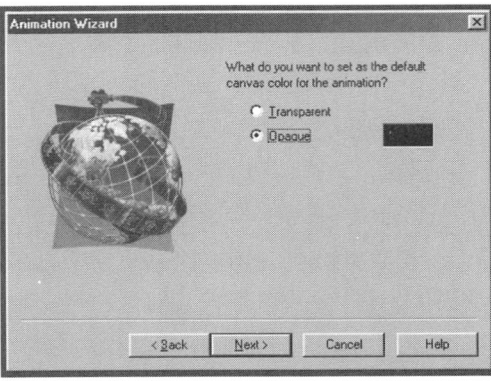

Figure C.2

Choose the background color for your animation and whether it will be transparent or opaque.

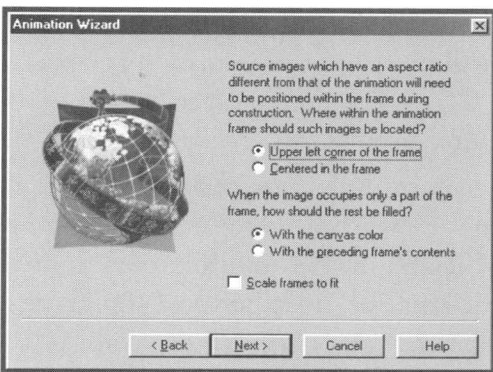

Figure C.3

For image frames of different sizes, set their alignment, how remaining space will be handled, and whether you want smaller images to be scaled to fit.

4. In the next dialog box, you can choose to loop your animation indefinitely or a certain number of times, and what the frame-rate will be (see Figure C.4). The default frame-rate is 10/100ths of a second; just increase this value to get a slower frame-rate or decrease it to get a faster frame-rate. Click on Next to go to the next dialog box.

5. In the next dialog box, you add the images that will be loaded into your animation's frames. To add your images, click on the Add Image button. In the Open dialog box, open the folder where the images you want to use are saved. To batch open your images, hold down the Control key and click on each image in the sequence that

Figure C.4

You can loop your animation indefinitely or a set number of times, as well as set the frame-rate at which your animation will display.

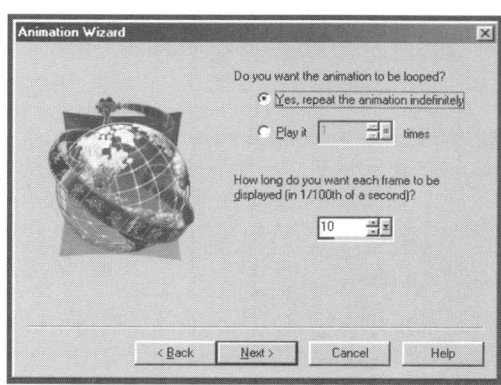

you want to include in your animation, starting with the last image to be displayed in the animation and ending with the first (see Figure C.5). Click on the Open button to add the images to your animation (see Figure C.6).

6. After you've added the images you want to use, you can add more images, remove images, or move images up or down in the image sequence. Click on the Next button to go to the next dialog box, and then click on the Finish button to build the actual animation.

7. You'll now see the animation frames displayed in Animation Shop's main window (see Figure C.7).

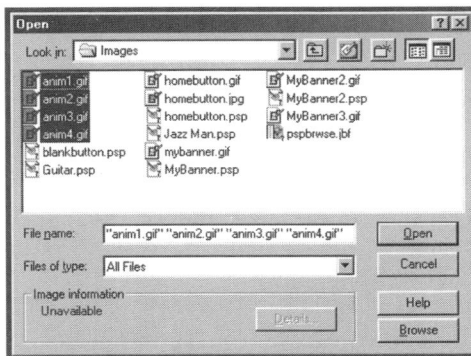

Figure C.5

Choose the images you want to use in your animation in the Open dialog box.

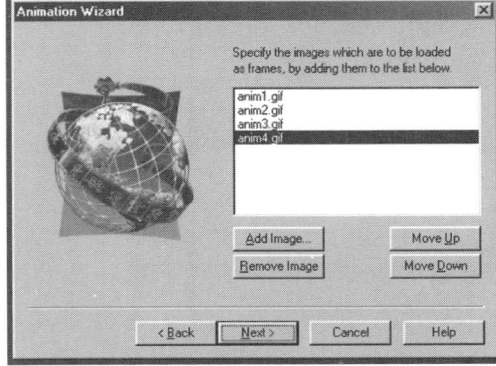

Figure C.6

Four images have been added to the animation.

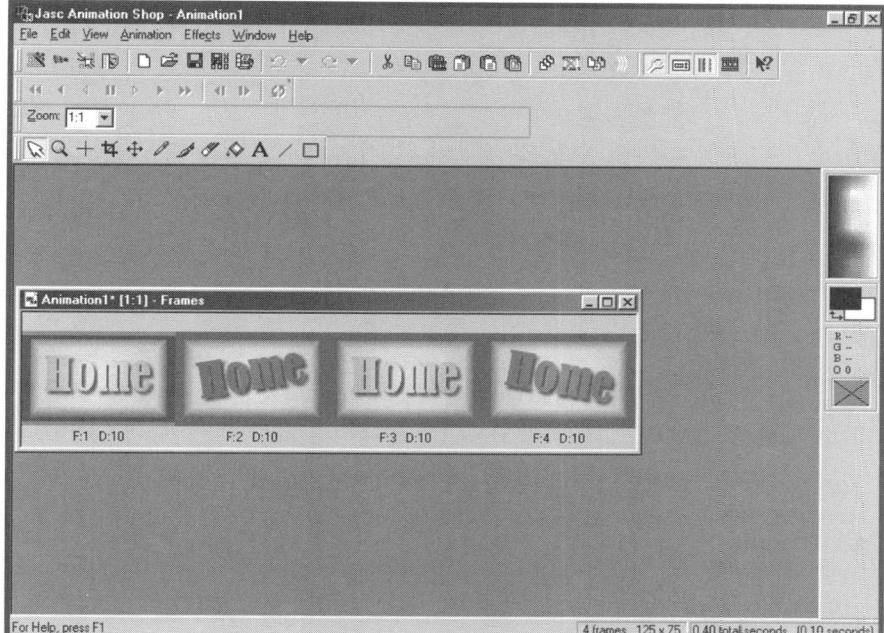

Figure C.7

The finished
animation is
displayed in
Animation Shop's
main window.

Viewing Your Animation

To view your animation, just select View, Animation. You'll see your animation playing in a separate window (see Figure C.8).

Saving Your Animation

Now that you've created your animation, you need to save it. To save your animation, follow these steps.

1. Select File, Save. Animation Shop defaults to the Anims folder located in the Paint Shop Pro 7 folder. To save your animation in that folder, just type a file name and then click on the Save button.

2. The next dialog box allows you to optimize your animation, balancing image quality against file size (see Figure C.9).

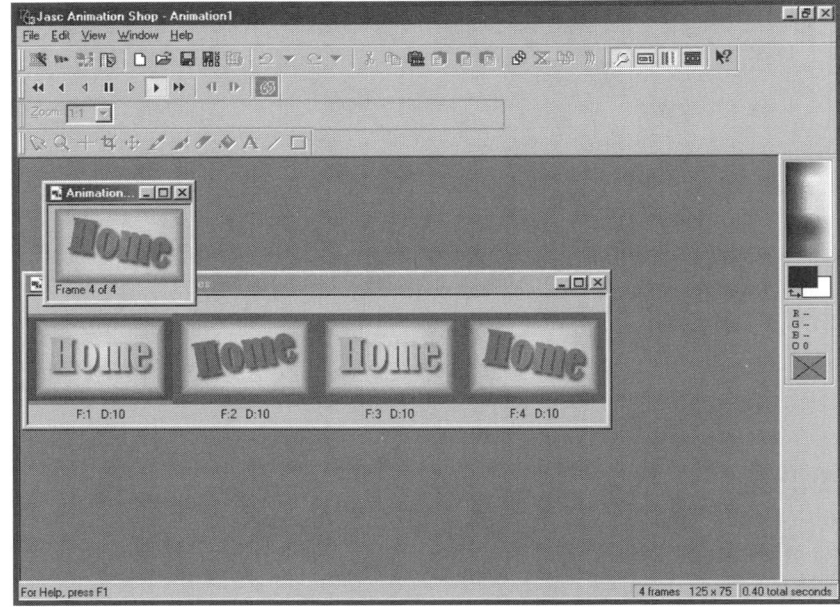

Figure C.8

You can preview your animation before you save it.

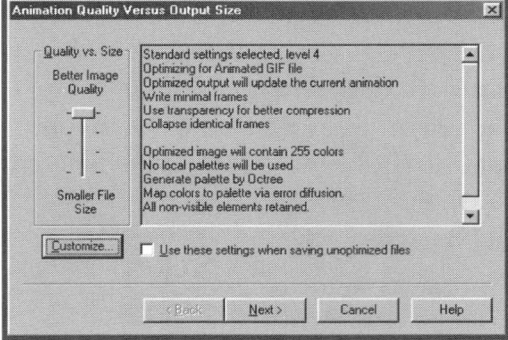

Figure C.9

Adjusting the slider lets you achieve a balance between image quality and file size.

3. You can use the slider control to adjust the balance between image quality and file size—the different slider stops will save your animation images with a palette of 255, 127, 63, or 31 colors, respectively. You can also click on the Customize button to create customized settings. For now, just click on Next to go to the next dialog box and then click on Next again.

4. At the Optimization Preview dialog box, you can compare the original and optimized animations (see Figure C.10). To choose different optimization settings, just click on the Back button. If you're satisfied with the result, click on Next.

5. The Optimization Results dialog box shows you the size of your optimized animation and the estimated amount of time to download it at various connection speeds. If you think your animation is too big, click on the Back button to go back and re-optimize your animation. If it's not too big, just click on the Finish button to finish saving your animation.

More Things You Can Do with Animation Shop

You can do much more with Animation Shop. There's a lot more to cover in this appendix, so I won't be covering these features in detail, but here's a brief list of some of your options. You can

○ Delete or duplicate a selected frame

○ Insert, mirror, or rotate an animation frame, as well as set animation or frame properties

○ Insert or apply image transitions, image effects, and text effects

○ Duplicate an animation

○ Run the Banner Wizard to create your own customized animated banner

Figure C.10

The Optimization Preview dialog box lets you see your original and optimized images side-by-side.

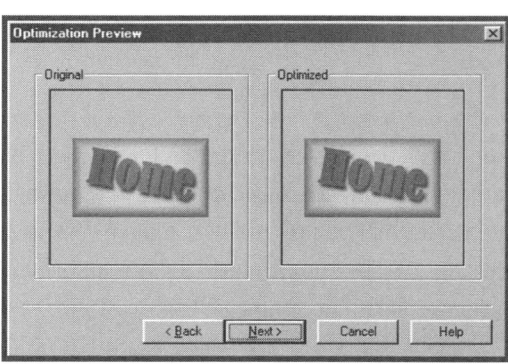

- ✪ Export image frames to Paint Shop Pro 7
- ✪ Edit the frame images using tools from the Tool palette, including the Brush, Eraser, Flood Fill, Text, Line, and Shape tools

Adding Background and Other Sounds

You can use FrontPage to automatically play a sound file in the background when your Web page is loaded into a browser. The only problem with this is that the background sound will only play in Internet Explorer. It won't play in Netscape Navigator, which does not support Microsoft's BGSOUND tag. To have your background sound also play in Netscape Navigator, use Netscape's EMBED tag. In the following sections, I'll show you how to use FrontPage to add a background sound to your Web page that will play in Internet Explorer. Then, I'll show you what codes you need to insert into your HTML file so that the background sound will also play in Netscape Navigator.

Before you can add a background sound, you'll need to choose or create the background sound that you want to use. WAV (*.wav) sound files are pretty easy to find. You can probably find quite a few in different locations on your hard drive. Just click on the Start button, point to Find, and select Files or Folders. In the Named box, type *.**wav** and click on New Search. MIDI (*.mid) sound files aren't nearly as common as WAV sound files, but they can provide better audio quality, especially for music files, while taking up fewer bytes. To search for MIDI files on your hard drive, type *.**mid** in the Named text box.

CAUTION

◆◆◆◆◆◆◆◆◆◆◆◆◆◆◆◆◆◆◆◆◆◆◆◆◆◆◆◆◆◆◆◆◆◆◆

Many sound files are available for download from the Internet. Be aware, however, that many of these files might be protected by copyright. Only download and use sound files on your site if you're sure that you're free to use them. This is especially true if you're creating a business site because you'd make a more attractive target for a copyright infringement suit than would a noncommercial site.

◆◆◆◆◆◆◆◆◆◆◆◆◆◆◆◆◆◆◆◆◆◆◆◆◆◆◆◆◆◆◆◆◆◆◆

Adding Background Sounds for Internet Explorer

The steps in FrontPage for adding background sound to your Web page will work with Internet Explorer but not with Netscape Navigator. In the next section, "Adding Background Sounds for Netscape Navigator," I'll show you how to edit your FrontPage Web's HTML code to add the codes for playing a background sound file in Navigator. To use FrontPage to add background sound to your Web page that will play in Internet Explorer, follow these steps.

1. Decide which WAV (*.wav) or MIDI (*.mid) file you want to use as your background sound.

2. Open the Web page to which you want to add the background sound in FrontPage. Right-click the mouse anywhere inside the Web page and then select Page Properties.

3. Click on the Browse button in the General tab and use the Look In menu to open the folder where the WAV or MIDI file that you want to use is located. Double-click on the audio file to select it.

4. Background sounds are set to play forever by default. I recommend that you always clear the Forever check box—background sounds that play forever are obnoxious, in my opinion. To have your background sound file play once, select 0 as the Loop value. Select 1 to play it twice, 2 to play it three times, and so on (see Figure C.11). Click on OK.

5. To preview your background sound, click on the Preview tab.

6. To save your Web page with its new embedded background sound file, select File, Save, and then click on OK at the Save Embedded Files dialog box (to save your sound file within your FrontPage Web).

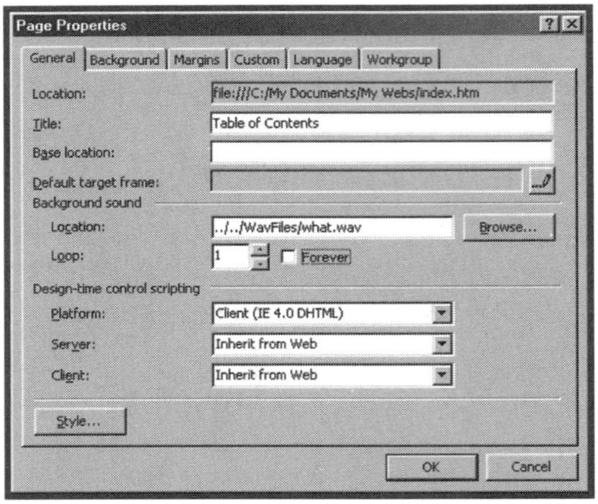

Figure C.11

The background sound file is set to play only twice.

Adding Background Sounds for Netscape Navigator

Netscape Navigator does not support the BGSOUND tag that FrontPage uses to add background sound to a FrontPage Web page. If you want your background sound to also play in Navigator, you have to use an entirely different HTML tag, the EMBED tag.

For this example, it is assumed that you have already added a background sound for Internet Explorer in the previous section. You'll be using the same sound file in this section. Otherwise, you'll need to first copy the sound file you want to use into the folder where you want to use it in your FrontPage Web—you should copy it into the same folder where the page in which you want to play the background sound is located. You can use Windows Explorer to do this, if you want. In the following steps, substitute the actual sound file you'll be using for *yoursound.wav*.

1. Choose the WAV (*.wav) or MIDI (*.mid) file you want to use as your background sound.

2. In FrontPage, open the Web page to which you want to add the background sound.

> **NOTE**
>
> Although MIDI sound files offer better audio quality and are smaller than WAV sound files, Navigator users are less likely to have a plug-in player installed for MIDI files than for WAV files. For that reason, you might want to stick to using WAV sound files when adding background sounds for Navigator.

3. If you previously set a background sound for playing in Internet Explorer (using the BGSOUND tag), first remove that setting. Right-click in your page's background, select Page Properties, and clear the Location box (under Background Sound). Click on OK.

4. Click on the HTML tab to edit the HTML code. Scroll down to the bottom of your Web page's code and click the mouse just above the </body> tag. Type the following code:

```
<embed src="yoursound.wav" autostart="true" hidden="true">
```

Figure C.12 shows the HTML code as typed directly into a Web page.

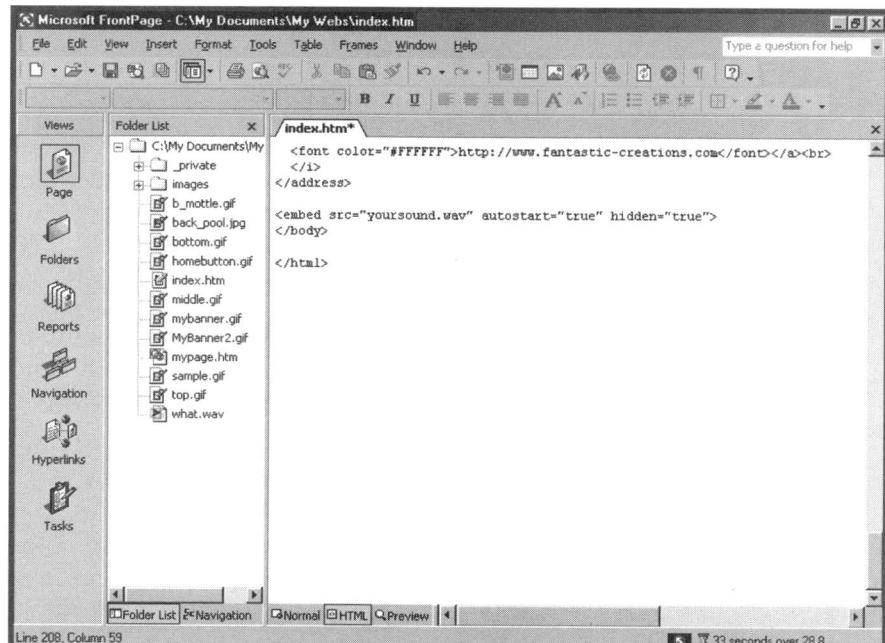

Figure C.12

For your background sound to play in Navigator, you have to insert the codes directly into your page's HTML.

To preview your background sound in FrontPage, just click on the Preview tab.

To preview your background sound in Netscape Navigator, first save your Web page (File, Save), and then run Navigator and open your Web page (in Navigator 4.7, select File, Open Page, Choose File).

Although the preceding codes should work in most instances, anyone viewing the page will need to have a plug-in player installed, capable of playing WAV or MIDI files. At least one plug-in player I know of, Quick-Time for Windows, doesn't support using the HIDDEN attribute. If you want to hide the player console, your only option that will work in all plug-in players is to set the height and width to two pixels each, like this:

```
<embed src="yoursound.wav" autostart="true" height="2"
➥ width="2">
```

By inserting this at the bottom of your page, you'll be less likely to have this affect your layout.

Displaying the Player Console

It is okay to hide the player console if you're not looping your background sound or music indefinitely. However, if you want to loop your background sound indefinitely, it is a good idea to display the player console so that visitors to your page can turn it off if they want.

You can usually incorporate the player console into your page's layout. You might choose to insert it inside a table cell, for example.

Because you'll be inserting the codes directly into your page's HTML, first copy the sound file you want to use to the folder where you want to use it in your FrontPage Web. Then, just click on the HTML tab and insert the following code as an example of displaying the player console for your background sound. (Make sure to delete any previous EMBED tag example you inserted.)

```
<embed src="mymusic.mid" autostart="true" width="200"
➥ height="50">
```

Of course, you'll need to substitute the actual name of the sound file you'll be using for *mymusic.mid* above. To preview how this will look in your browser, first save your page and then select File, Preview in Browser. Select the browser you want to preview your page in (Microsoft Internet Explorer 5.5, for instance) and click on Preview. Figure C.13 shows the Crescendo MIDI player console displayed in Internet Explorer.

The player console that is actually displayed will depend on the plug-in player a visitor to your page has installed. The default player console will have different default dimensions and startup options, depending on whether it is the Crescendo, Windows Media, or QuickTime player, for example. Here are the locations where you can download and install these plug-in players.

✿ Crescendo Player plays MIDI and MP3 files. You can download its free player from http://www.liveupdate.com/dl.html.

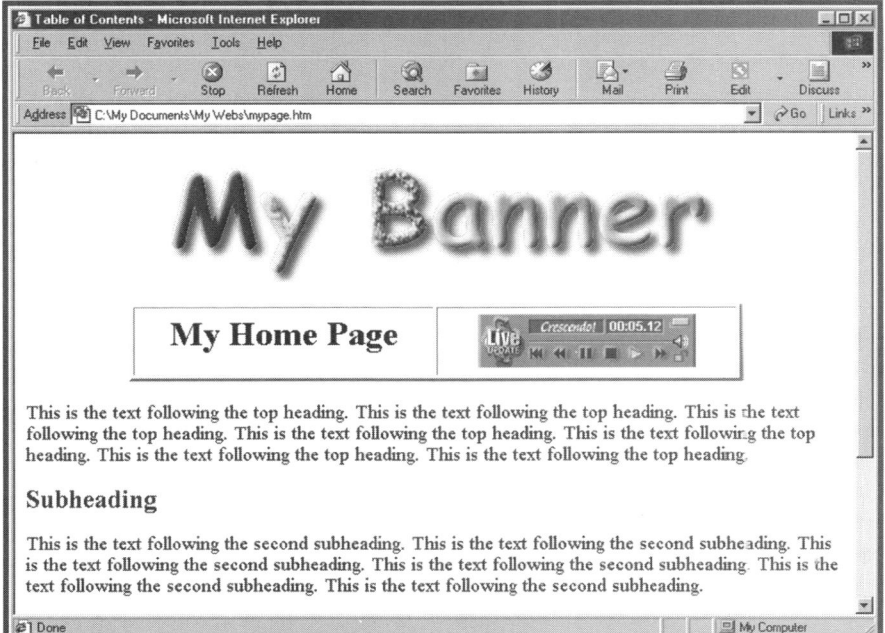

Figure C.13

Displaying the player console when automatically playing a sound file lets a visitor turn the sound file off.

- Windows Media Player plays practically all audio formats. You can download it from http://www.microsoft.com/windows/windows-media/en/download.

- QuickTime Player plays most audio formats. You can download it from http://www.apple.com/quicktime/download.

You can include additional attributes in the EMBED tag. Here's a brief rundown.

- **LOOP.** True (for infinite loop), false (to not loop), or a number (to loop a set of times).

- **ALIGN.** Top, right, left, middle, or bottom. To center the console, nest the EMBED tag inside a CENTER tag.

- **AUTOSTART.** True or false.

- **WIDTH and HEIGHT.** A number; sets the width and height of the player console in pixels.

- **VOLUME.** 0 to 100; the default volume is 100.

- **PLUGINSPAGE.** The URL where the appropriate plug-in player can be downloaded.

- **NOSAVE.** True or false; deactivates the console's save option.

- **BGCOLOR.** #rrggbb; a hexadecimal RGB color code.

- **BGTEXT.** #rrggbb; a hexadecimal RGB color code.

- **DELAY.** n; n = the number of seconds for the delay before the sound file starts to be downloaded (can speed up the display of other elements).

Linking Directly to Sound Files

The simplest way to add sound to your site is to simply link to a sound file. For example, if you link directly to a WAV file, when that link is clicked on, if there is a player installed that can play WAV files, it will open and play the sound file. If the visitor is using Internet Explorer to view the page, the Windows Media Player will likely play the sound file;

if the user is using Netscape Navigator, whichever plug-in WAV player is installed will play the sound file.

Because longer sound files, especially music clips, can be fairly large, it is a good idea to state the file size in kilobytes in conjunction with a link, allowing visitors to decide for themselves whether they want to take the time to download and play the file.

Adding Inline Video

You can use FrontPage to add inline video to your Web page. You can play the following formats: Video for Windows (*.avi), Windows Media (*.asf), and RealMedia (*.ra and *.ram).

NOTE Inline video will only play in Internet Explorer; it won't play in Netscape Navigator.

You can use the Find Utility option (discussed earlier in the section on adding background sounds) to search for any Video for Windows (*.avi) files that might be on your hard drive. If you don't have any on your hard drive, you can find one on the Internet and download it. Then, you can experiment with adding inline video clips to your Web pages. To add a Video for Windows (*.avi) video file to your FrontPage Web page, follow these steps.

1. In FrontPage, open the page to which you want to add the inline video and click the mouse in the page where you want the video to play.
2. Select Insert, Picture, Video.
3. Use the Look In box to open the folder on your hard drive where the AVI (*.avi) or ASF (*.asf) file that you want to use is located. Double-click on the file name to select it.
4. To center your inline video, click on the Center icon on the toolbar.
5. To preview your inline video, click on the Preview tab. Figure C.14 shows an inline video playing in FrontPage's Preview view.

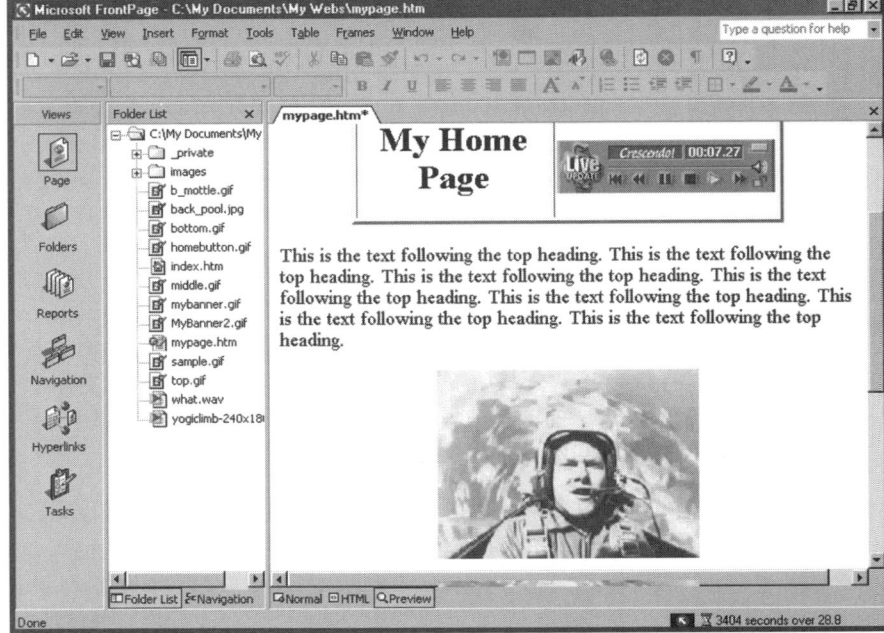

Figure C.14

You can insert and play inline video in your FrontPage Web page, as long as it is an ASF or AVI video file.

CAUTION

The same caution that was given for GIF animations and sound files also applies to any video files you might want to include in your site. Make sure that you're free to use a video file before you publish it to your site. Otherwise, you could be courting a copyright infringement suit (especially if you're a business site).

Other Ways to Add Video and Sound

You can create hypertext links to video files. To include video clips that will play in both Internet Explorer and Netscape Navigator, follow these steps.

1. Click the mouse where you want to create the hypertext link. Type the text you want to use for the link and then click and drag to select the text. (Or, select any text already on your page that you want to use as the link.)

2. Select Insert, Hyperlink.

3. You can select a video file from within your FrontPage Web, or you can use the Look In box to open the file's folder on your hard drive. Double-click on the video file to select it.

4. To check out the link, click on the Preview tab and then click on the link. You should see the video played by the Windows Media Player in a separate window.

NOTE You can create hypertext links to many different video and sound formats. The most common formats you are likely to run across are

- Video files (*.avi, *.mov, *.qt)
- Audio files (*.wav, *.mid, *.rmi, *.snd, *.au, *.aif)
- NetShow (Active Streaming Format) audio and video files (*.asf)
- MPEG audio and video files (*.mpeg, *.mpg, *.mpe, *.mp2)
- MPEG 3 audio files (*.mp3)
- RealMedia files (*.ra, *.ram)

Most of these file formats should play in Internet Explorer without any problem, but some might require extra plug-in support to play in Netscape Navigator.

Adding Streaming Media

Streaming media, like RealAudio and RealVideo, speeds up the process of downloading and playing an audio or video clip by starting to play it (or "streaming" it) before it has been entirely downloaded. RealAudio and RealVideo are not the only forms of streaming media available over the Internet, but they are the most common.

You can use FrontPage to display RealAudio or RealVideo either inline or through a hypertext link. The methods for doing this are the same as described previously for displaying inline video and for creating hypertext links to audio or video files.

Your server needs to have licensed and installed RealServer software to be able to stream RealMedia (RealAudio and RealVideo) files from your Web site. If your server does not support streaming of RealMedia files, you can still offer them. Visitors to your site won't be able to see or hear them until they've been completely downloaded from the Internet, though.

FIND IT ▶
ONLINE

If you want to create your own RealMedia clips, RealNetworks (http://www.real.com) offers a free tool, RealSystem Producer, that you can use for authoring your own RealMedia. You can download it from http://www.real.com/products/tools/producer. A number of shareware sound editors also are available that can convert sound files from other formats to RealMedia (*.ra) files. Two of these are Cool Edit 2000 (http://www.syntrillium.com) and WaveConvert Pro PC (http://www.waves.com). Microsoft also has a new streaming multimedia encoding tool available, the Windows Media 8 Encoding Utility (http://www.microsoft.com/windows/windowsmedia/en/wm8).

Using Other Streaming Media Types

RealMedia audio and video are not the only forms of streaming media you can add to your Web site. Here is a brief listing of some of the other available options.

- **TrueSpeech**. A streaming audio format that can be created using the Windows Sound Recorder and played by the Windows Media Player. A free TrueSpeech Player is available at http://www.dspg.com.

- **Shockwave**. A streaming media format available from Macromedia (http://www.macromedia.com), including audio, video, and animation. The production software and a free player can be downloaded.

- **Audioactive**. A free player that will stream Shockwave files, available at http://www.audioactive.com.

Web Site Promotion Tips and Tricks

There's little point in putting up your snazzy new FrontPage Web site if nobody is going to come to see it. Contrary to popular opinion, the world will not beat a path to your door, especially on the Internet. The fact of the matter is that with more people putting up their own Web sites, it is getting more difficult to get noticed. To make sure that your Web site is noticed, you need to know a few tips and tricks.

Snagging Search Engines

Some search engines have "robots" or "spiders" that crawl the Internet looking for new sites and pages, so you might not have to do anything to get your Web site indexed on those engines. For other search engines, indexes, and directories, you might have to first let them know that you exist before they'll index your site. (For more information on how to submit your Web site to the different search engines, see "Submitting Your Web Site to Search Engines and Indexes" later in this appendix.)

The trick is to prepare your Web pages so that you control how your site will be indexed. This helps ensure that when surfers do relevant Internet searches, your Web page lands at the top of the heap.

Using Keywords

You can increase the likelihood of your page showing up in an Internet search if your title, level-1 heading, and first paragraph contain keywords that searchers are likely to use when searching for the kind of content included in your Web site.

◄ ◄

When people search the Internet using a search form, such as at Yahoo! or NBCi, for example, they type one or more **_keywords_** for which they want to search. The search index then responds with a listing of Web pages that contain the keyword or keywords.

◄ ◄

Including Keywords in Your Title

The title of your page is very important. Many search engines are much more likely to list your page in the first few pages of responses if the keyword or keywords being searched for are included in your title. Make your title both informative and descriptive, and don't be afraid to be a little verbose. A good way to do this is to first state the title of your site and then follow it with a short description, including as many relevant keywords as you can. To edit the title for your Web page, follow these steps.

1. Open your page in FrontPage and then right-click the mouse inside the page and select Page Properties.

2. In the Title box, type a title and a description of your page. Try to include keywords in both the title and the description (see Figure D.1). Click on OK.

Always include an informative title in your Web page. Getting listed by a search engine won't do you any good if Internet searchers pass by the link to your site because your title doesn't provide any relevant information about your site.

The closer a keyword is to the beginning of your page's title, the more weight a search engine will give it. For example, a title like "Yo-Yo Kingdom" would probably get somewhat better search engine results than "John's Incredibly Wonderful Yo-Yo Page" when a search is done on the keyword "yo-yo."

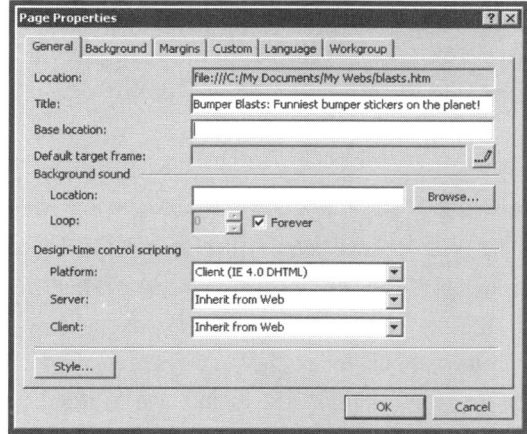

Figure D.1

You can edit your page properties to add a more descriptive title.

Including Keywords in Your Level-1 Headings

It is a good idea to start your Web page with a level-1 heading (the Heading 1 style in FrontPage). Many search engines give special weight to any level-1 heading included at the top of your page, so if you can sneak a few keywords into your level-1 heading, it will help to ensure that Internet searchers will find your site. Place your level-1 heading either at the top of your Web page or immediately following any banner or logo graphic you've inserted at the top of your page. To include a level-1 heading at the top of your page, follow these steps.

1. Click the mouse at the top of your page and press the Enter key to add a line.

2. Click on the line you just created and then select the Heading 1 style from the Style box.

3. Type the text for your level-1 heading. Try to include one or two keywords, if you can. To center your level-1 heading, click on the Center button on the Formatting toolbar.

Because search engines place special weight on any headings (Heading 1, Heading 2, and so on) that are in your Web page when indexing your site, avoid using these styles just to format your text in a bigger font. Only use the heading styles to designate the order of precedence within your page's hierarchical structure, and not as formatting devices. If you want to increase the font size for a section of text in your page, select the text and then click on the Font Size box and select a font size of 4, 5, or 6.

❖ ❖

CAUTION A trick that sneaky Web authors used to use to get listed higher in Internet search response lists was to include one or more choice keywords repeated multiple times at the top of a Web page. These were all neatly concealed from public view inside comment tags. Search engines, however, would index the comment text and pop the page to the top of their response list for searches using the commented keyword or keywords. Be aware, however, that search engines are aware of this trick. Now, if you try to do this, your page is liable to be demoted, if not eliminated, in a search engine's list of responses.

❖ ❖

Including Keywords in Your First Paragraph

Many search engines will index the text at the start of your Web page but ignore the rest. Others will weigh the first 30, 40, or more words higher than other words in your page when indexing your site. The more keywords you can strategically include in the first paragraph of your Web page, the more likely that Internet searchers will be able to find your page. Many search engines and directories will also display your page's initial 30 to 40 words when listing your site in a search response. Put special thought into composing the first couple of sentences on your page—the more informative you are right off the bat, the better.

Don't just include keywords in your introductory paragraph; include key phrases as well. Many people will use key phrases, such as "real estate," "nuclear energy," or "movie stars" when doing an Internet search. Try to anticipate the kinds of phrases someone might use when searching for a Web page like yours. Try to include those key phrases in your introductory paragraph.

NOTE

Some people recommend that you avoid using framed pages because a frameset page doesn't actually contain any content, just links to the page frames that make up your framed page. Because it doesn't have any real content to be indexed, a framed page is less likely to get listed among the top responses to an Internet search. If you do want to use a framed page, be sure to include an informative title. Also, always include a META tag (user-variable) description and list of keywords. See the next section, "Working with User-Variable Descriptions and Keywords," for directions on how to include these in your Web page.

Another trick is to type a description of your site, including keywords and key phrases, in the "noframes" section of the framed page. The "noframes" section is the part of the framed page that will be displayed by a browser that doesn't support frames, but won't be displayed by a browser that supports frames. That doesn't mean, however, that a search engine won't index it.

Working with User-Variable Descriptions and Keywords

User variables are commonly referred to as *META tag variables* because the META tag in HTML is used to add this information to your Web page's head section. You can define user variables for your Web page that can include a description of your Web page or Web site and a list of keywords.

Some search engines will give special priority to META tag descriptions and keywords when indexing your site. Also, some search engines will display your META tag description, rather than the first paragraph of your page, when listing your site. Always include a META tag description and a list of keywords in at least the front (index or default) Web page of your site.

Adding a META Tag Description

Adding a META tag description to your page is easy, so there's no reason not to do it. To add a META tag description to your Web page, follow these steps.

1. Right-click the mouse inside your page and select Page Properties.

2. Click on the Custom tab. Under User Variables, select Add. The User Meta Variable dialog box appears.

3. In the Name box, type **description**. In the Value box, type a concise description of your Web page. Try to include several keywords in your description that you think someone might use in trying to search for a page like yours (see Figure D.2). Click on OK.

4. The description META tag variable is added to your page's list of user variables. Click on OK.

Adding a META Tag List of Keywords

It is also a good idea to add a META tag list of keywords to your Web page. It's easy! To add a META tag list of keywords to your Web page, follow these steps.

1. Right-click the mouse inside your page and select Page Properties.

2. Click on the Custom tab. Under User Variables, select Add. The User Meta Variable dialog box appears.

3. In the Name box, type **keywords**. In the Value box, type a list of keywords separated by commas (see Figure D.3). Click on OK.

4. The keywords META tag variable is added to your page's list of user variables (see Figure D.4). Click on OK.

Figure D.2

You can add a META tag description that some search engines will use when indexing your Web page.

Figure D.3

You can define a META tag list of keywords that some search engines will use when indexing your site.

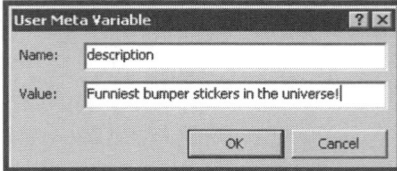

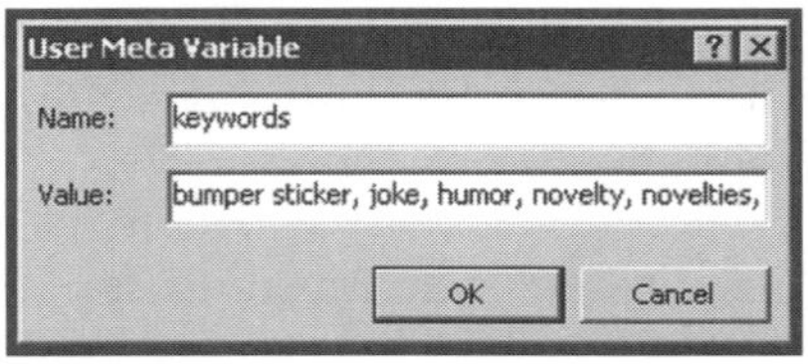

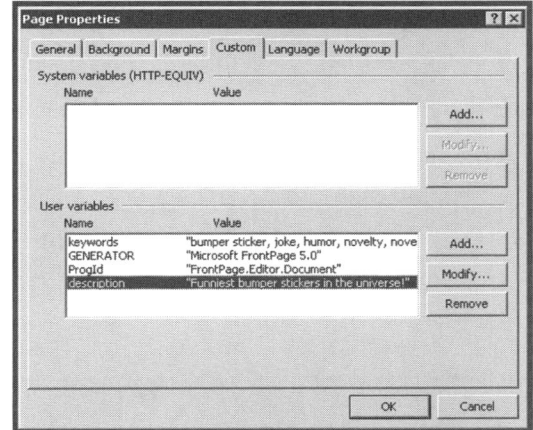

Figure D.4

The keywords
META tag variable
is added to your
page's list of
user variables.

TIP

■ ■
Another way to include words and phrases that might be indexed by a search engine is
to include alternative text for any images on your page. The alternative text is displayed
if visitors to your page have the display of graphics turned off or are using a text-only
browser. It can also be helpful to visitors using a Braille browser. Most browsers also
display alternative text when you pass the mouse over an image. To add alternative text
to an image, right-click on the image, select Picture Properties, and then click on the
General tab. In the Text box (under Alternative Representations), type the alternative text
that you want to attach to your image.
■ ■

Blocking a Search Engine from Indexing Your Web Pages

Sometimes you don't want your Web page to be indexed. It might be
under construction, or you might want to encourage visitors to come in
at your first page, rather than at pages deeper into your Web site. Many
search engines use robots to index Web sites on the Internet. It would be
nice if you could tell them which pages you want indexed and which ones
you don't. Well, you can, in a way. That is, you can tell some robots where
to go (primarily the AltaVista and Infoseek Guide robots, but there might

be more). To have some control over which of your pages are indexed and which aren't, follow these steps.

1. Right-click the mouse inside your page and select Page Properties.

2. Click on the Custom tab. Under User Variables, click on Add. The User Meta Variable dialog box appears.

3. In the Name box, type **robots**. Type **noindex** in the Value box to tell a robot or spider not to index the page. Click on OK twice.

BOSSING AROUND THE BOT

You can use other values with the robots variable, as shown in Figure D.5:

- **index.** Index the current page.

- **follow.** Continue to any following pages.

- **nofollow.** Don't continue to any following pages.

Figure D.5

The robots META tag variable is added to your page's list of user variables.

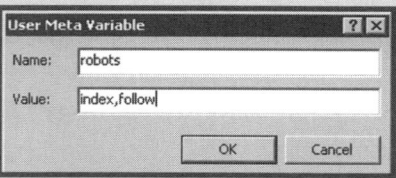

You can also combine values. You might try one of these combinations:

- **index,follow.** Index the current page and go on to any following pages.

- **noindex,follow.** Do not index the current page, but go on to any following pages.

- **noindex,nofollow.** Do not index the current page and do not index any following pages.

- **index,nofollow.** Index the current page, but do not go on to any following pages.

Announcing Your Web Site

After you've put up your Web site, you're going to want to announce it to the world. This can be done a couple of different ways on the Internet. You can

- Post an announcement on the newsgroup: comp.infosystems.www.announce

- Post announcements to appropriate online newsletters and mailing lists

Announcing Your Site to comp.infosystems.www.announce

The newsgroup comp.infosystems.www.announce has been created specifically for posting announcements about what's new on the Internet. This newsgroup is limited to announcing noncommercial Web sites, so if you have a commercial Web site, do not post to this newsgroup. It is considered poor etiquette to post new site announcements to other newsgroups, unless on topic announcements are allowed. Always check a newsgroup's FAQ or charter to see what kinds of announcements are allowed before posting any. To post to the comp.infosystems.www.announce newsgroup, you will need to have a newsreader configured and installed. This can be Netscape Messenger, Outlook Express, or Free Agent. You will need to subscribe to comp.infosystems.www.announce so that you can download messages from it and post your own announcement message. Be sure to read the newsgroup charter first at http://www.sangfroid.com/charter.html before posting any announcements.

Announcing Your Site to E-Mail Newsletters and Mailing Lists

You can also announce your site to a number of e-mail newsletters and mailing lists. These include Netsurfer Digest and Internet Scout Project.

Netsurfer Digest

FIND IT ► ONLINE

Netsurfer Digest is an e-mail newsletter that is a "guide to interesting news, places, and resources online." You can find out about it and how to subscribe to it at http://www.netsurf.com/nsd/index.html. Any announcement that you want to have considered for inclusion should be e-mailed to pressroom@netsurf.com.

Internet Scout Project

The National Science Foundation sponsors the Internet Scout Project to provide timely information to the education community about valuable Internet resources. It is composed of two services, Scout Report and Net-Happenings. More than 100,000 people receive the weekly Scout Report. More than 25,000 people receive Net-Happenings daily. Net-Happenings is also available as a newsgroup, www.internet.net-happenings.

To find out how to subscribe to Scout Report and Net-Happenings and to find out what their criteria are for accepting announcements, go to http://www.scout.cs.wisc.edu/scout (see Figure D.6).

FIND IT ► ONLINE

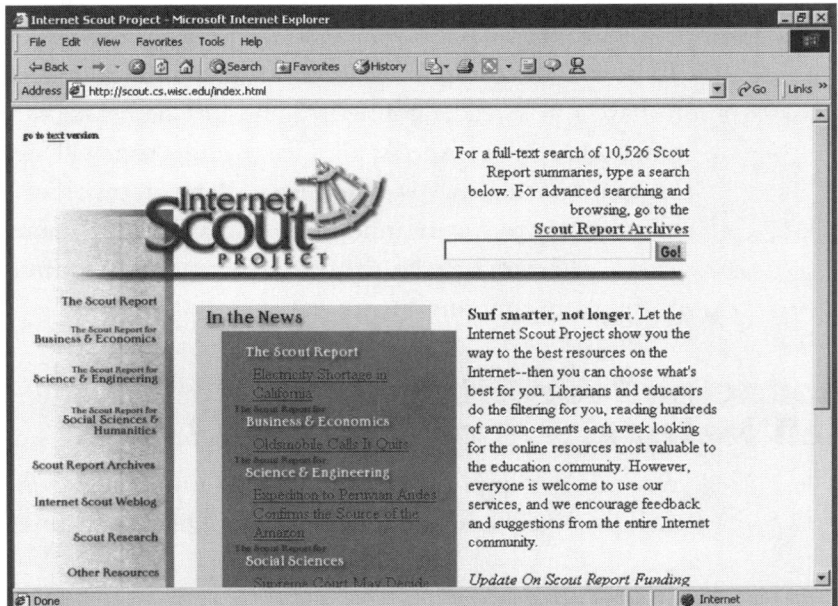

Figure D.6

Through the Internet Scout Project, you can submit announcements to both the Scout Report and Net-Happenings.

Submitting Your Web Site to Search Engines and Indexes

Some search engine robots and spiders roam freely around the Internet looking for new sites. However, the best way to get the most attention for your site in the shortest possible time is to submit information about your Web site to the major search engines and index directories.

Getting Your Site Listed on Yahoo!

If you don't get your site listed anywhere else, try to get it listed at Yahoo!. Getting listed at Yahoo! can make all the difference between whether you get a stream of new visitors each day or just a trickle. Here are some pointers on getting your site listed at Yahoo!.

FIND IT ▶
ONLINE

✿ Be sure to thoroughly read the guidelines on how to suggest a new site to Yahoo! at http://www.yahoo.com/info/suggest.

✿ Before actually starting, take the time to compose a description of your site in 30 words or less. Be sure to include as many appropriate keywords as you can in your description, but don't go overboard. The main thing is to have it accurately and informatively describe the content of your site. When you fill out Yahoo!'s site suggestion form, you can just paste in your description when you're asked for it. Save this description to use when you submit your site to other search engines and index directories.

✿ When you suggest your site for a category at Yahoo!, the form asks you what other categories you think would be appropriate for your Web site. So, before suggesting your site for a category, look through Yahoo! for other appropriate categories. A good way to do this is to open Windows Notepad and make a list of appropriate categories. Then, when you suggest your site to the first category, you can also include the other Yahoo! categories appropriate for your site. That way, you only need to fill out Yahoo!'s site suggestion form once.

✪ Don't suggest your site to too many or to inappropriate Yahoo! categories. Suggest your site to only the three or four of the most appropriate categories for your site.

✪ Be patient. Yahoo! has actual human beings (not robots or spiders) visit your site and review its contents. Then, if they feel it is appropriate, they might recommend your site for inclusion in the category that you've requested. There is no guarantee that you will get listed in the categories that you request. Also, the amount of time that it takes to get listed in different categories can vary—anywhere from a week to a couple months. This is because some categories get a lot of suggestions to review, whereas others only get a few. Suggesting your site again won't help—it'll only bump you to the back of the queue. So, before suggesting your site to a category again, wait at least three months. Then, if you still don't get listed, try another category.

Manually Submitting Your Site to the Other Top Search Engines and Indexes

There are many places other than Yahoo! where you'll want to submit your site. I recommend that you individually and manually submit your Web site to each of these search engines and directory indexes, rather than try to use an automatic submission service. You'll get better results if you can fine-tune your submission for each one. Later, you can use one of the automatic submission services to catch as many other submission sites as you can.

If you have already composed a description of your site (seeded with relevant keywords), you might want to open or paste it into Windows Notepad so you'll have it handy if you're asked to submit a description when you submit your site.

Table D.1 lists the main search engines and index directories, along with their Web addresses, to which you should submit your site.

TABLE D.1 SEARCH ENGINES AND INDEX DIRECTORIES

Search Engine or Index Directory	URL	Directions for Submitting Your Site
AltaVista	http://www.altavista.net	Click on the Submit a Site link at the bottom of the page.
Excite	http://www.excite.com	Click on the Submit a Site link at the bottom of the page.
GoTo	http://www.goto.com	Click on the List Sites and Products link at the bottom of the page.
WebCrawler	http://www.webcrawler.com	Click on the Add Your URL link at the bottom of the page.
Lycos	http://www.lycos.com	Click on the Add Your Site to Lycos link at the bottom of the page.
LookSmart	http://www.looksmart.com	Click on the Submit a Site link at the bottom of the page.
HotBot	http://www.hotbot.com	Click on the Submit Web Site link on the left side of the page.
Ask Jeeves	http://www.ask.com	See the AJ Editorial Guidelines at http://www.ask.com/docs/about/policy.html.
NBCi.com	http://www.nbci.com	Click on the Submit a Site link at the bottom of the page.

Using Free Site Submission Services

The Internet has many places where you can get your site listed. It would take forever to submit your site to them all. However, after you've manually submitted your site to the main search engines and index directories listed in the previous section, try one of the free site submission services available on the Internet.

TIP

You might want to keep a log of where you've submitted your site and when. The free site submission services let you select or clear the sites to which you want to submit your site, so having a log of where you've already submitted your site can help you avoid submitting your site more than once to the same place. If you also include when you submitted your site to a particular service, then you can remind yourself to update your listing every six months or so. This will ensure that the listing accurately represents your current site.

Table D.2 lists some of the free site submission services available on the Internet.

TABLE D.2 FREE SITE SUBMISSION SERVICES		
Submission Service	**URL**	**Details**
Submit It! Free Trial from Microsoft bCentral	http://submitit.bcentral.com/sitrial.htm	Fill out a form to submit your site to 19 different places.
Add Me!	http://www.addme.com	Add Me! can automatically submit your site to more than 30 different search engines and Web directories.
1 2 3 Add Masters Web Promotion Tool	http://www.123-add-masters.com	You can submit to their top 30 search sites for free.

Promoting Your Web Site

You can promote your Web site in many ways. You can get reciprocal links, use banner exchange networks, join Web rings, purchase banner ads, and use traditional promotional methods.

Getting Reciprocal Links

A great way to boost your traffic over time is to trade reciprocal links. Look for other sites related in some way to your own and offer to link to them if they will link to you. Others might also e-mail you that they want to link to you in return for your linking to them. Sometimes this takes a little negotiation because where and how you link to another site, or how they link to you, can make a difference. If someone just wants to link to you as one link among a hundred on a links page, then you probably wouldn't want to link back to that site prominently on your first page, unless you think it represents a significant value to your visitors. On the other hand, you might want to create a links page of your own if anyone asks for a reciprocal link.

Another thing you can do is put up a page of links that focuses on the general subject area of, or subject areas related to, your Web site. You might want to break up your links into different related areas. For example, if your Web site is called "The Michigan Weather Page," you could put up a couple of link pages, such as "Michigan Resources" and "Weather Resources," and then link to both prominently from your front page. That way, you won't just be sticking reciprocal links into a generic links page, and you should be able to get a better link back in return. In other words, when you design your page, think of ways that you can work in opportunities for being able to offer quality reciprocal links. If you're using a navigation bar on your page, for example, you might want to include links to your links pages there. Don't make it just an afterthought.

One key is to look for other sites with which you can form a relationship of synergy. The idea is that by prominently linking to each other (even swapping banner ads, for example), both sites can generate more traffic by sharing traffic. Establish two or three of these synergic relationships and you could see a significant boost to your traffic as a result.

Using Banner Exchange Networks

With a banner exchange network, you agree to display a banner ad on your page, in return for getting exposure through display of your banner ad on others' pages. Some banner exchange services allow you to restrict or focus the kinds of banner ads that will be displayed on your page. You can also suggest the type of pages on which your banner will be displayed. If your site is noncommercial, you might want to only display banner ads for other noncommercial Web sites.

The amount of exposure your banner ad will get on others' sites is determined by how many times the banner exchange's banner ad is displayed or clicked on in your own page or pages. The more traffic through your site, in other words, the more plays your banner ad will get on others' pages.

One trick here is to create an effective banner ad that will snag visitors for you. It doesn't do you any good to have your banner ad displayed on others' pages if no one clicks on it. It pays to put some forethought into the kind of banner ad you want to create. If you have completed the Sunday Evening session, "Creating Web Art Special Effects," you should be able to create a visually appealing banner ad. Of course, you can hire a graphics professional or advertising expert to create your banner ad for you, but that tends to be overkill for your basic "bootstrap" Web site.

Some banner exchange networks require a banner ad to be specific dimensions and not exceed a certain number of kilobytes in size (usually 10K or smaller). Transparent GIFs are usually discouraged or prohibited because you can't anticipate what the background color, tone, or texture might be on pages where your ad will be displayed. (If transparent GIFs are allowed, don't use any shadow or blended edges, and turn off smoothing.) A few banner exchange networks will allow you to use a GIF animation for your banner ad, but most won't.

Many banner exchange networks' terms and conditions state that their banner be the only banner ad displayed on your page. They also want it displayed prominently toward the top of your page ("above the fold").

Members who stack exchange banners from different services, or who artificially inflate traffic to their site to earn extra credits, might have their memberships terminated.

You can usually view statistics on how many credits you've received, how many times your banner ad has been displayed, and how many times it's been clicked.

Table D.3 lists some of the free banner exchange networks that you can use.

TABLE D.3 FREE BANNER EXCHANGE NETWORKS		
Banner Exchange	**URL**	**Details**
LinkExchange	http://adnetwork.bcentral.com	This was the first free banner exchange network and it is still probably the largest. Microsoft liked it so much they bought it and integrated it to the bCentral.com Internet business services. You can specify that you want only noncommercial banner ads displayed on your pages.
123Banners	http://www.123banners.com	A fairly straightforward banner exchange network that doesn't allow you to specify which kinds of ads get displayed on your page.
Exchange-it!	http://www.exchange-it.com	Exchange-it! accepts ads only from Web sites with content suitable for children.
CyberLink Exchange	http://www.cyberlinkexchange.com	CyberLink Exchange lets you create banner ads with multiple click-points, so one banner ad can link to several Web pages.

Joining Web Rings

A *Web ring* is a way of joining together Web sites that share a common theme. When you join a Web ring, you insert the code and banner for the Web ring on your page. Then visitors to your page can visit other pages in the ring. Because you are part of the ring, others can visit your Web page from other pages participating in the ring. Web rings can be a great way of generating traffic targeted to your particular area of interest.

Web rings exist for just about any imaginable theme or subject. For links to many Web rings, check out Yahoo!'s category for Web rings at http://dir.webring.yahoo.com/rw.

Purchasing Banner Ads

If you have a commercial site, you might want to consider advertising on other sites to get exposure. You could, for example, pay for a banner ad on a Web site that has many visitors who might also be interested in your Web site. Another option is to sponsor someone else's Web page. Sponsoring a Web page usually means that your banner ad will be displayed at the top of the page you're sponsoring.

Placing your own banner ad on other Web sites doesn't necessarily have to cost a bundle. If you find a Web site with a good amount of traffic that you think would also be interested in your service or product, simply make an offer. There are really no rules of thumb for what the right price is. It is simply whatever you can agree on. What's ten or twenty dollars a month, if it results in more than $1,000 in sales? Of course, it might also result in no sales at all, in which case you can drop your ad. You could also offer to exchange banner ads, which wouldn't cost you anything.

Some Web sites are essentially in the business of selling advertising. It makes sense that a high-traffic site will charge more to place a banner ad than a lower-traffic site will, just like buying commercial time for the SuperBowl broadcast is infinitely more expensive than buying time during a talk show that airs at 3:00am. If you want to advertise on Yahoo!, for example, expect to pay a bunch. Sites that are in the business of selling advertising usually also can provide daily or weekly statistical reports on how many times your banner ad has been displayed and how many click-throughs it has had.

Of course, after you start to attract enough traffic to your own site, you could start selling banner ads yourself.

Using Traditional Promotional Methods

Don't overlook using traditional promotional methods. Not everything you do to promote your Web site needs to be Web-based. Here are some traditional methods you can use to promote your Web site.

- Include your Web address (URL) on your letterhead and business cards.

- Include your Web address in any print or other advertising you might do. If you have an ad in the Yellow Pages, be sure to also include your Web address there.

- Send out press releases or press kits to local, regional, or national media outlets, as well as to any appropriate trade or professional media outlets.

- Get creative. Print your Web address on pens, notepads, buttons, T-shirts, and so on, then include them in your press kits or pass them out to customers or potential customers.

Implementing Special Features

Although a lot of information has been covered so far, covering absolutely everything you can do with FrontPage would take several weekends, at least. If you've done all the optional sections, you might already be suffering from information overload.

This appendix covers some of the more advanced things you can do with FrontPage. I won't be able to go into much detail here, but hopefully I can get you started along the right path. This appendix will cover the following topics:

- ❂ Installing a personal Web server (PWS)
- ❂ Setting up a password-protected Web site
- ❂ Creating a Discussion Web
- ❂ Using the Database Results Wizard
- ❂ Adding Java applets and ActiveX controls

Setting up a Personal Web Server

Unlike FrontPage 98, later versions of FrontPage do not require that a *personal Web server* (PWS) be installed on your local computer. For that reason, a personal Web server is not included with FrontPage.

◄ ◄

A *personal Web server* is a Web server you can install on your local computer, allowing you to publish and test your pages locally first, before publishing them to your remote server.

◄ ◄

If you are using Windows 98, you can install Microsoft Personal Web Server 4.0 from the Windows 98 CD-ROM. Just insert the Windows 98 disc in your CD-ROM drive, click on the Start button, and then select Run. In the Open box, type **d:\add-ons\pws\setup.exe** (substitute the drive letter of your CD-ROM drive for *d:*) and click on OK.

The Windows NT 4.0 Option Pack also includes a copy of MS PWS 4.0 that can be installed by both Windows 95 and Windows NT users. You can download the Windows NT 4.0 Option Pack from Microsoft's Web site.

NOTE Earlier versions of Microsoft PWS do not support ASP. Support for ASP is necessary if you want to do the Database Results Wizard example later in this appendix.

Installing the FrontPage 2000 Server Extensions on Your PWS

Microsoft PWS 4.0 comes with the FrontPage 98 server extensions already installed. Before you can publish your database to your personal Web server, you first need to upgrade its server extensions to the FrontPage 2000 (or later) server extensions. To do this, you need to run the Server Extensions Administrator from the Start menu.

- For Windows 95/98, select Start, Programs, Microsoft Office Tools, Server Extensions Administrator.

- For Windows NT Workstation, select Start, Programs, Administrative Tools, Server Extensions Administrator.

- For Windows NT Server 4.0 (without Microsoft Information Server 4.0 installed), select Start, Programs, Administrative Tools, Server Extensions Administrator.

- For Windows NT Server 4.0 (with Microsoft Information Server 4.0 installed), select Start, Programs, Windows NT 4.0 Option Pack, Microsoft Internet Information Server, Internet Service Manager.

With the Microsoft Management Console window open, do the following:

1. In the tree structure in the left pane, click on the + button to the left of FrontPage Server Extensions to expand the contents (if they aren't already expanded). Then, right-click on the selection listed under FrontPage Server Extensions.

2. If it isn't grayed out, select Task, Upgrade Server Extensions. If the Task option is grayed out, select New, Web to open the Server Extensions Configuration Wizard.

NOTE If the Task option is grayed out, it means that no FrontPage server extensions have been previously installed. If the Check Server Extensions option is displayed as the Task option, it means that the FrontPage 2000 server extensions have already been installed.

3. After you install the server extensions, right-click on the selection listed under FrontPage Server Extensions and select the Task option to display the Check Server Extensions option (see Figure E.1).

4. If you select the Check Server Extensions option, your server extensions will be checked in the Check Web dialog box (see Figure E.2). When the check is finished, click on Close.

5. Select Console, Exit. Click on Yes to save your new console settings.

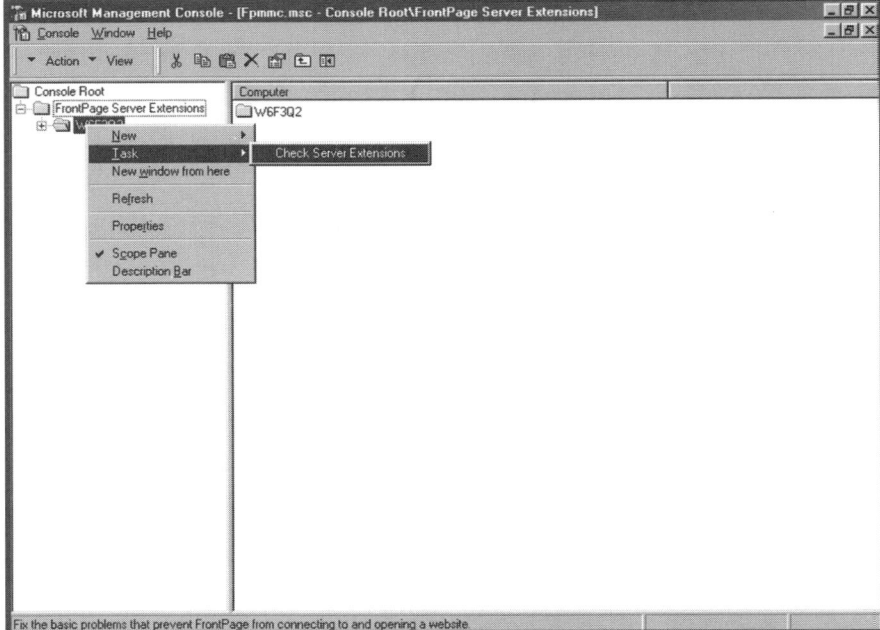

Figure E.1

The Check Server
Extensions option
is displayed if
the extensions
have been
successfully
installed for
your PWS.

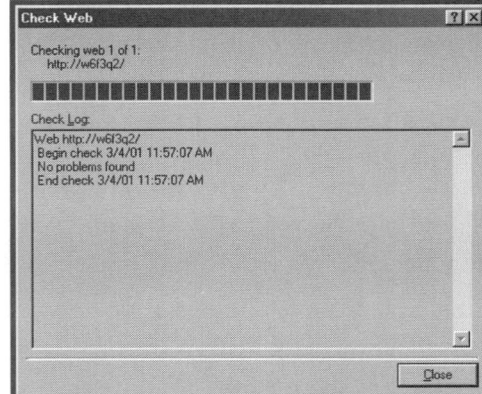

Figure E.2

You can check your
server extensions
to make sure that
they're working
properly.

Setting up a Password-Protected Web Site

With FrontPage, you can set permissions and control user access to the FrontPage Webs you create or edit on a Web server. The permissions that can be set by FrontPage are as follows:

- ✿ **Browse**. A user can browse the files in a Web.
- ✿ **Author**. A user can browse and edit files in a Web.
- ✿ **Administrator**. A user can administer a Web by adding and removing users.

You won't be able to test security restriction settings on your local Web. First, you'll have to publish your site to your remote Web server. To set permissions and assign user names and passwords, you'll need to have administrator rights for your Web folders. To test whether you have administrator rights, remotely open your site in FrontPage after you've published it to your Web server.

If the Servers option on the Tools menu is grayed out, either you don't have administrator rights assigned to you or your Web server does not support setting security restrictions. If the option is grayed out, request administrator rights for your Web site from your Web hosting service's support. If your Web Host isn't willing to do that, but you really need to set up security restrictions, you might want to consider finding another provider. As a last resort, you can request that your Web Host set the permissions and assign user names and passwords for you. This is not a good solution, though, if you'll need to revise the security permissions on an ongoing basis, rather than just once.

In FrontPage 98, you could only set security permissions for your entire site. With later versions of FrontPage, you can set separate security permissions for any subwebs you've created. This lets you assign different levels of permissions for different individuals (or lists of individuals or workgroups) for different subwebs.

Setting Permissions

After you've opened your remote Web in FrontPage, you can set permissions for your root Web by following these steps.

1. Click the mouse on your root Web folder (http://...) to select it. Select Tools, Server (if it is not grayed out), Permissions (see Figure E.3).

2. The Permissions dialog box opens (see Figure E.4). To restrict access to registered users only, select the Valid Username and Password Required to Browse this Web check box at the bottom of the dialog box.

3. To add a user to the list of authorized users for your site, click on the Add button.

4. Add a fictional user: In the Name box, type **Joe_Smith**. In the Password box, type a password. In the Confirm Password box, retype the password.

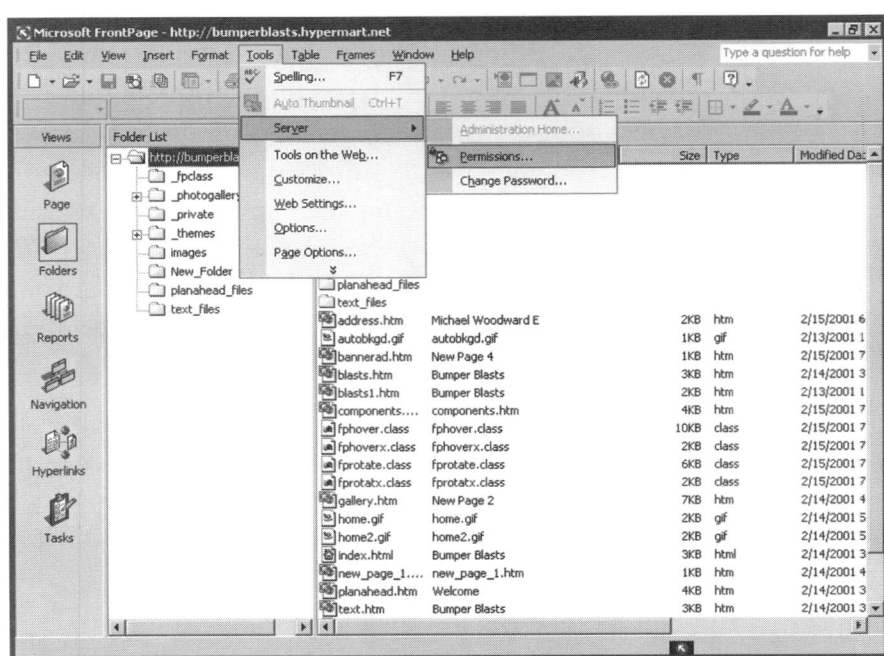

Figure E.3

Select Tools, Server, Permissions to set user access permissions for your Web.

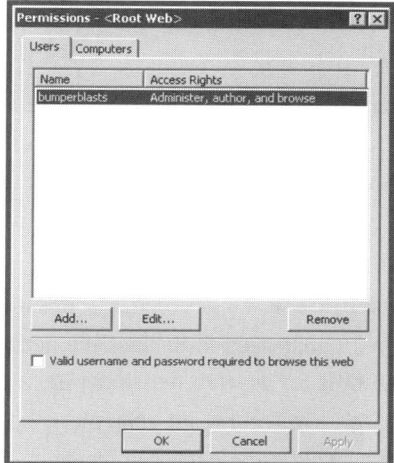

Figure E.4

The Permissions dialog box lets you assign user names and access rights.

Don't include any spaces in user names or passwords. In user names, substitute underscores (_) in place of spaces. Also, be aware that both user names and passwords are case-sensitive. When you provide user names and passwords to users, be sure to tell them to type the appropriate user name and password exactly as shown.

5. For this example, leave the Browse this Web radio button selected (to allow Joe Smith to only browse your pages). The other radio buttons allow you to assign either author or administer rights to Joe Smith (see Figure E.5).

Figure E.5

Specify a user name, password, and browsing rights.

6. Click on OK to add Joe Smith to the list of registered users for your site (see Figure E.6).

7. Repeat these steps for as many other users as you want to add. To change the settings for any user, highlight the user name and select Edit. To remove a user, highlight the user name and select Remove. When you're done, click on OK to close the Permissions dialog box.

◆ ◆

CAUTION When assigning passwords, you might need to balance the need for both security and convenience. The easiest passwords for users to remember are also often the easiest to crack. To ensure the highest degree of security for your site, especially if you're assigning author or administer rights, avoid using letter combinations that can be found in a dictionary and sequential numbers (1234, for example). Include both letters and numbers, and mix in both uppercase and lowercase letters. Needless to say, the longer the password, the more difficult it will be to crack.

◆ ◆

● ●

NOTE To reset the permissions for your Web so that everyone can browse it again, click the mouse on your root Web folder (http://...) to select it. Select Tools, Server, Permissions, and then deselect the check box at the bottom of the Permissions dialog box.

● ●

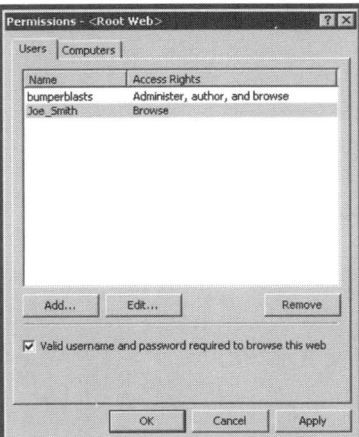

Figure E.6

A new user has been added to the list of registered users.

If you're planning to set up a password registration system that automatically assigns user names and passwords, your site must be located on a Unix server. Windows NT security and Microsoft Internet Information Services do not allow registration through a Web browser. For more information on this, see FrontPage's Help system or query your Web Host's technical support.

Creating a Discussion Web

A Discussion Web (or discussion forum) can be a nice feature to add to your site. For one thing, it'll help make your site "stickier," by getting visitors to come back multiple times just to participate in your forum. Adding a Discussion Web to your site is easy in FrontPage.

1. Select File, New, Page or Web.

2. Under New from Template, select Web Site Templates.

3. Click on the Discussion Web Wizard icon to highlight it. Check the Add to Current Web check box (see Figure E.7). Click on OK.

4. In the opening window for the Discussion Web Wizard, click on Next after reading the introduction.

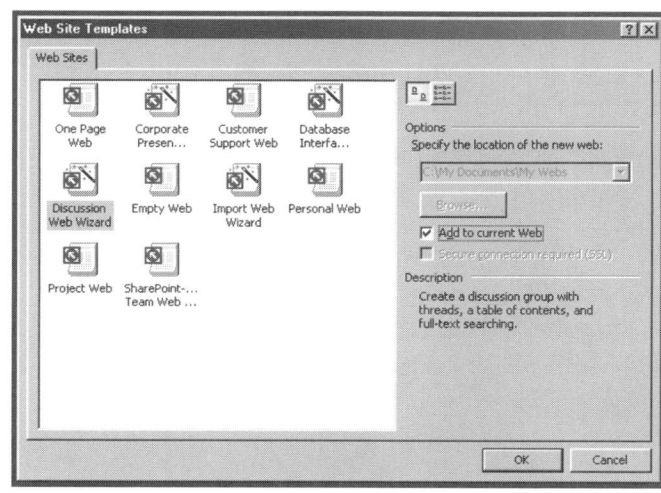

Figure E.7

The Discussion Web Wizard is included with FrontPage's Web site templates.

5. Specify the main features to be included in your Discussion Web. For this example, leave all the options checked (see Figure E.8). Click on Next.

6. The next dialog box asks you to specify a title for your Discussion Web and a name for the discussion folder (see Figure E.9). For this example, accept the default title and discussion folder name. Click on Next.

7. Specify the set of input fields for the discussion submission form. For this example, leave the first option (Subject, Comments) selected. (You can add more fields later if you want.) Click on Next.

8. Specify whether your Discussion Web will be located in a protected Web. For this example, leave the second radio button (No, Anyone Can Post Articles) selected. Click on Next.

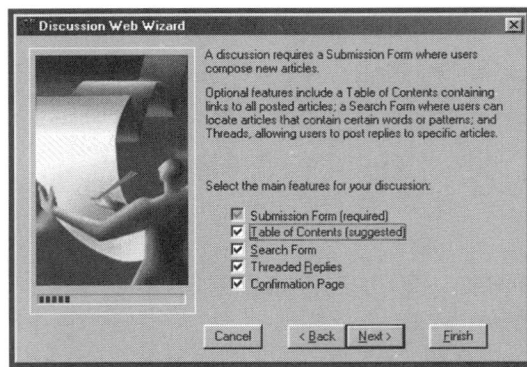

Figure E.8

Specify which features you want to include in your Discussion Web.

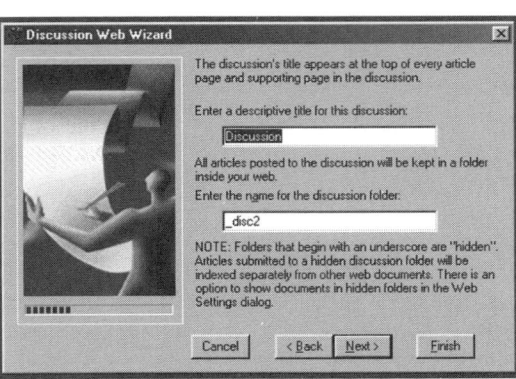

Figure E.9

Specify a title for your Discussion Web and a name for the discussion folder.

9. Specify how the list of posted articles will be sorted. For this example, leave the first radio button option (Oldest to Newest) selected. Click on Next.

10. Specify whether you want the Table of Contents page to be the home page for the Web. For this example, leave the No radio button selected. (You can change this later if you want.) Click on Next.

11. Specify the information to be reported by the Search Form for matching documents. Leave the default selected (Subject, Size, Date). Click on Next.

12. Specify how you want your Discussion Web to be laid out. For this example, leave the default selected (Dual Interface – Use Frames if Available), as shown in Figure E.10. Click on Next.

13. Read the information in the wizard's final dialog box. Click on Finish.

Linking to Your Discussion Web

Add any links to your site's pages that you want to connect to your Discussion Web. For example, you might include a link on your home page that says, "Participate in My Discussion Forum." Link it to the opening page of your Discussion Web (disc2_frm.htm, for example).

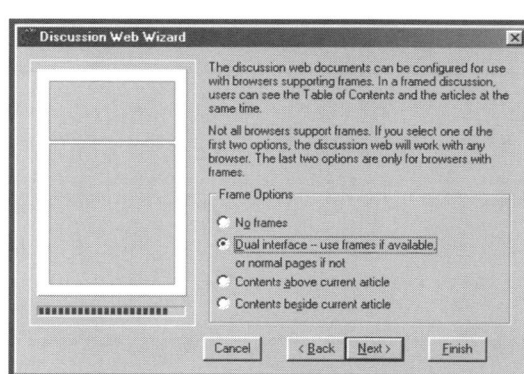

Figure E.10

Choose what frames layout you want to use (or choose not to use frames).

Testing Your Discussion Web

Although you can view your Discussion Web's opening pages without first publishing them, to fully check out your Discussion Web, you'll need to publish it to a server with the FrontPage server extensions installed. This can be either a remote server or a personal Web server on your local machine. Figure E.11 shows the Discussion Web's opening page after being published to a FrontPage server.

To start a new thread, click on the Post a New Article link. Fill out the form fields and then click on the Post Article button (see Figure E.12).

After you post your article, a confirmation page is displayed. If you refresh the main page, you'll see your new thread added to the top frame of the Discussion Web (see Figure E.13).

If visitors click on the new thread, they'll be able to respond to it by clicking on the Reply link.

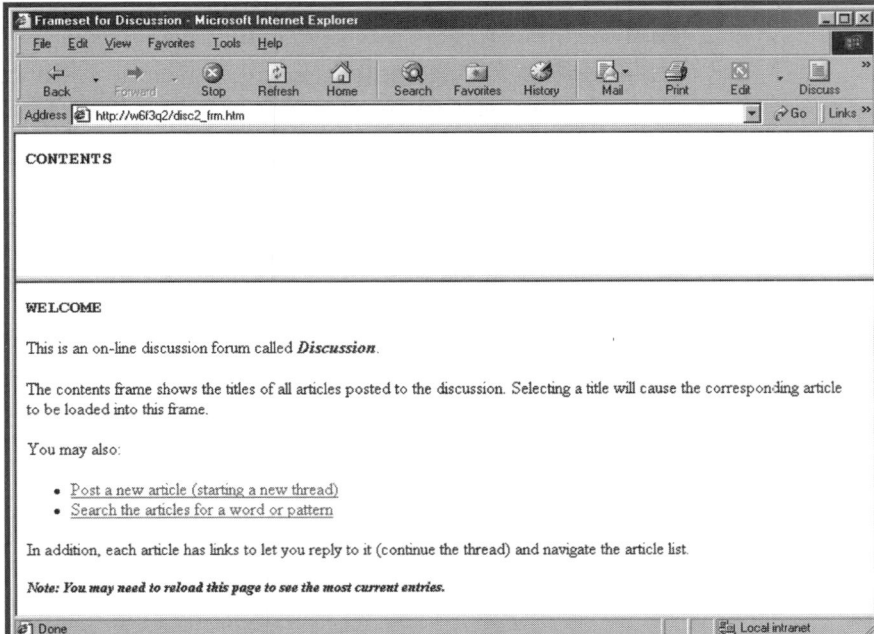

Figure E.11

The Discussion Web's opening page, viewed in a Web browser.

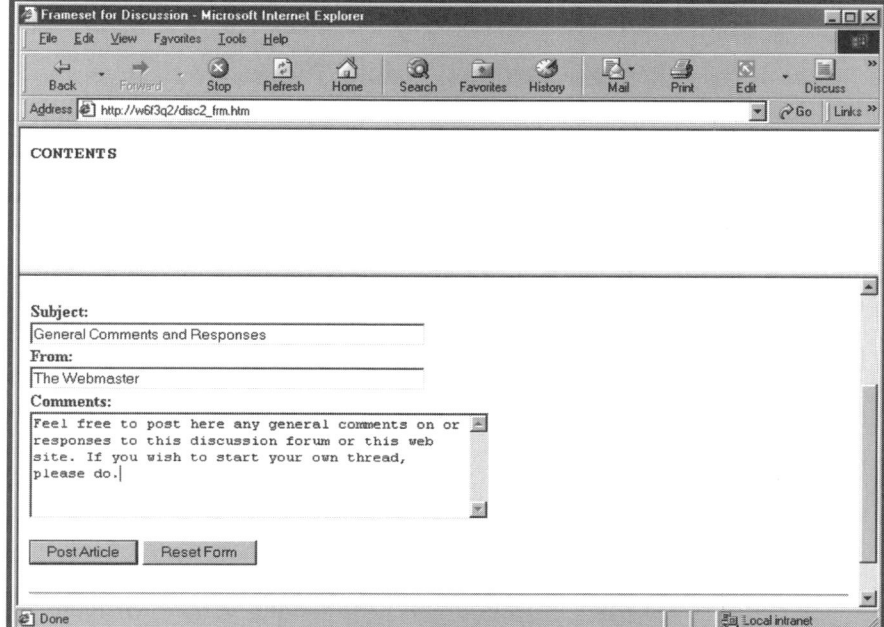

Figure E.12

Fill out the Subject, From, and Comments fields for a new article.

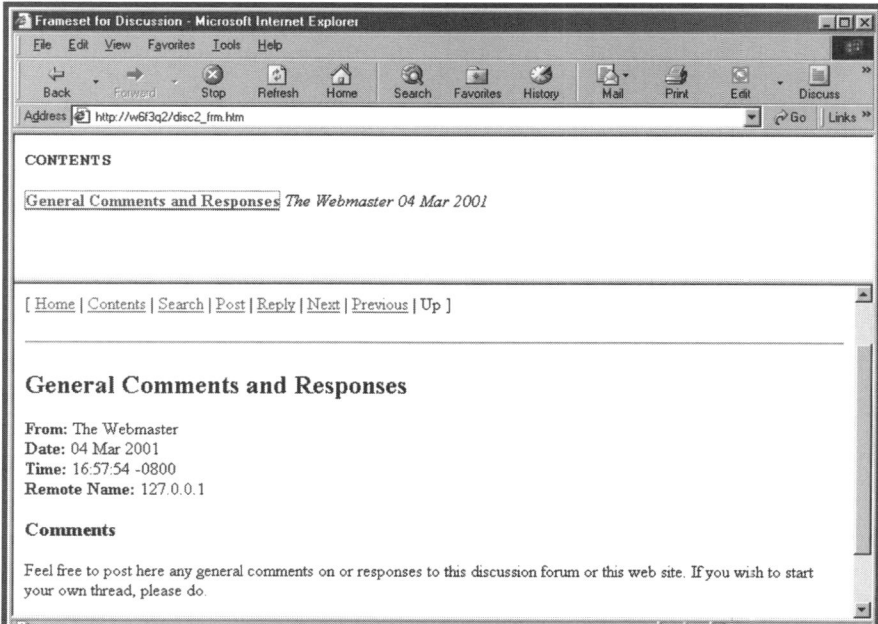

Figure E.13

The new thread is added to the Contents frame.

Using the Database Results Wizard

Using the Database Results Wizard, you can easily display information from an online Access or Excel database in your pages. Although the operation of the Database Results Wizard is deceptively simple, getting the actual database results to work can be a little tricky.

Before You Start

Before you start trying to use the Database Results Wizard, you'll need to install the following:

- Microsoft Personal Web Server (Version 4.0)
- The FrontPage 2000 server extensions on your PWS
- A 32-bit ODBC driver (if it is not already installed)

The Database Results Wizard creates an ASP page, rather than a regular HTML file. You'll need to install a version of PWS that supports ASP if you want to preview your database query results on your local computer. For information about installing a personal Web server that supports ASP and the FrontPage server extensions, see the "Setting up a Personal Web Server" section at the start of this appendix.

◄ ◄

ASP (*Active Server Pages*) is a means for dynamically generating Web pages on a Web server running Microsoft Internet Information Server (IIS) version 3.0 or higher. Support for ASP is also built into Microsoft Personal Web Server 4.0.

◄ ◄

● ●

The personal Web server software included on the FrontPage 98 CD-ROM, version 2.0, does not have built-in support for ASP.

● ●

You'll need a 32-bit ODBC (Online Database Connection) driver. Internet Explorer (versions 4.0 and later) automatically installs a 32-bit ODBC driver. 32-bit ODBC drivers are also included with Windows NT 4.0 SR Pack 2 (but not SR Pack 1).

To check whether ODBC drivers have been installed, click on the Start button and select Settings, Control Panel. Look for an icon labeled either as ODBC or ODBC Data Sources (32bit).

Only 32-bit ODBC applications are supported on Windows 95/98. Windows NT 4.0 supports both 16-bit and 32-bit ODBC applications, so if you're unable to get the Database Results Wizard to work, you might need to update your ODBC drivers.

FIND IT ▶
ONLINE

If you don't already have 32-bit ODBC drivers installed, you can download and install the latest versions, included in Microsoft Data Access Components 2.1, from http://www.microsoft.com/data/download.htm.

The first thing you need to do is create the database you want to use and then connect it to your FrontPage Web. FrontPage has included a sample Access database that you can use to test the Database Results Wizard. To use the Database Results Wizard and create a database connection, open or create the page where you want the database results to be displayed, and then follow these steps.

1. Select Insert, Database, Results.

2. If it is not already selected, select the first radio button to use the sample Northwind database connection (see Figure E.14). You can also use an existing database connection or create a new one. Click on Next.

3. Leave the Record source radio button selected. Leave Categories selected as the record source, as shown in Figure E.15. Click on Next.

4. The next dialog box provides two options that let you alter how your database results will be displayed (see Figure E.16). The Edit List button lets you edit the list of fields to be displayed (see Figure E.17),

and the More Options button lets you specify filtering criteria and how your database will be sorted (see Figure E.18). After checking out these options, click on Next.

Figure E.14

FrontPage includes a sample database connection you can use.

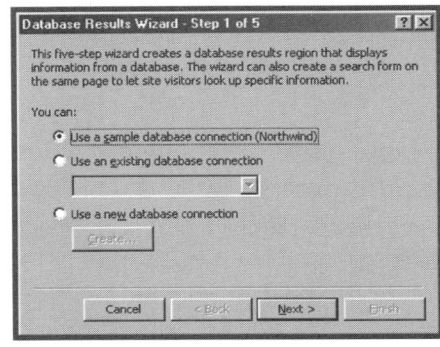

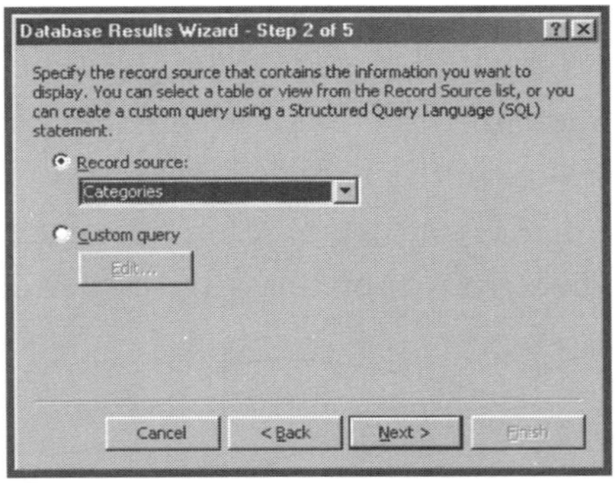

Figure E.15

The Categories record is selected as the record source.

Figure E.16

You can edit the list of fields or select from more options.

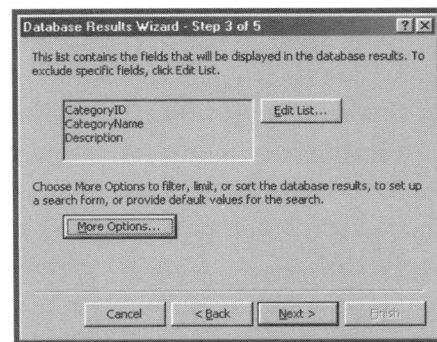

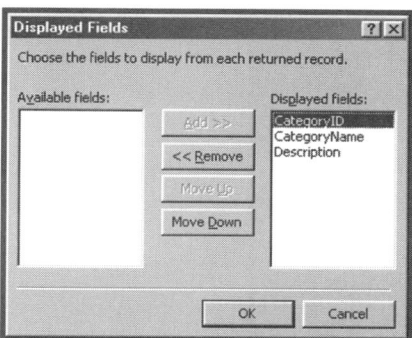

Figure E.17

You can add or remove fields, or you can rearrange their order.

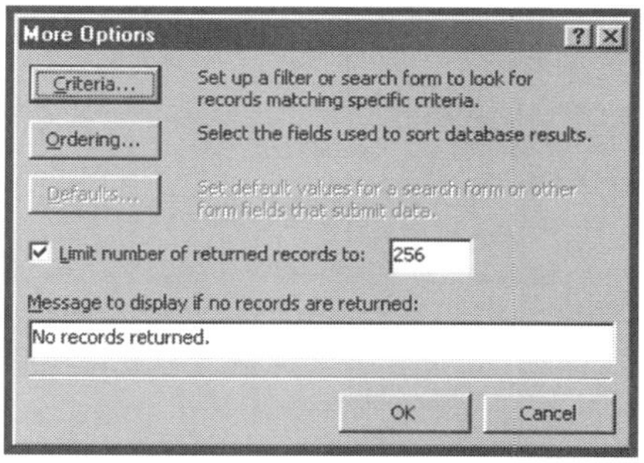

Figure E.18

You can specify filtering criteria and how your results will be sorted.

5. The next dialog box lets you specify how your database results will be formatted. From the drop-down menu, you can choose between three different basic formats (see Figure E.19) and then select different formatting options for each format type. For this example, select the Table – One Record per Row option and check all three check boxes (Use Table Border, Expand Table to Width of Page, and Include Header Row within Column Labels). Click on Next.

6. Leave the second radio button selected, to split the displayed records in groups of five. Click on the Finish button. At the message box telling you you'll need to rename the page with an .asp extension, click on OK.

7. Select File, Save As, then resave your page using .asp as the file extension (see Figure E.20).

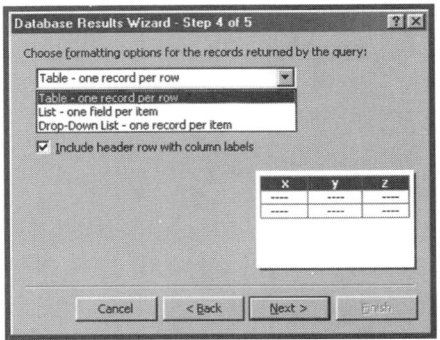

Figure E.19

You can choose between three basic formats for your database results.

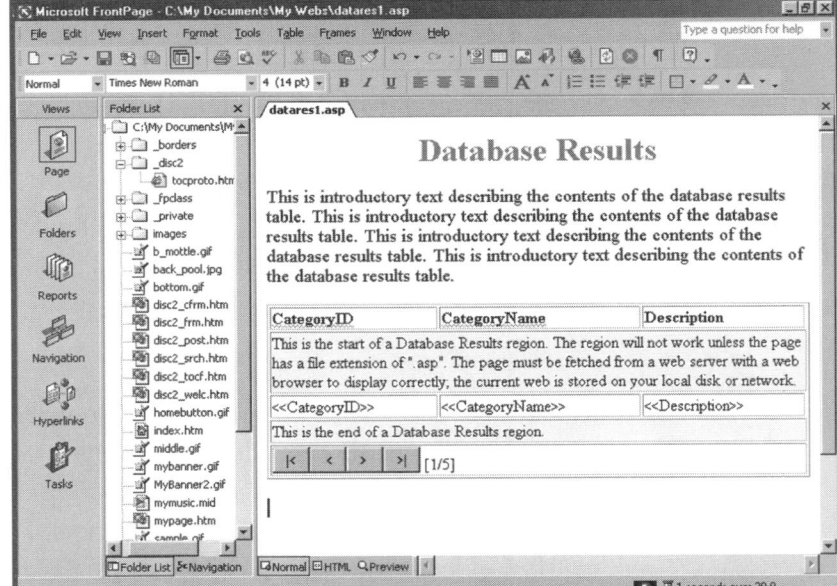

Figure E.20

The database results component is added to the page, and the page is saved as an ASP page.

Viewing the Database Results

As mentioned at the start of this section, to view your database results, you'll need to publish your page to a server that supports ASP pages and has the FrontPage 2000 server extensions installed. Figure E.21 shows the example database results created in this section after publishing the page to a local personal Web server.

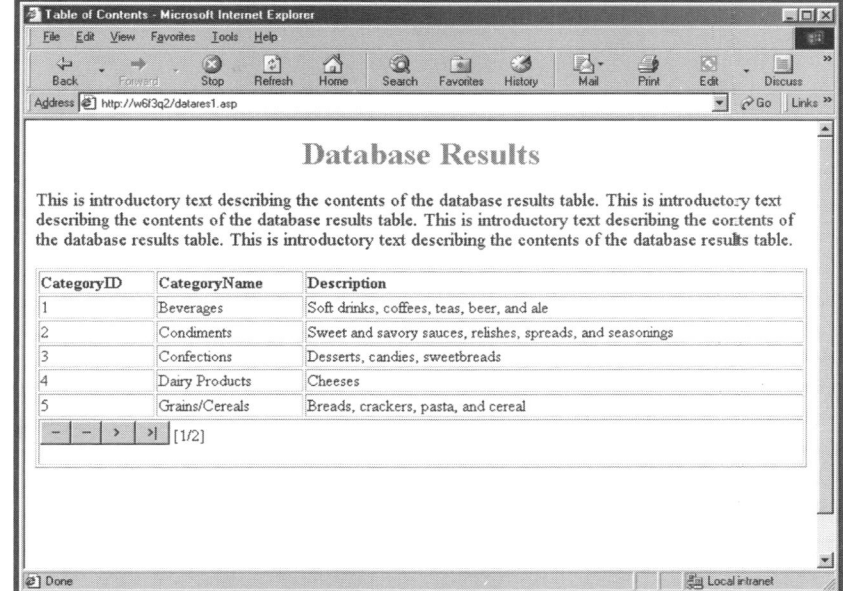

Figure E.21

To view your database results, you have to publish the page to a Web server that supports ASP and has the FrontPage 2000 server extensions installed.

If this has all worked for you the first time through, feel free to get up from your computer, walk into another room, and then jump up and down and scream a few times! If it hasn't worked for you, however, don't feel too bad. There are a lot of different pieces that need to fall into place. It took me several times through to figure it all out. Just go back over the steps detailed here and try to find out which step or steps didn't get done quite right.

Verifying Your Database Connection

You can verify that your database connection has been made properly. To do so, just follow these steps.

1. Select Tools, Web Settings. Click on the Database tab.

2. Click on the Sample database connection to select it, and then click on the Verify button. If the verification is successful, the question mark to the left of the connection changes to a check mark (see Figure E.22).

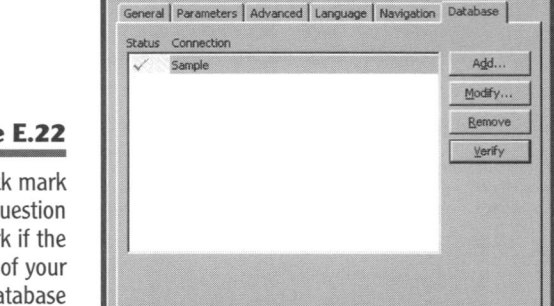

Figure E.22

The check mark replaces a question mark if the verification of your database connection is successful.

Publishing Your Database to a FrontPage Server on the Web

Publish your database only to a server with the FrontPage 2000 (or higher) server extensions installed. Your server also has to support publishing ASP pages and have Microsoft Data Access Components (MDAC) 2.1, SP1 installed. There is no need to have a System DSN assigned for your database connection, as long as your database does not reside outside your FrontPage Web.

If you are connecting to a database outside your FrontPage Web, you will need to have a System DSN assigned for your database connection. To specify the System DSN, follow these steps.

1. Publish your Web to your server and then open your remote Web in FrontPage. Open the ASP page that contains your database results region. Right-click on your database region and select Database Results Properties.

2. Select the Use a New Database Connection radio button, click on the Create button, and then click on the Add button.

3. Select the System Data Source on Web Server radio button. Type the name of the System DSN in the box to the left of the Browse

button. (You can also click on the Browse button to browse for a System DSN that resides on the server.) Click on OK.

4. Click on Verify to verify the new connection. Click on OK. Complete the dialog boxes to finish editing the database results properties.

Finding out More about Working with Online Databases and ASP Pages

FIND IT ▶
ONLINE

In this section, you've barely touched the surface of working with online databases and ASP pages. Even using the Database Results Wizard, there's a good deal more that can be done than what's been covered here, such as publishing an Excel database or creating custom queries. Still, you hopefully have learned enough in this section to begin using online databases and ASP pages. To find more information and guidance for using these FrontPage capabilities, check out Microsoft's FrontPage Web site at http://www.microsoft.com/frontpage for tips and tricks, FAQs, and white papers on online databases and ASP. For additional information on using databases and ASP in FrontPage, check out these resources on the Web.

- ☼ Online FrontPage Tutorials from SiteBuilder at http://www.net-sites.com/sitebuilder/tutorials/index.htm. This site includes visual tutorials on working with databases in FrontPage.

- ☼ ASP 101 at http://www.asp101.com. Look here for a discussion forum that includes questions and answers about working with databases and FrontPage.

- ☼ Thomas Brunt's Outfront: A Microsoft FrontPage Learning Community at http://www.outfront.net. Look here also for a discussion forum with questions and answers about working with databases and FrontPage.

- ☼ ZDNet Developer at http://www.zdnet.com/devhead/filters/0,9429,2133219,00.html. Look here for articles on ASP and databases, as well as ASP utilities you can download and use. Also, check out the Working with Access Data in FrontPage articles at

http://www.zdnet.com/devhead/stories/articles/
0,4413,2424704,00.html and http://www.zdnet.com/devhead/
stories/articles/0,4413,2458687,00.html. These useful online articles cover using Access and FrontPage to create online databases.

✿ LearnASP at http://www.LearnAsp.com. Look here for lots of
beginner lessons on using ASP.

✿ ASP Developer Network at http://www.aspdeveloper.net. This site
largely focuses on using Access and Visual InterDev to create ASP
pages.

✿ ASP-Help.com at http://asp-help.com. Look here for articles on
ASP and databases, as well as a discussion forum where you can
post questions.

NOTE When checking out other sources on publishing online databases, you should realize that
FrontPage 2000 and later versions use a different method for making database connec-
tions than FrontPage 98 used, so guides or tutorials on how to use FrontPage 98's Database Results Wizard might be misleading. Be sure that the information applies
specifically to using FrontPage 2000 or later.

Adding Java Applets and ActiveX Controls

A great way to add variety or interactivity to your FrontPage pages is to
include Java applets or ActiveX controls. Java applets are created using the
Java programming language, whereas ActiveX controls are created using
Microsoft's ActiveX technology. You don't have to be a Java or ActiveX
programmer, however, to include these features in your FrontPage pages.
There are many sources on the Web where you can find ready-made Java
applets or ActiveX controls that you can easily include in your pages.

◄ ◄

A *Java applet* is a small program (thus the word *applet*) created in the Java programming language that can be downloaded with a Web page and executed by any Java-enabled browser. All current Web browsers should support running Java applets.

◄ ◄

◄ ◄

An *ActiveX control* is a component that can be added to a Web page to provide extended functionality, such as animation sequences, transactions, calculations, and so on. ActiveX controls can be created using a variety of programming languages. Currently, only Internet Explorer 4.0 or later, or browsers that use its engine (such as Neoplanet, for example), support running ActiveX controls.

◄ ◄

Adding Java Applets

There are actually two ways in which you can add a Java applet to a FrontPage Web page. The first is to use FrontPage's Java Applet Web component, which uses a wizard that prompts you to fill in the details for your applet. The second is to manually paste the applet codes directly into your HTML code.

Getting the Example Java Applet

The example Java applet I'll be using in this section creates an analog clock (with real hour, minute, and second hands) that will display the current time. This is a free Java applet created by Sun Microsystems that you can use and include in your Web pages. If you want to follow along to add this Java applet to your own Web page, you can download it from http://javaboutique.internet.com/Clock or http://java.sun.com/openstudio/applets/clock.html.

To get ready to do the example, follow these steps.

1. In FrontPage, create a new folder named clock in your site's root Web.

2. Download the Clock Java applet. To save the applet's Zip file to a particular folder, just right-click on the link and then choose to save the file to a folder on your hard drive.

3. Open the applet's Zip file (clock.zip) in WinZip (or any other unzipping utility) and extract the contents to your new clock folder (C:\My Documents\My Webs\clock, for example).

◆ ◆

Not all Java animations available on the Web are free—many allow you only to try them out for a set period of time or have conditions you must meet before you are free to display them on your Web site. It is okay to try out different Java applets on your local machine, but before publishing them to your Web site, make sure that you have permission to do so and have met any conditions that might apply (such as providing a link back to the provider).

◆ ◆

Creating Your Example Page

Create a separate page for the Java animation example and save it in the clock folder. If you want, you can just open a page you've already created and then resave it in the clock folder. Then, follow the instructions given in the following section to insert the example Java applet into that page.

Using the Java Applet Web Component

To use FrontPage's Java Applet Web component, follow these steps.

1. Place the cursor where you want the Java applet to be inserted. Press Enter to create a blank line and then click on the Center icon to center-align it.

2. Select Insert, Web Component, and then scroll down in the Component type panel and click on Advanced Controls. Click on the Java Applet Web component to highlight it (see Figure E.23).

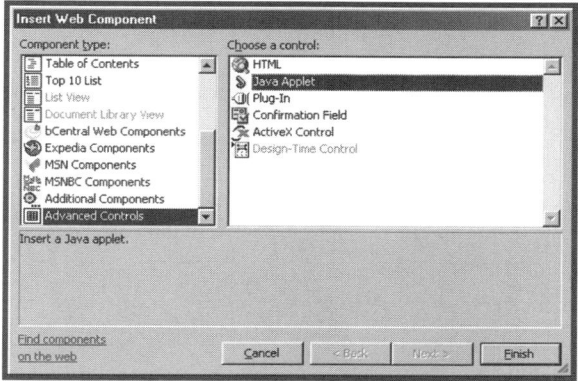

Figure E.23

The Java Applet Web component is included with FrontPage's advanced controls.

3. Click on the Finish button to open the Java Applet Properties dialog box.

4. In the Applet Source box, type the name of your Java applet's *.class file. This is case-sensitive, so type the file name exactly as it appears. For the example Java applet, type **JavaClock.class**.

5. As long as your applet files (*.class and *.jar) are in the same folder as the FrontPage Web page to which you are adding the applet, leave the Applet Base URL box blank. If the applet's HTML page is in your root Web, but the applet's other files are in a clock folder within the root Web, then type **clock/** in the Applet Base URL box.

6. In the next box, type any message you want displayed for browsers that don't support Java, or browsers in which display of Java has been turned off. For example, you might type **A Java-enabled Web browser is required to run this applet**.

7. The source for your Java applet should provide any parameters that need to be defined for the applet. To add the first parameter, click on the Add button and then type the parameter's name and value. For the example Clock applet, type **bgcolor** in the Name box, check the Specify Value check box, and then type **ffffff** in the Data box. This will specify a white background color. Click on OK to add the parameter.

Add the remaining parameters for the applet. Here are the parameters you need to add:

border	5
ccolor	dddddd
cfont	TimesRoman|BOLD|18
delay	100
hhcolor	0000ff
link	http://java.sun.com/
mhcolor	00ff00
ncolor	000000
nradius	80
shcolor	ff0000

NOTE Authors of Java applets often require that you include copyright and author parameters that must be typed exactly as specified. If not, the applet will not play.

Figure E.24 shows the applet's parameters added to the Web component.

8. The Layout options let you control how the applet window will be displayed on your page. The Horizontal Spacing value lets you add space to the left and right of the applet window. The Vertical Spacing value lets you add space above and below the applet window. The Alignment lets you specify the horizontal or vertical alignment of the applet window. For this example, leave all the settings as they are.

9. In the Size section, type **150** in both the Width and the Height boxes. Click on OK to add the Web component to your page (see Figure E.25).

To check out your Java applet, just click on the Preview tab. Figure E.26 shows the Clock applet running in FrontPage's Preview window.

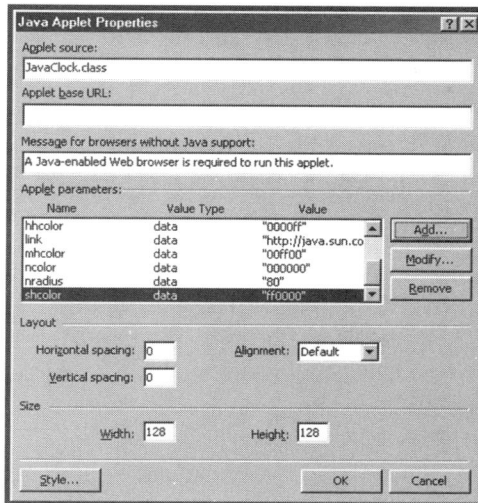

Figure E.24

The Java applet's parameters have been added in the Java Applet Properties dialog box.

Figure E.25

The Java Applet Web component has been added to the page.

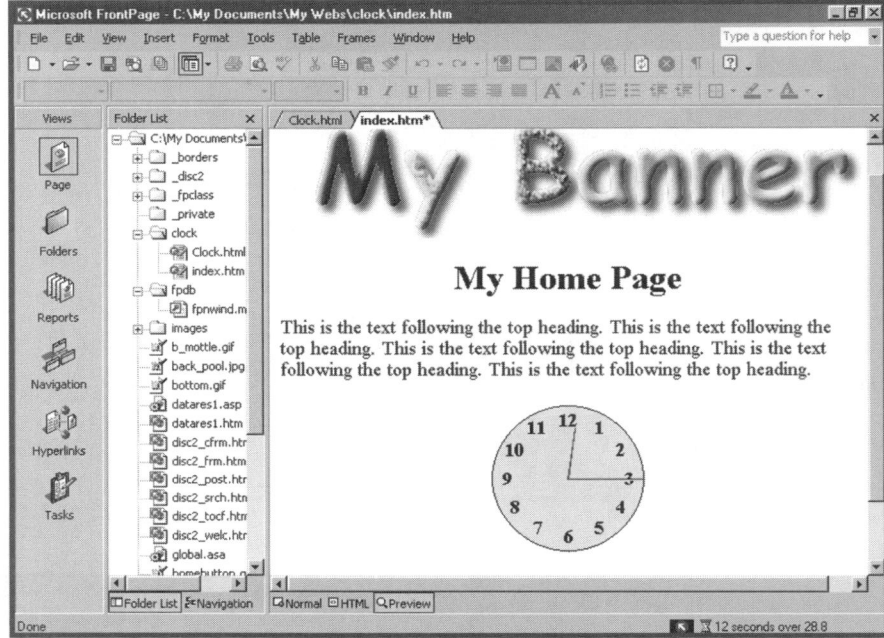

Figure E.26

The Clock Java applet is playing in FrontPage's Preview window.

Places Where You Can Get Java Applets

There are many places on the Web where you can find Java applets that you can download and use in your Web pages. Here are just a few of the sites where you'll find downloadable applets.

FIND IT ▶
ONLINE

- The Java Boutique at http://www.javaboutique.internet.com
- Applet Depot at http://www.ericharshbarger.org/java
- Gamelan at http://developer.earthWeb.com/dlink.index-jhtml. 72.1082.-.0.jhtml
- Freebie Applets You Can Use from Sun Microsystems at http://www.javasoft.com/openstudio/index.html

COPYING AND PASTING APPLETS

Filling out the Java Applet Properties dialog box can take some time, especially if your Java applet has many parameters that need to be added. If the source for your Java applet has the applet displayed on its Web site, it might be quicker to copy the Java animation's code from its Web page and paste it directly into your FrontPage Web page.

To view the source code for a page on the Web, in either Internet Explorer or Netscape Navigator, right-click on the applet's Web page and click on View Source. To copy the applet code, click and drag to highlight everything starting with <applet> and ending with </applet>, and press Ctrl+C.

To paste the applet code into your FrontPage Web page, click on the HTML tab, position the cursor where you want to place the applet, and press Ctrl+V to paste in the code.

To change the applet's parameters (to change colors, fonts, and so on), edit them directly in the HTML code.

You might need to edit the code slightly. For example, if you are placing all the Java applet files in the same folder as the applet's HTML file, then you should delete any codebase attribute included in the applet tag. If they are in separate folders, you'll need to enter the correct relative URL to point to the location of the Java applet's class files within your site.

Adding ActiveX Controls

Adding ActiveX controls is a good deal simpler than adding Java applets. The trade-off is that ActiveX controls will play only in Internet Explorer 4.0 or later, and not in Netscape Navigator, whereas Java applets will play in both browsers. To add an ActiveX control to a FrontPage Web page, follow these steps.

1. Select Insert, Web Component, and then scroll down in the Component Type panel and click on Advanced Controls.

2. Click on ActiveX Control and then click on the Next button.

3. Click on the Calendar Control 10.0 control (see Figure E.27).

4. Click on the Finish button to add the Calendar ActiveX control to your page (see Figure E.28).

5. To check out the Calendar control, click on the Preview tab. To see the calendar for a specific month, change the month and year accordingly.

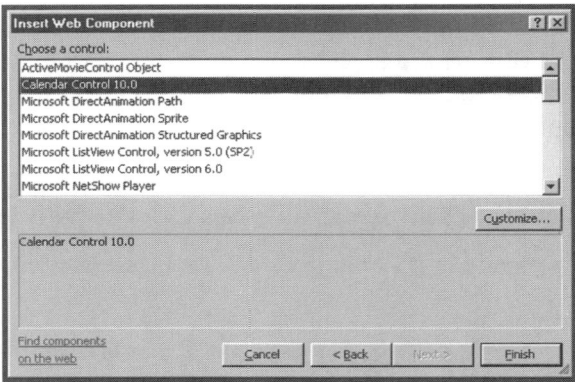

Figure E.27

Choose from a list of ActiveX controls that have been installed on your computer.

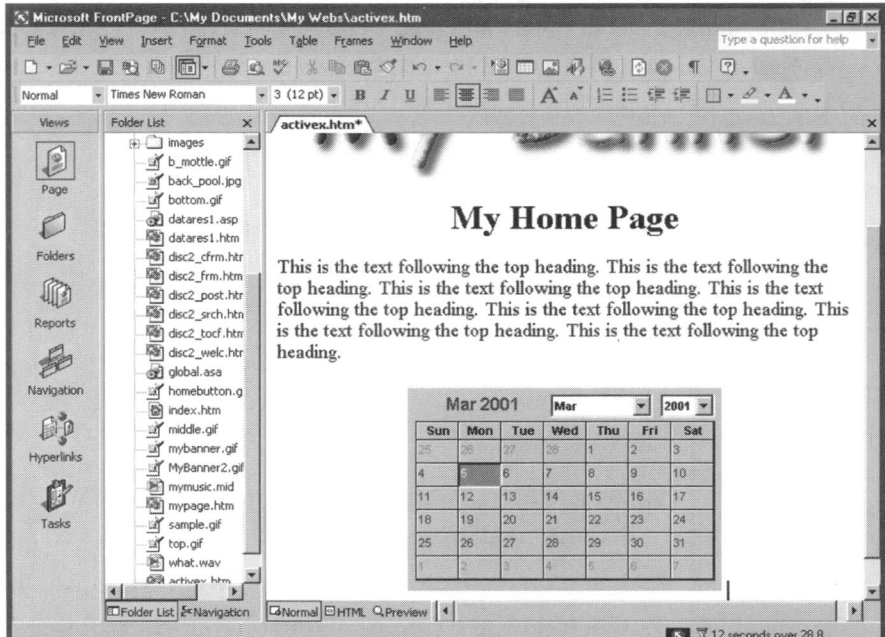

Figure E.28

The Calendar ActiveX control has been added to the page.

Enabling or Disabling ActiveX Controls

ActiveX controls only display in browsers that support ActiveX, which right now means in Internet Explorer 4.0 or later only. You can enable or disable ActiveX controls for your Web before publishing. You can also target your Web to a specific browser or browsers, which automatically enables or disables features (such as ActiveX controls) that don't work in all browsers. To do so, just follow these steps.

1. Select Tools, Page Options, and then click on the Compatibility tab.
2. To target your Web to a specific browser or browsers, click on the pull-down handle in the Browsers list.

ActiveX controls will be disabled and not published to your Web if you select any of these options from the Browsers list: Netscape Navigator only, Both Internet Explorer and Navigator, or Microsoft Web TV. To publish ActiveX controls to your Web, select either Internet Explorer Only or Custom.

ActiveX controls will also be disabled and not published to your Web if you select 3.0 Browsers and Later from the Browser Versions list. To publish Active X controls to your Web, select either 4.0 Browsers and Later or Custom.

You can also clear the ActiveX Controls check box under Technologies to disable publishing ActiveX controls to your Web.

Places Where You Can Get ActiveX Controls

There are many places on the Web where you can find ActiveX controls to download and use in your Web pages. Here are just a few of the sites from which you can download ActiveX controls.

○ ActiveX Control Library at http://www.download.com/PC/Activex
○ ZDNet Developer: ActiveX at http://www.zdnet.com/devhead/filters/0,,2133222,00.html
○ Active-X.com at http://www.active-x.com

APPENDIX F

Using the
CD-ROM

The CD-ROM that accompanies this book contains shareware and freeware that will help you use what you learned in the book more effectively.

Running the CD

To make the CD-ROM more user-friendly, and to take up less of your disk space, no installation is required. This means that the only files transferred to your hard disk are the ones you choose to copy or install.

 ●
CAUTION   This CD has been designed to run under Windows 95/98/2000/Me and Windows NT 4. Neither the CD itself nor the programs on the CD will run under earlier versions of Windows.
● ●

Windows 95/98/2000/Me/NT4

Since there is no install routine, running the CD-ROM in Windows 95/98/2000/Me/NT4 is a breeze. Simply follow these steps.

1. Insert the CD into the CD-ROM drive and close the tray.
2. Open Windows Explorer or double-click on My Computer, then double-click on the CD-ROM drive icon.
3. Double-click on the start.html file. Your default Web browser will open and load the Prima License Agreement.

The Prima License

The first window you will see is the Prima License Agreement. Take a moment to read the agreement, then click on the I Agree button to accept the license and proceed to the user interface. If you do not agree with the license, click on the I Disagree button to close the user interface and end the session.

The Prima User Interface

The opening screen of the Prima user interface contains a two-panel window. The left panel contains a directory of the programs and files on the CD. The right panel displays a description of the entry selected in the left panel.

Using the Left Panel

Click on one of the options in the left panel: Programs, Extras, Links, or Main. The right panel of the interface will display the appropriate information for the selected option.

Using the Right Panel

The right panel describes the entry you chose in the left panel. The information provided tells you about your selection, such as the functionality of an installable program. When you select Programs from the left panel, the right panel will display information about how to download the trial versions and programs from the CD.

Resizing and Closing the User Interface

To resize the window, position the mouse over any edge or corner, and click and hold the mouse button while dragging the edge or corner to a new position. Release the mouse button when the window has been sized to your requirements.

To close and exit the user interface, select File, Close.

GLOSSARY

A

absolute URL. A complete path or address of a file on the Internet (such as http://www. someserver.com/somedir/somepage.html). Sometimes called a *complete URL*. See also *relative URL*.

Active Server Pages. See *ASP*.

ActiveX. Microsoft's set of programming technologies for creating interactive software components in a networked environment.

ActiveX controls. Software components incorporating ActiveX technology, which can be used to add animation, pop-up menus, interactive forms, and other features to Web pages. ActiveX controls can be written in several languages, including C, C++, Visual Basic, and Java. They are currently only supported in Microsoft's Internet Explorer browser, version 4.0 or later.

Address. The format style in FrontPage that is usually used for formatting signature blocks.

alias. An e-mail address that has no Inbox of its own, but instead works as a forwarding address.

anchor. See *bookmark*.

antialiasing. The blending of colors to smooth out the jagged stair-stepped edges ("jaggies") in fonts and image graphics.

append. To add to the end of an existing file.

applet. A client-side program, such as a Java applet, that is downloaded from the Internet and executed in a Web browser. See also *Java*.

ASCII. The American Standard Code for Information Interchange, defining a standard minimum character set for computer text and data. ASCII files are sometimes called "DOS text" files, or "plain text" files.

ASP. Active Server Pages. A means for dynamically generating Web pages on a Web server running Microsoft Internet Information Server (IIS) version 3.0 or higher.

AU. A file format for audio files. Sound files used in FrontPage 2000's hover buttons must be 8-bit, mono, 8000Hz, mu-Law AU files.

AVI. Audio Video Interleaved. A multimedia format for sound and video that is common on the Windows platform.

B

background sound. A sound file that is played in the background when a Web page is displayed in a Web browser. Internet Explorer and Netscape Navigator use different methods for including background sounds in Web pages (see Appendix C, "Adding Multimedia").

bandwidth. The transmission capacity of a network, but also the amount of capacity consumed by a connection. A Web page containing many graphics consumes more bandwidth than one containing only text.

banner. Usually refers to an inline image displayed at the top of a Web page, often replacing the Heading 1 tag (H1).

Banner Ad Manager. A component in FrontPage that allows the timed display of sequential images, with transition effects definable between the image frames. Can be linked to a Web address or just used as a slide show.

bitmap. A graphic image format based on pixels. Also known as a raster image.

bookmark. In FrontPage, a named location in a Web page that serves as the target of a hyperlink. In Netscape Navigator, a saved URL, performing the same function as what is called a *favorite* in Internet Explorer.

browser. See *Web browser*.

Bulleted List. The style used in FrontPage to create a bulleted list. See also *unordered list*.

C

Cascading Style Sheets. A means for applying custom formatting characteristics to HTML elements in a Web page using the STYLE tag. A style sheet can either reside inside the HTML file or in a separate file downloaded along with the HTML file. Current versions are Cascading Style Sheets, level 1 (CSS1) and Cascading Style Sheets, level 2 (CSS2). You can find out more about Cascading Style Sheets at the World Wide Web Consortium's site at http://www.w3.org/Style.

CGI. The Common Gateway Interface, an interface to a gateway through which a Web server can run programs and scripts in response to requests from a Web browser.

CGI script. A server-side script or program executed on a Web server in response to a request from a Web browser. A common use of CGI scripts is the processing of form responses. CGI scripts are often written in the Perl programming language.

client. A computer on a network that makes a request to a server.

client-side image map. An image map that uses the Web browser, rather than a server script, to execute hotspot hyperlinks. Not supported by some older browsers.

client-side program. A program that is downloaded and executed on a client computer, rather than from a server. Java applets and ActiveX controls are examples of client-side programs.

clip art. The term originates from sheets of commonly used images that were printed and then literally clipped out and pasted into ad, magazine, or newspaper layouts. In the broader sense, it refers to any image inserted into a page design.

Clipboard. An area in memory, on the Windows platform for example, to which data can be copied or cut from one program or location and then pasted into another program or location.

component. A built-in object, inserted by FrontPage into a Web page, that can be evaluated and executed when a page is saved, published, or browsed. For more information on using components, see the Sunday Morning session, "Putting the Power of Components to Work." See also *WebBot*.

confirmation field. A component in FrontPage that can be used to insert the contents of a form field into a form confirmation page. It could be used to echo a user's name, e-mail address, and so on, from form fields that the user has filled out.

confirmation page. A page that confirms to a viewer that a form has been successfully submitted.

comment. A means of inserting text that will not be displayed in a browser into the body of an HTML file. See also *FrontPage comment*.

D

Database Results Wizard. A wizard in FrontPage for publishing an online database and database query results.

definition list. A list in HTML, often also called a *glossary*, created using the DL (Definition List), DT (Definition Term), and DD (Definition Description) tags. In FrontPage 2000, DT and DD tags are applied using the Defined Term and Definition styles, whereas the DL tags are automatically inserted for you.

DHTML. See *Dynamic HTML*.

discussion group. An interactive Web site that allows visitors to post discussion articles, reply to previous articles, search articles, or browse discussion threads from a table of contents. In FrontPage, discussion groups must be defined within their own Web or subweb.

dithering. A method for smoothing out color and tonal transitions. Dithering helps to eliminate "color banding" that is often evident in lower-resolution images displaying fewer than 256 colors or shades of gray. See also *antialiasing*.

domain category. A major grouping of domain names (such as .com, .org, .net, .edu, .mil, and .gov), as well as many national domain categories (.us, .uk, .ca, and so on).

domain name. An alphanumeric alternative to an IP address, registered with the InterNIC (Internet Network Information Center).

download. To transfer files from a server to a client. See also *upload*.

DPI. Dots per inch, used in combination with the number of pixels in an image to determine the size of an image. For instance, an image scanned at 75 DPI will be smaller than the same image scanned at 150 DPI.

Dynamic HTML. Various means of providing dynamic Web content that respond interactively to user actions, such as producing on-the-fly Web pages, starting and stopping animations, and so on. (Microsoft refers to its rendition of this as "Dynamic HTML" or DHTML, whereas Netscape refers to its rendition as "dynamic HTML.")

E

end tag. The end of a nonempty HTML element (...</P>, for example). See also *start tag*.

extension. An extension to standard HTML (as defined by the World Wide Web Consortium, or W3C) implemented by a particular browser (as in "Netscape extension" or "Microsoft extension") that may or may not be displayable in other browsers.

F

field validation. Default parameters or limits applied to a form field to help user efficiency and data accuracy.

float. The flow or wrap of text around an object on a Web page. You float an image to the left, for example, and text wraps around the right side of the image.

Folders view. Selected by clicking on the Folders icon from the Views pane in FrontPage. Displays the folder structure and contents of the current Web.

form. A grouping of data-entry fields, check boxes, radio buttons, and so on, that can be filled out by a visitor to a Web site. Forms created in FrontPage require that the site be published to a server that has the FrontPage server extensions installed.

form field. A data entry field on an HTML form.

frames. An extension to HTML pioneered by Netscape that has since been incorporated into HTML 4.0. Frames allow multiple HTML documents to be displayed at the same time in separate frame windows within a Web page.

frameset. A Web page that contains the HTML codes (defined within a FRAMESET tag) defining the layout for a framed Web site.

FrontPage comment. In FrontPage, a component that inserts a comment that will be visible when the page is being edited in FrontPage, but will not be displayed when the page is previewed in a browser (or in FrontPage's Preview view). Regular HTML comments, which are inserted into a Web page using HTML comment tags, are only viewable as part of a page's HTML code.

FrontPage server. A Web server that has the FrontPage server extensions installed.

FrontPage server extensions. A set of programs and scripts installed on a Web server that provide extended server-side functionality for Web sites created with FrontPage.

FrontPage Web. A collection of Web pages under the same root folder created in FrontPage. FrontPage Webs can be either disk-based Webs (C:\My Webs, for instance) or server-based Webs (http://*yourweb/*, for example). Server-based Webs can be located on a Web server or on a personal Web server (PWS) installed on a local hard drive.

FTP. File Transfer Protocol, the protocol used for downloading or uploading both ASCII and binary files on the Internet. FTP is the method FrontPage 2000 uses to transfer a FrontPage Web to a server that doesn't have the FrontPage server extensions installed. FTP should never be used to transfer a FrontPage Web to a FrontPage server. See also *FTP server*.

FTP server. A Web server that doesn't have the FrontPage server extensions installed.

G

GIF. Graphics Interchange Format. A popular Web graphics format developed by CompuServe. Each image can include up to 256 colors, transparency, interlacing, and multiple frames (GIF animation). See also *JPEG*.

GIF animation. A GIF-format image file containing multiple images that cumulatively create an animation. Such an animation is usually only viewable in a Web browser or a GIF animation editor.

global. Applicable to the entire Web site. A theme is applied globally, for example.

H

Heading *n*. A format style in FrontPage that specifies a paragraph as one of six heading levels—Heading 1, Heading 2, and so on. Corresponds to the HTML tags H1, H2, and so on.

hit counter. As the name implies, a hit counter counts the number of "hits" to a Web page. Each visit to a Web page is a hit.

home page. Usually, a Web page that is automatically displayed when a Web site or a Web folder in a Web site is accessed in a Web browser.

hotspot. An area within an image map that activates a hyperlink when clicked.

hover button. A FrontPage component that creates a button that can display visual effects and play sound effects when the mouse passes over the button. Clicking on the button can activate a hyperlink.

HTML. Hypertext Markup Language. A markup language for preparing documents for display on the World Wide Web. The current standard version of HTML is HTML 4.0 (previous versions were HTML 1.0, HTML 2.0, and HTML 3.2).

HTML attribute. A name-value pair in an HTML tag that defines additional display characteristics for an HTML element. For example, in the HTML tag, <P align="center">, the HTML attribute *align="center"* specifies that the paragraph should be centered when displayed in a browser.

HTML editor. A software program that edits HTML files. HTML editors cover a wide spectrum, from fairly simple Notepad-like editors, in which HTML codes can either be typed or selected using toolbars, menus, or wizards, to fancy WYSIWYG editors that do most of the coding for you, like FrontPage.

HTML element. Everything encompassed within a start and end tag in HTML. Stand-alone tags (such as the HR or IMG tag) are both tags and elements.

HTML tag. A markup code in HTML. There are two types of tags in HTML: container tags and empty tags (or stand-alone tags). Container tags start with a start tag (<H1>, for example) and end with an end tag (</H1>, for example). End tags always begin with a "/" (</P>,

</B>, and so on). Empty tags are single "stand-alone" tags that don't have end tags (<HR>, for example).

HTML view. Clicking on the HTML tab in FrontPage switches to HTML view. In HTML view, you can directly view and edit a page's HTML codes.

HTTP. Hypertext Transfer Protocol. The protocol used to exchange Web pages and other documents across the Internet. FrontPage 2000 uses the HTTP protocol (http://) to transfer FrontPage Webs to a FrontPage server.

hyperlink. FrontPage's term for a hypertext link. Hyperlinks can jump to any other object on the Web (a Web page, a graphic image, a text file, a CGI script, and so on) and also to a location (or *bookmark*) within either the same or another Web page. Also sometimes called a *hot link*.

Hyperlinks view. The Hyperlinks icon in the Views pane is used to turn on the Hyperlinks view. The Hyperlinks view displays a diagram of all pages linked to the default home page for a FrontPage Web.

hypermedia. A term coined by Ted Nelson, the inventor of hypertext. It generally refers to the interlinking of multiple media (text, images, sound, animation, video).

hypertext. Electronic documents that contain links to other documents, allowing nonsequential viewing of large amounts of information. Users can choose their own path through the material by clicking on the link to the topic that interests them. A Web site is a collection of hypertext documents.

I

image hyperlink. Also sometimes just called an *image link*. An inline image inserted inside a hypertext link, usually displayed with a blue border to show that it is an active link. However, if you select an image in FrontPage and then define a hyperlink for it, FrontPage automatically turns off the border. To make the border visible, in HTML view, just delete the *border="0"* attribute from the IMG tag, or edit the image properties to do the same thing.

image map. An image displayed in a Web browser with hidden "hotspots" that can be clicked on to link to their designated URLs. Older browsers only supported server-side image maps (image maps executed from a server), whereas newer browsers also support client-side image maps (image maps executed from the desktop, or client).

Include page. A component in FrontPage that automatically includes one Web page within another Web page. A handy feature, for example, when including a signature block page at the bottom of other pages.

inline frame. A single-paned frame window that appears embedded within another Web page.

inline image. An image (GIF, JPEG, or PNG) displayed on a Web page.

interlaced GIF. A GIF-format graphics file that can be gradually displayed in a browser while still being downloaded.

On each pass, only some of the lines of the image are displayed, allowing a viewer to see what the image is going to be long before it has been downloaded completely.

Internet. A set of protocols for transmitting and exchanging data among networks.

IP address. An Internet Protocol address. A unique number, such as 185.35.117.0, that is assigned to a server on the Internet.

ISP. An Internet service provider, also often called an *access provider*. A company that provides dial-up access to the Internet.

J

Java. Sun Microsystem's object-oriented programming language, designed to create programs that can be run securely on any platform, making it the ideal programming language for the World Wide Web. Because programs distributed across the Web need to be small (due to bandwidth constraints), Java programs, as well as ActiveX controls, are often called "applets."

JavaScript. A scripting language developed by Netscape and Sun that is loosely based on Java. Useful for adding behaviors to a Web page, such as mouse-over effects, for example. See also *JScript* and *VBScript*.

JPEG. Joint Photographic Experts Group. Besides GIF, the most common graphics format for the display of images on the Web. Images can use a palette of up to 16.7 million colors. Unlike GIF images, however, JPEG images cannot be transparent, interlaced, or animated. Often referred to as JPG format images, because the file extension for JPEG images under DOS/Windows is .jpg. JPEG images are generally best for images that require more than 256 colors, such as continuous tone photographs or images that use gradient fills, which blend one color into another in graduated steps. GIF images are best for images that have fewer than 256 colors. See also *GIF*.

JScript. A version of JavaScript developed by Microsoft for its Internet Explorer browser. It works with ActiveX controls, unlike JavaScript.

K

keyword. A word used in a search form, such as at AltaVista or Infoseek Guide, for example, to search for matching Web pages (pages that include the keyword).

L

line break. Forces a new line within an HTML element, without starting a new block element. Inserting line breaks is a common way of creating single-spaced lines in HTML.

link list. A list of hyperlinks, sometimes also called a *hotlist*.

link text. The text displayed in a hyperlink, usually in blue and underlined.

M

mailto link. A hyperlink that opens up a window where an e-mail message can be composed and sent to a specified e-mail address. Introduced originally by Netscape; versions of Internet Explorer earlier than 4.0 do not support mailto links.

marquee. An HTML element supported only by Microsoft Internet Explorer that displays scrolling text in a Web page. It is not included in standard HTML. In FrontPage, marquees can be created using the Marquee component.

META tag. A tag in HTML that is used to include meta-information in the header section of an HTML file. A common use is to include descriptions and keyword lists that can be used by search indexes to index a Web page.

Multimedia. Refers to the delivery of information that combines different content formats (motion video, audio, still images, graphics, animation, text and so on).

N

navigation bar. A set of text or button hyperlinks that link to other pages in a Web site.

Navigation view. Opened by clicking on the Navigation icon in the Views pane. Displays the navigational structure of a FrontPage Web.

nested list. A list indented inside another list. In nested bulleted lists (unordered lists), the

bullet character is automatically changed for the different nested list levels. Different types of lists can be nested inside each other—for example, you can nest a bulleted list inside a numbered list, or vice versa.

Numbered List. A specialized type of bulleted list in FrontPage that sequentially numbers the listed items, replacing the bullets with numbers.

O

ordered list. A numbered list created in HTML using the OL (Ordered List) tag. Applied in FrontPage by using the Numbered List style.

P

padding. In a Web page table, the amount of space between the inside border of a cell and the outer edge of the text.

personal Web server. A Web server you can install on your local computer, allowing you to publish and test your pages locally first, before publishing them to your remote server. Also called a PWS.

pixel. Short for picture element. Identifies a "point" in a graphic image, but also includes bytes that represent its color depth. The number of pixels does not determine the size of an image, only the resolution of the image. The size of the image (whether printed or displayed) is determined by the DPI (dots per inch) combined with its pixel dimensions.

plug-in. A software component that can be installed in a Web browser to enable the display or playing of document and media formats not otherwise supported.

PNG. Portable Network Graphics. The newest standard graphics format for the display of images on the Web. It supports up to 48-bit true color (JPEG supports up to 24-bit true color), as well as transparency and interlacing. Not supported on older browsers.

publish. To transfer a FrontPage Web to a server. A FrontPage web can be published to either a FrontPage server (with the FrontPage server extensions installed) or an FTP server (without the FrontPage server extensions installed).

R

radio button. A form field that allows a visitor to select an option by clicking on the button. The button is filled when it is selected, but empty when it is not.

raster image. Also called a bitmapped graphic. The image defined as a set of pixels or dots in a column and row format.

relative URL. Also called a partial URL. A relative URL is used to link to an object that resides within the same Web site (or FrontPage Web) as the linking page. An example of a relative URL, for example, would be *<IMG SRC="images/ myimage.jpg">*, which would display an inline image that is located in a subfolder, *images*, of the current folder (the folder where the linking page is saved). Other examples of relative URLs would be *<A HREF="../project1/welcome.htm">* (linking to a subfolder within the parent folder of the current folder). See also *absolute URL*.

root web. The root folder of a FrontPage Web. See also *subweb*.

S

sans serif. A font style that has flat, plain edges. Arial is an example of a sans serif font.

Scheduled Image. A FrontPage component that allows the display of an image only during a specified time period.

Scheduled Include page. A FrontPage component that allows the display of an Include page only during a specified time period.

Search form. A FrontPage component that allows a visitor to a Web page to do a full-text search of a Web site.

server. A computer on a network that responds to requests from clients. See also *client*.

shared borders. Regions in a Web page that are shared between pages. A common use for shared borders is to include common navigation bars for pages within a FrontPage Web. See also *navigation bar*.

smoothing. See *antialiasing*.

start tag. The start of a non-empty HTML element (<P>... for example). See also *end tag*.

style. Can refer either to a format style applied from the Formatting toolbar (Heading 1 or Numbered List, for example) or to a format defined as part of a style sheet. See also *Cascading Style Sheets*.

subweb. A FrontPage Web included within another FrontPage Web. FrontPage 2000 allows subwebs within other subwebs. See also *root web*.

T

tab order. The order in which form fields are selected as the user presses the Tab key to move through the form.

table. A means in HTML of displaying data in a tabular format using the TABLE tag. Table rows are defined by the TR (Table Row) tag, whereas table cells are defined by the TD (Table Data) tag.

Table of Contents. A FrontPage component that generates an outline of a FrontPage Web, with hypertext links to all pages included in the Web.

tag. A code in SGML, HTML, and XML used to define a document element. Tags can either be the start and end tags of a container element (such as a paragraph or a heading) or stand-alone tags that define an empty element (such as an inline image or a horizontal rule).

target anchor. Called a *bookmark* in FrontPage, a target anchor defines the "landing spot" for a hyperlink. See also *bookmark*.

target frame. The name of a frame in which a linked page will be displayed.

Tasks view. In FrontPage, clicking on the Tasks icon in the Views pane displays the task list that has been defined for the current Web.

TCP/IP. Transmission Control Protocol/ Internet Protocol. The standard protocol set for transmissions across the Internet.

template. A predesigned page that can contain page settings, formatting, and page elements. You can create your own page templates so that you can create pages for your Web quickly and consistently. In FrontPage, pages saved as templates have a *.tem file extension and are available under the General tab in the New dialog box.

theme. A unified set of design elements and color schemes that can be applied to multiple Web pages to give them a common look and feel. FrontPage users can apply any of the many themes provided with FrontPage, or they can create their own.

thumbnail. A miniature version of a graphic file. Typically, you click on a thumbnail to see a full-size view of a graphic. Thumbnails save your visitors time because they load into the browser more quickly.

Timestamp. A FrontPage component that, when included in a page, automatically displays the date and time when the page was last edited or updated.

toolbar. A collection of onscreen buttons or icons in a graphical user interface (GUI) that usually provides shortcuts to menu and other program functions.

transition. A special effect, such as Dissolve, Fade to Black, or Vertical Blinds, that can be assigned to take effect when a visitor enters or leaves a page. Transitions are Dynamic HTML (DHTML) effects and only play in Internet Explorer 4.0 or later.

U

Unix. A multiuser, multitasking operating system originally developed by AT&T Bell Laboratories. Versions include Linux, Xenix, AIX, and A/UX. The majority of servers on the World Wide Web run Unix, although Windows NT servers are also numerous.

unordered list. A bulleted list created in HTML using the UL (Unordered List) tag. See also *Bulleted List*.

upload. To transfer files from a client to a server. See also *client* or *server*.

URL. Uniform Resource Locator. For example, http://www.microsoft.com/frontpage is the URL for Microsoft's FrontPage support pages. See also *Web address*.

V

VBScript. Visual Basic Scripting Edition. Microsoft's scripting language for use on the World Wide Web. It is similar to JavaScript but only runs on Internet Explorer or on browsers that use the Internet Explorer engine (such as Neoplanet, for example).

Visual J++. Microsoft's implementation of the Java programming language.

Vector image. A graphic image composed of editable line objects, so the objects themselves can be edited individually and the image can be resized without quality loss. Vector images are only supported by newer browsers, as opposed to raster images, which are the de facto Web standard.

W

watermark. A non-scrolling background image, only displayable in Internet Explorer.

WAV. An audio file format common to Windows.

W3C. World Wide Web Consortium. The organization that oversees and regulates the development of international standards for Web technology and development.

Web. In FrontPage, a collection of Web pages, images, and other files developed for publishing online.

WebBot. Short for *WebBot component*. See also *component*.

Web address. A location on the Web. See also *URL*.

Web browser. A software program that browses (or "surfs") HTML and other files on the Internet. See also *client*.

Web Host. Also called a WPP (*Web Presence Provider*) or Web Service Provider. The company that you hire to store your Web site so that other users can access it on the Internet.

WYSIWYG. What You See Is What You Get. WYSIWYG HTML editors, such as FrontPage, allow you to edit a page in a display that shows how it will be shown in a Web browser.

X

XML. Extensible Markup Language. Slated by the W3C (World Wide Web Consortium) as the next-generation markup language for display of documents and data not only on the Web, but in all manner of media. Using XML, a single document can be marked up to be displayed on the Web, read in a Braille reader, printed in a book, or spoken by a speech application. The 5.0 versions of both Internet Explorer and Netscape Navigator should be able to display both HTML and XML documents. In many ways, XML is intended as the strict subset of SGML that HTML was supposed to have become. You can find out more about XML at the World Wide Web Consortium's site at http://www.w3.org/XML.

INDEX

License Agreement/Notice of Limited Warranty